Table of Contents

Business Analytics

6500:305

Authors

Shmueli • Linoff • Black

Printed in the United States of America 10 9 8 7 6 5 4 3 2

List of Titles

Business Statistics: For Contemporary Decision Making, 7th edition
by Ken Black
Copyright © 2012, ISBN: 978-0-470-93146-2

Data Mining for Business Intelligence: Concepts, Techniques, and Applications in Microsoft Office Excel® with XLMiner®, 2nd edition
by Galit Shmueli, Nitin R. Patel, and Peter C. Bruce
Copyright © 2010, ISBN: 978-0-470-52682-8

Data Mining Techniques: For Marketing, Sales, and Customer Relationship Management, 3rd edition
by Gordon S. Linoff and Michael J.A. Berry
Copyright © 2011, ISBN: 978-0-470-65093-6

HARVARD
BUSINESS
SCHOOL
PRESS

The Nature of Analytical Competition

Using Analytics to Build a Distinctive Capability

EXCERPTED FROM

*Competing on Analytics:
The New Science of Winning*

BY

Thomas H. Davenport, Jeanne G. Harris

Harvard Business School Press
Boston, Massachusetts

ISBN-13: 978-1-4221-2193-1
2193BC

You can purchase Harvard Business School Press books at booksellers worldwide.
You can order Harvard Business School Press books and book chapters online at
www.HBSPress.org, or by calling 888-500-1016 or, outside the U.S. and Canada, 617-783-7410.

I

THE NATURE OF ANALYTICAL COMPETITION

Using Analytics to Build a Distinctive Capability

IN 1997, A THIRTY-SOMETHING man whose resume included software geek, education reformer, and movie buff rented *Apollo 13* from the biggest video-rental chain on the block—Blockbuster—and got hit with $40 in late fees. That dent in his wallet got him thinking: why didn't video stores work like health clubs, where you paid a flat monthly fee to use the gym as much as you wanted? Because of this experience—and armed with the $750 million he received for selling his software company—Reed Hastings jumped into the frothy sea of the "new economy" and started Netflix, Inc.

Pure folly, right? After all, Blockbuster was already drawing in revenues of more than $3 billion per year from its thousands of stores across America and in many other countries—and it wasn't the only competitor in this space. Would people really order their movies online, wait for the U.S. Postal Service (increasingly being referred to as "snail mail" by the late 1990s) to deliver them, and then go back to the mailbox to return the films? Surely Netflix would go the route of the many Net-based companies that had a "business model" and a marketing pitch but no customers.

I

And yet we know that the story turned out differently, and a significant reason for Netflix's success today is that it is an analytical competitor. The movie delivery company, which has grown from $5 million in revenues in 1999 to about $1 billion in 2006, is a prominent example of a firm that competes on the basis of its mathematical, statistical, and data management prowess. Netflix offers free shipping of DVDs to its roughly 6 million customers and provides a return shipping package, also free. Customers watch their cinematic choices at their leisure; there are no late fees. When the DVDs are returned, customers select their next films.

Besides the logistical expertise that Netflix needs to make this a profitable venture, Netflix employs analytics in two important ways, both driven by customer behavior and buying patterns. The first is a movie-recommendation "engine" called Cinematch that's based on proprietary, algorithmically driven software. Netflix hired mathematicians with programming experience to write the algorithms and code to define clusters of movies, connect customer movie rankings to the clusters, evaluate thousands of ratings per second, and factor in current Web site behavior—all to ensure a personalized Web page for each visiting customer.

Netflix has also created a $1 million prize for quanitative analysts outside the company who can improve the cinematch algorithm by at least 10 percent. Netflix CEO Reed Hastings notes, "If the Starbucks secret is a smile when you get your latte, ours is that the Web site adapts to the individual's taste."[1] Netflix analyzes customers' choices and customer feedback on the movies they have rented—over 1 billion reviews of movies they liked, loved, hated, and so forth—and recommends movies in a way that optimizes both the customer's taste and inventory conditions. Netflix will often recommend movies that fit the customer's preference profile but that aren't in high demand. In other words, its primary territory is in "the long tail—the outer limits of the normal curve where the most popular products and offerings don't reside."[2]

Netflix also engages in a somewhat controversial, analytically driven practice called *throttling*. Throttling refers to how the company balances the distribution of shipping requests across frequent-use and infrequent-use customers. Infrequent-use customers are given priority in shipping over frequent-use customers. There are multiple reasons for this practice. Because shipping is free to customers and the monthly charge to the customer is fixed, infrequent-use customers are the most profitable to Netflix. Like all companies, Netflix wants to keep its most profitable customers satisfied and prevent them from leaving. And while frequent-use customers may feel they are being treated unfairly (there have been complaints by a small number of customers, according to Hastings), Netflix must distribute its shipping resources across its most and least profitable customers in a way that makes economic sense. Hastings refers to the practice as a *fairness algorithm*. Netflix recently settled a class action suit involving the practice, because it had advertised that most movies were shipped in a day.

Analytics also help Netflix decide what to pay for the distribution rights to DVDs. When the company bought the rights to *Favela Rising*, a documentary about musicians in Rio de Janeiro slums, Netflix executives were aware that a million customers had ordered from the company the 2003 movie *City of God*, a realistic drama set in the slums of Rio. It also knew that 500,000 customers had selected a somewhat related documentary about slum life in India, *Born into Brothels*, and 250,000 ordered both DVDs from Netflix. Therefore, the company's buyers felt safe in paying for 250,000 rentals. If more are ordered, both *Favela Rising's* producers and Netflix benefit.

Like most analytical competitors, Netflix has a strong culture of analytics and a "test and learn" approach to its business. The chief product officer, Neil Hunt, notes,

> From product management all the way down to the engineering team, we have hired for and have built a culture of quantitative tests. We typically have several hundred variations of consumer experience experiments running at once. For example, right now we're trying out the "Netflix Screening Room," which lets customers see previews of movies they haven't seen. We have built four different versions of that for the test. We put 20,000 subscribers into each of four test cells, and we have a control group that doesn't get the screening room at all. We measure how long they spend viewing previews, what the completion rate is, how many movies they add to their queue, how it affects ratings of movies they eventually order, and a variety of other factors. The initial data is quite promising.

Netflix's CEO, Hastings, has a master's in computer science from Stanford and is a former Peace Corps math teacher. The company has introduced science into a notably artistic industry. As a *BusinessWeek* article put it, "Netflix uses data to make decisions moguls make by gut. The average user rates more than 200 films, and Netflix crunches consumers' rental history and film ratings to predict what they'll like . . . 'It's *Moneyball* for movies [referring to the Oakland Athletics' usage of statistics in professional baseball], with geeks like Reed looking at movies as just another data problem,' says Netflix board member Richard N. Barton."

In its testing, Netflix employs a wide variety of quantitative and qualitative approaches, including primary surveys, Web site user testing, concept development and testing, advertising testing, data mining, brand awareness studies, subscriber satisfaction, channel analysis, marketing mix optimization, segmentation research, and marketing material effectiveness. The testing pervades the culture and extends from marketing to operations to customer service.

The company's analytical orientation has already led to a high level of success and growth. But the company is also counting on analytics to drive it through a major technological shift. It's already clear that the distribution of movies will eventually move to electronic channels—the Internet, cable, or over the air. The exact mix and timing aren't clear, but the long-term future of the mailed DVD isn't bright. Netflix, however, is counting on its analytics to help it prosper in a virtual distribution world. If Netflix knows more than anyone else about what movies its customers want to see, the logic goes, customers will stay with the company no matter how the movies get to their screens.

Netflix may seem unique, but in many ways it is typical of the companies and organizations—a small but rapidly growing number of them—that have recognized the potential of business analytics and have aggressively moved to realize it. They can be found in a variety of industries (see figure 1-1). Some, like Netflix, are not widely known as analytical competitors. Others, like Harrah's Entertainment in the gaming industry or the Oakland A's in baseball, have already been celebrated in books and articles. Some, such as Amazon.com, Yahoo!, and Google, are recent start-ups that have harnessed the power of the Internet to their analytical engines. Others, such as Mars and Procter & Gamble, have made familiar consumer goods for a century or more. These companies have only two things in common: they compete on the basis of their analytical capabilities, and they are highly successful in their industries. These two attributes, we believe, are not unrelated.

FIGURE 1-1

Analytic competitors are found in a variety of industries

Consumer products
- Anheuser-Busch
- E. & J. Gallo Winery
- Mars
- Procter & Gamble

Financial services
- Barclays Bank
- Capital One
- Royal Bank of Canada
- Progressive Casualty Insurance
- WellPoint

Hospitality and entertainment
- Oakland A's
- Boston Red Sox
- Harrah's Entertainment
- Marriott International
- New England Patriots

Industrial products
- CEMEX
- John Deere & Company

Pharmaceuticals
- AstraZeneca
- Solvay
- Vertex Pharmaceuticals, Inc.

Retail
- Amazon.com
- JCPenny
- Tesco
- Wal-Mart

Telecommunications
- Sprint
- O2
- Bouygues Telecom

Transport
- FedEx
- Schneider National
- United Parcel Service

eCommerce
- Google
- Netflix, Inc.
- Yahoo!

What Are Analytics?

By *analytics* we mean the extensive use of data, statistical and quantitative analysis, explanatory and predictive models, and fact-based management to drive decisions and actions. The analytics may be input for human decisions or may drive fully automated decisions. Analytics are a subset of what has come to be called *business intelligence*: a set of technologies and processes that use data to understand and analyze business performance. As figure 1-2 suggests, business intelligence includes both data access and reporting, and analytics. Each of these approaches addresses a range of questions about an organization's business activities. The questions that analytics can answer represent the higher-value and more proactive end of this spectrum.

In principle, analytics could be performed using paper, pencil, and perhaps a slide rule, but any sane person using analytics today would employ information technology. The range of analytical software goes from relatively simple statistical and optimization tools in spreadsheets (Excel being the primary example, of course), to statistical software packages (e.g., Minitab), to complex business intelligence suites (SAS,

6 • THE NATURE OF ANALYTICAL COMPETITION

FIGURE 1-2

Business intelligence and analytics

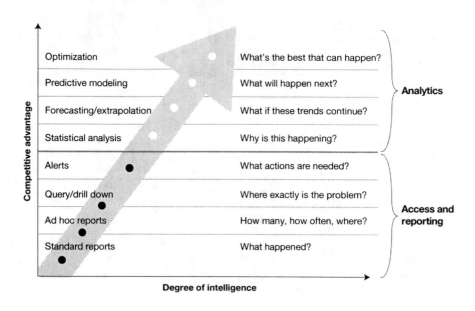

Source: Adapted from a graphic produced by SAS. Used with permission.

Cognos, BusinessObjects), predictive industry applications (Fair Isaac), and the reporting and analytical modules of major enterprise systems (SAP and Oracle). And as we'll describe later in the book, good analytical capabilities also require good information management capabilities to integrate, extract, transform, and access business transaction data. Some people, then, would simply equate analytics with analytical information technology. But this would be a huge mistake—as we'll argue throughout this book, it's the human and organizational aspects of analytical competition that are truly differentiating.

Why Compete on Analytics?

At a time when companies in many industries offer similar products and use comparable technology, high-performance business processes are among the last remaining points of differentiation. Many of the previous bases for competition are no longer available. Unique geographical advantage doesn't matter in global competition, and protective regulation is largely gone. Proprietary technologies are rapidly copied, and breakthrough innovation in products or services seems increasingly difficult to achieve. What's left as a basis for competition is to execute your business with maximum efficiency and effectiveness, and to make the smartest business decisions possible. And analytical competitors wring every last drop of value from business processes and key decisions.

Analytics can support almost any business process. Yet organizations that want to be competitive must have some attribute at which they are better than anyone else in their industry—a distinctive capability.[3] This usually involves some sort of business process or some type of decision. Maybe you strive to make money by being better at identifying profitable and loyal customers than your competition, and charging them the optimal price for your product or service. If so, analytics are probably the answer to being the best at it. Perhaps you sell commodity products and need to have the lowest possible level of inventory while preventing your customer from being unable to find your product on the shelf; if so, analytics are often the key to supply chain optimization. Perhaps you compete in a people-intensive business and are seeking to hire, retain, and promote the best people in the industry. There too, analytics can be the key (though thus far they have largely been used for this purpose in professional sports and not much in businesses).

On the other hand, perhaps your operational business processes aren't much different from anybody else's, but you feel you compete on making the best decisions. Maybe you can choose the best locations for your stores—if so, you're probably doing it analytically. You may build scale through mergers and acquisitions, and select only the best candidates for such combinations. Most don't work out well, according to widely publicized research, but yours do. If so, you're probably not making those decisions primarily on intuition. Good decisions usually have systematically assembled data and analysis behind them.

Analytical competitors, then, are organizations that have selected one or a few distinctive capabilities on which to base their strategies, and then have applied extensive data, statistical and quantitative analysis, and fact-based decision making to support the selected capabilities. Analytics themselves don't constitute a strategy, but using them to optimize a distinctive business capability certainly constitutes a strategy. Whatever the capabilities emphasized in a strategy, analytics can propel them to a higher level. Capital One, for example, calls its approach to analytical competition "information-based strategy." Harrah's distinctive capabilities are customer loyalty and service, and it has certainly optimized them with its analytically driven strategy.

Can any organization in any industry successfully compete on analytics? This is an interesting question that we've debated between ourselves. On the one hand, virtually any business would seem to have the potential for analytical competition. The cement business, for example, would seem to be as prosaic and nonanalytical an industry as one could find. But the global cement giant CEMEX has successfully applied analytics to its distinctive capability of optimized supply chains and delivery times.

On the other hand, some industries are clearly more amenable to analytics than others. If your business generates lots of transaction data—such as in financial services, travel and transportation, or gaming—competing on analytics is a natural strategy (though many firms still don't do it). If your business model is based on hard-to-measure factors—like style, as in the fashion business, or human relationships, as in the executive search industry—it would take much more groundbreaking work to compete on analytics. Still, virtually every day we find examples of businesses that were previously intuitive but are now becoming analytical. The wine business, for example, was once and (in some quarters) still is highly intuitive and built on unpredictable consumer preferences. Today, however, it's possible to quantitatively analyze and predict the appeal of any wine, and large winemakers such as E. & J. Gallo are competing on analytics in such domains as sales, agriculture, and understanding of consumer preferences.[4]

How This Book Can Help

We didn't invent the idea of competing on analytics, but we believe that this book (and the articles we wrote that preceded it) are the first to describe the phenomenon.[5] In this book, you'll find more on the topic than has ever been compiled: more discussion of the concept, more examples of organizations that are pursuing analytical competition, more management issues to be addressed, and more specific applications of analytics. Part I of the book lays out the definition and key attributes of analytical competition, and discusses (with some analytics!) how it can lead to better business performance. The end of this part describes a variety of applications of competitive analytics, first internally and then externally, with customers and suppliers.

Part II of the book is more of a how-to guide. It begins with an overall road map for organizations wishing to compete on their analytical capabilities. Whole chapters are devoted to each of the two key resources—human and technological—needed to make this form of competition a reality. We conclude by discussing some of the key directions for business analytics in the future.

There are a lot of words here, but we know they won't be the last on the topic. We know of several other authors planning books on it, and we hope there will be a raft of articles too. We hope that many academics and consultants will embrace the topic. If this field is to prosper, the world will have to spend a lot of time and energy focusing on it, and we'll need all the guidance we can get.

How Did We Get Here?
The Origins of Analytical Competition

The planets are clearly aligned for the move to analytical competition by organizations. At the same time that executives have been looking for new sources of advantage and differentiation, they have more data about their businesses than ever before. Enterprise resource planning (ERP) systems, point-of-sale (POS) systems, and Web sites, among other sources, have created more and better transaction data than in the history of humankind. A new generation of technically literate executives—the first to grow up with computers—is coming into organizations and looking for new ways to manage them with the help of technology. Finally, the ability to make sense of data through computers and software has finally come of age. Analytical software makers have dramatically expanded the functionality of their products over the past several years, and hardware providers have optimized their technologies for fast analysis and the management of large databases.

The use of analytics began as a small, out-of-the-way activity performed in a few data-intensive business functions. As early as the late 1960s, practitioners and researchers began to experiment with the use of computer systems to analyze data and support decision making. Called *decision support systems* (DSS), these applications were used for analytical, repetitive, and somewhat narrow activities such as production planning, investment portfolio management, and transportation routing. Two DSS pioneers, Peter Keen and Charles Stabell, argue that the concept of decision support arose from studies of organizational decision making done at Carnegie Tech (now Carnegie Mellon) by researchers such as Herbert Simon during the late 1950s and early '60s, and technical work on interactive computer systems, mainly carried out at MIT in the 1960s.[6] Others would argue that their origins were closely connected to military applications in and following World War II, although computers as we know them were not yet available for those applications.

Statistical analysis on computers became a much more mainstream activity in the 1970s, as companies such as SAS Institute and SPSS introduced packaged computer applications that made statistics accessible to many researchers and businesspeople. Yet despite the greater availability of statistics, DSS did not prosper in the period and evolved into *executive support systems*.[7] These applications involved direct use of computers and data by senior executives for monitoring and reporting of performance (with a lesser emphasis on decision making). This activity also never took off broadly, in part because of the reluctance of executives to engage in hands-on use.

Analytical technology became most frequently used for storing relatively small amounts of data and conducting ad hoc queries in support of decisions and performance monitoring. The focus on managing data became important because vast amounts of it were becoming available from transaction systems such as ERP and POS systems, and later from Internet transactions. Versions of this data-oriented focus were referred to as OLAP (online analytical processing) and later *data warehousing*. Smaller data warehouses were called *data marts*.

Today, as we mentioned, the entire field is often referred to with the term *business intelligence* and incorporates the collection, management, and reporting of decision-oriented data as well as the analytical techniques and computing approaches that are performed on the data. Business intelligence overall is a broad and popular field within the IT industry—in fact, a 2006 Gartner survey of 1,400 chief information officers suggests that business intelligence is the number one technology priority for IT organizations.[8] Two studies of large organizations using ERP systems that we did in 2002 and 2006 revealed that better decision making was the primary benefit sought, and (in 2006) analytics were the technology most sought to take advantage of the ERP data.

Despite the variation in terminology, these movements—each of which lasted about a decade—had several attributes in common. They were largely technically focused, addressing how computers could be used to store, analyze, and display data and results of analysis. They were focused on fairly narrow problems—with the exception of the executive and performance monitoring systems, which only displayed the condition of the business. They were also relegated to the "back office" of organizations—used by technicians and specialists, with little visibility to senior executives. With only a few exceptions, they could rarely be said to influence the nature of competition.

Today, most large organizations have some sort of analytical applications in place and some business intelligence tools installed. But they are typically marginal to the success of the business and are managed at the departmental level. An insurance company, for example, may have some analytical tools and approaches in the actuarial department, where pricing for policies is determined. A manufacturing company may use such tools for quality management. Marketing may have some capabilities for lifetime value analysis for customers. However valuable these activities are, they are invisible to senior executives, customers, and shareholders—and they can't be said to drive the company's competitive strategy. They are important to individual functions but insignificant to competition overall.

Our focus in this book, however, is on companies that have elevated data management, statistical and quantitative analysis, and fact-based decision making to a high art. These organizations have analytical activities that are hardly invisible; they are touted to every stakeholder and interested party by CEOs. Rather than being in the back room, analytics in these companies are found in the annual report and in the press clippings. These organizations have taken a resource that is ostensibly available to all, and refined it to such a degree that their strategies are built around it.

When Are Analytical Decisions Appropriate?

There is considerable evidence that decisions based on analytics are more likely to be correct than those based on intuition.[9] It's better to know—at least within the limits of data and analysis—than to believe or think or feel, and most companies can benefit from more analytical decision making. Of course, there are some circumstances in which decisions can't or shouldn't be based on analytics. Some of these circumstances are described in Malcolm Gladwell's popular book *Blink*, which is a paean to intuitive decision making.[10] It's ironic that a book praising intuition would arise and become popular just when many organizations are relying heavily on analytics, but then perhaps that's part of its romantic appeal. The book is fun and persuasive, but it doesn't make clear that intuition is only appropriate under certain circumstances. Gladwell is undoubtedly correct, for example, that human beings evolved a capability to make accurate and quick decisions about each other's personality and intentions, and it's rare for formal analysis to do that as well. Yet even Gladwell argues that intuition is a good guide to action only when it's backed by many years of expertise. And many of Gladwell's examples of intuition are only possible because of years of analytical research in the background, such as Dr. John Gottsman's rapid and seemingly intuitive judgments of whether a married couple he observes will stay together. He's only able to make such assessments because he observed and statistically analyzed thousands of hours of videotaped interactions by couples.

It's also clear that decision makers have to use intuition when they have no data and must make a very rapid decision—as in Gladwell's example of police officers deciding whether to shoot a suspect. Gary Klein, a consultant on decision making, makes similar arguments about firefighters making decisions about burning buildings.[11] Even firms that are generally quite analytical must sometimes resort to intuition when they have no data. For example, Jeff Bezos, CEO of Amazon.com, greatly prefers to perform limited tests of new features on Amazon.com, rigorously quantifying user reaction before rolling them out. But the company's "search inside the book" offering was impossible to test without applying it to a critical mass of books (Amazon.com started with 120,000). It was also expensive to develop, increasing the risk. In that case, Bezos trusted his instincts and took a flier. And the feature did prove popular when introduced.[12]

Of course, any quantitative analysis relies upon a series of assumptions. When the conditions behind the assumptions no longer apply, the analyses should no longer be employed. For example, Capital One and other credit card companies make analytical predictions about customers' willingness to repay their balances under conditions of general economic prosperity. If the economy took a sharp downturn, the predictions would no longer apply, and it would be dangerous to continue using them.

The key message is that the frontier of decisions that can be treated analytically is always moving forward. Areas of decision making that were once well suited for intuition accumulate data and analytical rigor over time, and intuition becomes suboptimal. Today, for example, some executives still consider it feasible to make major decisions about mergers and acquisitions from their gut. However, the best firms are already using detailed analytics to explore such decisions. Procter & Gamble, for example, used a variety of analytical techniques before its acquisition of Gillette, including those for logistics and supply chains, drivers of stock market value, and human resources. In a few years, firms that do not employ extensive analytics in making a major acquisition will be considered irresponsible.

Indeed, trends point to a more analytical future for virtually every firm. The amount of data available will only continue to increase. Radio frequency identification (RFID) devices will be put on virtually every pallet or carton that moves through the supply chain, generating vast amounts of new data for companies to collect and analyze. In retail, every shopping cart will be intelligent enough to gather data on "pickstreams," or a record of which products are taken off the shelves in what order. In oil exploration and mining, the amount of data—already massive—will expand geometrically. In advertising, more businesses are already shifting to media such as the Internet and cable television that can monitor which ads are seen by whom—again creating a huge new stream of data.

Analytical software will become more broadly available and will be in reach of every organization. Statistically oriented software firms such as SAS and SPSS have made increasingly sophisticated analyses available to average companies and users for over thirty years, and they will continue to do so. Business intelligence firms such as SAS, Business Objects, and Cognos are adding more analytical capabilities to their software toolsets. New industry applications targeting different business capabilities will become available from vendors such as Fair Isaac Corporation. Enterprise systems vendors such as SAP and Oracle are making it more possible to analyze their systems' data and monitor the performance of the business. And Microsoft is incorporating increasing amounts of analytical capability into basic office software. In the future, software availability will not be an issue in analytical competition, although the ability to use analytical software well won't ever be a commodity.

It's also safe to assume that hardware won't be a problem. Today the 64-bit processors from Intel and others that can do extensive quantitative analysis on large data sets are considered cutting-edge, but they won't be for long. Specialized computers from providers such as Teradata and Netezza can easily manage multiterabyte data warehouses. No doubt the personal computer of the near future will be able to perform serious analyses. The bigger issue will be how organizations control their data and analysis, and ensure that individual users make decisions on correct analyses and assumptions.

To remain an analytical competitor, however, means staying on the leading edge. Analytical competition will be something of an arms race, requiring continual development of new measures, new algorithms, and new decision-making approaches. Firms embracing it will systematically eliminate guesswork from their processes and business models. Analytical competitors will have to conduct experiments in many aspects of their businesses and learn from each one of them. In order for quantitative decisions to be implemented effectively, analysis will have to be a broad capability of employees, rather than the province of a few "rocket scientists" with quantitative expertise.

We've developed a road map describing the primary steps needed to build an effective analytical competitor. It involves key prerequisites, such as having at least a moderate amount and quality of data about the domain of business that analytics will support, and having the right types of hardware and software on hand. The key variables are human, however. One prerequisite is that some manager must have enough commitment to analytics to develop the idea further. But then the pivotal factor in how fast and how well an organization proceeds along the analytical path is sponsorship. Firms such as Netflix, Harrah's, and Capital One have CEO-level sponsorship and even passion for analytical competition that lets them proceed on a "full steam ahead" path.

Other organizations that lack passionate executive sponsorship must first go through a "prove it" path to demonstrate the value of analytical competition. This path is slower, and even those who take the prove-it path have to eventually arrive at strong executive sponsorship if they are to become true analytical competitors. We will discuss this road map—and the steps on each of the two paths—in greater detail in the second part of this book (chapter 6 in particular). For now, we simply want to emphasize that although analytics seem to be dispassionate and computer based, the most important factors leading to success involve passionate people.

Analytics in Professional Sports—and Their Implications for Business

We can perhaps best understand the progression of analytical competition across an industry by focusing on professional sports. While sports differ, of course, they have in common large amounts of data and talented but expensive human resources (the athletes). Sports also differ from businesses, but both domains of activity have in common the need to optimize critical resources and of course the need to win.

Perhaps the most analytical professional sport is baseball, which has long been the province of quantitative and statistical analysis. The use of statistics and new measures in baseball received considerable visibility with the publication of *Moneyball*, by Michael Lewis.[13] The book described the analytical orientation of the Oakland A's, a professional team that had a record of consistently making the playoffs despite a low overall payroll (including the 2006 playoffs—although, even the best analytical competitor doesn't win all the time, as in 2005). Lewis described the conversion of Oakland's general manager (GM), Billy Beane, to analytics for player selection when he realized that he himself had possessed all the traditional attributes of a great player, according to major league scouts. Yet Beane had not been a great player, so he began to focus more on actual player performance as revealed in statistics than on the potential to be great. Beane and the A's also began to make use of relatively new measures of player performance, eschewing the traditional "runs batted in," or RBIs, and focusing on "on-base percentage" and "on-base plus slugging percentage." Like analytical competitors in business, they invented new metrics that assessed and stretched their performance.

Yet Beane was not actually the first Oakland general manager to take a statistical orientation.[14] In the early 1980s, Sandy Alderson, then the GM (now CEO of the San Diego Padres, another 2006 playoff contender), adopted a more statistical approach for two reasons. First, Oakland had performed badly for a number of years before the decision and was on the brink of going out of business. Second, Alderson was offered an early version of a PC-based (actually, Apple II–based) statistical database and analysis package. Baseball statistics are widely available from firms such as STATS, Inc., and the Elias Sports Bureau, although the statistics were available to teams well before they started taking advantage of them. These reasons are typical of why businesses often adopt analytical competition: a combination of pressing business need, the availability of data, and IT that can crunch all the numbers.

The analytical approach to baseball has broadened considerably over the last few years. One team that has adopted the "moneyball" approach is the Boston Red Sox—a team with both analytical capabilities and the money to invest in expensive players. The Red Sox also had a business need, having failed to win the World Series for eighty-six years by the 2004 season. The Sox also exemplify another reason why organizations adopt analytical competition: new leadership. The team's two new principal owners in 2002 were John Henry, a quantitative hedge fund manager, and Tom Werner, a television producer who had previously owned the San Diego Padres. The appeal of analytics to Henry was obvious, but Werner had also realized with the Padres that the traditional baseball establishment didn't know as much about what led to championships as it purported to. As we mentioned earlier, the high level of executive sponsorship at the Sox let the team take the full-steam-ahead approach to analytical competition.

Like other organizations committed to analytical strategies, the Red Sox quickly hired as a consultant the best analytical talent: Bill James, who was widely regarded as the world's foremost practitioner of "sabermetrics," or baseball statistics (James even invented the term himself). The fact that no other team had seen fit to hire such an underemployed analytical genius suggests that analytical competition in baseball was not yet widespread. The analytical approach—along with some new and expensive talent—paid off for the Sox quickly, and they made the American League Championship Series (ALCS) against their perennial rivals, the New York Yankees, in 2003.

Yet one game in that series illustrates a key difficulty of analytical competition: it has to spread everywhere within an organization if analytical decisions are to be implemented. In the fifth and deciding game of the series, Red Sox ace Pedro Martinez was pitching. Sox analysts had demonstrated conclusively that Martinez became much easier for opposing batters to hit after about 7 innings or 105 pitches (that year, the opposing team's batting average against Martinez for pitches 91–105 was .231; for pitches 106–120 it was .370). They had warned manager Grady Little that by no means should Martinez be left in the game after that point. Yet when Martinez predictably began to falter late in the seventh, Little let him keep pitching into the eighth (even against the advice of his pitching coach), and the Yankees shelled Martinez. The

Yanks won the ALCS, but Little lost his job. It's a powerful story of what can happen if frontline managers and employees don't go along with the analytical program. Fortunately for long-suffering Red Sox fans (including one of the authors of this volume), the combination of numbers and money proved insurmountable in the 2004 season, and the Sox broke the eighty-six-year World Series championship drought.

Analytical competition has not fully triumphed in baseball, however. Some teams—including some perennially good teams, such as the Atlanta Braves—still rely heavily on traditional scouting criteria, although they use numbers too. The Braves' general manager, John Schuerholz, argued in an interview that "to suggest that new, statistical, chrome-plated, digitally enhanced, new-age-thinking statistics alone can replace scouting instincts and human judgment and analysis, I take great exception to that. So what we do is use both."[15] St. Louis Cardinals coach Tony La Russa (whose team won the 2006 World Series), one of the best coaches in the game, brilliantly combines analytics with intuition to decide when to substitute a charged-up player in the batting lineup or whether to hire a spark plug personality to improve morale. In his recent book, *Three Nights in August*, Buzz Bissinger describes that balance: "La Russa appreciated the information generated by computers. He studied the rows and the columns. But he also knew they could take you only so far in baseball, maybe even confuse you with a fog of overanalysis. As far as he knew, there was no way to quantify desire. And those numbers told him exactly what he needed to know when added to twenty-four years of managing experience."[16]

Analytics have also spread to professional football. The New England Patriots, for example, have been particularly successful of late, winning three Super Bowls in four years. The team uses data and analytical models extensively, both on and off the field. In-depth analytics help the team select its players and stay below the salary cap (last year the team had the twenty-fourth-highest payroll in the National Football League). The team selects players without using the scouting services that other teams employ, and it rates potential draft choices on such nontraditional factors as intelligence and willingness to subsume personal ego for the benefit of the team.

The Patriots also make extensive use of analytics for on-the-field decisions. They employ statistics, for example, to decide whether to punt or "go for it" on fourth down, whether to try for one point or two after a touchdown, and whether to challenge a referee's ruling. Both its coaches and players are renowned for their extensive study of game films and statistics, and head coach Bill Belichick has been known to peruse articles by academic economists on statistical probabilities of football outcomes. Off the field, the team uses detailed analytics to assess and improve the "total fan experience." At every home game, for example, twenty to twenty-five people have specific assignments to make quantitative measurements of the stadium food, parking, personnel, bathroom cleanliness, and other factors. External vendors of services are monitored for contract renewal and have incentives to improve their performance.[17]

Other NFL teams that make extensive usage of statistics include the Kansas City Chiefs, Tennessee Titans, and Green Bay Packers. The Titans, for example, have determined that the traditional performance measures of yards allowed or gained are relatively meaningless, and have come up with alternative measures. The Packers analyzed game films of one running back with a fumbling problem, and determined that the fumbles only happened when the player's elbow wasn't horizontal to the ground when he was hit.[18] Despite the success of the Patriots and these other teams, many teams in the NFL have yet to grasp the nature and value of analytical competition.

Professional basketball has historically been less quantitatively oriented than baseball or football, but the numeric approach is beginning to take off there as well. Several teams, including the high-performing San Antonio Spurs, have hired statistical consultants or statistically oriented executives. The Houston Rockets have recently selected as general manager a young, quantitatively oriented executive who previously managed information systems and analytics for the Boston Celtics. Daryl Morey, an MIT MBA, considers baseball sabermetrician Bill James to be his role model, and argues that analytics in basketball are similar to those for moneyball in baseball. "It's the same principle. Generate wins for fewer dollars."[19] As in baseball and football, teams and their analysts are pursuing new measures, such as a player's value to the team when on the court versus when off of it (called the Roland Rating after amateur statistician Roland Beech).

Analytical competition is taking root not only in U.S. sports. Some soccer teams in Europe have also begun to employ similar techniques. AC Milan, one of the leading teams in Europe, uses predictive models to prevent player injuries by analyzing physiological, orthopedic, and psychological data from a variety of sources. Its Milan Lab identifies the risk factors that are most likely to be associated with an injury for each player.

The lab also assesses potential players to add to the team. Several members of the World Cup–winning Italy national team trained at Milan Lab. The Bolton Wanderers, a fast-rising English soccer team, are known for the manager's use of extensive data to evaluate player performance and team strategies. The team also uses analytics to identify its most valuable customers and to offer them benefits that help build loyalty.

Why all this activity in professional sports, and what difference does it make for other types of organizations? There are many themes that could cut across sports and business. Perhaps the most important lesson from professional sports analytics is its focus on the human resource—on choosing and keeping the best players at the lowest price. This is not a widespread practice in the business "talent management" domain, but perhaps it should be. As executive and individual contributor salaries continue to rise, it may be time to begin to analyze and gather data on which people perform well under what circumstances, and to ensure that the right players are on the team. A few firms are beginning to adopt a more analytical approach to human resource management, but sports teams are still far ahead of other organizations.

Analytical competition in sports also illustrates the point that analysis rises first when sufficient data is present to analyze. If there is a business area in which large amounts of data are available for the first time, it will probably soon become a playing field for analytical competition. Analytical innovators in professional sports also often create new measures, and businesspeople should do the same.

While analytics is a somewhat abstract and complex subject, its adoption in professional sports illustrates the human nature of the process. When a team embraces analytical competition, it's because a leader makes a decision to do so. That decision can often be traced to the leader's own background and experiences. Analytical competition—whether in sports or business—is almost always a story involving people and leadership.

It's also no accident that the sports teams that have embraced analytical competition have generally done well. They won't win championships every year, of course, but analytical competitors have been successful in every sport in which they have arisen. However, as analytical competition spreads—and it spreads quickly—teams will have to continue innovating and building their analytical capabilities if they wish to stay in front. Whatever the approach to competition, no team (or firm) can afford to rest on its laurels.

What's in This Book

We've attempted to lay out the general outlines of analytical competition in this chapter and to provide a few examples in the worlds of business and sports. There are many more examples to come, and throughout part I of the book, we'll go into much more detail about what it means to compete on analytics and how companies can move in that direction. Chapter 2 describes the specific attributes of firms that compete on analytics and lays out a five-stage model of just how analytically oriented an organization is. Chapter 3 describes how analytics contribute to better business performance, and includes some data and analysis on that topic. Chapters 4 and 5 describe a number of applications of analytics in business; they are grouped into internally oriented applications and those primarily involving external relationships with customers and suppliers.

In part II of the book, our goal is to discuss the key steps and capabilities involved in analytical competition. We begin that part with a discussion in chapter 6 of the overall road map for analytical competition. Chapter 7 is about the most important factor in making a company analytical: its people. Chapter 8 is about the important resources of technology and data, and how they can be combined in an overall analytical architecture. We conclude the book in chapter 9 with a discussion of the future directions that analytical competition might take.

We do our best to help organizations embark upon this path to business and organizational success. However, it's important to remember that this is just an overview. There are many books on how to implement business intelligence, how to create and modify analytical models in such areas as supply chain and marketing, and how to do basic quantitative and statistical analysis. Our goal is not to give businesspeople all the knowledge they'll ever need to do serious analytical work, but rather to get you excited about the possibilities for analytical competition and motivated enough to pursue further study.

Notes

Chapter 1

1. Netflix quotation from Jena McGregor, "At Netflix, the Secret Sauce Is Software," *Fast Company*, October 2005, 50. Other Netflix information comes from the company Web site (http://www.netflix.com); Mark Hall, "Web Analytics Get Real," *Computerworld*, April 1, 2002; Timothy J. Mullaney, "Netflix: The Mail-Order Movie House That Clobbered Blockbuster," *BusinessWeek Online*, May 25, 2006, http://www.businessweek.com/smallbiz/content/may2006/sb20060525_268860.htm?campaign_id=search; and a telephone interview with chief product officer Neil Hunt on July 7, 2006.

2. The "long tail" concept has been popularized by Chris Anderson in *The Long Tail: Why the Future of Business Is Selling Less of More* (New York: Hyperion, 2006).

3. We define *distinctive capabilities* as the integrated business processes and capabilities that together serve customers in ways that are differentiated from competitors and that create an organization's formula for business success.

4. David Darlington, "The Chemistry of a 90+ Wine," *New York Times Sunday Magazine*, August 7, 2005.

5. Thomas H. Davenport, "Competing on Analytics," *Harvard Business Review*, January 2006; Thomas H. Davenport, "Analyze This," *CIO*, October 1, 2005, http://www.cio.com/archive/100105/comp_advantage.html; and Thomas H. Davenport and Jeanne G. Harris, "Automated Decision Making Comes of Age," *MIT Sloan Management Review*, Summer 2005.

6. One of the first books written on the subject of decision support was by Peter G. W. Keen and Michael S. Scott Morton, *Decision Support Systems: An Organizational Perspective* (Reading, MA: Addison-Wesley, 1978). A subsequent book written on the topic is by John W. Rockart and David W.

21

De Long, *Executive Support Systems: The Emergence of Top Management Computer Use* (Homewood, IL: Dow Jones-Irwin, 1988). Also note Tom Gerrity Jr.'s 1971 article, "The Design of Man-Machine Decision Systems: An Application to Portfolio Management," *MIT Sloan Management Review* 12, no. 2, (1971): 59–75; and Charles Stabell's 1974 work, "On the Development of Decision Support Systems on a Marketing Problem," *Information Processing*, as formative research in the field of DSS.

7. Rockart and De Long, *Executive Support Systems.*

8. Described in "Business Intelligence Software Market to Reach $3 Billion by 2009," *CRM Today*, February 8, 2006, http://www.crm2day.com/news/crm/117297.php.

9. For example, refer to Jeffrey Pfeffer and Robert Sutton's article "Evidence-Based Management," *Harvard Business Review*, January 2006; and Eric Bonabeau's article "Don't Trust Your Gut," *Harvard Business Review*, May 2003.

10. Malcolm Gladwell, *Blink: The Power of Thinking Without Thinking* (New York: Little, Brown, 2005).

11. Gary Klein, *Sources of Power: How People Make Decisions* (Cambridge, MA: MIT Press, 1999).

12. Alan Deutschman, "Inside the Mind of Jeff Bezos," *Fast Company*, August 2004, 52.

13. Michael Lewis, *Moneyball: The Art of Winning an Unfair Game* (New York: W. W. Norton & Company, 2004).

14. Alan Schwartz, *The Numbers Game: Baseball's Lifelong Fascination with Statistics* (New York: St. Martin's Griffin, 2005).

15. Russell Adams, "The Culture of Winning: Atlanta Braves Have Secured 14 Straight Division Titles, and Team's GM Tells Why," *Wall Street Journal*, October 5, 2005.

16. Buzz Bissinger, *Three Nights in August* (Boston: Houghton Mifflin, 2005), 201.

17. Andy Wasynczuk, then chief operating officer, New England Patriots, telephone interview with Tom Davenport, January 11, 2005.

18. From "Interview with Packers Director of Research and Development Mike Eayrs," *Football Outsiders*, June 22, 2004, http://www.football-outsiders.com/ramblings.php?p=226&cat=8.

19. Chris Ballard, "Measure of Success," *Sports Illustrated*, October 24, 2005.

HARVARD
BUSINESS
SCHOOL
PRESS

What Makes an Analytical Competitor?

Defining the Common Key Attributes of Such Companies

EXCERPTED FROM

Competing on Analytics: The New Science of Winning

BY

Thomas H. Davenport, Jeanne G. Harris

Harvard Business School Press
Boston, Massachusetts

ISBN-13: 978-1-4221-2196-2
2196BC

2

WHAT MAKES AN ANALYTICAL COMPETITOR?

Defining the Common
Key Attributes of Such Companies

WHAT DOES IT MEAN TO compete on analytics? We define an *analytical competitor* as an organization that uses analytics extensively and systematically to outthink and outexecute the competition. In this chapter, we'll describe the key attributes of companies that compete on analytics, and describe the levels and stages of these attributes that we found in researching actual organizations.

Among the firms we studied, we found that the most analytically sophisticated and successful had four common key characteristics: (1) analytics supported a strategic, distinctive capability; (2) the approach to and management of analytics was enterprise-wide; (3) senior management was committed to the use of analytics; and (4) the company made a significant strategic bet on analytics-based competition. We found each of these attributes present in the companies that were most aggressively pursuing analytical approaches to business.

We don't know, of course, exactly how many analytical competitors there are, but we do have data allowing a good estimate. In a global survey of 371 medium to large firms conducted in late 2005, we asked respondents (IT executives or business executives familiar with their companies' enterprise IT applications) how much analytical capability

I

their organizations had. The highest category was described by the statement "Analytical capability is a key element of strategy" for the business. Ten percent of the respondents selected that category. According to our detailed analysis of the data, perhaps half of these firms are full-bore analytical competitors. There may be slightly more or fewer, but we don't know of any better estimate.

Primary Attributes of Analytical Competitors

Next, we'll describe how several of the companies we studied exemplify the four attributes of analytical competition. True analytical competitors exhibit all four; less advanced organizations may have only one or two at best.

Support of a Strategic, Distinctive Capability

It stands to reason that if analytics are to support competitive strategy, they must be in support of an important and distinctive capability. As we mentioned in the first chapter, the capability varies by organization and industry, and might involve supply chains, pricing and revenue management, customer service, customer loyalty, or human resource management. At Netflix, of course, the primary focus for analytics is on predicting customer movie preferences. At Harrah's, it's on customer loyalty and service. Marriott International's primary analytical orientation is on revenue management. Wal-Mart obviously emphasizes supply chain analytics. Professional sports teams generally focus on human resources, or choosing the right players.

Having a distinctive capability means that the organization views this aspect of its business as what sets it apart from competitors and as what makes it successful in the marketplace. In companies without this strategic focus, analytical capabilities are just a utility to be applied to a variety of business problems without regard for their significance.

Of course, not all businesses have a distinctive capability. They usually suffer when they don't. It's not obvious, for example, what Kmart's, US Airways', or General Motors' distinctive capabilities are. To the outside observer, they don't do anything substantially better than their competitors—and their customers and potential shareholders have noticed. Without a distinctive capability, you can't be an analytical competitor, because there is no clear process or activity for analytics to support.

It's also possible that the distinctive capability an organization chooses would not be well supported by analytics—at least this has been true in the past. If the strategic decisions an organization makes are intuitive or experience based and cannot be made analytically, it wouldn't make sense to try to compete on statistics and fact-based decisions. We mentioned the fashion and executive search businesses in this regard in chapter 1. One might add management consulting to this list, in that most consulting advice is based on experience rather than analytics. We suspect, however, that in each of these industries there is the potential for analytical competition and that some firm will adopt it at some point in time. Fashion businesses could try to decompose and predict the elements of consumer taste. Executive search firms could build their businesses around a database of what kinds of executives perform well under certain circumstances. And consultants (and lawyers and investment bankers, for that matter) could base their advice to clients on detailed statistical analysis of what management approaches have been effective in specified business situations. They could perhaps transform their industries by taking an analytical approach to strategy.

A corollary of this factor is that analytical competitors pay careful attention to measures of the distinctive capabilities in their businesses. They engage in both *exploitation* and *exploration* of measures—they exploit existing measures to a considerable degree and are early to explore new measures. We've already discussed professional baseball, where teams like Oakland's have moved to new measures of player performance. Consumer finance is another industry with a strong emphasis on developing new metrics.

Because there are many quantitative transactions in consumer financial services, it's relatively easy to employ measures in decision making. Perhaps the most commonly used measure in consumer finance is the credit or FICO score, which is an indicator of the customer's creditworthiness. There are many possible credit scores, but only one official FICO score. (FICO scores are based on an algorithm developed by Fair, Isaac and Company [currently Fair Isaac Corporation] in 1989. Now, the three major credit bureaus have created a competitor, the Vantage Score, that, unlike the FICO score, is consistent with all credit ratings; in Europe, some financial services firms employ credit scores from Scorex.) Virtually every consumer finance firm in the United States uses the FICO score to make consumer credit decisions and to decide what interest rate to charge. Analytical banking competitors such as Capital One, however, adopted it earlier and more aggressively than other firms. Their distinctive capability was finding out which customers were most desirable in terms of paying considerable interest without defaulting on their loans. After FICO scores had become pervasive in banking, they began to spread to the insurance industry. Again, highly analytical firms such as Progressive determined that consumers with high FICO scores not only were more likely to pay back loans, but also were less likely to have automobile accidents. Therefore, they began to charge lower premiums for customers with higher FICO scores.

Today, however, there is little distinction in simply using a FICO score in banking or property and casualty insurance. The new frontiers are in applying credit scores in other industries and in mining data about them to refine decision making. Some analysts are predicting, for example, that credit scores will soon be applied in making life and health insurance decisions and pricing of premiums. At least one health insurance company is exploring whether the use of credit scores might make it possible to avoid requiring an expensive physical examination before issuing a health policy. One professor also notes that they might be used for employment screening:

> It is uncommon to counsel individuals with financial problems who don't have other kinds of problems. You're more likely to miss days at work, be less productive on the job, as well as have marriage and other relationship problems if you are struggling financially. It makes sense that if you have a low credit score that you are more likely to have problems in other areas of life. Employers looking to screen a large number of applicants could easily see a credit score as an effective way to narrow the field.[1]

Since credit scores are pervasive, some firms are beginning to try to disaggregate credit scores and determine which factors are most closely associated with the desired outcome. Progressive Insurance and Capital One, for example, are both reputed to be disaggregating and analyzing credit scores to determine which customers with relatively low scores might be better risks than their overall scores would predict.

One last point on the issue of distinctive capabilities. These mission-critical capabilities should be the organization's primary analytical target. Yet we've noticed that over time, analytical competitors tend to move into a variety of analytical domains. Marriott started its analytical work in the critical area of revenue management but later moved into loyalty program analysis and Web metrics analysis. At Netflix, the most strategic application may be predicting customer movie preferences, but the company also employs testing and detailed analysis in its supply chain and its advertising. Harrah's started in loyalty and service but also does detailed analyses of its slot machine pricing and placement, the design of its Web site, and many other issues in its business. Wal-Mart, Progressive Insurance, and the hospital supply distributor Owens & Minor are all examples of firms that started with an internal analytical focus but have broadened it externally—to suppliers in the case of Wal-Mart and to customers for the other two firms. Analytical competitors need a primary focus for their analytical activity, but once an analytical, test-and-learn culture has been created, it's impossible to stop it from spreading.

An Enterprise-Level Approach to and Management of Analytics

Companies and organizations that compete analytically don't entrust analytical activities just to one group within the company or to a collection of disparate employees across the organization. They manage analytics as an organization or enterprise and ensure that no process or business unit is optimized at the expense of another unless it is strategically important to do so. At Harrah's, for example, when Gary Loveman began the company's move into analytical competition, he had all the company's casino property heads report to him, and ensured that they implemented the company's marketing and customer service programs in the same way. Before this, each property had been a "fiefdom," managed by "feudal lords with occasional interruptions from the king or queen who passed through town."[2] This made it virtually impossible for Harrah's to implement marketing and loyalty initiatives encouraging cross-market play.

Enterprise-level management also means ensuring that the data and analyses are made available broadly throughout the organization and that the proper care is taken to manage data and analyses efficiently and effectively. If decisions that drive the company's success are made on overly narrow data, incorrect data, or faulty analysis, the consequences could be severe. Therefore, analytical competitors make the management of analytics and the data on which they are based an organization-wide activity. For example, one of the reasons that RBC Financial Group (the best-known unit of which is Royal Bank of Canada) has been a successful analytical competitor is that it decided early on (in the 1970s) that all customer data would be owned by the enterprise and held in a central customer information file. Bank of America attributes its analytical capabilities around asset and interest-rate risk exposure to the fact that risk was managed in a consistent way across the enterprise. Many other banks have been limited in their ability to assess the overall profitability or loyalty of customers because different divisions or product groups have different and incompatible ways to define and record customer data.

An enterprise approach is a departure from the past for many organizations. Analytics have largely been either an individual or a departmental activity in the past and largely remain so today in companies that don't compete on analytics. For example, in a 2005 survey of 220 organizations' approaches to the management of business intelligence (which, remember, also includes some nonanalytical activities, such as reporting), only 45 percent said that their use of business intelligence was either "organizational" or "global," with 53 percent responding "in my department," "departmental," "regional," or "individual." In the same survey, only 22 percent of firms reported a formal needs assessment process across the enterprise; 29 percent did no needs assessment at all; and 43 percent assessed business intelligence needs at the divisional or departmental level.[3] The reasons for this decentralization are easy to understand. A particular quantitatively focused department, such as quality, marketing, or pricing, may have used analytics in going about its work, without affecting the overall strategy or management approach of the enterprise. Perhaps its activities should have been elevated into a strategic resource, with broader access and greater management attention. Most frequently, however, these departmental analytical applications remained in the background.

Another possibility is that analytics might have been left entirely up to individuals within those departments. In such cases, analytics took place primarily on individual spreadsheets. While it's great for individual employees to use data and analysis to support their decisions, individually created and managed spreadsheets are not the best way to manage analytics for an enterprise. For one thing, they can contain errors. Research by one academic suggests that between 20 percent and 40 percent of user-created spreadsheets contain errors; the more spreadsheets, the more errors.[4] While there are no estimates of the frequency of errors for enterprise-level analytics, they could at least involve processes to control and eliminate errors that would be difficult to impose at the individual level.

A second problem with individual analytics is that they create "multiple versions of the truth," while most organizations seek only one. If, for example, there are multiple databases and calculations of the lifetime value of a company's customers across different individuals and departments, it will be difficult to focus the entire organization's attention on its best customers. If there are different versions of financial analytics across an organization, the consequences could be dire indeed—for example, extending to jail for senior executives under Sarbanes-Oxley legislation. Hence there are considerable advantages to managing key data and analytics at the enterprise level, so that there is only one version of critical business information and analytical results for decision making. Then, of course, the information and results can be distributed widely for use across the organization. Harrah's, for example, calls its management approach for customer analytics "centrally driven, broadly distributed."

Enterprise management may take a variety of forms. For some organizations, it may mean only that central IT groups manage the data and procure and install the needed business intelligence software. For others, it may mean that a central analytical services group assists executives with analysis and decision making. As we'll discuss in chapter 7, a number of firms have established such groups.

From an IT standpoint, another approach to enterprise-level management of analytics is the establishment of a *business intelligence competency center*, or BICC. According to SAS, a BICC is defined as "a cross-functional team with a permanent, formal organizational structure. It is owned and staffed by the [company] and has defined tasks, roles, responsibilities and processes for supporting and promoting the effective use of business intelligence across the organization."[5]

In the business intelligence survey of 220 firms described earlier, 23 percent of respondents said their firm already had a BICC. The purpose of such groups is often limited to IT-related issues. However, it could easily be extended to include development and refinement of analytical approaches and tools. For example, at Schneider National, a large trucking and logistics company, the central analytical group (called engineering and research) is a part of the chief information officer organization, and addresses BICC-type functions as well as working with internal and external customers on analytical applications and problems.

Senior Management Commitment

The adoption of a broad analytical approach to business requires changes in culture, process, behavior, and skills for multiple employees. Such changes don't happen by accident; they must be led by senior executives with a passion for analytics and fact-based decision making. Ideally, the primary advocate should be the CEO, and indeed we found several chief executives who were driving the shift to analytics at their firms. These included Gary Loveman, CEO of Harrah's; Jeff Bezos, the founder and CEO of Amazon.com; Rich Fairbank, the founder and CEO of Capital One; Reed Hastings of Netflix; and Barry Beracha, formerly CEO of Sara Lee Bakery Group. Each of these executives has stated both internally and publicly that their companies are engaged in some form of analytical competition. For example, Fairbank commented, "It's all about collecting information on 200 million people you'd never meet, and on the basis of that information, making a series of very critical long-term decisions about lending them money and hoping they would pay you back."[6]

Fairbank summarizes this approach as "information-based strategy." Beracha, before he retired as CEO of Sara Lee Bakery, simply kept a sign on his desk reading, "In God we trust; all others bring data" (a quote originally attributed to W. Edwards Deming). Loveman frequently asks employees, "Do we think, or do we know?" Anyone presenting ideas for initiatives or strategies is pressed for supporting evidence. Loveman has hired into Harrah's a number of very analytical senior and middle managers. He also listed three reasons why employees could be fired from Harrah's: ". . . you don't harass women, you don't steal, and you've got to have a control group."[7]

Loveman provides an excellent example of how a CEO—and ideally an entire executive team—who constantly pushes employees to use testing and analysis, and make fact-based decisions, can change an organization's culture. He's not just supportive of analytics—he's passionate on the subject.

Without the push from the top, it's rare to find a firm making the cultural changes necessary to become an analytical competitor. We know it's a bit of a cliché to say that an idea needs the passionate support of the CEO or other senior general managers, but in our research on analytical competitors, we simply didn't find any without such committed and broad support from the executive suite. We found some firms, for example, in which single functional or business unit leaders (such as heads of marketing or research) were trying to engineer an analytically oriented shift in their firms but weren't able to sufficiently change the culture by themselves. This doesn't mean, of course, that such an executive couldn't lead a change like this under other circumstances, and we did find organizations in which lower-level advocates were making progress on changing the culture. Any cross-functional or cross-department change, and certainly any enterprise-wide effort, clearly requires the support and attention of executives senior enough to direct and coordinate efforts in those separate units.

How does an executive develop a passion for analytics? It helps, of course, if they learn it in school. We've mentioned the math teacher background of Reed Hastings at Netflix. Loveman of Harrah's has a PhD in economics from MIT and taught at Harvard Business School. Bezos from Amazon.com was a quantitatively oriented A+ engineering and computer science student at Princeton. Fairbanks and New England Patriots COO Jonathan Kraft were MBAs and analytically oriented management consultants before taking their jobs at their respective analytical competitors. Chris Lofgren, the president and CEO of Schneider National, has a PhD in operations research. It's obviously a desirable situation when a CEO can go toe-to-toe with the "propeller heads" in the analytical department.

However, not every analytical executive has or needs such an extensive background. Statistics and data analysis are taught at virtually every college in the land. And a CEO doesn't have to be smarter or more quantitatively oriented than all of his or her employees. What is necessary is a willingness to delve into analytical approaches, the ability to engage in discussions with quantitative experts, and the fortitude to push others to think and act analytically.

There are several corollaries of the senior management commitment factor. CEO orientation drives not only the culture and mind share directed to analytics but also the level and persistence of the investment in people, IT, data, and so forth. It is no simple matter, as we will describe in subsequent chapters, to assemble these resources, and it can require substantial time.

Barclays's consumer finance organization, for example, had a "five-year plan" to build the unit's capabilities for analytical competition.[8] Executives in the consumer business had seen the powerful analytical transformations wrought by such U.S. banks as Capital One, and felt that Barclays was underleveraging its very large customer base in the United Kingdom. In adopting an analytical strategy, the company had to adjust virtually all aspects of its consumer business, including the interest rates it charges, the way it underwrites risk and sets credit limits, how it services accounts, its approach to controlling fraud, and how it cross-sells other products. It had to make its data on 13 million Barclay-Card customers integrated and of sufficient quality to support detailed analyses. It had to undertake a large number of small tests to begin learning how to attract and retain the best customers at the lowest price. New people with quantitative analysis skills had to be hired, and new systems had to be built. Given all these activities, it's no surprise that it took from 1998 to 2003 to put the information-based customer strategy in place. A single senior executive, Keith Coulter (now managing director for Barclays U.K. consumer cards and loans), oversaw these changes during the period. Coulter couldn't have worked out and executed on such a long-term plan without clear evidence of commitment from Barclays's most senior executives.

Large-Scale Ambition

A final way to define analytical competitors is by the results they aspire to achieve. The analytical competitors we studied had bet their future success on analytics-based strategies. In retrospect, the strategies appear very logical and rational. At the time, however, they were radical departures from standard industry practice. The founders of Capital One, for example, shopped their idea for "information-based strategy" to all the leaders of the credit card industry and found no takers. When Signet Bank accepted their terms and rebuilt its strategy and processes for credit cards around the new ideas, it was a huge gamble. The company was betting its future, at least in that business unit, on the analytical approach.

Not all attempts to create analytical competition will be successful, of course. But the scale and scope of results from such efforts should at least be large enough to affect organizational fortunes. Incremental, tactical uses of analytics will yield minor results; strategic, competitive uses should yield major ones.

There are many ways to measure the results of analytical activity, but the most obvious is with money. A single analytical initiative should result in savings or revenue increases in the hundreds of millions or billions for a large organization. There are many possible examples. One of the earliest was the idea of "yield management" at American Airlines, which greatly improved the company's fortunes in the 1980s. This technique, which involves optimizing the price at which each airline seat is sold to a passenger, is credited with bringing in $1.2 billion for American over three years and with putting some feisty competitors (such as People Express) out of business.[9] At Deere & Company, a new way of optimizing inventory (called "direct derivative estimation of nonstationary inventory") saved the company $1.2 billion in inventory costs between 2000 and 2005.[10] Procter & Gamble used operations research methods to reorganize sourcing and distribution approaches in the mid-1990s and saved the company $200 million in costs.[11]

The results of analytical competition can also be measured in overall revenues and profits, market share, and customer loyalty. If a company can't see any impact on such critical measures of its nonfinancial and financial performance, it's not really competing on analytics. At Harrah's, for example, the company increased its market share from 36 percent to 43 percent between 1998 (when it started its customer loyalty analytics initiative) and 2004.[12] Over that same time period, the company experienced "same store" sales gains in twenty-three of twenty-four quarters, and play by customers across multiple markets increased every year. Before the adoption of these approaches, the company had failed to meet revenue and profit expectations for seven straight years. Capital One, which became a public company in 1994, increased earnings per share and return on equity by at least 20 percent each year over its first decade. Barclays's information-based customer management strategy in its U.K. consumer finance business led to lower recruitment costs for customers, higher customer balances with lower risk exposure, and a 25 percent increase in revenue per customer account—all over the first three years of the program. As we'll discuss in chapter 3, the analytical competitors we've studied tend to be relatively high performers.

These four factors, we feel, are roughly equivalent in defining analytical competition. Obviously, they are not entirely independent of each other. If senior executive leadership is committed and has built the strategy around an analytics-led distinctive capability, it's likely that the organization will adopt an enterprise-wide approach and that the results sought from analytics will reflect the strategic orientation. Therefore, we view them as four pillars supporting an analytical platform (see figure 2-1). If any one fell, the others would have difficulty compensating.

12 • THE NATURE OF ANALYTICAL COMPETITION

FIGURE 2-1

Four pillars of analytical competition

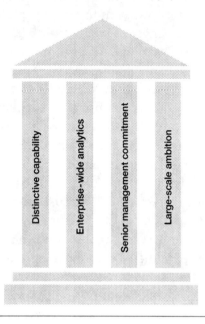

Of all the four, however, senior executive commitment is perhaps the most important because it can make the others possible. It's no accident that many of the organizations we describe became analytical competitors when a new CEO arrived (e.g., Loveman at Harrah's) or when they were founded by CEOs with a strong analytical orientation from the beginning (Hastings at Netflix or Bezos at Amazon.com). Sometimes the change comes from a new generation of managers in a family business. At the winemaker E. & J. Gallo, when Joe Gallo, the son of one of the firm's founding brothers, became CEO, he focused much more than the previous generation of leaders on data and analysis—first in sales and later in other functions, including the assessment of customer taste. At the New England Patriots National Football League team, the involvement in the team by Jonathan Kraft, the son of owner Bob Kraft and a former management consultant, helped move the team in a more analytical direction in terms of both on-field issues like play selection and team composition and off-field issues affecting the fan experience.

Assessing the Degree of Analytical Competition

If these four factors are the hallmarks or defining factors of analytical competition, we can begin to assess organizations by how much or how little they have of them. To do so, we have identified five stages of analytical competition, as seen in figure 2-2. The key attributes for each stage are listed in table 2-1. Like the well-known "capability maturity model" for software development, these stages can describe the path that an organization can follow from having virtually no analytical capabilities to being a serious analytical competitor. In chapter 6, we describe the overall road map for moving through these stages.

Stage 5 organizations are full-blown *analytical competitors*, with high degrees of each of the four factors described earlier. Their analytical activities are clearly in support of a distinctive capability, they are taking an enterprise-wide approach, their executives are passionate and driving, and their analytical initiatives are aimed at substantial results. Some of the firms that fall into this category include Google, Harrah's, Amazon.com, Capital One, Progressive, Netflix, Wal-Mart, and Yahoo!, as well as several sports teams we've discussed. These organizations could

FIGURE 2-2

The five stages of analytical competition

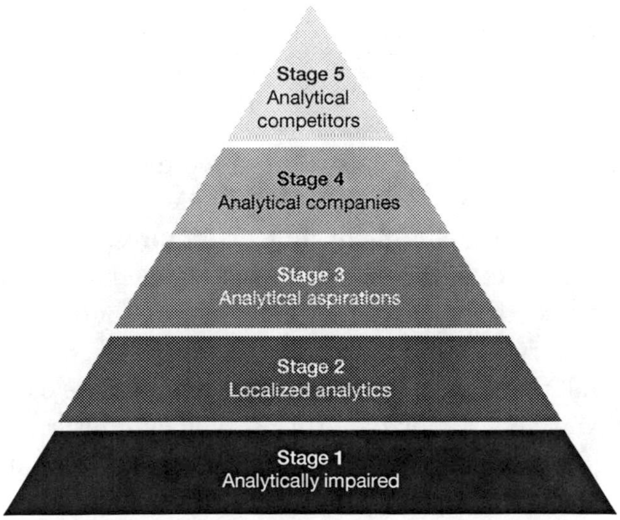

TABLE 2-1

Competing on analytics stages model

Stage	Distinctive capability/level of insights	Questions asked	Objective	Metrics/ measure/value
1 Analytically impaired	Negligible, "flying blind"	What happened in our business?	Get accurate data to improve operations	None
2 Localized analytics	Local and opportunistic— may not be supporting company's distinctive capabilities	What can we do to improve this activity? How can we understand our business better?	Use analytics to improve one or more functional activities	ROI of individual applications
3 Analytical aspirations	Begin efforts for more integrated data and analytics	What's happening now? Can we extrapolate existing trends?	Use analytics to improve a distinctive capability	Future performance and market value
4 Analytical companies	Enterprise-wide perspective, able to use analytics for point advantage, know what to do to get to next level, but not quite there	How can we use analytics to innovate and differentiate?	Build broad analytic capability— analytics for differentiation	Analytics are an important driver of performance and value
5 Analytical competitors	Enterprise-wide, big results, sustainable advantage	What's next? What's possible? How do we stay ahead?	Analytical master—fully competing on analytics	Analytics are the primary driver of performance and value

always apply their analytical capabilities even more broadly—and they are constantly doing so—but they already have them focused on the most significant capability their strategy requires. In our sample of thirty-two firms that are at least somewhat oriented to analytics, eleven were stage 5 analytical competitors. However, we sought out firms that fit in this category, so by no means should this be taken as an indicator of their overall prevalence. From our other research, we'd estimate that no more than 5 percent of large firms would be in this category overall (i.e., half of the percentage in our survey saying that "analytical capability is a key element of strategy"; the other half would be stage 4). Most of the stage 5 organizations we discovered, as might be predicted, were information-intensive services firms, with four firms in financial services. Several were also dot-com firms. However, it's difficult to generalize about industries for analytical competition, since we found stage 5 organizations in several industry categories.

Stage 4 organizations, our *analytical companies*, are on the verge of analytical competition but still face a few minor hurdles to get there in full measure. For example, they have the skill but lack the out-and-out will to compete on this basis. Perhaps the CEO and executive team are supportive of an analytical focus but are not passionate about competing on this basis. Or perhaps there is substantial analytical activity, but it is not targeted at a distinctive capability. With only a small increase in emphasis, the companies could move into analytical competitor status. We found seven organizations in this category.

For example, one stage 4 consumer products firm we studied had strong analytical activities in several areas of the business. However, it wasn't clear that analytics were closely bound to the organization's strategy, and neither analytics nor the likely synonyms for them were mentioned in the company's recent annual reports. Analytics or information was not mentioned as one of the firm's strategic competencies. Granted, there are people within this company—and all of the stage 4 companies we studied—who are working diligently to make the company an analytical competitor, but they aren't yet influential enough to make it happen.

The organizations at stage 3 do grasp the value and the promise of analytical competition, but they face major capability hurdles and are a long way from overcoming them. Because of the importance of executive awareness and commitment, we believe that just having that is enough to put the organization at a higher stage and on the full-steam-ahead path that we described in the first chapter. We found seven organizations in this position. Some have only recently articulated the vision and have not really begun implementing it. Others have very high levels of functional or business unit autonomy and are having difficulty mounting a cohesive approach to analytics across the enterprise.

One multiline insurance company, for example, had a CEO with the vision of using data, analytics, and a strong customer orientation in the fashion of the stage 5 firm Progressive, an auto insurance company with a history of technological and analytical innovation. But the multiline company had only recently begun to expand its analytical orientation beyond the traditionally quantitative actuarial function, and thus far there was little cooperation across the life and property and casualty business units.

We also interviewed executives from three different pharmaceutical firms, and we categorized two of the three into stage 3 at present. It was clear to all the managers that analytics were the key to the future of the industry. The combination of clinical, genomic, and proteomic data will lead to an analytical transformation and an environment of personalized medicine. Yet both the science and the application of informatics in these domains are as yet incomplete.[13] Each of our interviewees admitted that their company, and the rest of the industry, has a long way to go before mastering their analytical future. One of the companies, Vertex Pharmaceuticals, has made significant progress toward analytical competition—not by striving toward the analytical holy grail described earlier, but by making more analytical decisions in virtually every phase of drug development and marketing.

Despite the implementation issues faced by stage 3 firms, because executive demand is one of the most important aspects of a company's analytical orientation—and because sufficient interest from executives can drive a great deal of change relatively quickly—we'd put these firms ahead of those that may even have more analytical activity but less interest from executives. We refer to them as having *competitive aspirations* with regard to analytics.

Stage 2 organizations exhibit the typical *localized analytics* approach to "business intelligence" in the past—that is, an emphasis on reporting with pockets of analytical activity—but they don't measure up to the standard of competing on analytics. They do analytical work, but they have no intention of competing on it. We found six of these firms in our study, although they would be much more common in a random sample, and perhaps the largest group.

By no means have analytics transformed the way these organizations do business. Marketing, for example, may be identifying optimal customers or modeling demand, but the company still markets to all customers and creates supply independent of the demand models. Their business intelligence activities produce economic benefits but not enough to affect the company's competitive strategy. What they primarily lack is any vision of analytical competition from senior executives. Several of the firms have some of the same technology as firms at higher stages of analytical activity, but they have not put it to strategic use.

Stage 1 organizations have some desire to become more analytical, but thus far they lack both the will and the skill to do so. We call them *analytically impaired* organizations. They face some substantial barriers—both human and technical—to analytical competition and are still focused on putting basic, integrated transaction functionality and high-quality data in place. They may also lack the hardware, software, and skills to do substantial analysis. They certainly lack any interest in analytical competition on the part of senior executives. To the degree that they have any analytical activity at all, it is both small and local. At a state government organization we researched, for example, the following barriers were cited in our interview notes from April 4, 2005:

> [Manager interviewed] noted that there is not as great a sense in government that "time is money" and therefore that something needs to happen. Moreover, decision making is driven more by the budget and less by strategy. What this means is that decisions are as a rule very short-term focused on the current fiscal year and not characterized by a longer-term perspective. Finally, [interviewee] noted that one of the other impediments to developing a fact-based culture is that the technical tools today are not really adequate. Despite these difficulties, there is a great deal of interest on the part of the governor and the head of administration and finance to bring a new reform perspective to decision making and more of an analytical perspective. They are also starting to recruit staff with more of these analytical skills.

As a result of these deficiencies, stage 1 organizations are not yet even on the path to becoming analytical competitors, even though they have a desire to be. Because we only selected organizations to interview that wanted to compete on analytics, we included only two stage 1 organizations—a state government and an engineering firm (and even that firm is becoming somewhat more analytical about its human resources). However, such organizations, and those at stage 2, probably constitute the majority of all organizations in the world at large. Many firms today don't have a single definition of the customer, for example, and hence they can't use customer data across the organization to segment and select the best customers. They can't connect demand and supply information, so they can't optimize their supply chains. They can't understand the relationship between their nonfinancial performance indicators and their financial results. They may not even have a single definitive list of their employees—much less the ability to analyze employee traits. Such basic data issues are all too common among most firms today.

We have referred to these different categories as *stages* rather than *levels* because most organizations need to go through each one. However, with sufficiently motivated senior executives, it may be possible to skip a stage or at least move rapidly though them. We haven't yet observed the progress of analytical orientation within a set of firms over time. But we would bet that an organization that was in a hurry to get to stage 5 could hire the people, buy the technology, and pound data into shape within a year or two. The greatest constraint on rapid movement through the stages would be changing the basic business processes and behaviors of the organization and its people. That's always the most difficult and time-consuming part of any major organizational change.

In the next chapter, we describe the relationship between analytical activity and business performance. We discuss analytical applications for key processes in two subsequent chapters. The first, chapter 4, describes the role that analytics play in internally oriented processes, such as finance and human resource management. Chapter 5 focuses on using analytics to enhance organizations' externally oriented activities, including customer and supplier specific interactions. Before we get there, we will explore the link between organizations that have high analytical orientations and high-performance businesses.

Notes

Chapter 2

1. Professor Mark Oleson of the University of Missouri, quoted in Pat Curry, "The Future of FICO," Bankrate.com, November 1, 2005, http://www.bankrate.com/smrtpg/news/debt/debtcreditguide/fico-future1.asp.

19

2. Rajiv Lal and Patricia Matrone Carrolo, "Harrah's Entertainment, Inc.," Case 9-502-011 (Boston: Harvard Business School, 2002), 6.

3. Data from a BetterManagement survey and described in Gloria J. Miller, Dagmar Brautigam, and Stefanie V. Gerlach, *Business Intelligence Competency Centers: A Team Approach to Maximizing Competitive Advantage* (Hoboken, NJ: Wiley, 2006).

4. For more information on spreadsheet errors, see Raymond Panko's article, "What We Know About Spreadsheet Errors," *Journal of End User Computing* 10, no. 2 (Spring 1998): 15–21.

5. Definition of BICC from a SAS Web site, http://www.sas.com/consult/bicc.html.

6. Christopher H. Paige, "Capital One Financial Corporation," Case 9-700-124 (Boston: Harvard Business School, 2001).

7. Victoria Chang and Jeffrey Pfeffer, "Gary Loveman and Harrah's Entertainment," Case OB45 (Stanford, CA: Stanford Graduate School of Business, November 2003), 7.

8. Keith Coulter, managing director, U.K. cards and loans, Barclay, telephone interview with Tom Davenport, October 11, 2005.

9. Barry C. Smith, Dirk P. Gunther, B. Venkateshwara Rao, and Richard M. Ratliff, "E-Commerce and Operations Research in Airline Planning, Marketing, and Distribution," *Interfaces*, March–April 2001, 37–55.

10. Tallys H. Yunes, Dominic Napolitano, et al., "Building Efficient Product Portfolios at John Deere," working paper, Carnegie Mellon University, Pittsburgh, PA, April 2004.

11. Gary H. Anthes, "Modeling Magic," *Computerworld*, February 7, 2005.

12. Gary Loveman, CEO of Harrah's, from presentations and interviews with Tom Davenport, January 2005–June 2006.

13. The American Medical Informatics Association defines *informatics* as "the effective organization, analysis, management, and use of information in health care." See http://www.amia.org/informatics/.

## CHAPTER 1

Introduction

1.1 WHAT IS DATA MINING?

The field of data mining is still relatively new and in a state of evolution. The first International Conference on Knowledge Discovery and Data Mining (KDD) was held in 1995, and there are a variety of definitions of data mining.

A concise definition that captures the essence of *data mining* is:

> Extracting useful information from large data sets.
>
> (Hand et al., 2001)

A slightly longer version is:

> Data mining is the process of exploration and analysis, by automatic or semi-automatic means, of large quantities of data in order to discover meaningful patterns and rules.
>
> (Berry and Linoff, 1997, p. 5)

Berry and Linoff later had cause to regret the 1997 reference to "automatic and semi-automatic means," feeling that it shortchanged the role of data exploration and analysis analysis (Berry and Linoff, 2000).

Another definition comes from the Gartner Group, the information technology research firm:

> [Data Mining is] the process of discovering meaningful correlations, patterns and trends by sifting through large amounts of data stored in repositories. Data mining employs pattern recognition technologies, as well as statistical and mathematical techniques.
>
> (http://www.gartner.com/6_help/glossary, accessed May 14, 2010)

3

A summary of the variety of methods encompassed in the term *data mining* is given at the beginning of Chapter 2.

1.2 WHERE IS DATA MINING USED?

Data mining is used in a variety of fields and applications. The military use data mining to learn what roles various factors play in the accuracy of bombs. Intelligence agencies might use it to determine which of a huge quantity of intercepted communications are of interest. Security specialists might use these methods to determine whether a packet of network data constitutes a threat. Medical researchers might use it to predict the likelihood of a cancer relapse.

Although data mining methods and tools have general applicability, most examples in this book are chosen from the business world. Some common business questions that one might address through data mining methods include:

1. From a large list of prospective customers, which are most likely to respond? We can use classification techniques (logistic regression, classification trees, or other methods) to identify those individuals whose demographic and other data most closely matches that of our best existing customers. Similarly, we can use prediction techniques to forecast how much individual prospects will spend.

2. Which customers are most likely to commit, for example, fraud (or might already have committed it)? We can use classification methods to identify (say) medical reimbursement applications that have a higher probability of involving fraud and give them greater attention.

3. Which loan applicants are likely to default? We can use classification techniques to identify them (or logistic regression to assign a "probability of default" value).

4. Which customers are most likely to abandon a subscription service (telephone, magazine, etc.)? Again, we can use classification techniques to identify them (or logistic regression to assign a "probability of leaving" value). In this way, discounts or other enticements can be proffered selectively.

1.3 ORIGINS OF DATA MINING

Data mining stands at the confluence of the fields of statistics and machine learning (also known as artificial intelligence). A variety of techniques for exploring data and building models have been around for a long time in the world of statistics: linear regression, logistic regression, discriminant analysis, and principal components analysis, for example. But the core tenets of classical statistics—computing is difficult and data are scarce—do not apply in data mining applications where both data and computing power are plentiful.

This gives rise to Daryl Pregibon's description of data mining as "statistics at scale and speed" (Pregibon, 1999). A useful extension of this is "statistics at scale, speed, and simplicity." Simplicity in this case refers not to the simplicity of algorithms but, rather, to simplicity in the logic of inference. Due to the scarcity of data in the classical statistical setting, the same sample is used to make an estimate and also to determine how reliable that estimate might be. As a result, the logic of the confidence intervals and hypothesis tests used for inference may seem elusive for many, and their limitations are not well appreciated. By contrast, the data mining paradigm of fitting a model with one sample and assessing its performance with another sample is easily understood.

Computer science has brought us *machine learning techniques*, such as trees and neural networks, that rely on computational intensity and are less structured than classical statistical models. In addition, the growing field of database management is also part of the picture.

The emphasis that classical statistics places on inference (determining whether a pattern or interesting result might have happened by chance) is missing in data mining. In comparison to statistics, data mining deals with large datasets in open-ended fashion, making it impossible to put the strict limits around the question being addressed that inference would require.

As a result, the general approach to data mining is vulnerable to the danger of *overfitting*, where a model is fit so closely to the available sample of data that it describes not merely structural characteristics of the data but random peculiarities as well. In engineering terms, the model is fitting the noise, not just the signal.

1.4   RAPID GROWTH OF DATA MINING

Perhaps the most important factor propelling the growth of data mining is the growth of data. The mass retailer Wal-Mart in 2003 captured 20 million transactions per day in a 10-terabyte database (a terabyte is 1 million megabytes). In 1950, the largest companies had only enough data to occupy, in electronic form, several dozen megabytes. Lyman and Varian (2003) estimate that 5 exabytes of information were produced in 2002, double what was produced in 1999 (1 exabyte is 1 million terabytes); 40% of this was produced in the United States.

The growth of data is driven not simply by an expanding economy and knowledge base but by the decreasing cost and increasing availability of automatic data capture mechanisms. Not only are more events being recorded, but more information per event is captured. Scannable bar codes, point-of-sale

(POS) devices, mouse click trails, and global positioning satellite (GPS) data are examples.

The growth of the Internet has created a vast new arena for information generation. Many of the same actions that people undertake in retail shopping, exploring a library, or catalog shopping have close analogs on the Internet, and all can now be measured in the most minute detail. In marketing, a shift in focus from products and services to a focus on the customer and his or her needs has created a demand for detailed data on customers.

The operational databases used to record individual transactions in support of routine business activity can handle simple queries but are not adequate for more complex and aggregate analysis. Data from these operational databases are therefore extracted, transformed, and exported to a *data warehouse*, a large integrated data storage facility that ties together the decision support systems of an enterprise. Smaller *data marts* devoted to a single subject may also be part of the system. They may include data from external sources (e.g., credit rating data).

Many of the exploratory and analytical techniques used in data mining would not be possible without today's computational power. The constantly declining cost of data storage and retrieval has made it possible to build the facilities required to store and make available vast amounts of data. In short, the rapid and continuing improvement in computing capacity is an essential enabler of the growth of data mining.

1.5 WHY ARE THERE SO MANY DIFFERENT METHODS?

As can be seen in this book or any other resource on data mining, there are many different methods for prediction and classification. You might ask yourself why they coexist and whether some are better than others. The answer is that each method has advantages and disadvantages. The usefulness of a method can depend on factors such as the size of the dataset, the types of patterns that exist in the data, whether the data meet some underlying assumptions of the method, how noisy the data are, and the particular goal of the analysis. A small illustration is shown in Figure 1.1, where the goal is to find a combination of *household income level* and *household lot size* that separate buyers (solid circles) from nonbuyers (hollow circles) of riding mowers. The first method (left panel) looks only for horizontal and vertical lines to separate buyers from nonbuyers, whereas the second method (right panel) looks for a single diagonal line.

Different methods can lead to different results, and their performance can vary. It is therefore customary in data mining to apply several different methods and select the one that is most useful for the goal at hand.

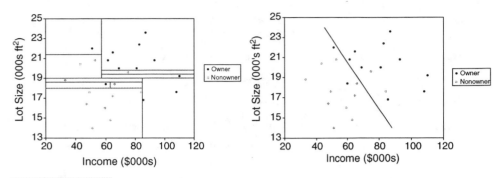

FIGURE 1.1   **TWO METHODS FOR SEPARATING BUYERS FROM NONBUYERS**

1.6   TERMINOLOGY AND NOTATION

Because of the hybrid parentry of data mining, its practitioners often use multiple terms to refer to the same thing. For example, in the machine learning (artificial intelligence) field, the variable being predicted is the output variable or target variable. To a statistician, it is the dependent variable or the response. Here is a summary of terms used:

Algorithm   Refers to a specific procedure used to implement a particular data mining technique: classification tree, discriminant analysis, and the like.

Attribute   See **Predictor**.

Case   See **Observation**.

Confidence   Has a specific meaning in association rules of the type "IF *A* and *B* are purchased, *C* is also purchased." Confidence is the conditional probability that *C* will be purchased IF *A* and *B* are purchased.

Confidence   Also has a broader meaning in statistics (*confidence interval*), concerning the degree of error in an estimate that results from selecting one sample as opposed to another.

Dependent Variable   See **Response**.

Estimation   See **Prediction**.

Feature   See **Predictor**.

Holdout Sample   Is a sample of data not used in fitting a model, used to assess the performance of that model; this book uses the term *validation set* or, if one is used in the problem, *test set* instead of *holdout sample*.

Input Variable   See **Predictor**.

Model   Refers to an algorithm as applied to a dataset, complete with its settings (many of the algorithms have parameters that the user can adjust).

Observation   Is the unit of analysis on which the measurements are taken (a customer, a transaction, etc.); also called *case*, *record*, *pattern*, or *row*. (Each row typically represents a record; each column, a variable.)

Outcome Variable   See **Response**.

Output Variable   See **Response**.

P (A | B)   Is the conditional probability of event *A* occurring given that event *B* has occurred. Read as "the probability that *A* will occur given that *B* has occurred."

Pattern   Is a set of measurements on an observation (e.g., the height, weight, and age of a person).

Prediction   The prediction of the value of a continuous output variable; also called *estimation*.

Predictor   Usually denoted by *X*, is also called a *feature*, *input variable*, *independent variable*, or from a database perspective, a *field*.

Record   See **Observation**.

Response   usually denoted by *Y*, is the variable being predicted in supervised learning; also called *dependent variable*, *output variable*, *target variable*, or *outcome variable*.

Score   Refers to a predicted value or class. *Scoring new data* means to use a model developed with training data to predict output values in new data.

Success Class   Is the class of interest in a binary outcome (e.g., *purchasers* in the outcome *purchase/no purchase*).

Supervised Learning   Refers to the process of providing an algorithm (logistic regression, regression tree, etc.) with records in which an output variable of interest is known and the algorithm "learns" how to predict this value with new records where the output is unknown.

Test Data (or **test set**)   Refers to that portion of the data used only at the end of the model building and selection process to assess how well the final model might perform on additional data.

Training Data (or **training set**)   Refers to that portion of data used to fit a model.

Unsupervised Learning   Refers to analysis in which one attempts to learn something about the data other than predicting an output value of interest (e.g., whether it falls into clusters).

Validation Data (or **validation set**)   Refers to that portion of the data used to assess how well the model fits, to adjust some models, and to select the best model from among those that have been tried.

Variable   Is any measurement on the records, including both the input (*X*) variables and the output (*Y*) variable.

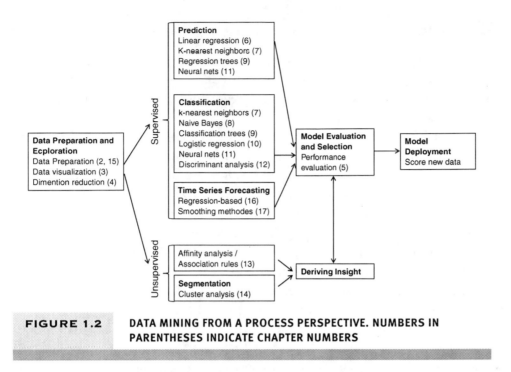

1.7 ROAD MAPS TO THIS BOOK

The book covers many of the widely used predictive and classification methods as well as other data mining tools. Figure 1.2 outlines data mining from a process perspective and where the topics in this book fit in. Chapter numbers are indicated beside the topic. Table 1.1 provides a different perspective: It organizes data mining procedures according to the type and structure of the data.

TABLE 1.1   **ORGANIZATION OF DATA MINING METHODS IN THIS BOOK, ACCORDING TO THE NATURE OF THE DATA[a]**

	Continuous Response	Categorical Response	No Response
Continuous Predictors	Linear regression (6) Neural nets (11) k Nearest neighbors (7)	Logistic regression (10) Neural nets (11) Discriminant analysis (12) k Nearest neighbors (7)	Principal components (4) Cluster analysis (14)
Categorical Predictors	Linear regression (6) Neural nets (11) Regression trees (9)	Neural nets (11) Classification trees (9) Logistic regression (10) Naive Bayes (8)	Association rules (13)

[a] Numbers in parentheses indicate chapter number.

Order of Topics

The book is divided into five parts: Part I (Chapters 1–2) gives a general overview of data mining and its components. Part II (Chapters 3–4) focuses on the early stage of data exploration and dimension reduction in which typically the most effort is expended.

Part III (Chapter 4) discusses performance evaluation. Although it contains a single chapter, we discuss a variety of topics, from predictive performance metrics to misclassification costs. The principles covered in this part are crucial for the proper evaluation and comparison of supervised learning methods.

Part IV includes eight chapters (Chapters 5–12), covering a variety of popular supervised learning methods (for classification and/or prediction). Within this part, the topics are generally organized according to the level of sophistication of the algorithms, their popularity, and ease of understanding.

Part V focuses on unsupervised learning, presenting association rules (Chapter 13) and cluster analysis (Chapter 14).

Part VI includes three chapters (Chapters 15–17), with the focus on forecasting time series. The first chapter covers general issues related to handling and understanding time series. The next two chapters present two popular forecasting approaches: regression–based forecasting and smoothing methods.

Finally, Part VII includes a set of cases.

Although the topics in the book can be covered in the order of the chapters, each chapter stands alone. It is advised, however, to read Parts I–III before proceeding to the chapters in Parts IV–V, and similarly Chapter 15 should precede other chapters in Part VI.

USING XLMINER SOFTWARE

To facilitate hands-on data mining experience, this book comes with access to XLMiner, a comprehensive data mining add-in for Excel. For those familiar with Excel, the use of an Excel add-in dramatically shortens the software learning curve. XLMiner will help you get started quickly on data mining and offers a variety of methods for analyzing data. The illustrations, exercises, and cases in this book are written in relation to this software. XLMiner has extensive coverage of statistical and data mining techniques for classification, prediction, affinity analysis, and data exploration and reduction. It offers a variety of data mining tools: neural nets, classification and regression trees, *k*-nearest neighbor classification, naive Bayes, logistic regression, multiple linear regression, and discriminant analysis, all for predictive modeling. It provides for automatic partitioning of data into training, validation, and test samples and for the deployment of the model to new data. It also offers association rules, principal components analysis, *k*-means clustering, and hierarchical clustering, as well as visualization tools and data-handling utilities. With its short learning curve, affordable price, and reliance on

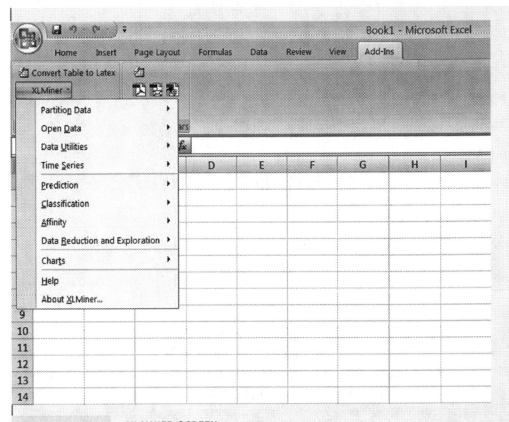

FIGURE 1.3   **XLMINER SCREEN**

the familiar Excel platform, it is an ideal companion to a book on data mining for the business student.

Installation   Click on setup.exe and installation dialog boxes will guide you through the installation procedure. After installation is complete, the XLMiner program group appears under *Start > Programs > XLMiner*. You can either invoke XLMiner directly or select the option to register XLMiner as an Excel add-In.

Use   Once opened, XLMiner appears as another menu in the top toolbar in Excel, as shown in Figure 1.3. By choosing the appropriate menu item, you can run any of XLMiner's procedures on the dataset that is open in the Excel worksheet.

CHAPTER 2

Overview of the Data Mining Process

In Kåre this chapter we give an overview of the steps involved in data mining, starting from a clear goal definition and ending with model deployment. The general steps are shown schematically in Figure 2.1. We also discuss issues related to data collection, cleaning, and preprocessing. We explain the notion of data partitioning, where methods are trained on a set of training data and then their performance is evaluated on a separate set of validation data, and how this practice helps avoid overfitting. Finally, we illustrate the steps of model building by applying them to data.

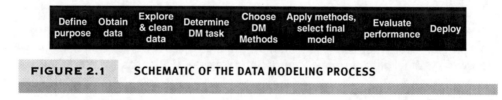

| Define purpose | Obtain data | Explore & clean data | Determine DM task | Choose DM Methods | Apply methods, select final model | Evaluate performance | Deploy |

FIGURE 2.1   **SCHEMATIC OF THE DATA MODELING PROCESS**

2.1 INTRODUCTION

In Chapter 1 we saw some very general definitions of data mining. In this chapter we introduce the variety of methods sometimes referred to as *data mining*. The core of this book focuses on what has come to be called *predictive analytics*, the tasks of classification and prediction that are becoming key elements of a

12

"business intelligence" function in most large firms. These terms are described and illustrated below.

Not covered in this book to any great extent are two simpler database methods that are sometimes considered to be data mining techniques: (1) OLAP (online analytical processing) and (2) SQL (structured query language). OLAP and SQL searches on databases are descriptive in nature ("find all credit card customers in a certain zip code with annual charges > $20,000, who own their own home and who pay the entire amount of their monthly bill at least 95% of the time") and do not involve statistical modeling.

2.2 CORE IDEAS IN DATA MINING

Classification

Classification is perhaps the most basic form of data analysis. The recipient of an offer can respond or not respond. An applicant for a loan can repay on time, repay late, or declare bankruptcy. A credit card transaction can be normal or fraudulent. A packet of data traveling on a network can be benign or threatening. A bus in a fleet can be available for service or unavailable. The victim of an illness can be recovered, still be ill, or be deceased.

A common task in data mining is to examine data where the classification is unknown or will occur in the future, with the goal of predicting what that classification is or will be. Similar data where the classification is known are used to develop rules, which are then applied to the data with the unknown classification.

Prediction

Prediction is similar to classification, except that we are trying to predict the value of a numerical variable (e.g., amount of purchase) rather than a class (e.g., purchaser or nonpurchaser). Of course, in classification we are trying to predict a class, but the term *prediction* in this book refers to the prediction of the value of a continuous variable. (Sometimes in the data mining literature, the term *estimation* is used to refer to the prediction of the value of a continuous variable, and *prediction* may be used for both continuous and categorical data.)

Association Rules

Large databases of customer transactions lend themselves naturally to the analysis of associations among items purchased, or "what goes with what." *Association rules*, or *affinity analysis*, can then be used in a variety of ways. For example, grocery stores can use such information after a customer's purchases have all been scanned to print discount coupons, where the items being discounted are determined by mapping the customer's purchases onto the association rules. Online merchants such as Amazon.com and Netflix.com use these methods as the heart of a "recommender" system that suggests new purchases to customers.

Predictive Analytics

Classification, prediction, and to some extent, affinity analysis constitute the analytical methods employed in *predictive analytics*.

Data Reduction

Sensible data analysis often requires distillation of complex data into simpler data. Rather than dealing with thousands of product types, an analyst might wish to group them into a smaller number of groups. This process of consolidating a large number of variables (or cases) into a smaller set is termed *data reduction*.

Data Exploration

Unless our data project is very narrowly focused on answering a specific question determined in advance (in which case it has drifted more into the realm of statistical analysis than of data mining), an essential part of the job is to review and examine the data to see what messages they hold, much as a detective might survey a crime scene. Here, full understanding of the data may require a reduction in its scale or dimension to allow us to see the forest without getting lost in the trees. Similar variables (i.e., variables that supply similar information) might be aggregated into a single variable incorporating all the similar variables. Analogously, records might be aggregated into groups of similar records.

Data Visualization

Another technique for exploring data to see what information they hold is through graphical analysis. This includes looking at each variable separately as well as looking at relationships between variables. For numerical variables, we use histograms and boxplots to learn about the distribution of their values, to detect outliers (extreme observations), and to find other information that is relevant to the analysis task. Similarly, for categorical variables we use bar charts. We can also look at scatterplots of pairs of numerical variables to learn about possible relationships, the type of relationship, and again, to detect outliers. Visualization can be greatly enhanced by adding features such as color, zooming, and interactive navigation.

2.3 SUPERVISED AND UNSUPERVISED LEARNING

A fundamental distinction among data mining techniques is between supervised and unsupervised methods. *Supervised learning algorithms* are those used in classification and prediction. We must have data available in which the value of the outcome of interest (e.g., purchase or no purchase) is known. These *training data* are the data from which the classification or prediction algorithm "learns," or is "trained," about the relationship between predictor variables and the outcome variable. Once the algorithm has learned from the training data, it is then applied to another sample of data (the *validation data*) where the outcome is known, to see how well it does in comparison to other models. If many different models are being tried out, it is prudent to save a third sample of known outcomes (the *test data*) to use with the model finally selected to predict how well it will do. The model can then be used to classify or predict the outcome of interest in new cases where the outcome is unknown. Simple linear regression analysis is an example of supervised learning (although rarely called that in the introductory statistics course where you probably first encountered it). The Y variable is the (known) outcome variable and the X variable is a predictor variable. A regression line is drawn to minimize the sum of squared deviations between the actual Y values and the values predicted by this line. The regression line can now be used to predict Y values for new values of X for which we do not know the Y value.

Unsupervised learning algorithms are those used where there is no outcome variable to predict or classify. Hence, there is no "learning" from cases where such an outcome variable is known. Association rules, dimension reduction methods, and clustering techniques are all unsupervised learning methods.

2.4 STEPS IN DATA MINING

This book focuses on understanding and using data mining algorithms (steps 4–7 below). However, some of the most serious errors in data analysis result from a poor understanding of the problem—an understanding that must be developed before we get into the details of algorithms to be used. Here is a list of steps to be taken in a typical data mining effort:

1. *Develop an understanding of the purpose of the data mining project* (if it is a one-shot effort to answer a question or questions) or application (if it is an ongoing procedure).

2. *Obtain the dataset to be used in the analysis.* This often involves random sampling from a large database to capture records to be used in an analysis. It may also involve pulling together data from different databases. The

databases could be internal (e.g., past purchases made by customers) or external (credit ratings). While data mining deals with very large databases, usually the analysis to be done requires only thousands or tens of thousands of records.

3. *Explore, clean, and preprocess the data.* This involves verifying that the data are in reasonable condition. How should missing data be handled? Are the values in a reasonable range, given what you would expect for each variable? Are there obvious outliers? The data are reviewed graphically: for example, a matrix of scatterplots showing the relationship of each variable with every other variable. We also need to ensure consistency in the definitions of fields, units of measurement, time periods, and so on.

4. *Reduce the data, if necessary, and* (where supervised training is involved) *separate them into training, validation, and test datasets.* This can involve operations such as eliminating unneeded variables, transforming variables (e.g., turning "money spent" into "spent > \$100" vs. "spent ≤ \$100"), and creating new variables (e.g., a variable that records whether at least one of several products was purchased). Make sure that you know what each variable means and whether it is sensible to include it in the model.

5. *Determine the data mining task* (classification, prediction, clustering, etc.). This involves translating the general question or problem of step 1 into a more specific statistical question.

6. *Choose the data mining techniques to be used* (regression, neural nets, hierarchical clustering, etc.).

7. *Use algorithms to perform the task.* This is typically an iterative process—trying multiple variants, and often using multiple variants of the same algorithm (choosing different variables or settings within the algorithm). Where appropriate, feedback from the algorithm's performance on validation data is used to refine the settings.

8. *Interpret the results of the algorithms.* This involves making a choice as to the best algorithm to deploy, and where possible, testing the final choice on the test data to get an idea as to how well it will perform. (Recall that each algorithm may also be tested on the validation data for tuning purposes; in this way the validation data become a part of the fitting process and are likely to underestimate the error in the deployment of the model that is finally chosen.)

9. *Deploy the model.* This involves integrating the model into operational systems and running it on real records to produce decisions or actions. For example, the model might be applied to a purchased list of possible customers, and the action might be "include in the mailing if the predicted amount of purchase is > \$10."

The foregoing steps encompass the steps in SEMMA, a methodology developed by SAS:

Sample   Take a sample from the dataset; partition into training, validation, and test datasets.

Explore   Examine the dataset statistically and graphically.

Modify   Transform the variables and impute missing values.

Model   Fit predictive models (e.g., regression tree, collaborative filtering).

Assess   Compare models using a validation dataset.

IBM Modeler (previously SPSS Clementine) has a similar methodology, termed CRISP-DM (cross-industry standard process for data mining).

2.5   PRELIMINARY STEPS

Organization of Datasets

Datasets are nearly always constructed and displayed so that variables are in columns and records are in rows. In the example shown in Section 2.6 (the Boston housing data), the values of 14 variables are recorded for a number of census tracts. The spreadsheet is organized such that each row represents a census tract—the first tract had a per capital crime rate (CRIM) of 0.00632, had 18% of its residential lots zoned for over 25,000 square feet (ZN), and so on. In supervised learning situations, one of these variables will be the outcome variable, typically listed at the end or the beginning (in this case it is median value, MEDV, at the end).

Sampling from a Database

Quite often, we want to perform our data mining analysis on less than the total number of records that are available. Data mining algorithms will have varying limitations on what they can handle in terms of the numbers of records and variables, limitations that may be specific to computing power and capacity as well as software limitations. Even within those limits, many algorithms will execute faster with smaller datasets.

From a statistical perspective, accurate models can often be built with as few as several hundred records (see below). Hence, we will often want to sample a subset of records for model building.

Oversampling Rare Events

If the event we are interested in is rare, however (e.g., customers purchasing a product in response to a mailing), sampling a subset of records may yield so few events (e.g., purchases) that we have little information on them. We would end up with lots of data on nonpurchasers but little on which to base a model that distinguishes purchasers from nonpurchasers. In such cases we would want our sampling procedure to overweight the purchasers relative to the nonpurchasers so that our sample would end up with a healthy complement of purchasers. This issue arises mainly in classification problems because those are the types of problems in which an overwhelming number of 0's is likely to be encountered in the response variable. Although the same principle could be extended to prediction, any prediction problem in which most responses are 0 is likely to raise the question of what distinguishes responses from nonresponses (i.e., a classification question). (For convenience below, we speak of responders and nonresponders as to a promotional offer, but we are really referring to any binary—0/1—outcome situation.)

Assuring an adequate number of responder or "success" cases to train the model is just part of the picture. A more important factor is the costs of misclassification. Whenever the response rate is extremely low, we are likely to attach more importance to identifying a responder than to identifying a nonresponder. In direct-response advertising (whether by traditional mail or via the Internet), we may encounter only one or two responders for every hundred records—the value of finding such a customer far outweighs the costs of reaching him or her. In trying to identify fraudulent transactions, or customers unlikely to repay debt, the costs of failing to find the fraud or the nonpaying customer are likely to exceed the cost of more detailed review of a legitimate transaction or customer.

If the costs of failing to locate responders were comparable to the costs of misidentifying responders as nonresponders, our models would usually be at their best if they identified everyone (or almost everyone, if it is easy to pick off a few responders without catching many nonresponders) as a nonresponder. In such a case, the misclassification rate is very low—equal to the rate of responders—but the model is of no value.

More generally, we want to train our model with the asymmetric costs in mind so that the algorithm will catch the more valuable responders, probably at the cost of "catching" and misclassifying more nonresponders as responders than would be the case if we assume equal costs. This subject is discussed in detail in Chapter 5.

Preprocessing and Cleaning the Data

Types of Variables   There are several ways of classifying variables. Variables can be numerical or text (character). They can be continuous (able to assume any real numerical value, usually in a given range), integer (assuming only integer values), or categorical (assuming one of a limited number of values). Categorical variables can be either numerical (1, 2, 3) or text (payments current, payments not current, bankrupt). Categorical variables can also be unordered (called *nominal variables*) with categories such as North America, Europe, and Asia; or they can be ordered (called *ordinal variables*) with categories such as high value, low value, and nil value.

Continuous variables can be handled by most data mining routines. In XLMiner, all routines take continuous variables, with the exception of the naive Bayes classifier, which deals exclusively with categorical variables. The machine learning roots of data mining grew out of problems with categorical outcomes; the roots of statistics lie in the analysis of continuous variables. Sometimes, it is desirable to convert continuous variables to categorical variables. This is done most typically in the case of outcome variables, where the numerical variable is mapped to a decision (e.g., credit scores above a certain level mean "grant credit," a medical test result above a certain level means "start treatment"). XLMiner has a facility for this type of conversion.

Handling Categorical Variables   Categorical variables can also be handled by most routines but often require special handling. If the categorical variable is ordered (age category, degree of creditworthiness, etc.), we can often use it as is, as if it were a continuous variable. The smaller the number of categories, and the less they represent equal increments of value, the more problematic this procedure becomes, but it often works well enough.

Categorical variables, however, often cannot be used as is. In those cases they must be decomposed into a series of dummy binary variables. For example, a single variable that can have possible values of "student," "unemployed," "employed," or "retired" would be split into four separate variables:

Student—Yes/No
Unemployed—Yes/No
Employed—Yes/No
Retired—Yes/No

Note that only three of the variables need to be used; if the values of three are known, the fourth is also known. For example, given that these four values are the only possible ones, we can know that if a person is neither student, unemployed, nor employed, he or she must be retired. In some routines (e.g., regression and logistic regression), you should not use all four variables—the redundant information will cause the algorithm to fail. XLMiner has a utility to convert categorical variables to binary dummies.

Variable Selection   More is not necessarily better when it comes to selecting variables for a model. Other things being equal, parsimony, or compactness, is a desirable feature in a model. For one thing, the more variables we include, the greater the number of records we will need to assess relationships among the

TABLE 2.1

Advertising	Sales
239	514
364	789
602	550
644	1386
770	1394
789	1440
911	1354

variables. Fifteen records may suffice to give us a rough idea of the relationship between Y and a single predictor variable X. If we now want information about the relationship between Y and 15 predictor variables $X_1 \cdots X_{15}$, 15 records will not be enough (each estimated relationship would have an average of only one record's worth of information, making the estimate very unreliable).

Overfitting   The more variables we include, the greater the risk of over-fitting the data. What is overfitting?

In Table 2.1 we show hypothetical data about advertising expenditures in one time period and sales in a subsequent time period (a scatterplot of the data is shown in Figure 2.2). We could connect up these points with a smooth but complicated function, one that explains all these data points perfectly and leaves no error (residuals). This can be seen in Figure 2.3. However, we can see that such a curve is unlikely to be accurate, or even useful, in predicting future sales on the basis of advertising expenditures (e.g., it is hard to believe that increasing expenditures from \$400 to \$500 will actually decrease revenue).

A basic purpose of building a model is to describe relationships among vari-ables in such a way that this description will do a good job of predicting future

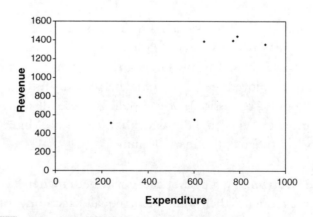

FIGURE 2.2   **SCATTERPLOT FOR ADVERTISING AND SALES DATA**

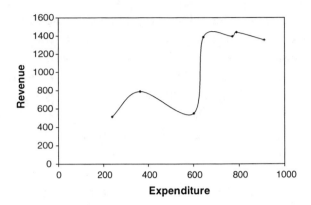

FIGURE 2.3   **SCATTERPLOT SMOOTHED**

outcome (dependent) values on the basis of future predictor (independent) values. Of course, we want the model to do a good job of describing the data we have, but we are more interested in its performance with future data.

In the example above, a simple straight line might do a better job than the complex function does of predicting future sales on the basis of advertising. Instead, we devised a complex function that fit the data perfectly, and in doing so, we overreached. We ended up "explaining" some variation in the data that was nothing more than chance variation. We mislabeled the noise in the data as if it were a signal.

Similarly, we can add predictors to a model to sharpen its performance with the data at hand. Consider a database of 100 individuals, half of whom have contributed to a charitable cause. Information about income, family size, and zip code might do a fair job of predicting whether or not someone is a contributor. If we keep adding additional predictors, we can improve the performance of the model with the data at hand and reduce the misclassification error to a negligible level. However, this low error rate is misleading because it probably includes spurious "explanations."

For example, one of the variables might be height. We have no basis in theory to suppose that tall people might contribute more or less to charity, but if there are several tall people in our sample and they just happened to contribute heavily to charity, our model might include a term for height—the taller you are, the more you will contribute. Of course, when the model is applied to additional data, it is likely that this will not turn out to be a good predictor.

If the dataset is not much larger than the number of predictor variables, it is very likely that a spurious relationship like this will creep into the model. Continuing with our charity example, with a small sample just a few of whom are tall, whatever the contribution level of tall people may be, the algorithm is tempted to attribute it to their being tall. If the dataset is very large relative to the number of predictors, this is less likely. In such a case, each predictor must help predict the outcome for a large number of cases, so the job it does is much less dependent on just a few cases, which might be flukes.

Somewhat surprisingly, even if we know for a fact that a higher degree curve is the appropriate model, if the model-fitting dataset is not large enough, a lower degree function (that is not as likely to fit the noise) is likely to perform better. Overfitting can also result from the application of many different models, from which the best performing is selected (see below).

How Many Variables and How Much Data?   Statisticians give us procedures to learn with some precision how many records we would need to achieve a given degree of reliability with a given dataset and a given model. Data miners' needs are usually not so precise, so we can often get by with rough rules of thumb. A good rule of thumb is to have 10 records for every predictor variable. Another, used by Delmaster and Hancock (2001, p. 68) for classification procedures, is to have at least $6 \times m \times p$ records, where m is the number of outcome classes and p is the number of variables.

Even when we have an ample supply of data, there are good reasons to pay close attention to the variables that are included in a model. Someone with domain knowledge (i.e., knowledge of the business process and the data) should be consulted, as knowledge of what the variables represent can help build a good model and avoid errors.

For example, the amount spent on shipping might be an excellent predictor of the total amount spent, but it is not a helpful one. It will not give us any information about what distinguishes high-paying from low-paying customers that can be put to use with future prospects because we will not have the information on the amount paid for shipping for prospects that have not yet bought anything.

In general, compactness or parsimony is a desirable feature in a model. A matrix of scatterplots can be useful in variable selection. In such a matrix, we can see at a glance scatterplots for all variable combinations. A straight line would be an indication that one variable is exactly correlated with another. Typically, we would want to include only one of them in our model. The idea is to weed out irrelevant and redundant variables from our model.

Outliers   The more data we are dealing with, the greater the chance of encountering erroneous values resulting from measurement error, data entry error, or the like. If the erroneous value is in the same range as the rest of the data, it may be harmless. If it is well outside the range of the rest of the data (e.g., a misplaced decimal), it may have a substantial effect on some of the data mining procedures we plan to use.

Values that lie far away from the bulk of the data are called *outliers*. The term *far away* is deliberately left vague because what is or is not called an outlier is basically an arbitrary decision. Analysts use rules of thumb such as "anything over 3 standard deviations away from the mean is an outlier," but no statistical rule can tell us whether such an outlier is the result of an error. In this statistical sense, an outlier is not necessarily an invalid data point; it is just a distant data point.

The purpose of identifying outliers is usually to call attention to values that need further review. We might come up with an explanation looking at the data—in the case of a misplaced decimal, this is likely. We might have no explanation but know that the value is wrong—a temperature of 178°F for a sick person. Or, we might conclude that the value is within the realm of possibility and leave it alone. All these are judgments best made by someone with *domain knowledge*, knowledge of the particular application being considered: direct mail, mortgage finance, and so on, as opposed to technical knowledge of statistical or data mining procedures. Statistical procedures can do little beyond identifying the record as something that needs review.

If manual review is feasible, some outliers may be identified and corrected. In any case, if the number of records with outliers is very small, they might be treated as missing data. How do we inspect for outliers? One technique in Excel is to sort the records by the first column, then review the data for very large or very small values in that column. Then repeat for each successive column. Another option is to examine the minimum and maximum values of each column using Excel's min and max functions. For a more automated approach that considers each record as a unit, clustering techniques could be used to identify clusters of one or a few records that are distant from others. Those records could then be examined.

Missing Values   Typically, some records will contain missing values. If the number of records with missing values is small, those records might be omitted. However, if we have a large number of variables, even a small proportion of missing values can affect a lot of records. Even with only 30 variables, if only 5% of the values are missing (spread randomly and independently among cases and variables), almost 80% of the records would have to be omitted from the analysis. (The chance that a given record would escape having a missing value is $0.95^{30} = 0.215$.)

An alternative to omitting records with missing values is to replace the missing value with an imputed value, based on the other values for that variable across all records. For example, if among 30 variables, household income is missing for a particular record, we might substitute the mean household income across all records. Doing so does not, of course, add any information about how household income affects the outcome variable. It merely allows us to proceed with the analysis and not lose the information contained in this record for the other 29 variables. Note that using such a technique will understate the variability in a dataset. However, we can assess variability and the performance of our data mining technique, using the validation data, and therefore this need not present a major problem.

Some datasets contain variables that have a very large number of missing values. In other words, a measurement is missing for a large number of records. In that case, dropping records with missing values will lead to a large loss of data. Imputing the missing values might also be useless, as the imputations are based on a small number of existing records. An alternative is to examine the importance of the predictor. If it is not very crucial, it can be dropped. If it is important, perhaps a proxy variable with fewer missing values can be used instead. When such a predictor is deemed central, the best solution is to invest in obtaining the missing data.

Significant time may be required to deal with missing data, as not all situations are susceptible to automated solution. In a messy dataset, for example, a 0 might mean two things: (1) the value is missing, or (2) the value is actually zero. In the credit industry, a 0 in the "past due" variable might mean a customer who is fully paid up, or a customer with no credit history at all—two very different situations. Human judgment may be required for individual cases or to determine a special rule to deal with the situation.

Normalizing (Standardizing) the Data Some algorithms require that the data be normalized before the algorithm can be implemented effectively. To normalize the data, we subtract the mean from each value and divide by the standard deviation of the resulting deviations from the mean. In effect, we are expressing each value as the "number of standard deviations away from the mean," also called a *z-score*.

To consider why this might be necessary, consider the case of clustering. Clustering typically involves calculating a distance measure that reflects how far each record is from a cluster center or from other records. With multiple variables, different units will be used: days, dollars, counts, and so on. If the dollars are in the thousands and everything else is in the tens, the dollar variable will come to dominate the distance measure. Moreover, changing units from (say) days to hours or months could alter the outcome completely.

Data mining software, including XLMiner, typically has an option that normalizes the data in those algorithms where it may be required. It is an option rather than an automatic feature of such algorithms because there are situations where we want each variable to contribute to the distance measure in proportion to its scale.

Use and Creation of Partitions

In supervised learning, a key question presents itself: How well will our prediction or classification model perform when we apply it to new data? We are particularly interested in comparing the performance among various models so that we can choose the one we think will do the best when it is actually implemented.

At first glance, we might think it best to choose the model that did the best job of classifying or predicting the outcome variable of interest with the data at hand. However, when we use the same data both to develop the model and to assess its performance, we introduce bias. This is because when we pick the model that works best with the data, this model's superior performance comes from two sources:

- A superior model
- Chance aspects of the data that happen to match the chosen model better than they match other models

The latter is a particularly serious problem with techniques (such as trees and neural nets) that do not impose linear or other structure on the data, and thus end up overfitting it.

To address this problem, we simply divide (partition) our data and develop our model using only one of the partitions. After we have a model, we try it out on another partition and see how it performs, which we can measure in several ways. In a classification model, we can count the proportion of held-back records that were misclassified. In a prediction model, we can measure the residuals (errors) between the predicted values and the actual values. We typically deal with two or three partitions: a training set, a validation set, and sometimes an additional test set. Partitioning the data into training, validation, and test sets is done either randomly according to predetermined proportions or by specifying which records go into which partitioning according to some relevant variable (e.g., in time-series forecasting, the data are partitioned according to their chronological order). In most cases, the partitioning should be done randomly to avoid getting a biased partition. It is also possible (although cumbersome) to divide the data into more than three partitions by successive partitioning (e.g., divide the initial data into three partitions, then take one of those partitions and partition it further).

Training Partition   The training partition, typically the largest partition, contains the data used to build the various models we are examining. The same training partition is generally used to develop multiple models.

Validation Partition   This partition (sometimes called the *test partition*) is used to assess the performance of each model so that you can compare models and pick the best one. In some algorithms (e.g., classification and regression trees), the validation partition may be used in automated fashion to tune and improve the model.

Test Partition   This partition (sometimes called the *holdout* or *evaluation partition*) is used if we need to assess the performance of the chosen model with new data.

Why have both a validation and a test partition? When we use the validation data to assess multiple models and then pick the model that does best with the validation data, we again encounter another (lesser) facet of the overfitting problem—chance aspects of the validation data that happen to match the chosen model better than they match other models.

The random features of the validation data that enhance the apparent performance of the chosen model will probably not be present in new data to which the model is applied. Therefore, we may have overestimated the accuracy of our model. The more models we test, the more likely it is that one of them will be particularly effective in explaining the noise in the validation data. Applying the model to the test data, which it has not seen before, will provide an unbiased estimate of how well it will do with new data. Figure 2.4 shows the three partitions and their use in the data mining process. When we are concerned mainly with finding the best model and less with exactly how well it will do, we might use only training and validation partitions.

Note that with some algorithms, such as nearest-neighbor algorithms, the training data itself is the model—records in the validation and test partitions, and in new data, are compared to records in the training data to find the nearest neighbor(s). As *k*-nearest neighbors is implemented in XLMiner and as discussed in this book, the use of two partitions is an essential part of the classification or prediction process, not merely a way to improve or assess it. Nonetheless, we

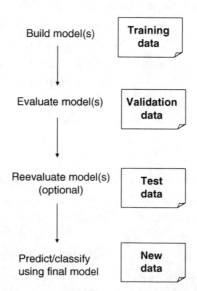

FIGURE 2.4   THREE DATA PARTITIONS AND THEIR ROLE IN THE DATA MINING PROCESS

can still interpret the error in the validation data in the same way that we would interpret error from any other model.

> XLMiner has a facility for partitioning a dataset randomly or according to a user-specified variable. For user-specified partitioning, a variable should be created that contains the value *t* (training), *v* (validation), or *s* (test), according to the designation of that record.

2.6   BUILDING A MODEL: EXAMPLE WITH LINEAR REGRESSION

Let us go through the steps typical to many data mining tasks using a familiar procedure: multiple linear regression. This will help us understand the overall process before we begin tackling new algorithms. We illustrate the Excel procedure using XLMiner.

Boston Housing Data

The Boston housing data contain information on neighborhoods in Boston for which several measurements are taken (e.g., crime rate, pupil/teacher ratio). The outcome variable of interest is the median value of a housing unit in the neighborhood. This dataset has 14 variables, and a description of each variable is given in Table 2.2. A sample of the data is shown in Figure 2.5.

The first row in the data represents the first neighborhood, which had an average per capita crime rate of 0.006, had 18% of the residential land zoned for lots over 25,000 square feet (ft^2), 2.31% of the land devoted to nonretail business, no border on the Charles River, and so on.

TABLE 2.2	DESCRIPTION OF VARIABLES IN BOSTON HOUSING DATASET
CRIM	Crime rate
ZN	Percentage of residential land zoned for lots over 25,000 ft^2
INDUS	Percentage of land occupied by nonretail business
CHAS	Charles River dummy variable ($= 1$ if tract bounds river; $= 0$ otherwise)
NOX	Nitric oxide concentration (parts per 10 million)
RM	Average number of rooms per dwelling
AGE	Percentage of owner-occupied units built prior to 1940
DIS	Weighted distances to five Boston employment centers
RAD	Index of accessibility to radial highways
TAX	Full-value property tax rate per $10,000
PTRATIO	Pupil/teacher ratio by town
B	$1000(Bk \text{ minus } 0.63)^2$, where Bk is the proportion of blacks by town
LSTAT	% Lower status of the population
MEDV	Median value of owner-occupied homes in $1000s

CRIM	ZN	INDUS	CHAS	NOX	RM	AGE	DIS	RAD	TAX	PTRATIO	B	LSTAT	MEDV	CAT. MEDV
0.00632	18	2.31	0	0.538	6.58	65.2	4.09	1	296	15.3	396.9	4.98	24	0
0.02731	0	7.07	0	0.469	6.42	78.9	4.97	2	242	17.8	396.9	9.14	21.6	0
0.02729	0	7.07	0	0.469	7.19	61.1	4.97	2	242	17.8	392.83	4.03	34.7	1
0.03237	0	2.18	0	0.458	7	45.8	6.06	3	222	18.7	394.63	2.94	33.4	1
0.06905	0	2.18	0	0.458	7.15	54.2	6.06	3	222	18.7	396.9	5.33	36.2	1
0.02985	0	2.18	0	0.458	6.43	58.7	6.06	3	222	18.7	394.12	5.21	28.7	0
0.08829	13	7.87	0	0.524	6.01	66.6	5.56	5	311	15.2	395.6	12.43	22.9	0
0.14455	13	7.87	0	0.524	6.17	96.1	5.95	5	311	15.2	396.9	19.15	27.1	0
0.21124	13	7.87	0	0.524	5.63	100	6.08	5	311	15.2	386.63	29.93	16.5	0

FIGURE 2.5   **FIRST NINE RECORDS IN THE BOSTON HOUSING DATA**

Modeling Process

We now describe in detail the various model stages using the Boston housing example.

1. *Purpose.* Let us assume that the purpose of our data mining project is to predict the median house value in small Boston area neighborhoods.

2. *Obtain the Data.* We will use the Boston housing data. The dataset in question is small enough that we do not need to sample from it—we can use it in its entirety.

3. *Explore, Clean, and Preprocess the Data.* Let us look first at the description of the variables (e.g., crime rate, number of rooms per dwelling) to be sure that we understand them all. These descriptions are available on the "description" tab on the worksheet, as is a Web source for the dataset. They all seem fairly straightforward, but this is not always the case. Often, variable names are cryptic and their descriptions may be unclear or missing.

   It is useful to pause and think about what the variables mean and whether they should be included in the model. Consider the variable TAX. At first glance, we consider that the tax on a home is usually a function of its assessed value, so there is some circularity in the model—we want to predict a home's value using TAX as a predictor, yet TAX itself is determined by a home's value. TAX might be a very good predictor of home value in a numerical sense, but would it be useful if we wanted to apply our model to homes whose assessed value might not be known? Reflect, though, that the TAX variable, like all the variables, pertains to the average in a neighborhood, not to individual homes. Although the purpose of our inquiry has not been spelled out, it is possible that at some stage we might want to apply a model to individual homes, and in such a case, the neighborhood TAX value would be a useful predictor. So we will keep TAX in the analysis for now.

RM	AGE	DIS
79.29	96.2	2.04
8.78	82.9	1.90
8.75	83	2.89
8.70	88.8	1.00

FIGURE 2.6   OUTLIER IN BOSTON HOUSING DATA

In addition to these variables, the dataset also contains an additional variable, CAT.MEDV, which has been created by categorizing median value (MEDV) into two categories, high and low. (There are a couple of aspects of MEDV, the median house value, that bear noting. For one thing, it is quite low, since it dates from the 1970s. For another, there are a lot of 50s, the top value. It could be that median values above $50, 000 were recorded as $50, 000.) The variable CAT.MEDV is actually a categorical variable created from MEDV. If MEDV $\geq$ $30,000, CAT.MEDV $= 1$. If MEDV $\leq$ $30,000, CAT.MEDV $= 0$. If we were trying to categorize the cases into high and low median values, we would use CAT.MEDV instead of MEDV. As it is, we do not need CAT.MEDV, so we leave it out of the analysis. We are left with 13 independent (predictor) variables, which can all be used.

It is also useful to check for outliers that might be errors. For example, suppose that the RM (number of rooms) column looked like the one in Figure 2.6, after sorting the data in descending order based on rooms. We can tell right away that the 79.29 is in error—no neighborhood is going to have houses that have an average of 79 rooms. All other values are between 3 and 9. Probably, the decimal was misplaced and the value should be 7.929. (This hypothetical error is not present in the dataset supplied with XLMiner.)

4. *Reduce the Data and Partition Them into Training, Validation, and Test Partitions.* Our dataset has only 13 variables, so data reduction is not required. If we had many more variables, at this stage we might want to apply a variable reduction technique such as principal components analysis to consolidate multiple similar variables into a smaller number of variables. Our task is to predict the median house value and then assess how well that prediction does. We will partition the data into a training set to build the model and a validation set to see how well the model does. This technique is part of the "supervised learning" process in classification and prediction problems. These are problems in which we know the class or value of the outcome variable for some data, and we want to use those data in developing a model that can then be applied to other data where that value is unknown.

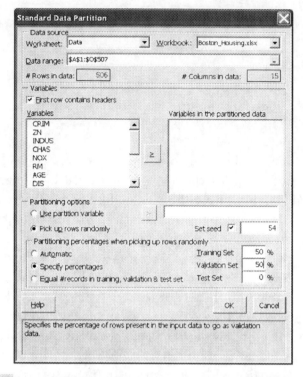

FIGURE 2.7	PARTITIONING THE DATA. THE DEFAULT IN XLMINER PARTITIONS THE DATA INTO 60% TRAINING DATA, 40% VALIDATION DATA, AND 0% TEST DATA. IN THIS EXAMPLE, A PARTITION OF 50% TRAINING AND 50% VALIDATION IS USED

In Excel, select *XLMiner > Partition* and the dialog box shown in Figure 2.7 appears. Here we specify which data range is to be partitioned and which variables are to be included in the partitioned dataset. The partitioning can be handled in one of two ways:

a. The dataset can have a partition variable that governs the division into training and validation partitions (e.g., 1 = training, 2 = validation).

b. The partitioning can be done randomly. If the partitioning is done randomly, we have the option of specifying a seed for randomization (which has the advantage of letting us duplicate the same random partition later should we need to). In this example, a seed of 54 is used.

In this case we divide the data into two partitions: training and validation. The training partition is used to build the model, and the validation partition is used to see how well the model does when applied to new data. We need to specify the percent of the data used in each partition.

Note: Although we are not using it here, a test partition might also be used.

Typically, a data mining endeavor involves testing multiple models, perhaps with multiple settings on each model. When we train just one model and try it out on the validation data, we can get an unbiased idea of how it might perform on more such data. However, when we train many models and use the validation data to see how each one does, then choose the best-performing model, the validation data no longer provide an unbiased estimate of how the model might do with more data. By playing a role in choosing the best model, the validation data have become part of the model itself. In fact, several algorithms (e.g., classification and regression trees) explicitly factor validation data into the model-building algorithm itself (e.g., in pruning trees). Models will almost always perform better with the data they were trained on than with fresh data. Hence, when validation data are used in the model itself, or when they are used to select the best model, the results achieved with the validation data, just as with the training data, will be overly optimistic.

The test data, which should not be used in either the model-building or model selection process, can give a better estimate of how well the chosen model will do with fresh data. Thus, once we have selected a final model, we apply it to the test data to get an estimate of how well it will actually perform.

5. *Determine the Data Mining Task.* In this case, as noted, the specific task is to predict the value of MEDV using the 13 predictor variables.

6. *Choose the Technique.* In this case, it is multiple linear regression. Having divided the data into training and validation partitions, we can use XLMiner to build a multiple linear regression model with the training data. We want to predict median house price on the basis of all the other values.

7. *Use the Algorithm to Perform the Task.* In XLMiner, we select *Prediction > Multiple Linear Regression*, as shown in Figure 2.8. The variable MEDV is selected as the output (dependent) variable, the variable CAT.MEDV is left unused, and the remaining variables are all selected as input (independent or predictor) variables. We ask XLMiner to show us the fitted values on the training data as well as the predicted values (scores) on the validation data, as shown in Figure 2.9. XLMiner produces standard regression output, but for now we defer that as well as the more advanced options displayed above. (See Chapter 6 or the user documentation for XLMiner for more information.) Rather, we review the predictions themselves. Figure 2.10 shows the predicted values for the first few records in the training data along with the actual values and the residual (prediction error). Note that the predicted values would often be called the *fitted values* since they are for the records to which the model was fit. The results for the validation

32 OVERVIEW OF THE DATA MINING PROCESS

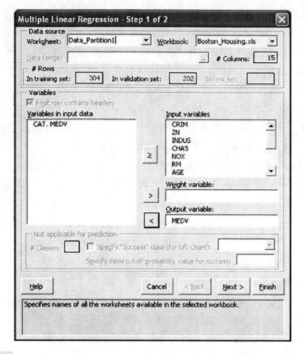

FIGURE 2.8   USING XLMINER FOR MULTIPLE LINEAR REGRESSION

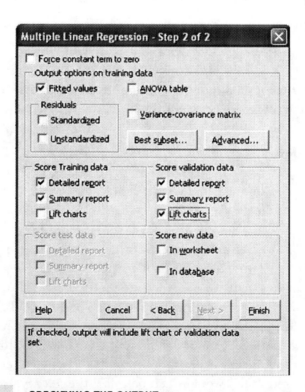

FIGURE 2.9   SPECIFYING THE OUTPUT

XLMiner : Multiple Linear Regression - Prediction of Training Data

| Data range | ['Boston_Housing']'Data_Partition2'!$C$19:$P$271 | | | | | Back to | | | | | | | | | | |

Row Id.	Predicted Value	Actual Value	Residual	CRIM	ZN	INDUS	CHAS	NOX	RM	AGE	DIS	RAD	TAX	PTRATIO	B	LSTAT
1	30.02788078	24	-6.027880779	0.00632	18	2.31	0	0.538	6.575	65.2	4.09	1	296	15.3	396.9	4.98
2	24.90910941	21.6	-3.309109407	0.02731	0	7.07	0	0.469	6.421	78.9	4.9671	2	242	17.8	396.9	9.14
3	30.9549987	34.7	3.745001299	0.02729	0	7.07	0	0.469	7.185	61.1	4.9671	2	242	17.8	392.83	4.03
4	28.07549961	33.4	5.324500385	0.03237	0	2.18	0	0.458	6.998	45.8	6.0622	3	222	18.7	394.63	2.94
5	27.9091436	36.2	8.290856402	0.06905	0	2.18	0	0.458	7.147	54.2	6.0622	3	222	18.7	396.9	5.33
7	23.65328843	22.9	-0.753288432	0.08829	12.5	7.87	0	0.524	6.012	66.6	5.5605	5	311	15.2	395.6	12.43
8	21.11420949	27.1	5.98579051	0.14455	12.5	7.87	0	0.524	6.172	96.1	5.9505	5	311	15.2	396.9	19.15
11	21.09801414	15	-6.09801414	0.22489	12.5	7.87	0	0.524	6.377	94.3	6.3467	5	311	15.2	392.52	20.45
12	22.12589464	18.9	-3.225894637	0.11747	12.5	7.87	0	0.524	6.009	82.9	6.2267	5	311	15.2	396.9	13.27
14	17.61047844	20.4	2.789521563	0.62976	0	8.14	0	0.538	5.949	61.8	4.7075	4	307	21	396.9	8.26
21	11.62929772	13.6	1.970702281	1.25179	0	8.14	0	0.538	5.57	98.1	3.7979	4	307	21	376.57	21.02

FIGURE 2.10   PREDICTIONS FOR THE TRAINING DATA

data are shown in Figure 2.11. The prediction error for the training and validation data are compared in Figure 2.12.

Prediction error can be measured in several ways. Three measures produced by XLMiner are shown in Figure 2.12. On the right is the *average error*, simply the average of the residuals (errors). In both cases it is quite small relative to the units of MEDV, indicating that, on balance, predictions average about right—our predictions are "unbiased." Of course, this simply means that the positive and negative errors balance out. It tells us nothing about how large these errors are.

The *total sum of squared errors* on the left adds up the squared errors, so whether an error is positive or negative, it contributes just the same. However, this sum does not yield information about the size of the typical error.

The *RMS error* (root-mean-squared error) is perhaps the most useful term of all. It takes the square root of the average squared error; thus, it gives an idea of the typical error (whether positive or negative) in the same scale as that used for the original data. As we might expect, the RMS error for the validation data (5.66 thousand $), which the model is

XLMiner : Multiple Linear Regression - Prediction of Validation Data

| Data range | ['Boston_Housing']'Data_Partition2'!$C$272:$P$524 | | | | | Back to | | | | | | | | | | |

Row Id.	Predicted Value	Actual Value	Residual	CRIM	ZN	INDUS	CHAS	NOX	RM	AGE	DIS	RAD	TAX	PTRATIO	B	LSTAT
6	24.09753481	28.7	4.602465185	0.02985	0	2.18	0	0.458	6.43	58.7	6.0622	3	222	18.7	394.12	5.21
9	14.04293006	16.5	2.457069944	0.21124	12.5	7.87	0	0.524	5.631	100	6.0821	5	311	15.2	386.63	29.93
10	20.02731265	18.9	-1.127312654	0.17004	12.5	7.87	0	0.524	6.004	85.9	6.5921	5	311	15.2	386.71	17.1
13	22.31053056	21.7	-0.610530557	0.09378	12.5	7.87	0	0.524	5.889	39	5.4509	5	311	15.2	390.5	15.71
15	17.56538825	18.2	0.634611749	0.63796	0	8.14	0	0.538	6.096	84.5	4.4619	4	307	21	380.02	10.26
16	17.30239527	19.9	2.597604726	0.62739	0	8.14	0	0.538	5.834	56.5	4.4986	4	307	21	395.62	8.47
17	18.71477307	23.1	4.385226932	1.05393	0	8.14	0	0.538	5.935	29.3	4.4986	4	307	21	386.85	6.58
18	15.81653483	17.5	1.683465174	0.7842	0	8.14	0	0.538	5.99	81.7	4.2579	4	307	21	386.75	14.67
19	14.38144028	20.2	5.818559715	0.80271	0	8.14	0	0.538	5.456	36.6	3.7965	4	307	21	288.99	11.69
20	16.554546	18.2	1.645453996	0.7258	0	8.14	0	0.538	5.727	69.5	3.7965	4	307	21	390.95	11.28
22	16.30306818	19.6	3.296931816	0.85204	0	8.14	0	0.538	5.965	89.2	4.0123	4	307	21	392.53	13.83
25	14.58925181	15.6	1.010748192	0.75026	0	8.14	0	0.538	5.924	94.1	4.3996	4	307	21	394.33	16.3

FIGURE 2.11   PREDICTIONS FOR THE VALIDATION DATA

Training Data scoring - Summary Report

Total sum of squared errors	RMS Error	Average Error
4136.091425	4.043289187	-1.12501E-06

(a)

Validation Data scoring - Summary Report

Total sum of squared errors	RMS Error	Average Error
8117.85953	5.66448597	0.961240934

(b)

FIGURE 2.12   **ERROR RATES FOR (A) TRAINING AND (B) VALIDATION DATA (ERROR FIGURES ARE IN THOUSANDS OF $)**

seeing for the first time in making these predictions, is larger than for the training data (4.04 thousand $), which were used in training the model.

8. *Interpret the Results.* At this stage we would typically try other prediction algorithms (e.g., regression trees) and see how they do errorwise. We might also try different "settings" on the various models (e.g., we could use the *best subsets* option in multiple linear regression to chose a reduced set of variables that might perform better with the validation data). After choosing the best model (typically, the model with the lowest error on the validation data while also recognizing that "simpler is better"), we use that model to predict the output variable in fresh data. These steps are covered in more detail in the analysis of cases.

9. *Deploy the Model.* After the best model is chosen, it is applied to new data to predict MEDV for records where this value is unknown. This was, of course, the overall purpose.

2.7 USING EXCEL FOR DATA MINING

An important aspect of this process to note is that the heavy-duty analysis does not necessarily require huge numbers of records. The dataset to be analyzed may have millions of records, of course, but in doing multiple linear regression or applying a classification tree, the use of a sample of 20,000 is likely to yield as accurate an answer as that obtained when using the entire dataset. The principle involved is the same as the principle behind polling: If sampled judiciously, 2000 voters can give an estimate of the entire population's opinion within one or two percentage points. (See How Many Variables and How Much Data in Section 2.5 for further discussion.)

Therefore, in most cases, the number of records required in each partition (training, validation, and test) can be accommodated within the rows allowed by Excel. Of course, we need to get those records into Excel, and for this purpose the standard version of XLMiner provides an interface for random sampling of records from an external database.

Similarly, we need to apply the results of our analysis to a large database, and for this purpose the standard version of XLMiner has a facility for storing models and scoring them to an external database. For example, XLMiner would write an additional column (variable) to the database consisting of the predicted purchase amount for each record.

XLMiner has a facility for drawing a sample from an external database. The sample can be drawn at random or it can be stratified. It also has a facility to score data in the external database using the model that was obtained from the training data.

DATA MINING SOFTWARE TOOLS: THE STATE OF THE MARKET By Herb Edelstein[1]

Data mining uses a variety of tools to discover patterns and relationships in data that can be used to explain the data or make meaningful predictions. The need for ever more powerful tools is driven by the increasing breadth and depth of analytical problems. In order to deal with tens of millions of cases (rows) and hundreds or even thousands of variables (columns), organizations need scalable tools. A carefully designed GUI (graphical user interface) also makes it easier to create, manage, and apply predictive models.

Data mining is a complete process, not just a particular technique or algorithm. Industrial-strength tools support all phases of this process, handle all sizes of databases, and manage even the most complex problems.

The software must first be able to pull all the data together. The data mining tool may need to access multiple databases across different database management systems. Consequently, the software should support joining and subsetting of data from a range of sources. Because some of the data may be a terabyte or more, the software also needs to support a variety of sampling methodologies.

Next, the software must facilitate exploring and manipulating the data to create understanding and suggest a starting point for model building. When a database has hundreds or thousands of variables, it becomes an enormous task to select the variables that best describe the data and lead to the most robust predictions. Visualization tools can make it easier to identify the most important variables and find meaningful patterns in very large databases. Certain algorithms are particularly suited to guiding the selection of the most relevant variables. However, often the best predictors are not the variables in the database themselves, but some mathematical combination of these variables. This not only increases the number of variables to be evaluated, but the more complex transformations require a scripting language. Frequently, the data access tools use the DBMS language itself to make transformations directly on the underlying database.

Because building and evaluating models is an iterative process, a dozen or more exploratory models may be built before settling on the best model. While any individual model may take only a modest amount of time for the software to construct, computer usage can really add up unless the tool is running on powerful hardware. Although some people consider this phase to be what data mining is all about, it usually represents a relatively small part of the total effort.

Finally, after building, testing, and selecting the desired model, it is necessary to deploy it. A model that was built using a small subset of the data may now be applied to millions of cases or integrated into a real-time application, processing hundreds of transactions each second. For example, the model may be integrated into credit scoring or fraud detection applications. Over time the model should be evaluated and refined as needed.

Data mining tools can be general purpose (either embedded in a DBMS or stand-alones) or they can be application specific.

All the major database management system vendors have incorporated data mining capabilities into their products. Leading products include IBM DB2 Intelligent Miner, Microsoft SQL Server 2005, Oracle Data Mining, and Teradata Warehouse Miner. The target user for embedded data mining is a database professional. Not surprisingly, these products take advantage of database functionality, including using the DBMS to transform variables, storing models in the database, and extending the data access language to include model building and scoring the database. A few products also supply a separate graphical interface for building data mining models. Where the DBMS has parallel processing capabilities, embedded data mining tools will generally take advantage of it, resulting in better performance. As with the data mining suites described below, these tools offer an assortment of algorithms.

Stand-alone data mining tools can be based on a single algorithm or a collection of algorithms called a suite. Target users include both statisticians and analysts. Well-known single-algorithm products include KXEN; RuleQuest Research C5.0; and Salford Systems CART, MARS, and Treenet. Most of the top single-algorithm tools have also been licensed to suite vendors. The leading suites include SAS Enterprise Miner, IBM Modeler (previously SPSS Clementine), and Spotfire Miner (previously Insightful Miner). Suites are characterized by providing a wide range of functionality and an interface designed to enhance model-building productivity. Many suites have outstanding visualization tools and links to statistical packages that extend the range of tasks they can perform, and most provide a procedural scripting language for more complex transformations. They use a graphical workflow interface to outline the entire data mining process. The suite vendors are working to link their tools more closely to underlying DBMSs; for example, data transformations might be handled by the DBMS. Data mining models can be exported to be incorporated into the DBMS either through generating SQL, procedural language code (e.g., C++ or Java), or a standardized data mining model language called Predictive Model Markup Language (PMML).

Application-specific tools, in contrast to the other types, are intended for particular analytic applications such as credit scoring, customer retention, or product marketing. Their focus may be further sharpened to address the needs of certain markets such as mortgage lending or financial services. The target user is an analyst with expertise in the applications domain. Therefore, the interfaces, the algorithms, and even the terminology are customized for that particular industry, application, or customer. While less flexible than general-purpose tools, they offer the advantage of already incorporating domain knowledge into the product design and can provide very good solutions with less effort. Data mining companies including SAS and SPSS offer vertical market tools, as do industry specialists such as Fair Isaac.

The tool used in this book, XLMiner, is a suite with both sampling and scoring capabilities. While Excel itself is not a suitable environment for dealing with thousands of columns and millions of rows, it is a familiar workspace to business analysts and can be used as a work platform to support other tools. An Excel add-in such as XLMiner (which uses non-Excel computational engines) is user friendly and can be used in conjunction with sampling techniques for prototyping, small-scale, and educational applications of data mining.

---

[1]Herb Edelstein is president of Two Crows Consulting (www.twocrows.com), a leading data mining consulting firm near Washington, D.C. He is an internationally recognized expert in data mining and data warehousing, a widely published author on these topics, and a popular speaker. 2006 Herb Edelstein.

SAS and *Enterprise Miner* are trademarks of SAS Institute, Inc. *CART, MARS*, and *TreeNet* are trademarks of Salford Systems. *XLMiner* is a trademark of Cytel Inc. *SPSS* and *Clementine* are trademarks of SPSS, Inc.

PROBLEMS

2.1 Assuming that data mining techniques are to be used in the following cases, identify whether the task required is supervised or unsupervised learning.

  a. Deciding whether to issue a loan to an applicant based on demographic and financial data (with reference to a database of similar data on prior customers).

  b. In an online bookstore, making recommendations to customers concerning additional items to buy based on the buying patterns in prior transactions.

  c. Identifying a network data packet as dangerous (virus, hacker attack) based on comparison to other packets whose threat status is known.

  d. Identifying segments of similar customers.

  e. Predicting whether a company will go bankrupt based on comparing its financial data to those of similar bankrupt and nonbankrupt firms.

  f. Estimating the repair time required for an aircraft based on a trouble ticket.

  g. Automated sorting of mail by zip code scanning.

  h. Printing of custom discount coupons at the conclusion of a grocery store checkout based on what you just bought and what others have bought previously.

2.2 Describe the difference in roles assumed by the validation partition and the test partition.

2.3 Consider the sample from a database of credit applicants in Figure 2.13. Comment on the likelihood that it was sampled randomly, and whether it is likely to be a useful sample.

2.4 Consider the sample from a bank database shown in Figure 2.14; it was selected randomly from a larger database to be the training set. Personal Loan indicates

OBS#	CHK_ACCT	DURATION	HISTORY	NEW_CAR	USED_CAR	FURNITURE	RADIO/TV	EDUCATION	RETRAINING	AMOUNT	SAV_ACCT	RESPONSE
1	0	6	4	0	0	0	1	0	0	1169	4	1
8	1	36	2	0	1	0	0	0	0	6948	0	1
16	0	24	2	0	0	0	1	0	0	1282	1	0
24	1	12	4	0	1	0	0	0	0	1804	1	1
32	0	24	2	0	0	1	0	0	0	4020	0	1
40	1	9	2	0	0	0	1	0	0	458	0	1
48	0	6	2	0	1	0	0	0	0	1352	2	1
56	3	6	1	1	0	0	0	0	0	783	4	1
64	1	48	0	0	0	0	0	0	1	14421	0	0
72	3	7	4	0	0	0	1	0	0	730	4	1
80	1	30	2	0	0	1	0	0	0	3832	0	1
88	1	36	2	0	0	0	0	1	0	12612	1	0
96	1	54	0	0	0	0	0	0	1	15945	0	0
104	1	9	4	0	0	1	0	0	0	1919	0	1
112	2	15	2	0	0	0	0	1	0	392	0	1

FIGURE 2.13 SAMPLE FROM A DATABASE OF CREDIT APPLICANTS

ID	Age	Experience	Income	ZIP Code	Family	CCAvg	Educ.	Mortgage	Personal Loan	Securities Account
1	25	1	49	91107	4	1.60	1	0	0	1
4	35	9	100	94112	1	2.70	2	0	0	0
5	35	8	45	91330	4	1.00	2	0	0	0
6	37	13	29	92121	4	0.40	2	155	0	0
9	35	10	81	90089	3	0.60	2	104	0	0
11	65	39	105	94710	4	2.40	3	0	0	0
12	29	5	45	90277	3	0.10	2	0	0	0
18	42	18	81	94305	4	2.40	1	0	0	0
20	55	28	21	94720	1	0.50	2	0	0	1
23	29	5	62	90277	1	1.20	1	260	0	0
26	43	19	29	94305	3	0.50	1	97	0	0
27	40	16	83	95064	4	0.20	3	0	0	0
29	56	30	48	94539	1	2.20	3	0	0	0
31	59	35	35	93106	1	1.20	3	122	0	0
32	40	16	29	94117	1	2.00	2	0	0	0
35	31	5	50	94035	4	1.80	3	0	0	0
36	48	24	81	92647	3	0.70	1	0	0	0
37	59	35	121	94720	1	2.90	1	0	0	0
38	51	25	71	95814	1	1.40	3	198	0	0
40	38	13	80	94115	4	0.70	3	285	0	0
41	57	32	84	92672	3	1.60	3	0	0	1

FIGURE 2.14   **SAMPLE FROM A BANK DATABASE**

whether a solicitation for a personal loan was accepted and is the response variable. A campaign is planned for a similar solicitation in the future, and the bank is looking for a model that will identify likely responders. Examine the data carefully and indicate what your next step would be.

2.5 Using the concept of overfitting, explain why when a model is fit to training data, zero error with those data is not necessarily good.

2.6 In fitting a model to classify prospects as purchasers or nonpurchasers, a certain company drew the training data from internal data that include demographic and purchase information. Future data to be classified will be lists purchased from other sources, with demographic (but not purchase) data included. It was found that "refund issued" was a useful predictor in the training data. Why is this not an appropriate variable to include in the model?

2.7 A dataset has 1000 records and 50 variables with 5% of the values missing, spread randomly throughout the records and variables. An analyst decides to remove records that have missing values. About how many records would you expect would be removed?

2.8 Normalize the data in Table 2.3, showing calculations.

TABLE 2.3

Age	Income ($)
25	49,000
56	156,000
65	99,000
32	192,000
41	39,000
49	57,000

2.9 Statistical distance between records can be measured in several ways. Consider Euclidean distance, measured as the square root of the sum of the squared differences. For the first two records in Table 2.3, it is

$$\sqrt{(25 - 56)^2 + (49,000 - 156,000)^2}.$$

Does normalizing the data change which two records are farthest from each other in terms of Euclidean distance?

2.10 Two models are applied to a dataset that has been partitioned. Model A is considerably more accurate than model B on the training data but slightly less accurate than model B on the validation data. Which model are you more likely to consider for final deployment?

2.11 The dataset ToyotaCorolla.xls contains data on used cars on sale during the late summer of 2004 in The Netherlands. It has 1436 records containing details on 38 attributes, including Price, Age, Kilometers, HP, and other specifications.

   a. Explore the data using the data visualization (matrix plot) capabilities of XLMiner. Which of the pairs among the variables seem to be correlated?

   b. We plan to analyze the data using various data mining techniques described in future chapters. Prepare the data for use as follows:

      i. The dataset has two categorical attributes, Fuel Type and Metallic.

         (a) Describe how you would convert these to binary variables.

         (b) Confirm this using XLMiner's utility to transform categorical data into dummies.

         (c) How would you work with these new variables to avoid including redundant information in models?

      ii. Prepare the dataset (as factored into dummies) for data mining techniques of supervised learning by creating partitions using XLMiner's data partitioning utility. Select all the variables and use default values for the random seed and partitioning percentages for training (50%), validation (30%), and test (20%) sets. Describe the roles that these partitions will play in modeling.

CHAPTER 3

Data Visualization

In this chapter we describe a set of plots that can be used to explore the multidimensional nature of a dataset. We present basic plots (bar charts, line graphs, and scatterplots), distribution plots (boxplots and histograms), and different enhancements that expand the capabilities of these plots to visualize more information. We focus on how the different visualizations and operations can support data mining tasks, from supervised (prediction, classification, and time series forecasting) to unsupervised tasks, and provide some guidelines on specific visualizations to use with each data mining task. We also describe the advantages of interactive visualization over static plots. The chapter concludes with a presentation of specialized plots that are suitable for data with special structure (hierarchical, network, and geographical).

3.1 USES OF DATA VISUALIZATION

The popular saying "a picture is worth a thousand words" refers to the ability to condense diffused verbal information into a compact and quickly understood graphical image. In the case of numbers, data visualization and numerical summarization provide us with both a powerful tool to explore data and an effective way to present results.

Where do visualization techniques fit into the data mining process, as described so far? Their use is primarily in the preprocessing portion of the data mining process. Visualization supports data cleaning by finding incorrect values (e.g., patients whose age is 999 or −1), missing values, duplicate rows, columns

Data Mining for Business Intelligence, By Galit Shmueli, Nitin R. Patel, and Peter C. Bruce

43

with all the same value, and the like. Visualization techniques are also useful for variable derivation and selection: they can help determine which variables to include in the analysis and which might be redundant. They can also help with determining appropriate bin sizes, should binning of numerical variables be needed (e.g., a numerical outcome variable might need to be converted to a binary variable, as was done in the Boston housing data, if a yes/no decision is required). They can also play a role in combining categories as part of the data reduction process. Finally, if the data have yet to be collected and collection is expensive (as with the Pandora project at its outset, see Chapter 7), visualization methods can help determine, using a sample, which variables and metrics are useful.

In this chapter we focus on the use of graphical presentations for the purpose of *data exploration*, in particular with relation to predictive analytics. Although our focus is not on visualization for the purpose of data reporting, this chapter offers ideas as to the effectiveness of various graphical displays for the purpose of data presentation. These offer a wealth of useful presentations beyond tabular summaries and basic bar charts, currently the most popular form of data presentation in the business environment. For an excellent discussion of using graphs to report business data, see Few (2004). In terms of reporting data mining results graphically, we describe common graphical displays elsewhere in the book, some of which are technique specific [e.g., dendrograms for hierarchical clustering (Chapter 14), and tree charts for classification and regression trees (Chapter 9)] while others are more general [e.g., receiver operating characteristic (ROC) curves and lift charts for classification (Chapter 5) and profile plots for clustering (Chapter 14)].

Data exploration is a mandatory initial step whether or not more formal analysis follows. Graphical exploration can support free-form exploration for the purpose of understanding the data structure, cleaning the data (e.g., identifying unexpected gaps or "illegal" values), identifying outliers, discovering initial patterns (e.g., correlations among variables and surprising clusters), and generating interesting questions. Graphical exploration can also be more focused, geared toward specific questions of interest. In the data mining context a combination is needed: free-form exploration performed with the purpose of supporting a specific goal.

Graphical exploration can range from generating very basic plots to using operations such as filtering and zooming interactively to explore a set of interconnected plots that include advanced features such as color and multiple panels. This chapter is not meant to be an exhaustive guidebook on visualization techniques but instead discusses main principles and features that support data exploration in a data mining context. We start by describing varying levels of sophistication in terms of visualization and show the advantages of different features and operations. Our discussion is from the perspective of how visualization supports the subsequent data mining goal. In particular, we distinguish between supervised and unsupervised learning; within supervised learning, we also further distinguish between classification (categorical Y) and prediction (numerical Y).

3.2 DATA EXAMPLES

To illustrate data visualization we use two datasets that are used in additional chapters in the book. This allows the reader to compare some of the basic Excel plots used in other chapters to the improved plots and easily see the merit of advanced visualization.

Example 1: Boston Housing Data

The Boston housing data contain information on census tracts in Boston for which several measurements are taken (e.g., crime rate, pupil/teacher ratio). It has 14 variables (a description of each variable and the data are given in Chapter 2, in Table 2.2 and Figure 2.5). We consider three possible tasks:

1. A supervised predictive task, where the outcome variable of interest is the median value of a home in the tract (MEDV)

2. A supervised classification task, where the outcome variable of interest is the binary variable CAT.MEDV that equals 1 for tracts with median home value above \$30,000 and equals 0 otherwise

3. An unsupervised task, where the goal is to cluster census tracts

(MEDV and CAT.MEDV are not used together in any of the three cases.)

Example 2: Ridership on Amtrak Trains

Amtrak, a U.S. railway company, routinely collects data on ridership. Here we focus on forecasting future ridership using the series of monthly ridership between January 1991 and March 2004. The data and their source are described in Chapter 15. Hence our task here is (numerical) time series forecasting.

3.3 BASIC CHARTS: BAR CHARTS, LINE GRAPHS, AND SCATTERPLOTS

The three most effective basic plots are bar charts, line graphs, and scatterplots. These plots are easy to create in Microsoft Excel and are the most commonly used in the current business world, in both data exploration and presentation (unfortunately, pie charts are also popular, although usually ineffective visualizations). Basic charts support data exploration by displaying one or two columns of data (variables) at a time. This is useful in the early stages of getting familiar with the data structure, the amount and types of variables, the volume and type of missing values, and the like.

The nature of the data mining task and domain knowledge about the data will affect the use of basic charts in terms of the amount of time and effort allocated to different variables. In supervised learning, there will be more focus on the outcome variable. In scatterplots, the outcome variable is typically associated with the y axis. In unsupervised learning (for the purpose of data reduction or clustering), basic plots that convey relationships (such as scatterplots) are preferred.

The top left panel in Figure 3.1 displays a line chart for the time series of monthly railway passengers on Amtrak. Line graphs are used primarily for showing time series. The choice of time frame to plot, as well as the temporal scale, should depend on the horizon of the forecasting task and on the nature of the data.

Bar charts are useful for comparing a single statistic (e.g., average, count, percentage) across groups. The height of the bar (or length, in a horizontal display) represents the value of the statistic, and different bars correspond to

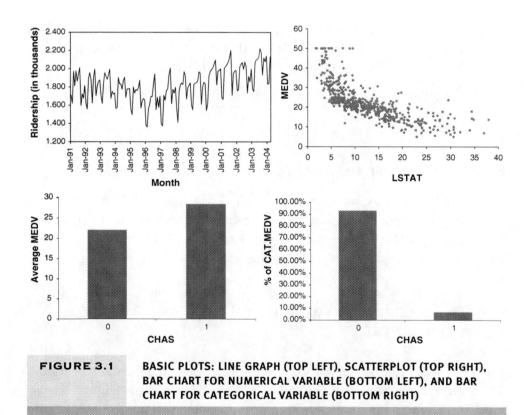

FIGURE 3.1   **BASIC PLOTS: LINE GRAPH (TOP LEFT), SCATTERPLOT (TOP RIGHT), BAR CHART FOR NUMERICAL VARIABLE (BOTTOM LEFT), AND BAR CHART FOR CATEGORICAL VARIABLE (BOTTOM RIGHT)**

different groups. Two examples are shown in the bottom panels in Figure 3.1. The left panel shows a bar chart for a numerical variable (MEDV) and the right panel shows a bar chart for a categorical variable (CAT.MEDV). In each, separate bars are used to denote homes in Boston that are near the Charles River versus those that are not (thereby comparing the two categories of CHAS). The chart with the numerical output MEDV (bottom left) uses the average MEDV on the y axis. This supports the predictive task: The numerical outcome is on the y axis and the x axis is used for a potential categorical predictor.[1] (Note that the x axis on a bar chart must be used only for categorical variables because the order of bars in a bar chart should be interchangeable.) For the classification task, CAT.MEDV is on the y axis (bottom right), but its aggregation is a percentage (the alternative would be a count). This graph shows us that the vast majority (over 90%) of the tracts do not border the Charles River (CHAS=0). Note that the labeling of the y axis can be confusing in this case: the value of CAT.MEDV plays no role and the y axis is simply a percentage of all records.

The top right panel in Figure 3.1 displays a scatterplot of MEDV versus LSTAT. This is an important plot in the prediction task. Note that the output MEDV is again on the y axis (and LSTAT on the x axis is a potential predictor). Because both variables in a basic scatterplot must be numerical, it cannot be used to display the relation between CAT.MEDV and potential predictors for the classification task (but we can enhance it to do so—see Section 3.4). For unsupervised learning, this particular scatterplot helps study the association between two numerical variables in terms of information overlap as well as identifying clusters of observations.

All three basic plots highlight global information such as the overall level of ridership or MEDV, as well as changes over time (line chart), differences between subgroups (bar chart), and relationships between numerical variables (scatterplot).

Distribution Plots: Boxplots and Histograms

Before moving on to more sophisticated visualizations that enable multidimensional investigation, we note two important plots that are usually not considered "basic charts" but are very useful in statistical and data mining contexts. The *boxplot* and the *histogram* are two plots that display the entire distribution of a numerical variable. Although averages are very popular and useful summary statistics, there is usually much to be gained by looking at additional statistics such as the median and standard deviation of a variable, and even more so by examining the entire distribution. Whereas bar charts can only use a single

---

[1] We refer here to a bar chart with vertical bars. The same principles apply if using a bar chart with horizontal bars, except that the x axis is now associated with the numerical variable and the y axis with the categorical variable.

aggregation, boxplots and histograms display the entire distribution of a numerical variable. Boxplots are also effective for comparing subgroups by generating side-by-side boxplots, or for looking at distributions over time by creating a series of boxplots.

Distribution plots are useful in supervised learning for determining potential data mining methods and variable transformations. For example, skewed numerical variables might warrant transformation (e.g., moving to a logarithmic scale) if used in methods that assume normality (e.g., linear regression, discriminant analysis).

A histogram represents the frequencies of all x values with a series of vertical connected bars. For example, in the top left panel of Figure 3.2, there are about 20 tracts where the median value (MEDV) is between $7500 and $12,500.

A boxplot represents the variable being plotted on the y axis (although the plot can potentially be turned in a 90° angle, so that the boxes are parallel to the x axis). In the top right panel of Figure 3.2 there are two boxplots (called a side-by-side boxplot). The box encloses 50% of the data—for example, in the right-hand box half of the tracts have median values (MEDV) between $20,000 and $33,000. The horizontal line inside the box represents the median (50th percentile). The top and bottom of the box represent the 75th and 25th percentiles, respectively. Lines extending above and below the box cover the rest of the data range; outliers may be depicted as points or circles. Sometimes the average is marked by a + (or similar) sign, as in the top right panel of Figure 3.2. Comparing the average and the median helps in assessing how skewed the data are. Boxplots are often arranged in a series with a different plot for each of the various values of a second variable, shown on the x axis.

Because histograms and boxplots are geared toward numerical variables, in their basic form they are useful for prediction tasks. Boxplots can also support unsupervised learning by displaying relationships between a numerical variable (y axis) and a categorical variable (x axis). To illustrate these points, see Figure 3.2. The top panel shows a histogram of MEDV, revealing a skewed distribution. Transforming the output variable to log(MEDV) would likely improve results of a linear regression predictor.

The right panel in Figure 3.2 shows side-by-side boxplots comparing the distribution of MEDV for homes that border the Charles River (1) or not (0), (similar to Figure 3.1). We see that not only is the average MEDV for river-bounding homes higher than the non-river-bounding homes, the entire distribution is higher (median, quartiles, min, and max). We also see that all river-bounding homes have MEDV above $10,000, unlike non-river-bounding homes. This information is useful for identifying the potential importance of this predictor (CHAS) and for choosing data mining methods that can capture the nonoverlapping area between the two distributions (e.g., trees). Boxplots and histograms applied to numerical variables can also provide directions for

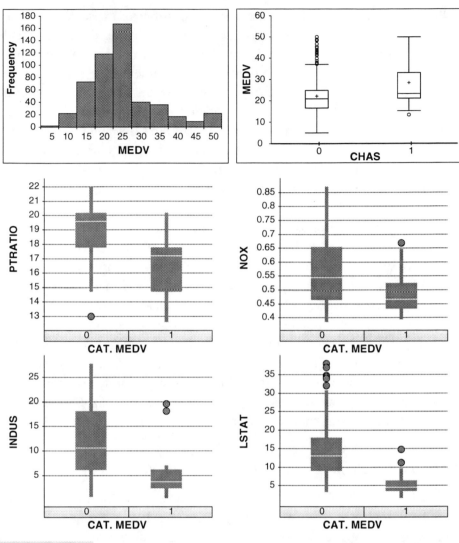

FIGURE 3.2   EXAMPLES OF HISTOGRAM (TOP LEFT) AND SIDE-BY-SIDE BOXPLOTS CREATED WITH XLMINER (TOP RIGHT) AND SPOTFIRE (CENTER AND BOTTOM ROWS). NOTE THAT IN A SIDE-BY-SIDE BOXPLOT, ONE AXIS IS USED FOR A CATEGORICAL VARIABLE, AND THE OTHER FOR A NUMERICAL VARIABLE. A NUMERICAL OUTCOME VARIABLE, IF IT IS PLOTTED, WILL APPEAR ON THE CATEGORICAL AXIS (IN WHICH CASE WE ARE PLOTTING THE DISTRIBUTION OF ONE OF THE NUMERICAL PREDICTORS). A NUMERICAL OUTCOME VARIABLE, IF IT IS PLOTTED, WILL APPEAR ON THE NUMERICAL AXIS (IN WHICH CASE WE ARE PLOTTING THE DISTRIBUTION OF THE OUTCOME VARIABLE ITSELF, WITH A CATEGORICAL PREDICTOR ON THE CATEGORICAL AXIS)

deriving new variables, for example, they can indicate how to bin a numerical variable (e.g., binning a numerical outcome in order to use a naive Bayes classifier, or in the Boston housing example, choosing the cutoff to convert MEDV to CAT.MEDV).

Finally, side-by-side boxplots are useful in classification tasks for evaluating the potential of numerical predictors. This is done by using the x axis for the categorical outcome and the y axis for a numerical predictor. An example is shown in the center and bottom rows of Figure 3.2, where we can see the effects of four numerical predictors on CAT.MEDV. The pairs that are most separated (e.g., PTRATIO and INDUS) indicate potentially useful predictors.

Boxplots and histograms are not readily available in Microsoft Excel (although they can be constructed through a tedious manual process). They are available in a wide range of statistical software packages. In XLMiner they can be generated through the *Charts* menu (we note the current limitation of five categories for side-by-side boxplots).

The main weakness of basic charts and distribution plots, in their basic form (i.e., using position in relation to the axes to encode values), is that they can only display two variables and therefore cannot reveal high-dimensional information. Each of the basic charts has two dimensions, where each dimension is dedicated to a single variable. In data mining, the data are usually multivariate by nature, and the analytics are designed to capture and measure multivariate information. Visual exploration should therefore also incorporate this important aspect. In the next section we describe how to extend basic charts (and distribution charts) to multidimensional data visualization by adding features, employing manipulations, and incorporating interactivity. We then present several specialized charts that are geared toward displaying special data structures (Section 3.5).

Heatmaps: Visualizing Correlations and Missing Values

A *heatmap* is a graphical display of numerical data where color is used to denote values. In a data mining context, heatmaps are especially useful for two purposes: for visualizing correlation tables and for visualizing missing values in the data. In both cases the information is conveyed in a two-dimensional table. A correlation table for p variables has p rows and p columns. A data table contains p columns (variables) and n rows (records). If the number of rows is huge, then a subset can be used. In both cases it is much easier and faster to scan the color coding rather than the values. Note that heatmaps are useful when examining a large number of values, but they are not a replacement for more precise graphical display, such as bar charts, because color differences cannot be perceived accurately.

An example of a correlation table heatmap is shown in Figure 3.3, showing all the pairwise correlations between 14 variables (MEDV and 13 predictors). Darker shades correspond to stronger (positive or negative) correlation. It is easy to quickly spot the high and low correlations. This heatmap was produced using Excel's *Conditional Formatting*.

In a missing value heatmap rows correspond to records and columns to variables. We use a binary coding of the original dataset where 1 denotes a

	CRIM	ZN	INDUS	CHAS	NOX	RM	AGE	DIS	RAD	TAX	PTRATIO	B	LSTAT	MEDV
CRIM	1.00													
ZN	-0.20	1.00												
INDUS	0.41	-0.53	1.00											
CHAS	-0.06	-0.04	0.06	1.00										
NOX	0.42	-0.52	0.76	0.09	1.00									
RM	-0.22	0.31	-0.39	0.09	-0.30	1.00								
AGE	0.35	-0.57	0.64	0.09	0.73	-0.24	1.00							
DIS	-0.38	0.66	-0.71	-0.10	-0.77	0.21	-0.75	1.00						
RAD	0.63	-0.31	0.60	-0.01	0.61	-0.21	0.46	-0.49	1.00					
TAX	0.58	-0.31	0.72	-0.04	0.67	-0.29	0.51	-0.53	0.91	1.00				
PTRATIO	0.29	-0.39	0.38	-0.12	0.19	-0.36	0.26	-0.23	0.46	0.46	1.00			
B	-0.39	0.18	-0.36	0.05	-0.38	0.13	-0.27	0.29	-0.44	-0.44	-0.18	1.00		
LSTAT	0.46	-0.41	0.60	-0.05	0.59	-0.61	0.60	-0.50	0.49	0.54	0.37	-0.37	1.00	
MEDV	-0.39	0.36	-0.48	0.18	-0.43	0.70	-0.38	0.25	-0.38	-0.47	-0.51	0.33	-0.74	1.00

FIGURE 3.3   **HEATMAP OF A CORRELATION TABLE. DARKER VALUES DENOTE STRONGER CORRELATION**

missing value and 0 otherwise. This new binary table is then colored such that only missing value cells (with value 1) are colored. Figure 3.4 shows an example of a missing value heatmap for a dataset with over 1000 columns. The data include economic, social, political and "well-being" information on different countries around the world (each row is a country). The variables were merged from multiple sources, and for each source information was not always available on every country. The missing data heatmap helps visualize the level and amount of "missingness" in the merged data file. Some patterns of "missingness" easily emerge: variables that are missing for nearly all observations, as well as clusters of rows (countries) that are missing many values. Variables with little missingness are

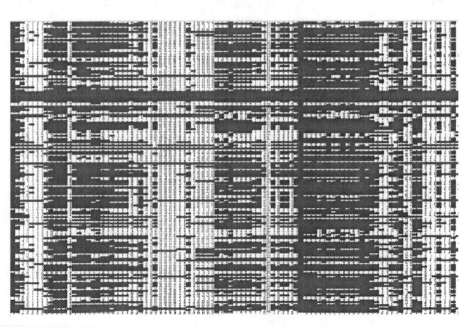

FIGURE 3.4   **HEATMAP OF MISSING VALUES IN A DATASET. BLACK DENOTES MISSING VALUE**

also visible. This information can then be used for determining how to handle the missingness (e.g., dropping some variables, dropping some records, imputing, or via other techniques).

3.4 MULTIDIMENSIONAL VISUALIZATION

Basic plots can convey richer information with features such as color, size, and multiple panels, and by enabling operations such as rescaling, aggregation, and interactivity. These additions allow looking at more than one or two variables at a time. The beauty of these additions is their effectiveness in displaying complex information in an easily understandable way. Effective features are based on understanding how visual perception works [see Few (2009) for a discussion]. The purpose is to make the information more understandable, not just represent the data in higher dimensions (such as three-dimensional plots that are usually ineffective visualizations).

Adding Variables: Color, Size, Shape, Multiple Panels, and Animation

In order to include more variables in a plot, we must consider the type of variable to include. To represent additional categorical information, the best way is to use hue, shape, or multiple panels. For additional numerical information we can use color intensity or size. Temporal information can be added via animation.

Incorporating additional categorical and/or numerical variables into the basic (and distribution) plots means that we can now use all of them for both prediction and classification tasks! For example, we mentioned earlier that a basic scatterplot cannot be used for studying the relationship between a categorical outcome and predictors (in the context of classification). However, a very effective plot for classification is a scatterplot of two numerical predictors color coded by the categorical outcome variable. An example is shown in the left panel of Figure 3.5, with color denoting CAT.MEDV.

In the context of prediction, color coding supports the exploration of the conditional relationship between the numerical outcome (on the y axis) and a numerical predictor. Color-coded scatterplots then help assess the need for creating interaction terms (e.g., is the relationship between MEDV and LSTAT different for homes near versus away from the river?).

Color can also be used to include further categorical variables into a bar chart, as long as the number of categories is small. When the number of categories is large, a better alternative is to use multiple panels. Creating multiple panels (also called "trellising") is done by splitting the observations according to a categorical variable and creating a separate plot (of the same type) for each category. An example is shown in the right panel of Figure 3.5, where a bar chart

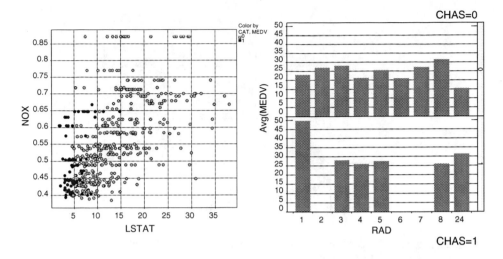

FIGURE 3.5	ADDING CATEGORICAL VARIABLES BY COLOR CODING AND MULTIPLE PANELS. (LEFT) SCATTERPLOT OF TWO NUMERICAL PREDICTORS, COLOR CODED BY THE CATEGORICAL OUTCOME (CAT.MEDV). (RIGHT) BAR CHART OF MEDV BY TWO CATEGORICAL PREDICTORS (CHAS AND RAD), USING MULTIPLE PANELS FOR CHAS. (CHAS = 0 FOR UPPER PANEL, CHAS = 1 FOR LOWER PANEL)

of average MEDV by RAD is broken down into two panels by CHAS. We see that the average MEDV for different highway accessibility levels (RAD) behaves differently for homes near the river (lower panel) compared to homes away from the river (upper panel). This is especially salient for RAD=1. We also see that there are no near-river homes in RAD levels 2, 6, and 7. Such information might lead us to create an interaction term between RAD and CHAS and to consider condensing some of the bins in RAD. All these explorations are useful for prediction and classification.

A special plot that uses scatterplots with multiple panels is the *scatterplot matrix*. In it, all pairwise scatterplots are shown in a single display. The panels in a scatterplot matrix are organized in a special way, such that each column corresponds to a variable and each row corresponds to a variable, thereby the intersections create all the possible pairwise scatterplots. The scatterplot matrix plot is useful in unsupervised learning for studying the associations between numerical variables, detecting outliers and identifying clusters. For supervised learning, it can be used for examining pairwise relationships (and their nature) between predictors to support variable transformations and variable selection (see Section 4.4). For prediction it can also be used to depict the relationship of the outcome with the numerical predictors.

An example of a scatterplot matrix is shown in Figure 3.6, with MEDV and three predictors. To identify which pair is plotted, variable names are shown along the diagonal cells; plots in the row corresponding to a variable show the

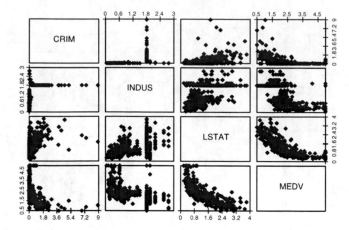

| FIGURE 3.6 | **SCATTERPLOT MATRIX FOR MEDV AND THREE NUMERICAL PREDICTORS** |

variable's values along the y axis while plots in the corresponding column show the variable's values along the x axis. For example, the plots in the bottom row all have MEDV on the y axis (which allows studying the individual outcome–predictor relations). We can see different types of relationships from the different shapes (e.g., an exponential relationship between MEDV and LSTAT and a highly skewed relationship between CRIM and INDUS), which can indicate needed transformations. Note that the plots above and to the right of the diagonal are mirror images of those below and to the left.

Once hue is used, further categorical variables can be added via shape and multiple panels. However, one must proceed cautiously in adding multiple variables, as the display can become overcluttered and then visual perception is lost.

Adding a numerical variable via size is useful especially in scatterplots (thereby creating "bubble plots") because in a scatterplot, points represent individual observations. In plots that aggregate across observations (e.g., boxplots, histograms, bar charts) size and hue are not normally incorporated.

Finally, adding a temporal dimension to a plot to show how the information changes over time can be achieved via animation. A famous example is Rosling's animated scatterplots showing how world demographics changed over the years (www.gapminder.org). However, while animations of this type work for "statistical storytelling," they are not very effective for data exploration.

Manipulations: Rescaling, Aggregation and Hierarchies, Zooming, and Panning, and Filtering

Most of the time spent in data mining projects is spent in preprocessing. Typically, considerable effort is expended getting all the data in a format that can actually be used in the data mining software. Additional time is spent processing the data in ways that improve the performance of the data mining procedures. This pre-processing step in data mining includes variable transformation and derivation of new variables to help models perform more effectively. Transformations include changing the numeric scale of a variable, binning numerical variables, condensing categories in categorical variables, and the like. The following manipulations support the preprocessing step as well as the choice of adequate data mining methods. They do so by revealing patterns and their nature.

Rescaling   Changing the scale in a display can enhance the plot and illuminate relationships. For example, in Figure 3.7 we see the effect of changing both axes of the scatterplot (top) and the y axis of a boxplot (bottom) to logarithmic (log) scale. Whereas the original plots (left) are hard to understand, the patterns become visible in log scale (right). In the scatterplot, the nature of the relationship between MEDV and CRIM is hard to determine in the original scale because too many of the points are "crowded" near the y axis. The rescaling removes this crowding and allows a better view of the linear relationship between the two log-scaled variables (indicating a log–log relationship). In the boxplot displays the crowding toward the x axis in the original units does not allow us to compare the two box sizes, their locations, lower outliers, and most of the distribution information. Rescaling removes the "crowding to the x axis" effect, thereby allowing a comparison of the two boxplots.

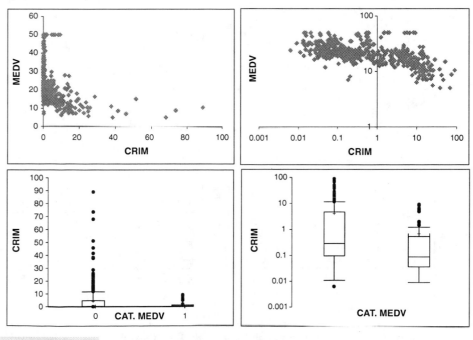

FIGURE 3.7   **RESCALING CAN ENHANCE PLOTS AND REVEAL PATTERNS. (LEFT) ORIGINAL SCALE. (RIGHT) LOG SCALE**

Aggregation and Hierarchies Another useful manipulation of scaling is changing the level of aggregation. For a temporal scale, we can aggregate by different granularity (e.g., monthly, daily, hourly) or even by a "seasonal" factor of interest such as month of year or day of week. A popular aggregation for time series is a moving average, where the average of neighboring values within a given window size is plotted. Moving-average plots enhance global trend visualization (see Chapter 15).

Nontemporal variables can be aggregated if some meaningful hierarchy exists: geographical (tracts within a zip code in the Boston housing example), organizational (people within departments within units), and so on. Figure 3.8 illustrates two types of aggregation for the railway ridership time series. The original monthly series is shown in the top left panel. Seasonal aggregation (by month of year) is shown in the top right panel, where it is easy to see the peak in ridership in July–Aug and the dip in Jan–Feb. The bottom right panel shows temporal aggregation, where the series is now displayed in yearly aggregates. This plot reveals the global long-term trend in ridership and the generally increasing trend from 1996 on.

Examining different scales, aggregations, or hierarchies supports both supervised and unsupervised tasks in that it can reveal patterns and relationships at various levels and can suggest new sets of variables with which to work.

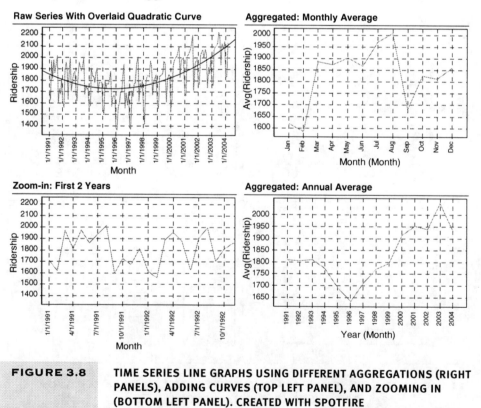

FIGURE 3.8 TIME SERIES LINE GRAPHS USING DIFFERENT AGGREGATIONS (RIGHT PANELS), ADDING CURVES (TOP LEFT PANEL), AND ZOOMING IN (BOTTOM LEFT PANEL). CREATED WITH SPOTFIRE

Zooming and Panning The ability to zoom in and out of certain areas of the data on a plot is important for revealing patterns and outliers. We are often interested in more detail on areas of dense information or of special interest. Panning refers to the operation of moving the zoom window to other areas (popular in mapping applications such as Google Maps). An example of zooming is shown in the bottom left panel of Figure 3.8, where the ridership series is zoomed in to the first 2 years of the series.

Zooming and panning support supervised and unsupervised methods by detecting areas of different behavior, which may lead to creating new interaction terms, new variables, or even separate models for data subsets. In addition, zooming and panning can help choose between methods that assume global behavior (e.g., regression models) and data-driven methods (e.g., exponential smoothing forecasters and k-nearest neighbors classifiers) and indicate the level of global–local behavior (as manifested by parameters such as k in k-nearest neighbors, the size of a tree, or the smoothing parameters in exponential smoothing).

Filtering Filtering means removing some of the observations from the plot. The purpose of filtering is to focus the attention on certain data while eliminating "noise" created by other data. Filtering supports supervised and unsupervised learning in a similar way to zooming and panning: It assists in identifying different or unusual local behavior.

Reference: Trend Lines and Labels

Trend lines and using in-plot labels also help to detect patterns and outliers. Trend lines serve as a reference and allow us to more easily assess the shape of a pattern. Although linearity is easy to visually perceive, more elaborate relationships such as exponential and polynomial trends are harder to assess by eye. Trend lines are useful in line graphs as well as in scatterplots. An example is shown in the top left panel of Figure 3.8, where a polynomial curve is overlaid on the original line graph (see also Chapter 15).

In displays that are not overcrowded, the use of in-plot labels can be useful for better exploration of outliers and clusters. An example is shown in Figure 3.9 (a reproduction of Figure 14.1 with the addition of labels). The figure shows different utilities on a scatterplot that compares fuel cost with total sales. We might be interested in clustering the data, and using clustering algorithms to identify clusters that differ markedly with respect to fuel cost and sales. Figure 14.1, with the labels, helps visualize these clusters and their members (e.g., Nevada and Puget are part of a clear cluster with low fuel costs and high sales). For more on clustering, and this example, see Chapter 14.

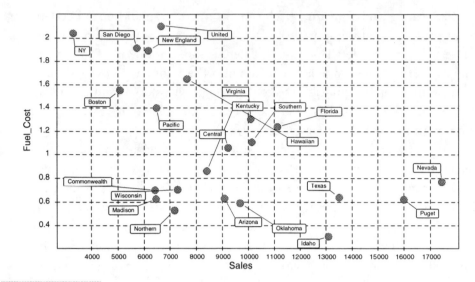

FIGURE 3.9   **SCATTERPLOT WITH LABELED POINTS (CREATED WITH SPOTFIRE). COMPARE TO FIGURE 14.1**

Scaling up: Large Datasets

When the number of observations (rows) is large, plots that display each individual observation (e.g., scatterplots) can become ineffective. Aside from applying aggregated charts such as boxplots, some alternatives are:

1. Sampling: drawing a random sample and using it for plotting (XLMiner has a sampling utility)

2. Reducing marker size

3. Using more transparent marker colors and removing fill

4. Breaking down the data into subsets (e.g., by creating multiple panels)

5. Using aggregation (e.g., bubble plots where size corresponds to number of observations in a certain range)

6. Using jittering (slightly moving each marker by adding a small amount of noise)

An example of the advantage of plotting a sample over the large dataset is shown in Figure 12.2 in Chapter 12, where a scatterplot of 5000 records is plotted alongside a scatterplot of a sample. Those plots were generated in Excel. We illustrate (Figure 3.10) an improved plot of the full dataset by applying smaller markers, using jittering to uncover overlaid points, and more transparent colors. We can see that larger areas of the plot are dominated by the gray class, the black class is mainly on the right, while there is a lot of overlap in the top right area.

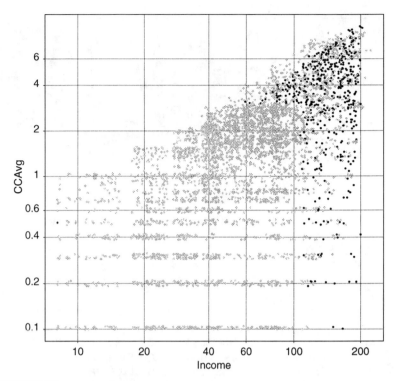

FIGURE 3.10   **REPRODUCTION OF FIGURE 12.2 WITH REDUCED MARKER SIZE, JITTERING, AND MORE TRANSPARENT COLORING**

Multivariate Plot: Parallel Coordinates Plot

Another approach toward presenting multidimensional information in a two-dimensional plot is via specialized plots such as the *parallel coordinates plot*. In this plot a vertical axis is drawn for each variable. Then each observation is represented by drawing a line that connects its values on the different axes, thereby creating a "multivariate profile." An example is shown in Figure 3.11 for the Boston housing data. In this display separate panels are used for the two values of CAT.MEDV in order to compare the profiles of homes in the two classes (for a classification task). We see that the more expensive homes (bottom panel) consistently have low CRIM, low LSAT, high B, and high RM compared to cheaper homes (top panel), which are more mixed on CRIM, LSAT, and B, and have a medium level of RM. This observation gives an indication of useful predictors and suggests possible binning for some numerical predictors.

Parallel coordinate plots are also useful in unsupervised tasks. They can reveal clusters, outliers, and information overlap across variables. A useful manipulation is to reorder the columns to better reveal observation clusterings. Parallel coordinate plots are not implemented in Excel. However, a free Excel add-in is currently available at http://ibmi.mf.uni-lj.si/ibmi-english/biostat-center/programje/excel/ParallelCoordinates.xls.

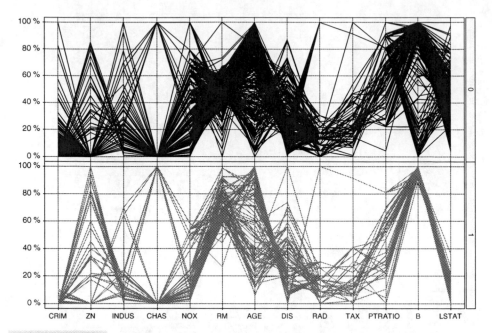

FIGURE 3.11   PARALLEL COORDINATES PLOT FOR BOSTON HOUSING DATA. EACH OF THE VARIABLES (SHOWN ON THE HORIZONTAL AXIS) IS SCALED TO 0--100%. PANELS ARE USED TO DISTINGUISH CAT.MEDV (TOP PANEL = HOMES BELOW $30,000). CREATED USING SPOTFIRE

Interactive Visualization

Similar to the interactive nature of the data mining process, interactivity is key to enhancing our ability to gain information from graphical visualization. In the words of Stephen Few (Few, 2009, p. 55), an expert in data visualization,

> We can only learn so much when staring at a static visualization such as a printed graph . . . If we can't interact with the data . . . we hit the wall.

By interactive visualization we mean an interface that supports the following principles:

1. Making changes to a plot is *easy, rapid, and reversible.*
2. Multiple concurrent plots can be easily combined and displayed on a single screen.
3. A set of visualizations can be linked such that operations in one display are reflected in the other displays.

Let us consider a few examples where we contrast a static plot generator (e.g., Excel) with an interactive visualization interface.

Histogram rebinning   Consider the need to bin a numerical variable using a histogram. A static histogram would require replotting for each new binning choice (in Excel it would require creating the new bins manually). If the user generates multiple plots, then the screen becomes cluttered. If the same plot is recreated, then it is hard to compare to other binning choices. In contrast, an interactive visualization would provide an easy way to change bin width interactively (see, e.g., the slider below the histogram in Figure 3.12), and then the histogram would automatically and rapidly replot as the user changes the bin width.

Aggregation and Zooming   Consider a time series forecasting task, given a long series of data. Temporal aggregation at multiple levels is needed for determining short- and long-term patterns. Zooming and panning are used to identify unusual periods. A static plotting software requires the user to create new data columns for each temporal aggregation (e.g., aggregate daily data to obtain weekly aggregates). Zooming and panning in Excel requires manually changing the min and max values on the axis scale of interest (thereby losing the ability to quickly move between different areas without creating multiple charts). An interactive visualization would provide immediate temporal hierarchies between which the

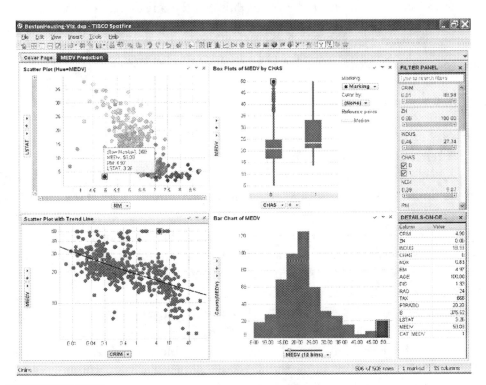

FIGURE 3.12   **MULTIPLE INTERLINKED PLOTS IN A SINGLE VIEW (IN SPOTFIRE). NOTE THE MARKED OBSERVATION IN THE TOP LEFT PANEL, WHICH IS ALSO HIGHLIGHTED IN ALL OTHER PLOTS**

user can easily switch. Zooming would be enabled as a slider near the axis (see, e.g., the sliders on the top left panel in Figure 3.12), thereby allowing direct manipulation and rapid reaction.

Combining Multiple Linked Plots That Fit in a Single Screen   To support a classification task, multiple plots are created of the outcome variable versus potential categorical and numerical predictors. These can include side-by-side boxplots, color-coded scatterplots, multipanel bar charts, and the like. The user wants to detect multidimensional relationships (and identify outliers) by selecting a certain subset of the data (e.g., a single category of some variable) and locating the observations on the other plots. In a static interface, the user would have to manually organize the plots of interest and resize them in order to fit within a single screen. A static interface would usually not support interplot linkage, and even if so, the entire set of plots would have to be regenerated each time that a selection is made. In contrast, an interactive visualization would provide an easy way to automatically organize and resize the set of plots to fit within a screen. Linking the set of plots would be easy, and in response to the users selection on one plot, the appropriate selection would be automatically highlighted in the other plots (see example in Figure 3.12).

In earlier sections we used plots to illustrate the advantages of visualizations because "a picture is worth a thousand words." The advantages of an interactive visualization are even greater. As Ben Shneiderman, a well-known researcher in information visualization and interfaces, notes:

> A picture is worth a thousand words. An interface is worth a thousand pictures.

Interactive Visualization Software   Some added features such as color, shape, and size are often available in software that produces static plots, while others (multiple panels, hierarchies, labels) are only available in more advanced visualization tools. Even when a feature is available (e.g., color), the ease of applying it to a plot can widely vary. For example, incorporating color into an Excel scatterplot is a daunting task.[2] Plot manipulation possibilities (e.g., zooming, filtering, and aggregation) and ease of implementation are also quite limited in standard "static plot" software.

Although we do not intend to provide a market survey of interactive visualization tools, we do mention a few prominent packages. Spotfire (http://spotfire.tibco.com) and Tableau (www.tableausoftware.com) are two dedicated data visualization tools (several of the plots in this chapter were created using Spotfire). They both provide a high level of interactivity, can support large datasets, and produce high-quality plots that are also easy to export. JMP

---

[2] See http://blog.bzst.com/2009/08/creating-color-coded-scatterplots-in.html.

by SAS (www.jmp.com) is a "statistical discovery" software that also has strong interactive visualization capabilities. All three offer free trial versions. Finally, we mention Many Eyes by IBM (http://manyeyes.alphaworks.ibm.com/manyeyes) that allows uploading your data and visualizing it via different interactive visualizations.

3.5 SPECIALIZED VISUALIZATIONS

In this section we mention a few specialized visualizations that are able to capture data structures beyond the standard time series and cross-sectional structures—special types of relationships that are usually hard to capture with ordinary plots. In particular, we address hierarchical data, network data, and geographical data—three types of data that are becoming more available.

Visualizing Networked Data

With the explosion of social and product network data, network analysis has become a hot topic. Examples of social networks include networks of sellers and buyers on eBay and networks of people on Facebook. An example of a product network is the network of products on Amazon (linked through the recommendation system). Network data visualization is available in various network-specialized software, and also in general-purpose software.

A network diagram consists of actors and relations between them. "Nodes" are the actors (e.g., people in a social network or products in a product network) and represented by circles. "Edges" are the relations between nodes and are represented by lines connecting nodes. For example, in a social network such as Facebook, we can construct a list of users (nodes) and all the pairwise relations (edges) between users who are "Friends." Alternatively, we can define edges as a posting that one user posts on another user's Facebook page. In this setup we might have more than a single edge between two nodes. Networks can also have nodes of multiple types. A common structure is networks with two types of nodes. An example of a two-type node network is shown in Figure 3.13, where we see a set of transactions between a network of sellers and buyers on the online auction site www.eBay.com [the data are for auctions selling Swarowski beads and took place during a period of several months; from Jank and Yahav (2010)]. The circles on the left side represent sellers and on the right side buyers. Circle size represents the number of transactions that the node (seller or buyer) was involved in within this network. Line width represents the number of auctions that the bidder–seller pair interacted in (in this case we use arrows to denote the directional relationship from buyer to seller). We can see that this marketplace is dominated by three or four high-volume sellers. We can also see that many

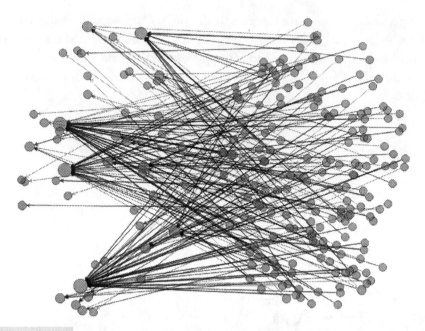

FIGURE 3.13	NETWORK GRAPH OF EBAY SELLERS (LEFT SIDE) AND BUYERS (RIGHT SIDE) OF SWAROSKI BEADS. CIRCLE SIZE REPRESENTS THE NODE'S NUMBER OF TRANSACTIONS. LINE WIDTH REPRESENTS THE NUMBER OF TRANSACTIONS BETWEEN THAT PAIR OF SELLER--BUYER (CREATED WITH SPOTFIRE)

buyers interact with a single seller. The market structures for many individual products could be reviewed quickly in this way. Network providers could use the information, for example, to identify possible partnerships to explore with sellers.

Figure 3.13 was produced using Spotfire's network visualization. An Excel-based tool is NodeXL (http://nodexl.codeplex.com), which is a template for Excel 2007 that allows entering a network edge list. The graph's appearance can be customized and various interactive features are available such as zooming, scaling and panning the graph, dynamically filtering nodes and edges, altering the graph's layout, finding clusters of related nodes, and calculating graph metrics. Networks can be imported from and exported to a variety of data formats, and built-in connections for getting networks from Twitter, Flickr, and your local e-mail are provided.

Network graphs can be potentially useful in the context of association rules (see Chapter 13). For example, consider a case of mining a dataset of consumers' grocery purchases to learn which items are purchased together ("what goes with what"). A network can be constructed with items as nodes and edges connecting items that were purchased together. After a set of rules is generated by the data mining algorithm (which often contains an excessive number of rules, many of which are unimportant), the network graph can help visualize different rules for the purpose of choosing the interesting ones. For example, a popular "beer and diapers" combination would appear in the network graph as a pair of nodes with very high connectivity. An item that is almost always purchased regardless of other items (e.g., milk) would appear as a very large node with high connectivity to all other nodes.

Visualizing Hierarchical Data: Treemaps

We discussed hierarchical data and the exploration of data at different hierarchy levels in the context of plot manipulations. *Treemaps* are useful visualizations for exploring large data sets that are hierarchically structured (tree structured). They enable exploration of various dimensions of the data while maintaining the data's hierarchical nature. An example is shown in Figure 3.14, which displays a large set of eBay auctions, hierarchically ordered by item category, subcategory, and brand. The levels in the hierarchy of the treemap are visualized as rectangles containing subrectangles. Categorical variables can be included in the display by using hue. Numerical variables can be included via rectangle size and color intensity (ordering of the rectangles is sometimes used to reinforce size). In Figure 3.14 size is used to represent the average closing price (which reflects item value), and color intensity represents the percent of sellers with negative feedback

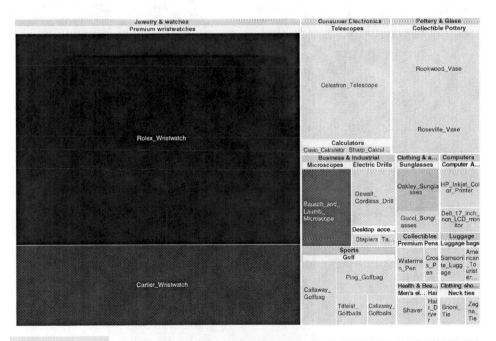

FIGURE 3.14   **TREEMAP SHOWING NEARLY 11,000 EBAY AUCTIONS, ORGANIZED BY ITEM CATEGORY, SUBCATEGORY, AND BRAND. RECTANGLE SIZE REPRESENTS AVERAGE CLOSING PRICE (REFLECTING ITEM VALUE). SHADE REPRESENTS % OF SELLERS WITH NEGATIVE FEEDBACK (DARKER = HIGHER %)**

(a negative seller feedback indicates buyer dissatisfaction in past transactions and often indicative of fraudulent seller behavior). Consider the task of classifying ongoing auctions in terms of a fraudulent outcome. From the treemap we see that the highest proportion of sellers with negative ratings (black) is concentrated in expensive item auctions (Rolex and Cartier wristwatches).

Ideally, treemaps should be explored interactively, zooming to different levels of the hierarchy. An interactive online application of treemaps is "Map of the Market" by Smart-Money (www.smartmoney.com/map-of-the-market), which displays stock market information in an interactive treemap display.

A free treemap add-in for Excel was developed by Microsoft research and is available at http://research.microsoft.com/apps/dp/dl/downloads.aspx (search for "Treemapper").

Visualizing Geographical Data: Map Charts

With the growing availability of location data, many datasets used for data mining now include geographical information. Zip codes are one example of a categorical variable with many categories, where creating meaningful variables for analysis is not straightforward. Plotting the data on a geographical map can often reveal patterns that are otherwise harder to identify. A map chart uses a

FIGURE 3.15   WORLD MAPS COMPARING "WELL-BEING" TO GDP. (TOP) SHADING BY AVERAGE "GLOBAL WELL-BEING" SCORE OF COUNTRY (DARKER CORRESPONDS TO HIGHER SCORE OR LEVEL). (BOTTOM) SHADING ACCORDING TO GDP. DATA FROM VEENHOVEN'S WORLD DATABASE OF HAPPINESS

geographical map as its background, and then color, hue, and other features can be used to include categorical or numerical variables. Besides specialized mapping software, maps are now becoming part of general-purpose software. Figure 3.15 shows two world maps (created with Spotfire), comparing countries' "well-being" (according to a 2006 Gallup survey) in the top map to gross domestic product (GDP) in the bottom map. A darker shade means higher value (white areas are missing data).

3.6 SUMMARY OF MAJOR VISUALIZATIONS AND OPERATIONS, ACCORDING TO DATA MINING GOAL

Prediction

- Plot outcome on the y axis of vertical boxplots, vertical bar charts, and scatterplots.
- Study relation of outcome to categorical predictors via side-by-side boxplots, bar charts, and multiple panels.
- Study relation of outcome to numerical predictors via scatterplots.
- Use distribution plots (boxplot, histogram) for determining needed transformations of the outcome variable (and/or numerical predictors).
- Examine scatterplots with added color/panels/size to determine the need for interaction terms.
- Use various aggregation levels and zooming to determine areas of the data with different behavior, and to evaluate the level of global versus local patterns.

Classification

- Study relation of outcome to categorical predictors using bar charts with the outcome on the y axis.
- Study relation of outcome to pairs of numerical predictors via color-coded scatterplots (color denotes the outcome).
- Study relation of outcome to numerical predictors via side-by-side boxplots: Plot boxplots of a numerical variable by outcome. Create similar displays for each numerical predictor. The most separable boxes indicate potentially useful predictors.
- Use color to represent the outcome variable on a parallel coordinate plot.
- Use distribution plots (boxplot, histogram) for determining needed transformations of the outcome variable.

- Examine scatterplots with added color/panels/size to determine the need for interaction terms.
- Use various aggregation levels and zooming to determine areas of the data with different behavior, and to evaluate the level of global versus local patterns.

Time Series Forecasting

- Create line graphs at different temporal aggregations to determine types of patterns.
- Use zooming and panning to examine various shorter periods of the series to determine areas of the data with different behavior.
- Use various aggregation levels to identify global and local patterns.
- Identify missing values in the series (that require handling).
- Overlay trend lines of different types to determine adequate modeling choices.

Unsupervised Learning

- Create scatterplot matrices to identify pairwise relationships and clustering of observations.
- Use heatmaps to examine the correlation table.
- Use various aggregation levels and zooming to determine areas of the data with different behavior.
- Generate a parallel coordinate plot to identify clusters of observations.

PROBLEMS ▬▬▬▬▬▬▬▬▬▬▬▬▬▬■

3.1 **Shipments of Household Appliances: Line Graphs.** The file ApplianceShipments.xls contains the series of quarterly shipments (in million $) of U.S. household appliances between 1985 and 1989 (data courtesy of Ken Black).

    a. Create a well-formatted time plot of the data using Excel.

    b. Does there appear to be a quarterly pattern? For a closer view of the patterns, zoom in to the range of 3500–5000 on the y axis.

    c. Create four separate lines for Q1, Q2, Q3, and Q4, using Excel. In each, plot a line graph. In Excel, order the data by Q1, Q2, Q3, Q4 (alphabetical sorting will work), and plot them as separate series on the line graph. Zoom in to the range of 3500–5000 on the y axis. Does there appear to be a difference between quarters?

    d. Using Excel, create a line graph of the series at a yearly aggregated level (i.e., the total shipments in each year).

    e. Re-create the above plots using an interactive visualization tool. Make sure to enter the quarter information in a format that is recognized by the software as a date.

    f. Compare the two processes of generating the line graphs in terms of the effort as well as the quality of the resulting plots. What are the advantages of each?

3.2 **Sales of Riding Mowers: Scatterplots.** A company that manufactures riding mowers wants to identify the best sales prospects for an intensive sales campaign. In particular, the manufacturer is interested in classifying households as prospective owners or nonowners on the basis of Income (in $1000s) and Lot Size (in 1000 ft^2). The marketing expert looked at a random sample of 24 households, included in the file RidingMowers.xls.

    a. Using Excel, create a scatterplot of Lot Size vs. Income, color coded by the outcome variable owner/nonowner. Make sure to obtain a well-formatted plot (remove excessive background and gridlines; create legible labels and a legend, etc.). The result should be similar to Figure 9.2. *Hint:* First sort the data by the outcome variable, and then plot the data for each category as separate series.

    b. Create the same plot, this time using an interactive visualization tool.

    c. Compare the two processes of generating the plot in terms of the effort as well as the quality of the resulting plots. What are the advantages of each?

3.3 **Laptop Sales at a London Computer Chain: Bar Charts and Boxplots.** The file LaptopSalesJanuary2008.xls contains data for all sales of laptops at a computer chain in London in January 2008. This is a subset of the full dataset that includes data for the entire year.

    a. Create a bar chart, showing the average retail price by store. Which store has the highest average? Which has the lowest?

    b. To better compare retail prices across stores, create side-by-side boxplots of retail price by store. Now compare the prices in the two stores above. Do you see a difference between their price distributions? Explain.

3.4 **Laptop Sales at a London Computer Chain: Interactive Visualization.** *The next exercises are designed for use with an interactive visualization tool. The file LaptopSales.txt is a comma-separated file with nearly 300,000 rows. ENBIS (the European Network for Business and Industrial Statistics) provided these data as part of a contest organized in the fall of 2009.*

Scenario: You are a new analyst for Acell, a company selling laptops. You have been provided with data about products and sales. Your task is to help the company to plan product strategy and pricing policies that will maximize Acell's projected revenues in 2009. Using an interactive visualization tool, answer the following questions.

a. **Price Questions**

   i. At what prices are the laptops actually selling?

   ii. Does price change with time? (*Hint*: Make sure that the date column is recognized as such. The software should then enable different temporal aggregation choices, e.g., plotting the data by weekly or monthly aggregates, or even by day of week.)

   iii. Are prices consistent across retail outlets?

   iv. How does price change with configuration?

b. **Location Questions**

   i. Where are the stores and customers located?

   ii. Which stores are selling the most?

   iii. How far would customers travel to buy a laptop?

   ○ *Hint 1*: you should be able to aggregate the data, for example, plot the sum or average of the prices.

   ○ *Hint 2*: Use the coordinated highlighting between multiple visualizations in the same page, for example, select a store in one view to see the matching customers in another visualization.

   ○ *Hint 3*: Explore the use of filters to see differences. Make sure to filter in the zoomed out view. For example, try to use a "store location" slider as an alternative way to dynamically compare store locations. This is especially useful for spotting outlier patterns if there are many store locations to compare.

   iv. Try an alternative way of looking at how far customers traveled. Do this by creating a new data column that computes the distance between customer and store.

c. **Revenue Questions**

   i. How do the sales volume in each store relate to Acell's revenues?

   ii. How does this depend on the configuration?

d. **Configuration Questions**

   i. What are the details of each configuration? How does this relate to price?

   ii. Do all stores sell all configurations?

CHAPTER 5

Evaluating Classification and Predictive Performance

In this chapter we discuss how the predictive performance of data mining methods can be assessed. We point out the danger of overfitting to the training data and the need for testing model performance on data that were not used in the training step. We discuss popular performance metrics. For prediction, metrics include Average Error, MAPE, and RMSE (based on the validation data). For classification tasks, metrics include the classification matrix, specificity and sensitivity, and metrics that account for misclassification costs. We also show the relation between the choice of cutoff value and method performance, and present the receiver operating characteristic (ROC) curve, which is a popular plot for assessing method performance at different cutoff values. When the goal is to accurately classify the top tier of a new sample rather than accurately classify the entire sample (e.g., the 10% of customers most likely to respond to an offer), lift charts are used to assess performance. We also discuss the need for oversampling rare classes and how to adjust performance metrics for the oversampling. Finally, we mention the usefulness of comparing metrics based on the validation data to those based on the training data for the purpose of detecting overfitting. While some differences are expected, extreme differences can be indicative of overfitting.

5.1 INTRODUCTION

In supervised learning we are interested in predicting the class (classification) or continuous value (prediction) of an outcome variable. In Chapter 2 we worked

Data Mining for Business Intelligence, By Galit Shmueli, Nitin R. Patel, and Peter C. Bruce

93

through a simple example. Let us now examine the questions of how to judge the usefulness of a classifier or predictor and how to compare different ones.

5.2   JUDGING CLASSIFICATION PERFORMANCE

The need for performance measures arises from the wide choice of classifiers and predictive methods. Not only do we have several different methods, but even within a single method there are usually many options that can lead to completely different results. A simple example is the choice of predictors used within a particular predictive algorithm. Before we study these various algorithms in detail and face decisions on how to set these options, we need to know how we will measure success.

A natural criterion for judging the performance of a classifier is the probability of making a *misclassification error*. Misclassification means that the observation belongs to one class but the model classifies it as a member of a different class. A classifier that makes no errors would be perfect, but we do not expect to be able to construct such classifiers in the real world due to "noise" and to not having all the information needed to classify cases precisely. Is there a minimal probability of misclassification that we should require of a classifier?

Benchmark: The Naive Rule

A very simple rule for classifying a record into one of m classes, ignoring all predictor information $(X_1, X_2, ..., X_p)$ that we may have, is to classify the record as a member of the majority class. In other words, "classify as belonging to the most prevalent class." The *naive rule* is used mainly as a baseline or benchmark for evaluating the performance of more complicated classifiers. Clearly, a classifier that uses external predictor information (on top of the class membership allocation) should outperform the naive rule. There are various performance measures based on the naive rule that measure how much better than the naive rule a certain classifier performs. One example is the multiple R^2 reported by XLMiner, which measures the distance between the fit of the classifier to the data and the fit of the naive rule to the data (for further details, see Section 10.5.

The equivalent of the naive rule for classification when considering a quantitative response is to use $\hat{y}$, the sample mean, to predict the value of y for a new record. In both cases the predictions rely solely on the y information and exclude any additional predictor information.

Class Separation

If the classes are well separated by the predictor information, even a small dataset will suffice in finding a good classifier, whereas if the classes are not separated at all by the predictors, even a very large dataset will not help. Figure 5.1 illustrates this for a two–class case. Figure 5.1(*a*) includes a small dataset ($n = 24$ observations) where two predictors (income and lot size) are used for separating owners from nonowners [we thank Dean Wichern for this example, described in Johnson and Wichern (2002)]. Here, the predictor information seems useful in that it separates the two classes (owners/nonowners). Figure 5.1(*b*) shows a much larger dataset ($n = 5000$ observations) where the two predictors (income and average credit card spending) do not separate the two classes well in most of the higher ranges (loan acceptors/nonacceptors).

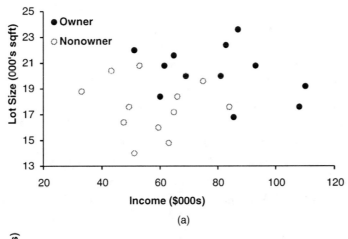

(a)

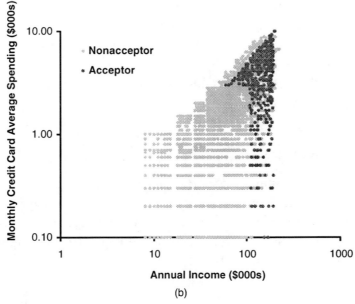

(b)

FIGURE 5.1   (*A*) HIGH AND (*B*) LOW LEVELS OF SEPARATION BETWEEN TWO CLASSES, USING TWO PREDICTORS

Classification Confusion Matrix		
	Predicted Class	
Actual Class	1	0
1	201	85
0	25	2689

FIGURE 5.2 CLASSIFICATION MATRIX BASED ON 3000 OBSERVATIONS AND TWO CLASSES

Classification Matrix

In practice, most accuracy measures are derived from the *classification matrix* (also called the *confusion matrix*). This matrix summarizes the correct and incorrect classifications that a classifier produced for a certain dataset. Rows and columns of the classification matrix correspond to the true and predicted classes, respectively. Figure 5.2 shows an example of a classification (confusion) matrix for a two-class (0/1) problem resulting from applying a certain classifier to 3000 observations. The two diagonal cells (upper left, lower right) give the number of correct classifications, where the predicted class coincides with the actual class of the observation. The off-diagonal cells give counts of misclassification. The top right cell gives the number of class 1 members that were misclassified as 0's (in this example, there were 85 such misclassifications). Similarly, the lower left cell gives the number of class 0 members that were misclassified as 1's (25 such observations).

The classification matrix gives estimates of the true classification and misclassification rates. Of course, these are estimates and they can be incorrect, but if we have a large enough dataset and neither class is very rare, our estimates will be reliable. Sometimes, we may be able to use public data such as U.S. Census data to estimate these proportions. However, in most practical business settings, we will not know them.

Using the Validation Data

To obtain an honest estimate of classification error, we use the classification matrix that is computed from the *validation data*. In other words, we first partition the data into training and validation sets by random selection of cases. We then construct a classifier using the training data and apply it to the validation data. This will yield the predicted classifications for observations in the validation set (see Figure 2.4). We then summarize these classifications in a classification matrix. Although we can summarize our results in a classification matrix for training data as well, the resulting classification matrix is not useful for getting an honest estimate of the misclassification rate for new data due to the danger of overfitting.

In addition to examining the validation data classification matrix to assess the classification performance on new data, we compare the training data classification matrix to the validation data classification matrix, in order to detect overfitting: although we expect inferior results on the validation data, a large discrepancy in training and validation performance might be indicative of overfitting.

Accuracy Measures

Different accuracy measures can be derived from the classification matrix. Consider a two-class case with classes C_0 and C_1 (e.g., buyer/nonbuyer). The schematic classification matrix in Table 5.1 uses the notation $n_{i,j}$ to denote the number of cases that are class C_i members and were classified as C_j members. Of course, if $i \neq j$, these are counts of misclassifications. The total number of observations is $n = n_{0,0} + n_{0,1} + n_{1,0} + n_{1,1}$.

A main accuracy measure is the *estimated misclassification rate*, also called the *overall error rate*. It is given by

$$\text{err} = \frac{n_{0,1} + n_{1,0}}{n},$$

where n is the total number of cases in the validation dataset. In the example in Figure 5.2, we get err $= (25 + 85)/3000 = 3.67\%$.

We can measure accuracy by looking at the correct classifications instead of the misclassifications. The *overall accuracy* of a classifier is estimated by

$$\text{Accuracy} = 1 - \text{err} = \frac{n_{0,0} + n_{1,1}}{n}.$$

In the example we have $(201 + 2689)/3000 = 96.33$.

Cutoff for Classification

The first step in most classification algorithms is to estimate the probability that a case belongs to each of the classes. If overall classification accuracy (involving all the classes) is of interest, the case can be assigned to the class with the highest

TABLE 5.1   CLASSIFICATION MATRIX: MEANING OF EACH CELL

Actual Class	Predicted Class	
	C_0	C_1
C_0	$n_{0,0}$ = number of C_0 cases classified correctly	$n_{0,1}$ = number of C_0 cases classified incorrectly as C_1
C_1	$n_{1,0}$ = number of C_1 cases classified incorrectly as C_0	$n_{1,1}$ = number of C_1 cases classified correctly

probability. In many cases, a single class is of special interest, so we will focus on that particular class and compare the estimated probability of belonging to that class to a *cutoff value*. This approach can be used with two classes or more than two classes, though it may make sense in such cases to consolidate classes so that you end up with two: the class of interest and all other classes. If the probability of belonging to the class of interest is above the cutoff, the case is assigned to that class.

The default cutoff value in two-class classifiers is 0.5. Thus, if the probability of a record being a class 1 member is greater than 0.5, that record is classified as a 1. Any record with an estimated probability of less than 0.5 would be classified as a 0. It is possible, however, to use a cutoff that is either higher or lower than 0.5. A cutoff greater than 0.5 will end up classifying fewer records as 1's, whereas a cutoff less than 0.5 will end up classifying more records as 1. Typically, the misclassification rate will rise in either case.

Consider the data in Table 5.2, showing the actual class for 24 records, sorted by the probability that the record is a 1 (as estimated by a data mining algorithm). If we adopt the standard 0.5 as the cutoff, our misclassification rate is 3/24, whereas if we instead adopt a cutoff of 0.25, we classify more records as 1's and the misclassification rate goes up (comprising more 0's misclassified as 1's) to 5/24. Conversely, if we adopt a cutoff of 0.75, we classify fewer records as 1's. The misclassification rate goes up (comprising more 1's misclassified as 0's) to 6/24. All this can be seen in the classification tables in Figure 5.3.

To see the entire range of cutoff values and how the accuracy or misclassification rates change as a function of the cutoff, we can use one-variable tables in Excel (see the accompanying box), and then plot the performance measure of interest versus the cutoff. The results for the data above are shown in Figure 5.4.

TABLE 5.2   24 RECORDS WITH THEIR ACTUAL CLASS AND PROBABILITY OF BEING CLASS 1 MEMBERS, AS ESTIMATED BY A CLASSIFIER

Actual Class	Probability of Class 1	Actual Class	Probability of Class 1
1	0.995976726	1	0.505506928
1	0.987533139	0	0.47134045
1	0.984456382	0	0.337117362
1	0.980439587	1	0.21796781
1	0.948110638	0	0.199240432
1	0.889297203	0	0.149482655
1	0.847631864	0	0.047962588
0	0.762806287	0	0.038341401
1	0.706991915	0	0.024850999
1	0.680754087	0	0.021806029
1	0.656343749	0	0.016129906
0	0.622419543	0	0.003559986

Cut off Prob.Val. for Success (Updatable)	**0.5**

Classification Confusion Matrix

	Predicted Class	
Actual Class	Owner	Nonowner
Owner	11	1
Nonowner	2	10

Cut off Prob.Val. for Success (Updatable)	**0.25**

Classification Confusion Matrix

	Predicted Class	
Actual Class	Owner	Nonowner
Owner	11	1
Nonowner	4	8

Cut off Prob.Val. for Success (Updatable)	**0.75**

Classification Confusion Matrix

	Predicted Class	
Actual Class	Owner	Nonowner
Owner	7	5
Nonowner	1	11

FIGURE 5.3   **CLASSIFICATION MATRICES BASED ON CUTOFFS OF 0.5, 0.25, AND 0.75**

We can see that the accuracy level is pretty stable around 0.8 for cutoff values between 0.2 and 0.8.

Why would we want to use cutoffs different from 0.5 if they increase the misclassification rate? The answer is that it might be more important to classify 1's properly than 0's, and we would tolerate a greater misclassification of the latter. Or the reverse might be true; in other words, the costs of misclassification might be asymmetric. We can adjust the cutoff value in such a case to classify more records as the high-value class (in other words, accept more misclassifications where the misclassification cost is low). Keep in mind that we are doing so after the data mining model has already been selected—we are not changing that model. It is also possible to incorporate costs into the picture before deriving the model. These subjects are discussed in greater detail below.

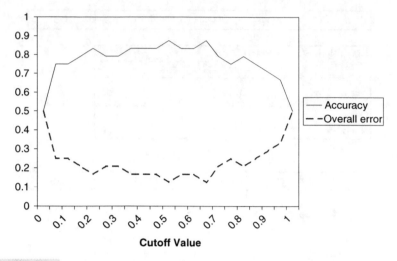

Cutoff Value

FIGURE 5.4 **PLOTTING RESULTS FROM ONE-WAY TABLE: ACCURACY AND OVERALL ERROR AS A FUNCTION OF THE CUTOFF VALUE**

ONE-VARIABLE TABLES IN EXCEL

Excel's one-variable data tables are very useful for studying how the cutoff affects different performance measures. It will change the cutoff values to values in a user-specified column and calculate different functions based on the corresponding classification matrix. To create a one-variable data table (see Figure 5.5):

1. In the top row, create column names for each of the measures you wish to compute. (We created "overall error" and "accuracy" in B11 and C11.) The leftmost column should be titled "cutoff" (A11).

2. In the row below, add formulas, using references to the relevant classification matrix cells. [The formula in B12 is $= (B6 + C7)/(B6 + C6 + B7 + C7)$.]

3. In the leftmost column, list the cutoff values that you want to evaluate. (We chose 0, 0.05, . . . , 1 in B13 to B33.)

4. Select the range excluding the first row (B12:C33). In Excel 2007 go to *Data ›*
   Whatif Analysis › Data Table (in Excel 2003 select *Table* from the *Data* menu).

5. In "column input cell," select the cell that changes (here, the cell with the cutoff value, D1). Click OK.

6. The table will now be automatically completed.

Performance in Unequal Importance of Classes

Suppose that it is more important to predict membership correctly in class 1 than in class 0. An example is predicting the financial status (bankrupt/solvent) of firms. It may be more important to predict correctly a firm that is going bankrupt than to predict correctly a firm that is going to stay solvent. The

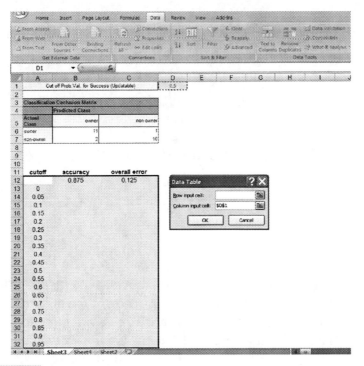

FIGURE 5.5	CREATING ONE-VARIABLE TABLES IN EXCEL. ACCURACY AND OVERALL ERROR ARE COMPUTED FOR DIFFERENT VALUES OF THE CUTOFF

classifier is essentially used as a system for detecting or signaling bankruptcy. In such a case, the overall accuracy is not a good measure for evaluating the classifier. Suppose that the important class is C_1. The following pair of accuracy measures are the most popular:

> **The sensitivity** of a classifier is its ability to detect the important class members correctly. This is measured by $n_{1,1}/(n_{1,0} + n_{1,1})$, the percentage of C_1 members classified correctly.

> **The specificity** of a classifier is its ability to rule out C_0 members correctly. This is measured by $n_{0,0}/(n_{0,0} + n_{0,1})$, the percentage of C_0 members classified correctly.

It can be useful to plot these measures versus the cutoff value (using one-variable tables in Excel, as described above) in order to find a cutoff value that balances these measures.

ROC Curve   A more popular method for plotting the two measures is through *ROC* (receiver operating characteristic) *curves*. The ROC curve plots the pairs {sensitivity, 1-specificity} as the cutoff value increases from 0 and 1.

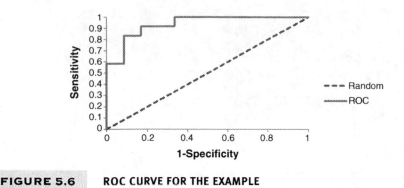

FIGURE 5.6   ROC CURVE FOR THE EXAMPLE

Better performance is reflected by curves that are closer to the top left corner. The comparison curve is the diagonal, which reflects the performance of the naive rule, using varying cutoff values (i.e., setting different thresholds on the level of majority used by the majority rule). The ROC curve for our 24-case example above is shown in Figure 5.6.

FALSE-POSITIVE AND FALSE-NEGATIVE RATES

Sensitivity and specificity measure the performance of a classifier from the point of view of the "classifying agency" (e.g., a company classifying customers or a hospital classifying patients). They answer the question: How well does the classifier segregate the important class members? It is also possible to measure accuracy from the perspective of the entity that is being predicted (e.g., the customer or the patient), who asks: What is my chance of belonging to the important class? This question, however, is usually less relevant in a data mining application. The terms *false-positive rate* and *false-negative rate*, which are sometimes used erroneously to describe 1-sensitivity and 1-specificity, are measures of performance from the perspective of the individual entity. They are defined as:

The *false-positive rate* is the proportion of C_1 predictions that are wrong: $n_{0,1}/(n_{0,1} + n_{1,1})$. Notice that this is a ratio within the column of C_1 predictions (i.e., it uses only records that were classified as C_1).

The *false-negative rate* is the proportion of C_0 predictions that are wrong: $n_{1,0}/(n_{0,0} + n_{1,0})$. Notice that this is a ratio within the column of C_0 predictions (i.e., it uses only records that were classified as C_0).

Lift Charts   Let us continue further with the case in which a particular class is relatively rare and of much more interest than the other class: tax cheats, debt defaulters, or responders to a mailing. We would like our classification model to sift through the records and sort them according to which ones are most likely to be tax cheats, responders to the mailing, and so on. We can then make more informed decisions. For example, we can decide how many, and which tax returns to examine, looking for tax cheats. The model will give us an estimate of the extent to which we will encounter more and more noncheaters as we proceed through the sorted data starting with the records most likely to be tax cheats. Or we can use the sorted data to decide to which potential customers a limited-budget mailing should be targeted. In other words, we are describing the case when our goal is to obtain a rank ordering among the records according to their estimated probabilities of class membership.

In such cases, when the classifier gives a probability of belonging to each class and not just a binary classification to C_1 or C_0, we can use a very useful device known as the *lift curve*, also called a *gains curve* or *gains chart*. The lift curve is a popular technique in direct marketing. One useful way to think of a lift curve is to consider a data mining model that attempts to identify the likely responders to a mailing by assigning each case a "probability of responding" score. The lift curve helps us determine how effectively we can "skim the cream" by selecting a relatively small number of cases and getting a relatively large portion of the responders. The input required to construct a lift curve is a validation dataset that has been "scored" by appending to each case the estimated probability that it will belong to a given class.

Let us return to the example in Table 5.2. We have shown that different choices of a cutoff value lead to different classification matrices (as in Figure 5.3). Instead of looking at a large number of classification matrices, it is much more convenient to look at the *cumulative lift curve* (sometimes called a *gains chart*), which summarizes all the information in these multiple classification matrices into a graph. The graph is constructed with the cumulative number of cases (in descending order of probability) on the x axis and the cumulative number of true positives on the y axis. Figure 5.7 gives the table of cumulative values of the class 1 classifications and the corresponding lift chart. The line joining the points (0,0) to (24,12) is a reference line. For any given number of cases (the x-axis value), it represents the expected number of C_1 predictions if we did not have a model but simply selected cases at random. It provides a benchmark against which we can see performance of the model. If we had to choose 10 cases as class 1 (the important class) members and used our model to pick the ones most likely to be 1's, the lift curve tells us that we would be right about 9 of them. If we simply select 10 cases at random, we expect to be right for $10 \times 12/24 = 5$ cases. The model gives us a "lift" in predicting class 1 of 9/5 = 1.8. The lift will vary with the number of cases on which we choose to act. A good classifier will give us a high lift when we act on only a few cases (i.e., use the prediction for those at the top). As we include more cases, the lift will decrease. The lift curve for the best possible classifier—a classifier that makes no errors—would overlap the existing curve at the start, continue with a slope of

Serial no.	Predicted prob of 1	Actual Class	Cumulative Actual class
1	0.995976726	1	1
2	0.987533139	1	2
3	0.984456382	1	3
4	0.980439587	1	4
5	0.948110638	1	5
6	0.889297203	1	6
7	0.847631864	1	7
8	0.762806287	0	7
9	0.706991915	1	8
10	0.680754087	1	9
11	0.656343749	1	10
12	0.622419543	0	10
13	0.505506928	1	11
14	0.47134045	0	11
15	0.337117362	0	11
16	0.21796781	1	12
17	0.199240432	0	12
18	0.149482655	0	12
19	0.047962588	0	12
20	0.038341401	0	12
21	0.024850999	0	12
22	0.021806029	0	12
23	0.016129906	0	12
24	0.003559986	0	12

FIGURE 5.7   **TABLE AND LIFT CHART FOR THE EXAMPLE**

1 until it reached 12 successes (all the successes), then continue horizontally to the right.

The same information can be portrayed as a *decile chart*, shown in Figure 5.8, which is widely used in direct marketing predictive modeling. The bars show the factor by which our model outperforms a random assignment of 0's and 1's, taking one decile at a time. Reading the first bar on the left, we see that taking

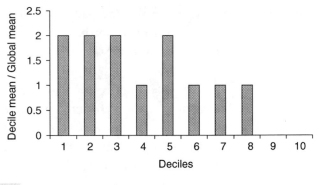

FIGURE 5.8 **DECILE LIFT CHART**

the 10% of the records that are ranked by the model as "the most probable 1's" yields twice as many 1's as would a random selection of 10% of the records.

> XLMiner automatically creates lift (and decile) charts from probabilities predicted by classifiers for both training and validation data. Of course, the lift curve based on the validation data is a better estimator of performance for new cases.

Asymmetric Misclassification Costs

Implicit in our discussion of the lift curve, which measures how effective we are in identifying the members of one particular class, is the assumption that the error of misclassifying a case belonging to one class is more serious than for the other class. For example, misclassifying a household as unlikely to respond to a sales offer when it belongs to the class that would respond incurs a greater cost (the opportunity cost of the foregone sale) than the converse error. In the former case, you are missing out on a sale worth perhaps tens or hundreds of dollars. In the latter, you are incurring the costs of mailing a letter to someone who will not purchase. In such a scenario, using the misclassification rate as a criterion can be misleading.

Note that we are assuming that the cost (or benefit) of making correct classifications is zero. At first glance, this may seem incomplete. After all, the benefit (negative cost) of classifying a buyer correctly as a buyer would seem substantial. And in other circumstances (e.g., scoring our classification algorithm to fresh data to implement our decisions), it will be appropriate to consider the actual net dollar impact of each possible classification (or misclassification). Here, however, we are attempting to assess the value of a classifier in terms of classification error, so it greatly simplifies matters if we can capture all cost–benefit information in the misclassification cells. So, instead of recording the benefit of classifying a respondent household correctly, we record the cost of failing to classify it as a respondent household. It amounts to the same thing and our goal becomes the minimization of costs, whether the costs are actual costs or missed benefits (opportunity costs).

Consider the situation where the sales offer is mailed to a random sample of people for the purpose of constructing a good classifier. Suppose that the offer is accepted by 1% of those households. For these data, if a classifier simply classifies every household as a nonresponder, it will have an error rate of only 1% but it will be useless in practice. A classifier that misclassifies 2% of buying households as nonbuyers and 20% of the nonbuyers as buyers would have a higher error rate but would be better if the profit from a sale is substantially higher than the cost of sending out an offer. In these situations, if we have estimates of the cost of both types of misclassification, we can use the classification matrix to compute the expected cost of misclassification for each case in the validation data. This enables us to compare different classifiers using overall expected costs (or profits) as the criterion.

Suppose that we are considering sending an offer to 1000 more people, 1% of whom respond (1), on average. Naively classifying everyone as a 0 has an error rate of only 1%. Using a data mining routine, suppose that we can produce these classifications:

	Predict Class 0	Predict Class 1
Actual 0	970	20
Actual 1	2	8

These classifications have an error rate of $100 \times (20 + 2)/1000 = 2.2\%$—higher than the naive rate.

Now suppose that the profit from a 1 is \$10 and the cost of sending the offer is \$1. Classifying everyone as a 0 still has a misclassification rate of only 1% but yields a profit of \$0. Using the data mining routine, despite the higher misclassification rate, yields a profit of \$60.

The matrix of profit is as follows (nothing is sent to the predicted 0's so there are no costs or sales in that column):

Profit	Predict Class 0	Predict Class 1
Actual 0	0	− \$20
Actual 1	0	\$80

Looked at purely in terms of costs, when everyone is classified as a 0, there are no costs of sending the offer; the only costs are the opportunity costs of failing to make sales to the ten 1's = \$100. The cost (actual costs of sending the offer, plus the opportunity costs of missed sales) of using the data mining routine to select people to send the offer to is only \$48, as follows:

Costs	Predict Class 0	Predict Class 1
Actual 0	0	\$20
Actual 1	\$20	\$8

However, this does not improve the actual classifications themselves. A better method is to change the classification rules (and hence the misclassification rates), as discussed in the preceding section, to reflect the asymmetric costs.

A popular performance measure that includes costs is the *average misclassification cost*, which measures the average cost of misclassification per classified observation. Denote by q_0 the cost of misclassifying a class 0 observation (as belonging to class 1) and by q_1 the cost of misclassifying a class 1 observation (as belonging to class 0). The average misclassification cost is

$$\frac{q_0 n_{0,1} + q_1 n_{1,0}}{n}.$$

Thus, we are looking for a classifier that minimizes this quantity. This can be computed, for instance, for different cutoff values.

It turns out that the optimal parameters are affected by the misclassification costs only through the ratio of these costs. This can be seen if we write the foregoing measure slightly differently:

$$\frac{q_0 n_{0,1} + q_1 n_{1,0}}{n} = \frac{n_{0,1}}{n_{0,0} + n_{0,1}} \frac{n_{0,0} + n_{0,1}}{n} q_0 + \frac{n_{1,0}}{n_{1,0} + n_{1,1}} \frac{n_{1,0} + n_{1,1}}{n} q_1.$$

Minimizing this expression is equivalent to minimizing the same expression divided by a constant. If we divide by q_0, it can be seen clearly that the minimization depends only on q_1/q_0 and not on their individual values. This is very practical because in many cases it is difficult to assess the cost associated with misclassifying a 0 member and that associated with misclassifying a 1 member, but estimating the ratio is easier.

This expression is a reasonable estimate of future misclassification cost if the proportions of classes 0 and 1 in the sample data are similar to the proportions of classes 0 and 1 that are expected in the future. If instead of a random sample, we draw a sample such that one class is oversampled (as described in the next section), then the sample proportions of 0's and 1's will be distorted compared to the future or population. We can then correct the average misclassification cost measure for the distorted sample proportions by incorporating estimates of the true proportions (from external data or domain knowledge), denoted by $p(C_0)$ and $p(C_1)$, into the formula:

$$\frac{n_{0,1}}{n_{0,0} + n_{0,1}} p(C_0) \, q_0 + \frac{n_{1,0}}{n_{1,0} + n_{1,1}} p(C_1) \, q_1.$$

Using the same logic as above, it can be shown that optimizing this quantity depends on the costs only through their ratio (q_1/q_0) and on the prior probabilities only through their ratio $[p(C_0)/p(C_1)]$. This is why software packages that incorporate costs and prior probabilities might prompt the user for ratios rather than actual costs and probabilities.

Generalization to More Than Two Classes   All the comments made above about two-class classifiers extend readily to classification into more than two classes. Let us suppose that we have m classes $C_0, C_1, C_2, \ldots, C_{m-1}$. The classification matrix has m rows and m columns. The misclassification cost associated with the diagonal cells is, of course, always zero. Incorporating prior probabilities of the various classes (where now we have m such numbers) is still done in the same manner. However, evaluating misclassification costs becomes much more complicated: For an m-class case we have $m(m - 1)$ types of misclassifications. Constructing a matrix of misclassification costs thus becomes prohibitively complicated.

A lift chart cannot be used with a multiclass classifier, unless a single "important class" is defined, and the classifications are reduced to "important" and "unimportant" classes.

Lift Charts Incorporating Costs and Benefits   When the benefits and costs of correct and incorrect classification are known or can be estimated, the lift chart is still a useful presentation and decision tool. As before, a classifier is needed that assigns to each record a probability that it belongs to a particular class. The procedure is then as follows:

1. Sort the records in order of predicted probability of success (where *success* = belonging to the class of interest).

2. For each record, record the cost (benefit) associated with the actual outcome.

3. For the highest probability (i.e., first) record, the value in step 2 is the y coordinate of the first point on the lift chart. The x coordinate is index number 1.

4. For the next record, again calculate the cost (benefit) associated with the actual outcome. Add this to the cost (benefit) for the previous record.

This sum is the y coordinate of the second point on the lift curve. The x coordinate is index number 2.

5. Repeat step 4 until all records have been examined. Connect all the points, and this is the lift curve.

6. The reference line is a straight line from the origin to the point $y =$ total net benefit and $x = N(N =$ number of records).

Note: It is entirely possible for a reference line that incorporates costs and benefits to have a negative slope if the net value for the entire dataset is negative. For example, if the cost of mailing to a person is \$0.65, the value of a responder is \$25, and the overall response rate is 2%, the expected net value of mailing to a list of 10,000 is $(0.02 \times \$25 \times 10,000) - (\$0.65 \times 10,000) = \$5000 - \$6500 = -\$1500$. Hence, the y value at the far right of the lift curve $(x = 10,000)$ is -1500, and the slope of the reference line from the origin will be negative. The optimal point will be where the lift curve is at a maximum (i.e., mailing to about 3000 people) in Figure 5.9.

Lift as Function of Cutoff   We could also plot the lift as a function of the cutoff value. The only difference is the scale on the x axis. When the goal is to select the top records based on a certain budget, the lift versus number of records is preferable. In contrast, when the goal is to find a cutoff that distinguishes well between the two classes, the lift versus cutoff value is more useful.

Oversampling and Asymmetric Costs

As we saw briefly in Chapter 2, when classes are present in very unequal proportions, simple random sampling may produce too few of the rare class to yield useful information about what distinguishes them from the dominant class. In such cases, stratified sampling is often used to oversample the cases from the more rare class and improve the performance of classifiers. It is often the case that the

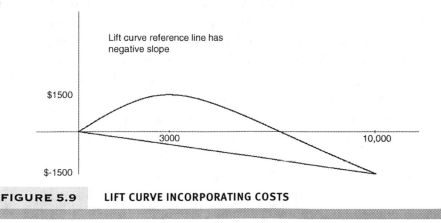

FIGURE 5.9   **LIFT CURVE INCORPORATING COSTS**

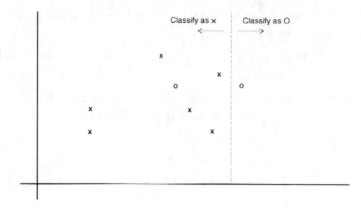

FIGURE 5.10 **CLASSIFICATION ASSUMING EQUAL COSTS OF MISCLASSIFICATION**

more rare events are the more interesting or important ones: responders to a mailing, those who commit fraud, defaulters on debt, and the like.

> In all discussions of *oversampling* (also called *weighted sampling*), we assume the common situation in which there are two classes, one of much greater interest than the other. Data with more than two classes do not lend themselves to this procedure.

Consider the data in Figure 5.10, where × represents nonresponders, and O, responders. The two axes correspond to two predictors. The dashed vertical line does the best job of classification under the assumption of equal costs: It results in just one misclassification (one O is misclassified as an ×). If we incorporate more realistic misclassification costs—let us say that failing to catch an O is five times as costly as failing to catch a ×—the costs of misclassification jump to 5. In such a case, a horizontal line as shown in Figure 5.11, does a better job: It results in misclassification costs of just 2.

Oversampling is one way of incorporating these costs into the training process. In Figure 5.12, we can see that classification algorithms would automatically determine the appropriate classification line if four additional O's were present at each existing O. We can achieve appropriate results either by taking five times as many o's as we would get from simple random sampling (by sampling with replacement if necessary), or by replicating the existing o's fourfold.

Oversampling without replacement in accord with the ratio of costs (the first option above) is the optimal solution but may not always be practical. There may not be an adequate number of responders to assure that there will be enough nonresponders to fit a model if the latter constitutes only a small proportion of the former. Also, it is often the case that our interest in discovering responders is known to be much greater than our interest in discovering nonresponders, but the exact ratio of costs is difficult to determine. When faced with very low response

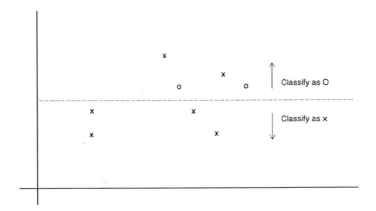

**CLASSIFICATION ASSUMING UNEQUAL COSTS OF
MISCLASSIFICATION**

rates in a classification problem, practitioners often sample equal numbers of responders and nonresponders as a relatively effective and convenient approach. Whatever approach is used, when it comes time to assess and predict model performance, we will need to adjust for the oversampling in one of two ways:

1. Score the model to a validation set that has been selected without oversampling (i.e., via simple random sampling).

2. Score the model to an oversampled validation set, and reweight the results to remove the effects of oversampling.

The first method is more straightforward and easier to implement. We describe how to oversample and how to evaluate performance for each of the two methods.

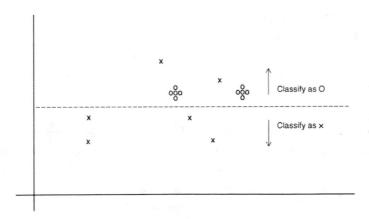

**CLASSIFICATION USING OVERSAMPLING TO ACCOUNT FOR UNEQUAL
COSTS**

When classifying data with very low response rates, practitioners typically:

- Train models on data that are 50% responder, 50% nonresponder.
- Validate the models with an unweighted (simple random) sample from the original data.

Oversampling the Training Set   How is weighted sampling done? One common procedure, where responders are sufficiently scarce that you will want to use all of them, follows:

1. First, the response and nonresponse data are separated into two distinct sets, or *strata*.
2. Records are then randomly selected for the training set from each stratum. Typically, one might select half the (scarce) responders for the training set, then an equal number of nonresponders.
3. The remaining responders are put in the validation set.
4. Nonresponders are randomly selected for the validation set in sufficient numbers to maintain the original ratio of responders to nonresponders.
5. If a test set is required, it can be taken randomly from the validation set.

XLMiner has a utility for this purpose.

Evaluating Model Performance Using a Nonoversampled Validation Set   Although the oversampled data can be used to train models, they are often not suitable for predicting model performance because the number of responders will (of course) be exaggerated. The most straightforward way of gaining an unbiased estimate of model performance is to apply the model to regular data (i.e., data not oversampled). To recap: Train the model on oversampled data, but validate it with regular data.

Evaluating Model Performance If Only Oversampled Validation Set Exists   In some cases, very low response rates may make it more practical to use oversampled data not only for the training data, but also for the validation data. This might happen, for example, if an analyst is given a data sample for exploration and prototyping, and it is more convenient to transfer and work with a smaller dataset in which a sizable proportion of cases are those with the rare response (typically the response of interest). In such cases it is still possible to assess how well the model will do with real data, but this requires the oversampled validation set to be reweighted, in order to restore the class of observations that were underrepresented in the sampling process. This adjustment should be made to the classification matrix and to the lift chart in order to derive good accuracy measures. These adjustments are described next.

I. Adjusting the Confusion Matrix for Oversampling   Let us say that the response rate in the data as a whole is 2%, and that the data were oversampled, yielding a sample in which the response rate is 25 times as great = 50%. Assume that the validation classification matrix looks like this:

CLASSIFICATION MATRIX, OVERSAMPLED DATA (VALIDATION)

	Predicted 0	Predicted 1	Total
Actual 0	390	110	500
Actual 1	80	420	500
Total	470	530	1000

At this point, the (inaccurate) misclassification rate appears to be $(80 + 110)/1000 = 19\%$, and the model ends up classifying 53% of the records as 1's.

There were 500 (actual) 1's in the sample and 500 (actual) 0's. If we had not oversampled, there would have been far fewer 1's. Put another way, there would be many more 0's for each 1. So we can either take away 1's or add 0's to reweight the sample. The calculations for the latter are shown: We need to add enough 0's so that the 1's constitute only 2% of the total, and the 0's, 98% (where X is the total):

$$500 + 0.98X = X.$$

Solving for X, we find that $X = 25,000$.

The total is 25,000, so the number of 0's is $(0.98)(25,000) = 24,500$. We can now redraw the classification matrix by augmenting the number of (actual) nonresponders, assigning them to the appropriate cells in the same ratio in which they appear in the classification table above (3.545 predicted 0's for every predicted 1):

CLASSIFICATION MATRIX, REWEIGHTED

	Predicted 0	Predicted 1	Total
Actual 0	19,110	5,390	24,500
Actual 1	80	420	500
Total	19,190	5,810	25,000

The adjusted misclassification rate is $(80 + 5390)/25,000 = 21.9\%$, and the model ends up classifying 5810/25,000 of the records as 1's, or 21.4%.

II. Adjusting the Lift Curve for Oversampling   The lift curve is likely to be a more useful measure in low-response situations, where our interest lies not so much in classifying all the records correctly as in finding a model that guides us toward those records most likely to contain the response of interest (under the assumption that scarce resources preclude examining or contacting all the records). Typically, our interest in such a case is in maximizing value or minimizing cost, so we will show the adjustment process incorporating the cost-benefit element. The following procedure can be used (and easily implemented in Excel):

1. Sort the validation records in order of the predicted probability of success (where success = belonging to the class of interest).

2. For each record, record the cost (benefit) associated with the actual outcome.

3. Multiply that value by the proportion of the original data having this outcome; this is the adjusted value.

4. For the highest probability (i.e., first) record, the value above is the y coordinate of the first point on the lift chart. The x coordinate is index number 1.

5. For the next record, again calculate the adjusted value associated with the actual outcome. Add this to the adjusted cost (benefit) for the previous record. This sum is the y coordinate of the second point on the lift curve. The x coordinate is index number 2.

6. Repeat step 5 until all records have been examined. Connect all the points, and this is the lift curve.

7. The reference line is a straight line from the origin to the point y = total net benefit and $x = N(N =$ number of records).

Classification Using a Triage Strategy

In some cases it is useful to have a "cannot say" option for the classifier. In a two-class situation, this means that for a case, we can make one of three predictions: The case belongs to C_0, or the case belongs to C_1, or we cannot make a prediction because there is not enough information to pick C_0 or C_1 confidently. Cases that the classifier cannot classify are subjected to closer scrutiny either by using expert judgment or by enriching the set of predictor variables by gathering additional information that is perhaps more difficult or expensive to obtain. This is analogous to the strategy of triage, which is often employed during retreat in battle. The wounded are classified into those who are well enough to retreat, those who are too ill to retreat even if treated medically under the prevailing conditions, and those who arc likely to become well enough to retreat if given medical attention. An example is in processing credit card transactions, where a classifier may be used to identify clearly legitimate cases and obviously fraudulent ones while referring the remaining cases to a human decision maker who may look up a database to form a judgment. Since the vast majority of transactions are legitimate, such a classifier would substantially reduce the burden on human experts.

5.3 EVALUATING PREDICTIVE PERFORMANCE

When the response variable is continuous, the evaluation of model performance is slightly different from the categorical response case. First, let us emphasize that predictive accuracy is not the same as goodness of fit. Classical measures of performance are aimed at finding a model that fits the data well, whereas in data mining we are interested in models that have high predictive accuracy. Measures such as R^2 and standard error of estimate are very popular strength of fit measures in classical regression modeling, and residual analysis is used to gauge goodness of fit where the goal is to find the best fit for the data. However, these measures do not tell us much about the ability of the model to predict new cases.

For prediction performance, there are several measures that are used to assess the predictive accuracy of a regression model. In all cases, the measures are based on the validation set, which serves as a more objective ground than the training set to assess predictive accuracy. This is because records in the validation set are not used to select predictors or to estimate the model coefficients. Measures of accuracy use the prediction error that results from predicting the validation data with the model (that was trained on the training data).

Benchmark: The Average

Recall that the benchmark criterion in prediction is using the average outcome (thereby ignoring all predictor information). In other words, the prediction for a new record is simply the average outcome of the records in the training set. A good predictive model should outperform the benchmark criterion in terms of predictive accuracy.

Prediction Accuracy Measures

The prediction error for record i is defined as the difference between its actual y value and its predicted y value: $e_i = y_i - \hat{y}_i$. A few popular numerical measures of predictive accuracy are:

- *MAE* or *MAD* (mean absolute error/deviation) $= 1/n \sum_{i=1}^{n} |e_i|$. This gives the magnitude of the average absolute error.

- *Average error* $= 1/n \sum_{i=1}^{n} e_i$. This measure is similar to MAD except that it retains the sign of the errors, so that negative errors cancel out positive errors of the same magnitude. It therefore gives an indication of whether the predictions are on average over- or underpredicting the response.

- *MAPE* (mean absolute percentage error) $= 100\% \times 1/n \sum_{i=1}^{n} |e_i/y_i|$. This measure gives a percentage score of how predictions deviate (on average) from the actual values.

- *RMSE* (root-mean-squared error) $= \sqrt{1/n \sum_{i=1}^{n} e_i^2}$. This is similar to the standard error of estimate, except that it is computed on the validation data rather than on the training data. It has the same units as the variable predicted.

- Total *SSE* (total sum of squared errors) $= \sum_{i=1}^{n} e_i^2$.

Such measures can be used to compare models and to assess their degree of prediction accuracy. Notice that all these measures are influenced by outliers. To check outlier influence, we can compute median-based measures (and compare to the mean-based measures) or simply plot a histogram or boxplot of the errors. It is important to note that a model with high predictive accuracy might not coincide with a model that fits the training data best.

Finally, a graphical way to assess predictive performance is through a lift chart. This compares the model's predictive performance to a baseline model that has no predictors. Predictions from the baseline model are simply the average $\bar{y}$. A lift chart for a continuous response is relevant only when we are searching for a set of records that gives the highest cumulative predicted values.

To illustrate this, consider a car rental firm that renews its fleet regularly so that customers drive late-model cars. This entails disposing of a large quantity of used vehicles on a continuing basis. Since the firm is not primarily in the used car sales business, it tries to dispose of as much of its fleet as possible through volume sales to used car dealers. However, it is profitable to sell a limited number of cars through its own channels. Its volume deals with the used car dealers leave it flexibility to pick and choose which cars to sell in this fashion, so it would like to have a model for selecting cars for resale through its own channels. Since all cars were purchased some time ago and the deals with the used car dealers are for fixed prices (specifying a given number of cars of a certain make and model class), the cars' costs are now irrelevant and the dealer is interested only in maximizing revenue. This is done by selecting for its own resale the cars likely to generate the most revenue. The lift chart in this case gives the predicted lift for revenue.

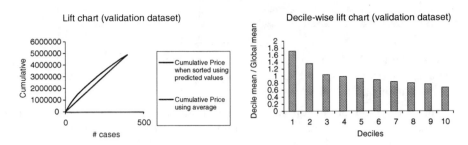

FIGURE 5.13   LIFT CHARTS FOR CONTINUOUS RESPONSE (SALES)

Figure 5.13 shows a lift chart based on fitting a linear regression model to a dataset that includes the car prices (y) and a set of predictor variables that describe a car's features (mileage, color, etc.) The lift chart is based on the validation data of 400 cars. It can be seen that the model's predictive performance is better than the baseline model since its lift curve is higher than that of the baseline model. The lift (and decile-wise) charts in Figure 5.13 would be useful in the following scenario: Choosing the top 10% of the cars that gave the highest predicted sales, for example, we would gain 1.7 times the amount compared to choosing 10% of the cars at random. This can be seen from the decile chart (Figure 5.13). This number can also be computed from the lift chart by comparing the sales predicted for 40 random cars (the value of the baseline curve at $x = 40$), which is \$486,871 (= the sum of the predictions of the 400 validation set cars divided by 10) with the sales of the 40 cars that have the highest predicted values by the model (the value of the lift curve at $x = 40$), \$835,883. The ratio between these numbers is 1.7.

PROBLEMS

5.1 A data mining routine has been applied to a transaction dataset and has classified 88 records as fraudulent (30 correctly so) and 952 as nonfraudulent (920 correctly so). Construct the classification matrix and calculate the error rate.

5.2 Suppose that this routine has an adjustable cutoff (threshold) mechanism by which you can alter the proportion of records classified as fraudulent. Describe how moving the cutoff up or down would affect the following:

a. The classification error rate for records that are truly fraudulent

b. The classification error rate for records that are truly nonfraudulent

5.3 Consider Figure 5.14, the decile-wise lift chart for the transaction data model, applied to new data

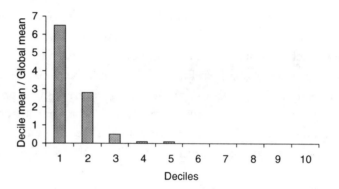

FIGURE 5.14 DECILE-WISE LIFT CHART FOR TRANSACTION DATA

a. Interpret the meaning of the first and second bars from the left.

b. Explain how you might use this information in practice.

c. Another analyst comments that you could improve the accuracy of the model by classifying everything as nonfraudulent. If you do that, what is the error rate?

d. Comment on the usefulness, in this situation, of these two metrics of model performance (error rate and lift).

5.4 A large number of insurance records are to be examined to develop a model for predicting fraudulent claims. Of the claims in the historical database, 1% were judged to be fraudulent. A sample is taken to develop a model, and oversampling is used to provide a balanced sample in light of the very low response rate. When applied to this sample ($N = 800$), the model ends up correctly classifying 310 frauds, and 270 nonfrauds. It missed 90 frauds, and classified 130 records incorrectly as frauds when they were not.

a. Produce the classification matrix for the sample as it stands.

b. Find the adjusted misclassification rate (adjusting for the oversampling).

c. What percentage of new records would you expect to be classified as fraudulent?

CHAPTER 9

Classification and Regression Trees

This chapter describes a flexible data-driven method that can be used for both classification (called *classification tree*) and prediction (called *regression tree*). Among the data-driven methods, trees are the most transparent and easy to interpret. Trees are based on separating observations into subgroups by creating splits on predictors. These splits create logical rules that are transparent and easily understandable, for examples "If Age < 55 AND Education > 12 THEN class $= 1$." The resulting subgroups should be more homogeneous in terms of the outcome variable, thereby creating useful prediction or classification rules. We discuss the two key ideas underlying trees: recursive partitioning (for constructing the tree) and pruning (for cutting the tree back). In the context of tree construction, we also describe a few metrics of homogeneity that are popular in tree algorithms, for determining the homogeneity of the resulting subgroups of observations. We explain that pruning is a useful strategy for avoiding overfitting and show how it is done. We also describe alternative strategies for avoiding overfitting. As with other data-driven methods, trees require large amounts of data. However, once constructed, they are computationally cheap to deploy even on large samples. They also have other advantages such as being highly automated, robust to outliers, and can handle missing values. Finally, we describe how trees can be used for dimension reduction.

9.1 INTRODUCTION

If one had to choose a classification technique that performs well across a wide range of situations without requiring much effort from the analyst while being

Data Mining for Business Intelligence, By Galit Shmueli, Nitin R. Patel, and Peter C. Bruce
Copyright © 2010 John Wiley & Sons Inc.

164

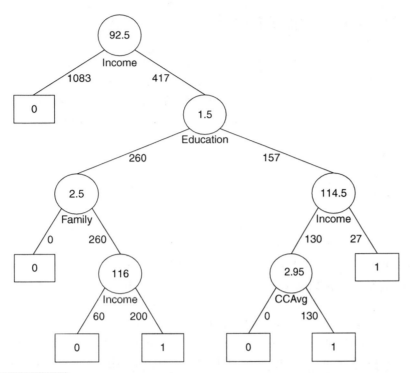

FIGURE 9.1 BEST PRUNED TREE OBTAINED BY FITTING A FULL TREE TO THE TRAINING DATA AND PRUNING IT USING THE VALIDATION DATA

readily understandable by the consumer of the analysis, a strong contender would be the tree methodology developed by Breiman et al. (1984). We discuss this classification procedure first; then in later sections we show how the procedure can be extended to prediction of a numerical outcome. The program that Breiman et al. created to implement these procedures was called CART (classification and regression trees). A related procedure is called C4.5.

What is a classification tree? Figure 9.1 describes a tree for classifying bank customers who receive a loan offer as either acceptors or nonacceptors, as a function of information such as their income, education level, and average credit card expenditure. One of the reasons that tree classifiers are very popular is that they provide easily understandable classification rules (at least if the trees are not too large). Consider the tree in the example. The square *terminal nodes* are marked with 0 or 1 corresponding to a nonacceptor (0) or acceptor (1). The values in the circle nodes give the splitting value on a predictor. This tree can easily be translated into a set of rules for classifying a bank customer. For example, the middle left square node in this tree gives us the following rule:

IF(Income > 92.5) AND (Education < 1.5) AND (Family ≤ 2.5)
THEN Class = 0 (nonacceptor).

In the following we show how trees are constructed and evaluated.

9.2 CLASSIFICATION TREES

There are two key ideas underlying classification trees. The first is the idea of recursive partitioning of the space of the predictor variables. The second is the idea of pruning using validation data. In the next few sections we describe recursive partitioning and in subsequent sections explain the pruning methodology.

Recursive Partitioning

Let us denote the dependent (response) variable by y and the predictor variables by $x_1, x_2, x_3, \ldots, x_p$. In classification, the outcome variable will be a categorical variable. Recursive partitioning divides up the p-dimensional space of the x variables into nonoverlapping multidimensional rectangles. The X variables here are considered to be continuous, binary, or ordinal. This division is accomplished recursively (i.e., operating on the results of prior divisions). First, one of the variables is selected, say x_i, and a value of x_i, say s_i, is chosen to split the p-dimensional space into two parts: one part that contains all the points with $x_i \leq s_i$ and the other with all the points with $x_i > s_i$. Then one of these two parts is divided in a similar manner by choosing a variable again (it could be x_i or another variable) and a split value for the variable. This results in three (multidimensional) rectangular regions. This process is continued so that we get smaller and smaller rectangular regions. The idea is to divide the entire x space up into rectangles such that each rectangle is as homogeneous or "pure" as possible. By *pure* we mean containing points that belong to just one class. (Of course, this is not always possible, as there may be points that belong to different classes but have exactly the same values for every one of the predictor variables.)

Let us illustrate recursive partitioning with an example.

Example 1: Riding Mowers

We again use the riding-mower example presented in Chapter 7. A riding-mower manufacturer would like to find a way of classifying families in a city into those likely to purchase a riding mower and those not likely to buy one. A pilot random sample of 12 owners and 12 nonowners in the city is undertaken. The data are shown and plotted in Table 9.1 and Figure 9.2.

If we apply the classification tree procedure to these data, the procedure will choose Lot Size for the first split with a splitting value of 19. The (x_1, x_2) space is now divided into two rectangles, one with Lot Size $\leq$ 19 and the other with Lot Size $>$ 19. This is illustrated in Figure 9.3.

Notice how the split has created two rectangles, each of which is much more homogeneous than the rectangle before the split. The upper rectangle contains points that are mostly owners (nine owners and three nonowners) and the lower rectangle contains mostly nonowners (nine nonowners and three owners).

| TABLE 9.1 | LOT SIZE, INCOME, AND OWNERSHIP OF A RIDING MOWER FOR 24 HOUSEHOLDS |

Household Number	Income ($000s)	Lot Size (000s ft²)	Ownership of Riding Mower
1	60	18.4	Owner
2	85.5	16.8	Owner
3	64.8	21.6	Owner
4	61.5	20.8	Owner
5	87	23.6	Owner
6	110.1	19.2	Owner
7	108	17.6	Owner
8	82.8	22.4	Owner
9	69	20	Owner
10	93	20.8	Owner
11	51	22	Owner
12	81	20	Owner
13	75	19.6	Nonowner
14	52.8	20.8	Nonowner
15	64.8	17.2	Nonowner
16	43.2	20.4	Nonowner
17	84	17.6	Nonowner
18	49.2	17.6	Nonowner
19	59.4	16	Nonowner
20	66	18.4	Nonowner
21	47.4	16.4	Nonowner
22	33	18.8	Nonowner
23	51	14	Nonowner
24	63	14.8	Nonowner

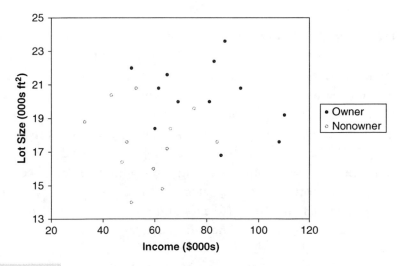

| FIGURE 9.2 | SCATTERPLOT OF LOT SIZE VS. INCOME FOR 24 OWNERS AND NONOWNERS OF RIDING MOWERS |

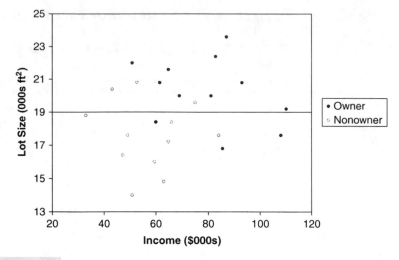

FIGURE 9.3   SPLITTING THE 24 OBSERVATIONS BY LOT SIZE VALUE OF 19

How was this particular split selected? The algorithm examined each variable (in this case, Income and Lot Size) and all possible split values for each variable to find the best split. What are the possible split values for a variable? They are simply the midpoints between pairs of consecutive values for the variable. The possible split points for Income are {38.1, 45.3, 50.1, . . . , 109.5} and those for Lot Size are {14.4, 15.4, 16.2, . . . , 23}. These split points are ranked according to how much they reduce impurity (heterogeneity) in the resulting rectangle. A pure rectangle is one that is composed of a single class (e.g., owners). The reduction in impurity is defined as overall impurity before the split minus the sum of the impurities for the two rectangles that result from a split.

Categorical Predictors   The above description used numerical predictors. However, categorical predictors can also be used in the recursive partitioning context. To handle categorical predictors, the split choices for a categorical predictor are all ways in which the set of categories can be divided into two subsets. For example, a categorical variable with four categories, say {a,b,c,d}, can be split in seven ways into two subsets: {a} and {b,c,d}; {b} and {a,c,d}; {c} and {a,b,d}; {d} and {a,b,c}; {a,b} and {c,d}; {a,c} and {b,d}; and {a,d} and {b,c}. When the number of categories is large, the number of splits becomes very large. XLMiner supports only binary categorical variables (coded as numbers). If you have a categorical predictor that takes more than two values, you will need to replace the variable with several dummy variables, each of which is binary in a manner that is identical to the use of dummy variables in regression.[1]

---

[1] This is a difference between CART and C4.5; the former performs only binary splits, leading to binary trees, whereas the latter performs splits that are as large as the number of categories, leading to "bushlike" structures.

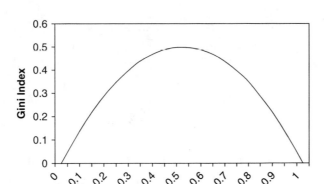

FIGURE 9.4   **VALUES OF THE GINI INDEX FOR A TWO-CLASS CASE AS A FUNCTION OF THE PROPORTION OF OBSERVATIONS IN CLASS 1 (P_1)**

9.3 MEASURES OF IMPURITY

There are a number of ways to measure impurity. The two most popular measures are the *Gini index* and an *entropy measure*. We describe both next. Denote the m classes of the response variable by $k = 1, 2, \ldots, m$.

The Gini impurity index for a rectangle A is defined by

$$I(A) = 1 - \sum_{k=1}^{m} p_k^2,$$

where p_k is the proportion of observations in rectangle A that belong to class k. This measure takes values between 0 (if all the observations belong to the same class) and $(m-1)/m$ (when all m classes are equally represented). Figure 9.4 shows the values of the Gini index for a two-class case as a function of p_k. It can be seen that the impurity measure is at its peak when $p_k = 0.5$ (i.e., when the rectangle contains 50% of each of the two classes).[2]

A second impurity measure is the entropy measure. The entropy for a rectangle A is defined by

$$\text{Entropy}(A) = -\sum_{k=1}^{m} p_k \log_2(p_k)$$

[to compute $\log_2(x)$ in Excel, use the function $= \log(x, 2)$]. This measure ranges between 0 (most pure, all observations belong to the same class) and $\log_2(m)$ (when all m classes are represented equally). In the two-class case, the entropy measure is maximized (like the Gini index) at $p_k = 0.5$.

---

[2] XLMiner uses a variant of the Gini index called the *delta splitting rule*; for details, see XLMiner documentation.

170 **CLASSIFICATION AND REGRESSION TREES**

Let us compute the impurity in the riding-mower example before and after the first split (using Lot Size with the value of 19). The unsplit dataset contains 12 owners and 12 nonowners. This is a two-class case with an equal number of observations from each class. Both impurity measures are therefore at their maximum value: Gini $= 0.5$ and entropy $= \log_2(2) = 1$. After the split, the upper rectangle contains nine owners and three nonowners. The impurity measures for this rectangle are Gini $= 1 - 0.25^2 - 0.75^2 = 0.375$ and entropy $= -0.25\log_2(0.25) - 0.75\log_2(0.75) = 0.811$. The lower rectangle contains three owners and nine nonowners. Since both impurity measures are symmetric, they obtain the same values as for the upper rectangle.

The combined impurity of the two rectangles that were created by the split is a weighted average of the two impurity measures, weighted by the number of observations in each (in this case we ended up with 12 observations in each rectangle, but in general the number of observations need not be equal): Gini $= (12/24)(0.375) + (12/24)(0.375) = 0.375$ and entropy $= (12/24)(0.811) + (12/24)(0.811) = 0.811$. Thus, the Gini impurity index decreased from 0.5 before the split to 0.375 after the split. Similarly, the entropy impurity measure decreased from 1 before the split to 0.811 after the split.

By comparing the reduction in impurity across all possible splits in all possible predictors, the next split is chosen. If we continue splitting the mower data, the next split is on the Income variable at the value 84.75. Figure 9.5 shows that once again the tree procedure has astutely chosen to split a rectangle to increase the purity of the resulting rectangles. The left lower rectangle, which contains data points with Income ≤ 84.75 and Lot Size ≤ 19, has all points that are nonowners (with one exception); whereas the right lower rectangle,

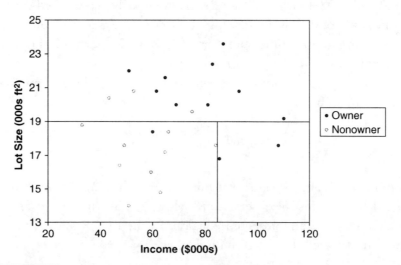

FIGURE 9.5 SPLITTING THE 24 OBSERVATIONS BY LOT SIZE VALUE OF $19K, AND THEN INCOME VALUE OF $84.75K

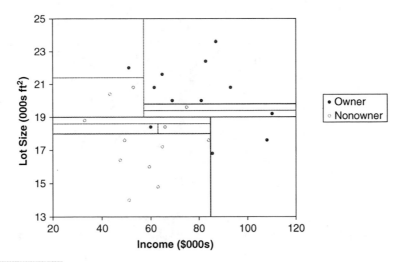

FIGURE 9.6   **FINAL STAGE OF RECURSIVE PARTITIONING; EACH RECTANGLE CONSISTING OF A SINGLE CLASS (OWNERS OR NONOWNERS)**

which contains data points with Income > 84.75 and Lot Size $\leq$ 19, consists exclusively of owners. We can see how the recursive partitioning is refining the set of constituent rectangles to become purer as the algorithm proceeds. The final stage of the recursive partitioning is shown in Figure 9.6.

Notice that each rectangle is now pure: It contains data points from just one of the two classes.

The reason the method is called a *classification tree algorithm* is that each split can be depicted as a split of a node into two successor nodes. The first split is shown as a branching of the root node of a tree in Figure 9.7. The tree representing the first three splits is shown in Figure 9.8. The full-grown tree is shown in Figure 9.9.

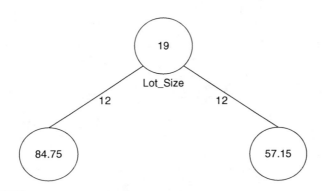

FIGURE 9.7   **TREE REPRESENTATION OF FIRST SPLIT (CORRESPONDS TO FIGURE 9.3)**

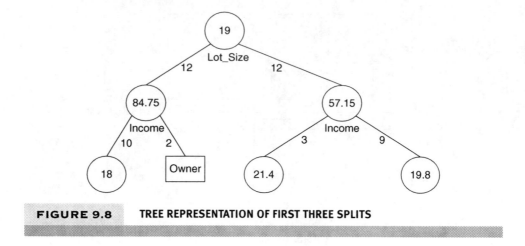

FIGURE 9.8 **TREE REPRESENTATION OF FIRST THREE SPLITS**

Tree Structure

We represent the nodes that have successors by circles. The numbers inside the circles are the splitting values and the name of the variable chosen for splitting at that node is shown below the node. The numbers on the left fork at a decision node are the number of records in the decision node that had values less than or equal to the splitting value, and the numbers on the right fork show the number

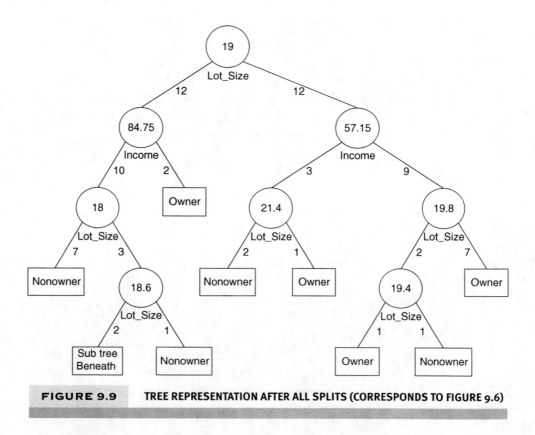

FIGURE 9.9 **TREE REPRESENTATION AFTER ALL SPLITS (CORRESPONDS TO FIGURE 9.6)**

that had a greater value. These are called *decision nodes* because if we were to use a tree to classify a new observation for which we knew only the values of the predictor variables, we would "drop" the observation down the tree in such a way that at each decision node the appropriate branch is taken until we get to a node that has no successors. Such terminal nodes are called the *leaves* of the tree. Each leaf node is depicted with a rectangle rather than a circle, and corresponds to one of the final rectangles into which the x space is partitioned.

Classifying a New Observation

To classify a new observation, it is "dropped" down the tree. When it has dropped all the way down to a terminal leaf, we can assign its class simply by taking a "vote" of all the training data that belonged to the leaf when the tree was grown. The class with the highest vote is assigned to the new observation. For instance, a new observation reaching the rightmost leaf node in Figure 9.9, which has a majority of observations that belong to the owner class, would be classified as "owner." Alternatively, if a single class is of interest, the algorithm counts the number of "votes" for this class, converts it to a proportion (estimated probability), then compares it to a user-specified cutoff value. See Chapter 5 for further discussion of the use of a cutoff value in classification, for cases where a single class is of interest.

In a binary classification situation (typically, with a *success* class that is relatively rare and of particular interest), we can also establish a lower cutoff to better capture those rare successes (at the cost of lumping in more nonsuccesses as successes). With a lower cutoff, the votes for the *success* class only need attain that lower cutoff level for the entire leaf to be classified as a *success*. The cutoff therefore determines the proportion of votes needed for determining the leaf class. It is useful to note that the type of trees grown by CART (called *binary trees*) have the property that the number of leaf nodes is exactly one more than the number of decision nodes.

9.4 EVALUATING THE PERFORMANCE OF A CLASSIFICATION TREE

To assess the accuracy of a tree in classifying new cases, we use the tools and criteria that were discussed in Chapter 5. We start by partitioning the data into training and validation sets. The training set is used to grow the tree, and the validation set is used to assess its performance. In the next section we discuss an important step in constructing trees that involves using the validation data. In that case, a third set of test data is preferable for assessing the accuracy of the final tree.

Each observation in the validation (or test) data is dropped down the tree and classified according to the leaf node it reaches. These predicted classes can then be compared to the actual memberships via a classification matrix. When a particular class is of interest, a lift chart is useful for assessing the model's ability to capture those members. We use the following example to illustrate this.

Example 2: Acceptance of Personal Loan

Universal Bank is a relatively young bank that is growing rapidly in terms of overall customer acquisition. The majority of these customers are liability customers with varying sizes of relationship with the bank. The customer base of asset customers is quite small, and the bank is interested in growing this base rapidly to bring in more loan business. In particular, it wants to explore ways of converting its liability customers to personal loan customers.

A campaign the bank ran for liability customers showed a healthy conversion rate of over 9% successes. This has encouraged the retail marketing department to devise smarter campaigns with better target marketing. The goal of our analysis is to model the previous campaign's customer behavior to analyze what combination of factors make a customer more likely to accept a personal loan. This will serve as the basis for the design of a new campaign.

The bank's dataset includes data on 5000 customers. The data include customer demographic information (age, income, etc.), customer response to the last personal loan campaign (Personal Loan), and the customer's relationship with the bank (mortgage, securities account, etc.). Among these 5000 customers, only 480 (= 9.6%) accepted the personal loan that was offered to them in the earlier campaign. Table 9.2 contains a sample of the bank's customer database for 20 customers, to illustrate the structure of the data.

After randomly partitioning the data into training (2500 observations), validation (1500 observations), and test (1000 observations) sets, we use the training data to construct a full-grown tree. The first four levels of the tree are shown in Figure 9.10, and the complete results are given in a form of a table in Figure 9.11.

Even with just four levels, it is difficult to see the complete picture. A look at the top tree node or the first row of the table reveals that the first predictor that is chosen to split the data is Income, with a value of 92.5 ($000s).

Since the full-grown tree leads to completely pure terminal leaves, it is 100% accurate in classifying the training data. This can be seen in Figure 9.12. In contrast, the classification matrix for the validation and test data (which were not used to construct the full-grown tree) show lower classification accuracy. The main reason is that the full-grown tree overfits the training data (to complete accuracy!). This motivates the next section, where we describe ways to avoid overfitting by either stopping the growth of the tree before it is fully grown or by pruning the full-grown tree.

TABLE 9.2   SAMPLE OF DATA FOR 20 CUSTOMERS OF UNIVERSAL BANK

ID	Age	Professional Experience	Income	Family Size	CC Avg	Education	Mortgage	Personal Loan	Securities Account	CD Account	Online Banking	Credit Card
1	25	1	49	4	1.60	UG	0	No	Yes	No	No	No
2	45	19	34	3	1.50	UG	0	No	Yes	No	No	No
3	39	15	11	1	1.00	UG	0	No	No	No	No	No
4	35	9	100	1	2.70	Grad	0	No	No	No	No	No
5	35	8	45	4	1.00	Grad	0	No	No	No	No	Yes
6	37	13	29	4	0.40	Grad	155	No	No	No	Yes	No
7	53	27	72	2	1.50	Grad	0	No	No	No	Yes	No
8	50	24	22	1	0.30	Prof	0	No	No	No	No	Yes
9	35	10	81	3	0.60	Grad	104	No	No	No	Yes	No
10	34	9	180	1	8.90	Prof	0	Yes	No	No	No	No
11	65	39	105	4	2.40	Prof	0	No	No	No	No	No
12	29	5	45	3	0.10	Grad	0	No	Yes	No	Yes	No
13	48	23	114	2	3.80	Prof	0	No	No	No	No	No
14	59	32	40	4	2.50	Grad	0	No	Yes	No	Yes	No
15	67	41	112	1	2.00	UG	0	No	No	No	No	No
16	60	30	22	1	1.50	Prof	0	No	No	No	Yes	Yes
17	38	14	130	4	4.70	Prof	134	Yes	No	No	No	No
18	42	18	81	4	2.40	UG	0	No	No	No	No	No
19	46	21	193	2	8.10	Prof	0	Yes	No	No	No	No
20	55	28	21	1	0.50	Grad	0	No	Yes	No	No	Yes

175

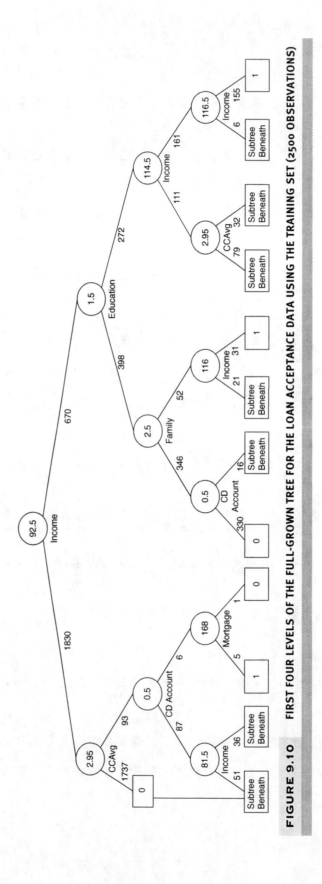

FIGURE 9.10   FIRST FOUR LEVELS OF THE FULL-GROWN TREE FOR THE LOAN ACCEPTANCE DATA USING THE TRAINING SET (2500 OBSERVATIONS)

176

#Decision Nodes	41		#Terminal Nodes	42

Level	NodeID	ParentID	SplitVar	SplitValue	Cases	LeftChild	RightChild	Class	Node Type
0	0	N/A	Income	92.5	2500	1	2	0	Decision
1	1	0	CCAvg	2.95	1830	3	4	0	Decision
1	2	0	Education	1.5	670	5	6	0	Decision
2	3	1	N/A	N/A	1737	N/A	N/A	0	Terminal
2	4	1	CD Account	0.5	93	7	8	0	Decision
2	5	2	Family	2.5	398	9	10	0	Decision
2	6	2	Income	114.5	272	11	12	1	Decision
3	7	4	Income	81.5	87	13	14	0	Decision
3	8	4	Mortgage	168	6	15	16	1	Decision
3	9	5	CD Account	0.5	346	17	18	0	Decision
3	10	5	Income	116	52	19	20	1	Decision
3	11	6	CCAvg	2.95	111	21	22	0	Decision
3	12	6	Income	116.5	161	23	24	1	Decision
4	13	7	Age	28	51	25	26	0	Decision
4	14	7	CCAvg	3.75	36	27	28	0	Decision
4	15	8	N/A	N/A	5	N/A	N/A	1	Terminal
4	16	8	N/A	N/A	1	N/A	N/A	0	Terminal
4	17	9	N/A	N/A	330	N/A	N/A	0	Terminal
4	18	9	Mortgage	350.5	16	29	30	0	Decision
4	19	10	CCAvg	1.7	21	31	32	0	Decision
4	20	10	N/A	N/A	31	N/A	N/A	1	Terminal
4	21	11	Income	106.5	79	33	34	0	Decision
4	22	11	EducProf	0.5	32	35	36	1	Decision
4	23	12	CCAvg	1.1	6	37	38	1	Decision
4	24	12	N/A	N/A	155	N/A	N/A	1	Terminal
5	25	13	N/A	N/A	1	N/A	N/A	1	Terminal
5	26	13	N/A	N/A	50	N/A	N/A	0	Terminal
5	27	14	CCAvg	3.35	16	39	40	0	Decision
5	28	14	Mortgage	93.5	20	41	42	0	Decision
5	29	18	N/A	N/A	15	N/A	N/A	0	Terminal
5	30	18	N/A	N/A	1	N/A	N/A	1	Terminal
5	31	19	N/A	N/A	13	N/A	N/A	0	Terminal
5	32	19	Income	109.5	8	43	44	0	Decision
5	33	21	N/A	N/A	49	N/A	N/A	0	Terminal
5	34	21	CCAvg	1.75	30	45	46	0	Decision
5	35	22	Age	60	17	47	48	1	Decision
5	36	22	CCAvg	3.7	15	49	50	0	Decision
5	37	23	Online	0.5	2	51	52	1	Decision
5	38	23	N/A	N/A	4	N/A	N/A	1	Terminal
6	39	27	N/A	N/A	7	N/A	N/A	0	Terminal
6	40	27	CCAvg	3.65	9	53	54	1	Decision
6	41	28	N/A	N/A	16	N/A	N/A	0	Terminal
6	42	28	Mortgage	104.5	4	55	56	0	Decision
6	43	32	Experience	6.5	4	57	58	1	Decision
6	44	32	N/A	N/A	4	N/A	N/A	0	Terminal
6	45	34	Family	1.5	13	59	60	0	Decision
6	46	34	ZIP Code	94206.5	17	61	62	0	Decision
6	47	35	N/A	N/A	13	N/A	N/A	1	Terminal
6	48	35	Age	64	4	63	64	1	Decision
6	49	36	N/A	N/A	3	N/A	N/A	1	Terminal
6	50	36	Family	2.5	12	65	66	0	Decision
6	51	37	N/A	N/A	1	N/A	N/A	1	Terminal
6	52	37	N/A	N/A	1	N/A	N/A	0	Terminal
7	53	40	Age	61.5	5	67	68	1	Decision
7	54	40	EducProf	0.5	4	69	70	0	Decision
7	55	42	N/A	N/A	1	N/A	N/A	1	Terminal
7	56	42	N/A	N/A	3	N/A	N/A	0	Terminal
7	57	43	N/A	N/A	1	N/A	N/A	0	Terminal
7	58	43	N/A	N/A	3	N/A	N/A	1	Terminal
7	59	45	EducProf	0.5	7	71	72	0	Decision
7	60	45	ZIP Code	91409	6	73	74	1	Decision
7	61	46	Income	111	7	75	76	0	Decision
7	62	46	N/A	N/A	10	N/A	N/A	0	Terminal
7	63	48	N/A	N/A	2	N/A	N/A	0	Terminal
7	64	48	N/A	N/A	2	N/A	N/A	1	Terminal
7	65	50	N/A	N/A	9	N/A	N/A	0	Terminal
7	66	50	N/A	N/A	3	N/A	N/A	1	Terminal
8	67	53	N/A	N/A	4	N/A	N/A	1	Terminal
8	68	53	N/A	N/A	1	N/A	N/A	0	Terminal
8	69	54	N/A	N/A	1	N/A	N/A	1	Terminal
8	70	54	N/A	N/A	3	N/A	N/A	0	Terminal
8	71	59	Online	0.5	2	77	78	1	Decision
8	72	59	N/A	N/A	5	N/A	N/A	0	Terminal
8	73	60	Family	2.5	3	79	80	0	Decision
8	74	60	N/A	N/A	3	N/A	N/A	1	Terminal
8	75	61	Mortgage	54.5	3	81	82	1	Decision
8	76	61	N/A	N/A	4	N/A	N/A	0	Terminal
9	77	71	N/A	N/A	1	N/A	N/A	0	Terminal
9	78	71	N/A	N/A	1	N/A	N/A	1	Terminal
9	79	73	N/A	N/A	1	N/A	N/A	1	Terminal
9	80	73	N/A	N/A	2	N/A	N/A	0	Terminal
9	81	75	N/A	N/A	2	N/A	N/A	1	Terminal
9	82	75	N/A	N/A	1	N/A	N/A	0	Terminal

FIGURE 9.11 DESCRIPTION OF EACH SPLITTING STEP OF THE FULL-GROWN TREE FOR THE LOAN ACCEPTANCE DATA

177

Training Data Scoring - Summary Report (Using Full Tree)

Cut off Prob.Val. for Success (Updatable)	0.5

Classification Confusion Matrix		
	Predicted Class	
Actual Class	1	0
1	235	0
0	0	2265

Error Report			
Class	# Cases	# Errors	% Error
1	235	0	0.00
0	2265	0	0.00
Overall	2500	0	0.00

Validation Data Scoring - Summary Report (Using Full Tree)

Cut off Prob.Val. for Success (Updatable)	0.5

Classification Confusion Matrix		
	Predicted Class	
Actual Class	1	0
1	128	15
0	17	1340

Error Report			
Class	# Cases	# Errors	% Error
1	143	15	10.49
0	1357	17	1.25
Overall	1500	32	2.13

Test Data Scoring - Summary Report (Using Full Tree)

Cut off Prob.Val. for Success (Updatable)	0.5

Classification Confusion Matrix		
	Predicted Class	
Actual Class	1	0
1	88	14
0	8	890

Error Report			
Class	# Cases	# Errors	% Error
1	102	14	13.73
0	898	8	0.89
Overall	1000	22	2.20

FIGURE 9.12   CLASSIFICATION MATRIX AND ERROR RATES FOR THE TRAINING AND VALIDATION DATA

9.5 AVOIDING OVERFITTING

As the last example illustrated, using a full-grown tree (based on the training data) leads to complete overfitting of the data. As discussed in Chapter 5, overfitting will lead to poor performance on new data. If we look at the overall error at the various levels of the tree, it is expected to decrease as the number of levels grows until the point of overfitting. Of course, for the training data the overall error decreases more and more until it is zero at the maximum level of the tree. However, for new data, the overall error is expected to decrease until the point where the tree models the relationship between class and the predictors. After that, the tree starts to model the noise in the training set, and we expect the overall error for the validation set to start increasing. This is depicted in Figure 9.13. One intuitive reason for the overfitting at the high levels of the tree is that these splits are based on very small numbers of observations. In such cases, class difference is likely to be attributed to noise rather than predictor information.

Two ways to try and avoid exceeding this level, thereby limiting overfitting, are by setting rules to stop tree growth or, alternatively, by pruning the full-grown tree back to a level where it does not overfit. These solutions are discussed below.

Stopping Tree Growth: CHAID

One can think of different criteria for stopping the tree growth before it starts overfitting the data. Examples are tree depth (i.e., number of splits), minimum number of observations in a node, and minimum reduction in impurity. The problem is that it is not simple to determine what is a good stopping point using such rules.

Previous methods developed were based on the idea of recursive partitioning, using rules to prevent the tree from growing excessively and overfitting the training data. One popular method called *CHAID* (chi-squared automatic interaction detection) is a recursive partitioning method that predates classification

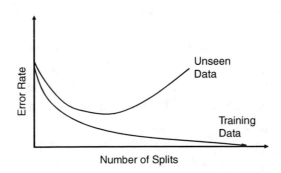

FIGURE 9.13   **ERROR RATE AS A FUNCTION OF THE NUMBER OF SPLITS FOR TRAINING VS. VALIDATION DATA: OVERFITTING**

and regression tree (CART) procedures by several years and is widely used in database marketing applications to this day. It uses a well-known statistical test (the chi-square test for independence) to assess whether splitting a node improves the purity by a statistically significant amount. In particular, at each node we split on the predictor that has the strongest association with the response variable. The strength of association is measured by the p-value of a chi-squared test of independence. If for the best predictor the test does not show a significant improvement, the split is not carried out, and the tree is terminated. This method is more suitable for categorical predictors, but it can be adapted to continuous predictors by binning the continuous values into categorical bins.

Pruning the Tree

An alternative solution that has proven to be more successful than stopping tree growth is pruning the full-grown tree. This is the basis of methods such as CART [developed by Breiman et al. (1984), implemented in multiple data mining software packages such as SAS Enterprise Miner, CART, MARS, and in XLMiner] and C4.5 implemented in packages such as IBM Modeler (previously Clementine by SPSS). In C4.5 the training data are used both for growing and pruning the tree. In CART the innovation is to use the validation data to prune back the tree that is grown from training data. CART and CART-like procedures use validation data to prune back the tree that has deliberately been overgrown using the training data. This approach is also used by XLMiner.

The idea behind pruning is to recognize that a very large tree is likely to be overfitting the training data and that the weakest branches, which hardly reduce the error rate, should be removed. In the mower example the last few splits resulted in rectangles with very few points (indeed, four rectangles in the full tree had just one point). We can see intuitively that these last splits are likely simply to be capturing noise in the training set rather than reflecting patterns that would occur in future data, such as the validation data. Pruning consists of successively selecting a decision node and redesignating it as a leaf node [lopping off the branches extending beyond that decision node (its *subtree*) and thereby reducing the size of the tree]. The pruning process trades off misclassification error in the validation dataset against the number of decision nodes in the pruned tree to arrive at a tree that captures the patterns but not the noise in the training data. Returning to Figure 9.13, we would like to find the point where the curve for the unseen data begins to increase.

To find this point, the CART algorithm uses a criterion called the *cost complexity* of a tree to generate a sequence of trees that are successively smaller to the point of having a tree with just the root node. (What is the classification rule for a tree with just one node?). This means that the first step is to find the best subtree of each size (1, 2, 3, ...). Then, to chose among these, we want the tree that minimizes the error rate of the validation set. We then pick as our best tree the one tree in the sequence that gives the smallest misclassification error in the validation data.

Constructing the best tree of each size is based on the cost complexity (CC) criterion, which is equal to the misclassification error of a tree (based on the training data) plus a penalty factor for the size of the tree. For a tree T that has $L(T)$ leaf nodes, the cost complexity can be written as

$$CC(T) = \mathrm{Err}(T) + \alpha L(T),$$

where err(T) is the fraction of training data observations that are misclassified by tree T and α is a penalty factor for tree size. When $\alpha = 0$, there is no penalty for having too many nodes in a tree, and the best tree using the cost complexity criterion is the full-grown unpruned tree. When we increase α to a very large value, the penalty cost component swamps the misclassification error component of the cost complexity criterion function, and the best tree is simply the tree with the fewest leaves: namely, the tree with simply one node. The idea is therefore to start with the full-grown tree and then increase the penalty factor α gradually until the cost complexity of the full tree exceeds that of a subtree. Then the same procedure is repeated using the subtree. Continuing in this manner, we generate a succession of trees with a diminishing number of nodes all the way to a trivial tree consisting of just one node.

From this sequence of trees it seems natural to pick the one that gave the minimum misclassification error on the validation dataset. We call this the *minimum error tree*. To illustrate this, Figure 9.14 shows the error rate for both the training and validation data as a function of the tree size. It can be seen that the training set error steadily decreases as the tree grows, with a noticeable drop in error rate between two and three nodes. The validation set error rate, however, reaches a minimum at 11 nodes and then starts to increase as the tree grows. At this point the tree is pruned and we obtain the minimum error tree.

A further enhancement is to incorporate the sampling error, which might cause this minimum to vary if we had a different sample. The enhancement uses the estimated standard error of the error rate to prune the tree even further (to the validation error rate, which is one standard error above the minimum.) In other words, the "best pruned tree" is the smallest tree in the pruning sequence that has an error within one standard error of the minimum error tree. The best pruned tree for the loan acceptance example is shown in Figure 9.15.

Returning to the loan acceptance example, we expect that the classification accuracy of the validation set using the pruned tree would be higher than using the full-grown tree (compare Figure 9.12 with Figure 9.16). However, the performance of the pruned tree on the validation data is not fully reflective of the performance on completely new data because the validation data were actually used for the pruning. This is a situation where it is particularly useful to evaluate

# Decision Nodes	% Error Training	% Error Validation			
41	0	2.133333			
40	0.04	2.2			
39	0.08	2.2			
38	0.12	2.2			
37	0.16	2.066667			
36	0.2	2.066667			
35	0.2	2.066667			
34	0.24	2.066667			
33	0.28	2.066667			
32	0.4	2.066667			
31	0.48	2.133333			
30	0.48	2.133333			
29	0.56	2.133333			
28	0.6	1.866667			
27	0.64	1.866667			
26	0.72	1.866667			
25	0.76	1.866667			
24	0.88	1.866667			
23	0.88	1.733333			
22	0.88	1.733333			
21	0.96	1.733333			
20	0.96	1.733333			
19	1	1.733333			
18	1	1.733333			
17	1.12	1.733333			
16	1.12	1.533333			
15	1.12	1.533333			
14	1.16	1.533333			
13	1.16	1.6			
12	1.2	1.6			
11	1.2	1.466667	<-- Min. Err. Tree	Std. Err.	0.003103929
10	1.6	1.666667			
9	2.2	1.666667			
8	2.2	1.866667			
7	2.24	1.866667			
6	2.24	1.6	<-- Best Pruned Tree		
5	4.44	1.8			
4	5.08	2.333333			
3	5.24	3.466667			
2	9.4	9.533333			
1	9.4	9.533333			
0	9.4	9.533333			

FIGURE 9.14   **ERROR RATE AS A FUNCTION OF THE NUMBER OF SPLITS FOR TRAINING VS. VALIDATION DATA FOR THE LOAN EXAMPLE**

the performance of the chosen model, whatever it may be, on a third set of data, the test set, which has not been used at all. In our example, the pruned tree applied to the test data yields an overall error rate of 1.7% (compared to 0% for the training data and 1.6% for the validation data). Although in this example the

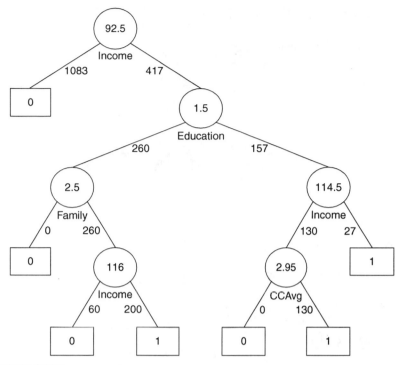

BEST PRUNED TREE OBTAINED BY FITTING A FULL TREE TO THE TRAINING DATA AND PRUNING IT USING THE VALIDATION DATA

performance on the validation and test sets is similar, the difference can be larger for other datasets.

9.6 CLASSIFICATION RULES FROM TREES

As described in Section 9.1, classification trees provide easily understandable *classification rules* (if the trees are not too large). Each leaf is equivalent to a classification rule. Returning to the example, the middle left leaf in the best pruned tree gives us the rule

IF(Income > 92.5) AND (Education < 1.5) AND (Family ≤ 2.5) THEN
Class = 0.

However, in many cases the number of rules can be reduced by removing redundancies. For example, the rule

IF(Income > 92.5) AND (Education > 1.5) AND (Income > 114.5) THEN
Class = 1

Training Data Scoring - Summary Report (Using Full Tree)

Cut off Prob.Val. for Success (Updatable)	0.5

Classification Confusion Matrix

	Predicted Class	
Actual Class	1	0
1	235	0
0	0	2265

Error Report

Class	# Cases	# Errors	% Error
1	235	0	0.00
0	2265	0	0.00
Overall	2500	0	0.00

Validation Data Scoring - Summary Report (Using Best Pruned Tree)

Cut off Prob.Val. for Success (Updatable)	0.5

Classification Confusion Matrix

	Predicted Class	
Actual Class	1	0
1	127	16
0	8	1349

Error Report

Class	# Cases	# Errors	% Error
1	143	16	11.19
0	1357	8	0.59
Overall	1500	24	1.60

Test Data Scoring - Summary Report (Using Best Pruned Tree)

Cut off Prob.Val. for Success (Updatable)	0.5

Classification Confusion Matrix

	Predicted Class	
Actual Class	1	0
1	88	14
0	3	895

Error Report

Class	# Cases	# Errors	% Error
1	102	14	13.73
0	898	3	0.33
Overall	1000	17	1.70

FIGURE 9.16   CLASSIFICATION MATRIX AND ERROR RATES FOR THE TRAINING, VALIDATION, AND TEST DATA BASED ON THE PRUNED TREE

184

can be simplified to

IF(Income > 114.5) AND (Education > 1.5) THEN Class = 1.

This transparency in the process and understandability of the algorithm that leads to classifying an observation as belonging to a certain class is very advantageous in settings where the final classification is not solely of interest. Berry and Linoff (2000) give the example of health insurance underwriting, where the insurer is required to show that coverage denial is not based on discrimination. By showing rules that led to denial (e.g., income < \$20K AND low credit history), the company can avoid lawsuits. Compared to the output of other classifiers, such as discriminant functions, tree-based classification rules are easily explained to managers and operating staff. Their logic is certainly far more transparent than that of weights in neural networks!

9.7 CLASSIFICATION TREES FOR MORE THAN TWO CLASSES

Classification trees can be used with an outcome that has more than two classes. In terms of measuring impurity, the two measures that were presented earlier (the Gini impurity index and the entropy measure) were defined for m classes and hence can be used for any number of classes. The tree itself would have the same structure, except that its terminal nodes would take one of the m–class labels.

9.8 REGRESSION TREES

The tree method can also be used for numerical response variables. Regression trees for prediction operate in much the same fashion as classification trees. The output variable, Y, is a numerical variable in this case, but both the principle and the procedure are the same: Many splits are attempted, and for each, we measure "impurity" in each branch of the resulting tree. The tree procedure then selects the split that minimizes the sum of such measures. To illustrate a regression tree, consider the example of predicting prices of Toyota Corolla automobiles (from Chapter 6). The dataset includes information on 1000 sold Toyota Corolla cars (we use the first 1000 cars from the dataset ToyotoCorolla.xls). The goal is to find a predictive model of price as a function of 10 predictors (including mileage, horsepower, number of doors, etc.). A regression tree for these data was built using a training set of 600. The best pruned tree is shown in Figure 9.17.

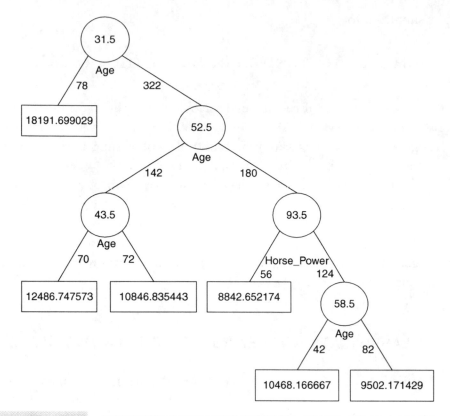

FIGURE 9.17   BEST PRUNED REGRESSION TREE FOR TOYOTA COROLLA PRICES

It can be seen that only two predictors show up as useful for predicting price: the age of the car and its horsepower. There are three details that are different in regression trees than in classification trees: prediction, impurity measures, and evaluating performance. We describe these next.

Prediction

Predicting the value of the response Y for an observation is performed in a fashion similar to the classification case: The predictor information is used for "dropping" down the tree until reaching a leaf node. For instance, to predict the price of a Toyota Corolla with Age = 55 and Horsepower = 86, we drop it down the tree and reach the node that has the value $8842.65. This is the price prediction for this car according to the tree. In classification trees the value of the leaf node (which is one of the categories) is determined by the "voting" of the training data that were in that leaf. In regression trees the value of the leaf node is determined by the average of the training data in that leaf. In the example above, the value $8842.6 is the average of the 56 cars in the training set that fall in the category of Age > 52.5 AND Horsepower < 93.5.

Measuring Impurity

We described two types of impurity measures for nodes in classification trees: the Gini index and the entropy-based measure. In both cases the index is a function of the ratio between the categories of the observations in that node. In regression trees a typical impurity measure is the sum of the squared deviations from the mean of the leaf. This is equivalent to the squared errors because the mean of the leaf is exactly the prediction. In the example above, the impurity of the node with the value \$8842.6 is computed by subtracting \$8842.6 from the price of each of the 56 cars in the training set that fell in that leaf, then squaring these deviations and summing them up. The lowest impurity possible is zero, when all values in the node are equal.

Evaluating Performance

As stated above, predictions are obtained by averaging the values of the responses in the nodes. We therefore have the usual definition of predictions and errors. The predictive performance of regression trees can be measured in the same way that other predictive methods are evaluated, using summary measures such as RMSE and charts such as lift charts.

9.9 ADVANTAGES, WEAKNESSES, AND EXTENSIONS

Tree methods are good off-the-shelf classifiers and predictors. They are also useful for variable selection, with the most important predictors usually showing up at the top of the tree. Trees require relatively little effort from users in the following senses: First, there is no need for transformation of variables (any monotone transformation of the variables will give the same trees). Second, variable subset selection is automatic since it is part of the split selection. In the loan example notice that the best pruned tree has automatically selected just four variables (Income, Education, Family, and CCAvg) out of the set 14 variables available.

Trees are also intrinsically robust to outliers since the choice of a split depends on the *ordering* of observation values and not on the absolute *magnitudes* of these values. However, they are sensitive to changes in the data, and even a slight change can cause very different splits!

Unlike models that assume a particular relationship between the response and predictors (e.g., a linear relationship such as in linear regression and linear discriminant analysis), classification and regression trees are nonlinear and non-parametric. This allows for a wide range of relationships between the predictors and the response. However, this can also be a weakness: Since the splits are done on single predictors rather than on combinations of predictors, the tree is likely to miss relationships between predictors, in particular linear structures such as those in linear or logistic regression models. Classification trees are useful classifiers in

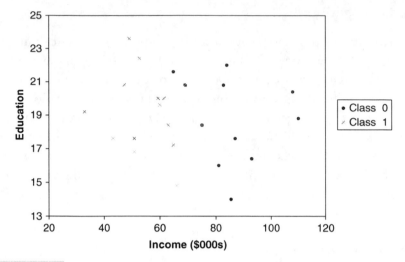

FIGURE 9.18   **SCATTERPLOT DESCRIBING A TWO-PREDICTOR CASE WITH TWO CLASSES**

cases where horizontal and vertical splitting of the predictor space adequately divides the classes. But consider, for instance, a dataset with two predictors and two classes, where separation between the two classes is most obviously achieved by using a diagonal line (as shown in Figure 9.18). A classification tree is therefore expected to have lower performance than methods such as discriminant analysis. One way to improve performance is to create new predictors that are derived from existing predictors, which can capture hypothesized relationships between predictors (similar to interactions in regression models).

Another performance issue with classification trees is that they require a large dataset in order to construct a good classifier. Recently, Breiman and Cutler introduced *random forests*,[3] an extension to classification trees that tackles these issues. The basic idea is to create multiple classification trees from the data (and thus obtain a "forest") and combine their output to obtain a better classifier.

An appealing feature of trees is that they handle missing data without having to impute values or delete observations with missing values. The method can be extended to incorporate an importance ranking for the variables in terms of their impact on the quality of the classification. From a computational aspect, trees can be relatively expensive to grow because of the multiple sorting involved in computing all possible splits on every variable. Pruning the data using the validation set adds further computation time. Finally, a very important practical advantage of trees is the transparent rules that they generate. Such transparency is often useful in managerial applications.

---

[3] For further details on random forests see www.stat.berkeley.edu/users/breiman/RandomForests/cc_home.htm.

PROBLEMS

9.1 **Competitive Auctions on eBay.com.** The file eBayAuctions.xls contains information on 1972 auctions transacted on eBay.com during May–June 2004. The goal is to use these data to build a model that will classify competitive auctions from noncompetitive ones. A *competitive auction* is defined as an auction with at least two bids placed on the item auctioned. The data include variables that describe the item (auction category), the seller (his/her eBay rating), and the auction terms that the seller selected (auction duration, opening price, currency, day-of-week of auction close). In addition, we have the price at which the auction closed. The goal is to predict whether or not the auction will be competitive.

Data Preprocessing. Create dummy variables for the categorical predictors. These include Category (18 categories), Currency (USD, GBP, Euro), EndDay (Monday–Sunday), and Duration (1, 3, 5, 7, or 10 days). Split the data into training and validation datasets using a 60% : 40% ratio.

   a. Fit a classification tree using all predictors, using the best pruned tree. To avoid overfitting, set the minimum number of observations in a leaf node to 50. Also, set the maximum number of levels to be displayed at seven (the maximum allowed in XLminer). To remain within the limitation of 30 predictors, combine some of the categories of categorical predictors. Write down the results in terms of rules.

   b. Is this model practical for predicting the outcome of a new auction?

   c. Describe the interesting and uninteresting information that these rules provide.

   d. Fit another classification tree (using the best-pruned tree, with a minimum number of observations per leaf node = 50 and maximum allowed number of displayed levels), this time only with predictors that can be used for predicting the outcome of a new auction. Describe the resulting tree in terms of rules. Make sure to report the smallest set of rules required for classification.

   e. Plot the resulting tree on a scatterplot: Use the two axes for the two best (quantitative) predictors. Each auction will appear as a point, with coordinates corresponding to its values on those two predictors. Use different colors or symbols to separate competitive and noncompetitive auctions. Draw lines (you can sketch these by hand or use Excel) at the values that create splits. Does this splitting seem reasonable with respect to the meaning of the two predictors? Does it seem to do a good job of separating the two classes?

   f. Examine the lift chart and the classification table for the tree. What can you say about the predictive performance of this model?

   g. Based on this last tree, what can you conclude from these data about the chances of an auction obtaining at least two bids and its relationship to the auction settings set by the seller (duration, opening price, ending day, currency)? What would you recommend for a seller as the strategy that will most likely lead to a competitive auction?

9.2 **Predicting Delayed Flights.** The file FlightDelays.xls contains information on all commercial flights departing the Washington, D.C., area and arriving at New York during January 2004. For each flight there is information on the departure and arrival airports, the distance of the route, the scheduled time and date of the flight, and so on. The variable that we are trying to predict is whether or not a flight is delayed. A delay is defined as an arrival that is at least 15 minutes later than scheduled.

Data Preprocessing. Create dummies for day of week, carrier, departure airport, and arrival airport. This will give you 17 dummies. Bin the scheduled departure time into 2-hour bins (in XLMiner use *Data Utilities > Bin Continuous Data* and select 8 bins with equal width). After binning DEP_TIME into 8 bins, this new variable should be broken down into 7 dummies (because the effect will not be linear due to the morning and afternoon rush hours). This will avoid treating the departure time as a continuous predictor because it is reasonable that delays are related to rush-hour times. Partition the data into training and validation sets.

a. Fit a classification tree to the flight delay variable using all the relevant predictors. Do not include DEP_TIME (actual departure time) in the model because it is unknown at the time of prediction (unless we are doing our predicting of delays after the plane takes off, which is unlikely). In the third step of the classification tree menu, choose "Maximum # levels to be displayed = 6". Use the best pruned tree without a limitation on the minimum number of observations in the final nodes. Express the resulting tree as a set of rules.

b. If you needed to fly between DCA and EWR on a Monday at 7 AM, would you be able to use this tree? What other information would you need? Is it available in practice? What information is redundant?

c. Fit another tree, this time excluding the day-of-month predictor. (Why?) Select the option of seeing both the full tree and the best pruned tree. You will find that the best pruned tree contains a single terminal node.

    i. How is this tree used for classification? (What is the rule for classifying?)

    ii. To what is this rule equivalent?

    iii. Examine the full tree. What are the top three predictors according to this tree?

    iv. Why, technically, does the pruned tree result in a tree with a single node?

    v. What is the disadvantage of using the top levels of the full tree as opposed to the best pruned tree?

    vi. Compare this general result to that from logistic regression in the example in Chapter 10. What are possible reasons for the classification tree's failure to find a good predictive model?

9.3 **Predicting Prices of Used Cars (Regression Trees).** The file ToyotaCorolla.xls contains the data on used cars (Toyota Corolla) on sale during late summer of 2004 in The Netherlands. It has 1436 observations containing details on 38 attributes, including Price, Age, Kilometers, HP, and other specifications. The goal is to predict the price of a used Toyota Corolla based on its specifications. (The example in Section 9.8 is a subset of this dataset.)

Data Preprocessing. Create dummy variables for the categorical predictors (Fuel Type and Color). Split the data into training (50%), validation (30%), and test (20%) datasets.

a. Run a regression tree (RT) using the prediction menu in XLMiner with the output variable Price and input variables Age_08_04, KM, Fuel_Type, HP, Automatic, Doors, Quarterly_Tax, Mfg_Guarantee, Guarantee_Period, Airco, Automatic_Airco, CD_Player, Powered_Windows, Sport_Model, and Tow_Bar. Normalize the variables. Keep the minimum number of observations in a terminal node to 1 and the scoring option to Full Tree, to make the run least restrictive.

    i. Which appear to be the three or four most important car specifications for predicting the car's price?

ii. Compare the prediction errors of the training, validation, and test sets by examining their RMS error and by plotting the three boxplots. What is happening with the training set predictions? How does the predictive performance of the test set compare to the other two? Why does this occur?

iii. How can we achieve predictions for the training set that are not equal to the actual prices?

iv. If we used the best pruned tree instead of the full tree, how would this affect the predictive performance for the validation set? (*Hint:* Does the full tree use the validation data?)

b. Let us see the effect of turning the price variable into a categorical variable. First, create a new variable that categorizes price into 20 bins. Use *Data Utilities > Bin Continuous Data* to categorize Price into 20 bins of equal intervals (leave all other options at their default). Now repartition the data keeping Binned_ Price instead of Price. Run a classification tree (CT) using the Classification menu of XLMiner with the same set of input variables as in the RT, and with Binned_Price as the output variable. Keep the minimum number of observations in a terminal node to 1 and uncheck the Prune Tree option, to make the run least restrictive. Select "Normalize input data."

i. Compare the tree generated by the CT with the one generated by the RT. Are they different? (Look at structure, the top predictors, size of tree, etc.) Why?

ii. Predict the price, using the RT and the CT, of a used Toyota Corolla with the specifications listed in Table 9.3.

TABLE 9.3   SPECIFICATIONS FOR A PARTICULAR TOYOTA COROLLA

Variable	Value
Age_-08_-04	77
KM	117,000
Fuel_Type	Petrol
HP	110
Automatic	No
Doors	5
Quarterly_Tax	100
Mfg_Guarantee	No
Guarantee_Period	3
Airco	Yes
Automatic_Airco	No
CD_Player	No
Powered_Windows	No
Sport_Model	No
Tow_Bar	Yes

iii. Compare the predictions in terms of the variables that were used, the magnitude of the difference between the two predictions, and the advantages and disadvantages of the two methods.

CHAPTER 10

Logistic Regression

In this chapter we describe the highly popular and powerful classification method called logistic regression. Like linear regression, it relies on a specific model relating the predictors with the outcome. The user must specify the predictors to include and their form (e.g., including any interaction terms). This means that even small datasets can be used for building logistic regression classifiers, and that once the model is estimated, it is computationally fast and cheap to classify even large samples of new observations. We describe the logistic regression model formulation and its estimation from data. We also explain the concepts of "logit," "odds," and "probability" of an event that arise in the logistic model context and the relations among the three. We discuss variable importance using coefficient and statistical significance and also mention variable selection algorithms for dimension reduction. All this is illustrated on an authentic dataset of flight information where the goal is to predict flight delays. Our presentation is strictly from a data mining perspective, where classification is the goal and performance is evaluated on a separate validation set. However, because logistic regression is heavily used also in statistical analyses for purposes of inference, we give a brief review of key concepts related to coefficient interpretation, goodness-of-fit evaluation, inference, and multiclass models in the Appendix at the end of this chapter.

10.1 INTRODUCTION

Logistic regression extends the ideas of linear regression to the situation where the dependent variable, Y, is categorical. We can think of a categorical variable

192

as dividing the observations into classes. For example, if Y denotes a recommendation on holding/selling/buying a stock, we have a categorical variable with three categories. We can think of each of the stocks in the dataset (the observations) as belonging to one of three classes: the *hold* class, the *sell* class, and the *buy* class. Logistic regression can be used for classifying a new observation, where the class is unknown, into one of the classes, based on the values of its predictor variables (called *classification*). It can also be used in data (where the class is known) to find similarities between observations within each class in terms of the predictor variables (called *profiling*). Logistic regression is used in applications such as:

1. Classifying customers as returning or nonreturning (classification)
2. Finding factors that differentiate between male and female top executives (profiling)
3. Predicting the approval or disapproval of a loan based on information such as credit scores (classification)

In this chapter we focus on the use of logistic regression for classification. We deal only with a binary dependent variable having two possible classes. At the end we show how the results can be extended to the case where Y assumes more than two possible outcomes. Popular examples of binary response outcomes are success/failure, yes/no, buy/don't buy, default/don't default, and survive/die. For convenience we often code the values of a binary response Y as 0 and 1.

Note that in some cases we may choose to convert continuous data or data with multiple outcomes into binary data for purposes of simplification, reflecting the fact that decision making may be binary (approve the loan/don't approve, make an offer/don't make an offer). As with multiple linear regression, the independent variables $X_1, X_2, \ldots, X_k$ may be categorical or continuous variables or a mixture of these two types. While in multiple linear regression the aim is to predict the value of the continuous Y for a new observation, in logistic regression the goal is to predict which class a new observation will belong to or simply to *classify* the observation into one of the classes. In the stock example, we would want to classify a new stock into one of the three recommendation classes: sell, hold, or buy.

In logistic regression we take two steps: the first step yields estimates of the *probabilities* of belonging to each class. In the binary case we get an estimate of $P(Y = 1)$, the probability of belonging to class 1 (which also tells us the probability of belonging to class 0). In the next step we use a cutoff value on these probabilities in order to classify each case in one of the classes. For example, in a binary case, a cutoff of 0.5 means that cases with an estimated probability of $P(Y = 1) > 0.5$ are classified as belonging to class 1, whereas cases with $P(Y = 1) < 0.5$ are classified as belonging to class 0. This cutoff need not be set at 0.5. When the event in question is a low-probability event, a higher-than-average cutoff value, although still below 0.5, may be sufficient to classify a case as belonging to class 1.

10.2 LOGISTIC REGRESSION MODEL

The logistic regression model is used in a variety of fields: whenever a structured model is needed to explain or predict categorical (in particular, binary) outcomes. One such application is in describing choice behavior in econometrics, which is useful in the context of the example above (see the accompanying box).

LOGISTIC REGRESSION AND CONSUMER CHOICE THEORY

In the context of choice behavior, the logistic model can be shown to follow from the *random utility theory* developed by Manski (1977) as an extension of the standard economic theory of consumer behavior. In essence, the consumer theory states that when faced with a set of choices, a consumer makes the choice that has the highest utility (a numerical measure of worth with arbitrary zero and scale). It assumes that the consumer has a preference order on the list of choices that satisfies reasonable criteria such as transitivity. The preference order can depend on the person (e.g., socioeconomic characteristics) as well as attributes of the choice. The random utility model considers the utility of a choice to incorporate a random element. When we model the random element as coming from a "reasonable" distribution, we can logically derive the logistic model for predicting choice behavior.

The idea behind logistic regression is straightforward: Instead of using Y as the dependent variable, we use a function of it, which is called the *logit*. The logit, it turns out, can be modeled as a linear function of the predictors. Once the logit has been predicted, it can be mapped back to a probability.

To understand the logit, we take several intermediate steps: First, we look at p, the probability of belonging to class 1 (as opposed to class 0). In contrast to Y, the class number, which only takes the values 0 and 1, p can take any value in the interval [0, 1]. However, if we express p as a linear function of the q predictors[1] in the form

$$p = \beta_0 + \beta_1 x_1 + \beta_2 x_2 + \cdots + \beta_q x_q, \tag{10.1}$$

---

[1] Unlike elsewhere in the book, where p denotes the number of predictors, in this chapter we indicate predictors by q, to avoid confusion with the probability p.

it is not guaranteed that the right-hand side will lead to values within the interval [0, 1]. The fix is to use a nonlinear function of the predictors in the form

$$p = \frac{1}{1 + e^{-(\beta_0 + \beta_1 x_1 + \beta_2 x_2 + \cdots + \beta_q x_q)}}. \tag{10.2}$$

This is called the *logistic response function*. For any values of $x_1, \ldots, x_q$, the right-hand side will always lead to values in the interval [0, 1]. Next, we look at a different measure of belonging to a certain class, known as *odds*. The odds of belonging to class 1 ($Y = 1$) is defined as the ratio of the probability of belonging to class 1 to the probability of belonging to class 0:

$$\text{Odds} = \frac{p}{1 - p}. \tag{10.3}$$

This metric is very popular in horse races, sports, gambling in general, epidemiology, and many other areas. Instead of talking about the *probability* of winning or contacting a disease, people talk about the *odds* of winning or contacting a disease. How are these two different? If, for example, the probability of winning is 0.5, the odds of winning are $0.5/0.5 = 1$. We can also perform the reverse calculation: Given the odds of an event, we can compute its probability by manipulating equation (10.3):

$$p = \frac{\text{odds}}{1 + \text{odds}}. \tag{10.4}$$

Substituting (10.2) into (10.4), we can write the relationship between the odds and the predictors as

$$\text{Odds} = e^{\beta_0 + \beta_1 x_1 + \beta_2 x_2 + \cdots + \beta_q x_q}. \tag{10.5}$$

This last equation describes a multiplicative (proportional) relationship between the predictors and the odds. Such a relationship is interpretable in terms of percentages, for example, a unit increase in predictor x_j is associated with an average increase of $\beta_j \times 100\%$ in the odds (holding all other predictors constant).

Now, if we take a log on both sides, we get the standard formulation of a logistic model:

$$\log(\text{odds}) = \beta_0 + \beta_1 x_1 + \beta_2 x_2 + \cdots + \beta_q x_q. \tag{10.6}$$

The log(odds) is called the *logit*, and it takes values from $-\infty$ to ∞. Thus, our final formulation of the relation between the response and the predictors uses the logit as the dependent variable and models it as a *linear function* of the q predictors.

To see the relation between the probability, odds, and logit of belonging to class 1, look at Figure 10.1, which shows the odds (*a*) and logit (*b*) as a function of p. Notice that the odds can take any nonnegative value, and that the logit can take any real value. Let us examine some data to illustrate the use of logistic regression.

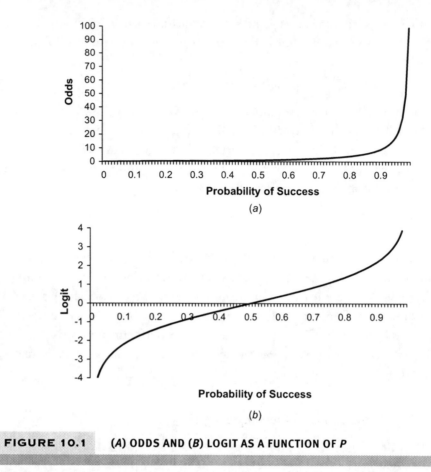

FIGURE 10.1   **(A) ODDS AND (B) LOGIT AS A FUNCTION OF P**

Example: Acceptance of Personal Loan

Recall the example described in Chapter 9, of acceptance of a personal loan by Universal Bank. The bank's dataset includes data on 5000 customers. The data include customer demographic information (Age, Income, etc.), customer response to the last personal loan campaign (Personal Loan), and the customer's relationship with the bank (mortgage, securities account, etc.). Among these 5000 customers, only 480 (=9.6%) accepted the personal loan that was offered to them in a previous campaign. The goal is to find characteristics of customers who are most likely to accept the loan offer in future mailings.

Data Preprocessing   We start by partitioning the data randomly using a standard 60% : 40% rate into training and validation sets. We use the training set to fit a model and the validation set to assess the model's performance.

Next, we create dummy variables for each of the categorical predictors. Except for education, which has three categories, the remaining four categorical variables have two categories. We therefore need $6 = 2 + 1 + 1 + 1 + 1$ dummy variables to describe these five categorical predictors. In XLMiner's classification functions, the response can remain in text form (Yes, No, etc.), but the predictor variables must be coded into dummy variables. We use the following coding:

$$\text{EducProf} = \begin{cases} 1 \text{ if education is Professional} \\ 0 \text{ otherwise} \end{cases}$$

$$\text{EducGrad} = \begin{cases} 1 \text{ if education is at Graduate level} \\ 0 \text{ otherwise} \end{cases}$$

$$\text{Securities} = \begin{cases} 1 \text{ if customer has securities account in bank} \\ 0 \text{ otherwise} \end{cases}$$

$$\text{CD} = \begin{cases} 1 \text{ if customer has CD account in bank} \\ 0 \text{ otherwise} \end{cases}$$

$$\text{Online} = \begin{cases} 1 \text{ if customer uses online banking} \\ 0 \text{ otherwise} \end{cases}$$

$$\text{CreditCard} = \begin{cases} 1 \text{ if customer holds Universal Bank credit card} \\ 0 \text{ otherwise} \end{cases}$$

Model with a Single Predictor

Consider first a simple logistic regression model with just one independent variable. This is analogous to the simple linear regression model in which we fit a straight line to relate the dependent variable, Y, to a single independent variable, X.

Let us construct a simple logistic regression model for classification of customers using the single predictor Income. The equation relating the dependent variable to the explanatory variable in terms of probabilities is

$$\text{Prob(Personal Loan = Yes | Income} = x) = \frac{1}{1 + e^{-(\beta_0 + \beta_1 x)}},$$

or equivalently, in terms of odds,

$$\text{Odds(Personal Loan = Yes)} = e^{\beta_0 + \beta_1 x}. \tag{10.7}$$

The estimated coefficients for the model are $b_0 = -6.3525$ and $b_1 = 0.0392$. So the fitted model is

$$P(\text{Personal Loan = Yes | Income} = x) = \frac{1}{1 + e^{6.3525 - 0.0392x}}. \tag{10.8}$$

Although logistic regression can be used for prediction in the sense that we predict the *probability* of a categorical outcome, it is most often used for classification. To see the difference between the two, consider predicting the probability of a customer accepting the loan offer as opposed to classifying the customer as an accepter/nonaccepter. From Figure 10.2 it can be seen that the loan acceptance can yield numbers between 0 and 1. To end up with classifications into either 0

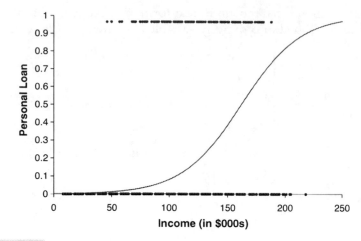

FIGURE 10.2   **PLOT OF DATA POINTS (PERSONAL LOAN AS A FUNCTION OF INCOME) AND THE FITTED LOGISTIC CURVE**

or 1 (e.g., a customer either accepts the loan offer or not), we need a threshold, or "cutoff value." This is true in the case of multiple predictor variables as well.

Cutoff Value   Given the values for a set of predictors, we can predict the probability that each observation belongs to class 1. The next step is to set a cutoff on these probabilities so that each observation is classified into one of the two classes. This is done by setting a cutoff value, c, such that observations with probabilities above c are classified as belonging to class 1, and observations with probabilities below c are classified as belonging to class 0.

In the Universal Bank example, in order to classify a new customer as an acceptor/nonacceptor of the loan offer, we use the information on his/her income by plugging it into the fitted equation (10.8). This yields an estimated probability of accepting the loan offer. We then compare it to the cutoff value. The customer is classified as an acceptor if the probability of his/her accepting the offer is above the cutoff. [2]

Different cutoff values lead to different classifications and, consequently, different classification matrices. There are several approaches to determining the "optimal" cutoff probability: A popular cutoff value for a two-class case is 0.5. The rationale is to assign an observation to the class in which its probability of membership is highest. A cutoff can also be chosen to maximize overall accuracy. This can be determined using a one-way data table in Excel (see Chapter 5).

---

[2] If we prefer to look at *odds* of accepting rather than the probability, an equivalent method is to use equation (10.7) and compare the odds to $c/(1 - c)$. If the odds are higher than this number, the customer is classified as an acceptor. If it is lower, we classify the customer as a nonacceptor.

The overall accuracy is computed for various values of the cutoff value, and the cutoff value that yields maximum accuracy is chosen. The danger is, of course, overfitting.

Alternatives to maximizing accuracy are to maximize sensitivity subject to some minimum level of specificity, or to minimize false positives subject to some maximum level of false negatives, and so on. Finally, a cost-based approach is to find a cutoff value that minimizes the expected cost of misclassification. In this case one must specify the misclassification costs and the prior probabilities of belonging to each class.

Estimating the Logistic Model from Data: Computing Parameter Estimates

In logistic regression, the relation between Y and the β parameters is nonlinear. For this reason the β parameters are not estimated using the method of least squares (as in multiple linear regression). Instead, a method called *maximum likelihood* is used. The idea, in brief, is to find the estimates that maximize the chance of obtaining the data that we have. This requires iterations using a computer program.[3]

Algorithms to compute the coefficient estimates are less robust than algorithms for linear regression. Computed estimates are generally reliable for well-behaved datasets where the number of observations with outcome variable values of both 0 and 1 are large, their ratio is "not too close" to either 0 or 1, and when the number of coefficients in the logistic regression model is small relative to the sample size (say, no more than 10%). As with linear regression, collinearity (strong correlation among the independent variables) can lead to computational difficulties. Computationally intensive algorithms have been developed recently that circumvent some of these difficulties. For technical details on the maximum-likelihood estimation in logistic regression, see Hosmer and Lemeshow (2000).

To illustrate a typical output from such a procedure, look at the output in Figure 10.3 for the logistic model fitted to the training set of 3000 Universal Bank customers. The dependent variable is Personal Loan, with Yes defined as the *success* (this is equivalent to setting the variable to 1 for an acceptor and 0 for a nonacceptor). Here we use all 12 predictors.

---

[3] The method of maximum likelihood ensures good asymptotic (large sample) properties for the estimates. Under very general conditions, maximum-likelihood estimators are: (1) *Consistent*—the probability of the estimator differing from the true value approaches zero with increasing sample size. (2) *Asymptotically efficient*—the variance is the smallest possible among consistent estimators. (3) *Asymptotically normally distributed*—this allows us to compute confidence intervals and perform statistical tests in a manner analogous to the analysis of linear multiple regression models, provided that the sample size is *large*.

Input variables	Coefficient	Std. Error	p-value	Odds
Constant term	-13.20165825	2.46772742	0.00000009	*
Age	-0.04453737	0.09096102	0.62439483	0.95643985
Experience	0.05657264	0.09005365	0.5298661	1.05820346
Income	0.0657607	0.00422134	0	1.06797111
Family	0.57155931	0.10119002	0.00000002	1.77102649
CCAvg	0.18724874	0.06153848	0.00234395	1.20592725
Mortgage	0.00175308	0.00080375	0.02917421	1.00175464
Securities Account	-0.85484785	0.41863668	0.04115349	0.42534789
CD Account	3.46900773	0.44893095	0	32.10486984
Online	-0.84355801	0.22832377	0.00022026	0.43017724
CreditCard	-0.96406376	0.28254223	0.00064463	0.38134006
EducGrad	4.58909273	0.38708162	0	98.40509796
EducProf	4.52272701	0.38425466	0	92.08635712

FIGURE 10.3   **LOGISTIC REGRESSION COEFFICIENT TABLE FOR PERSONAL LOAN ACCEPTANCE AS A FUNCTION OF 12 PREDICTORS**

Ignoring p-values for the coefficients, a model based on all 12 predictors would have the following estimated logistic equation:

$$\text{logit} = -13.201 - 0.045\,\text{Age} + 0.057\,\text{Experience} + 0.066\,\text{Income} + 0.572\,\text{Family}$$
$$+ 0.18724874\,\text{CCAvg} + 0.002\,\text{Mortgage} - 0.855\,\text{Securities} + 3.469\,\text{CD}$$
$$- 0.844\,\text{Online} - 0.964\,\text{Credit Card} + 4.589\,\text{EducGrad} + 4.523\,\text{EducProf}$$

$$(10.9)$$

The positive coefficients for the dummy variables CD, EducGrad, and EducProf mean that holding a CD account and having graduate or professional education (all marked by 1 in the dummy variables) are associated with higher probabilities of accepting the loan offer. On the other hand, having a securities account, using online banking, and owning a Universal Bank credit card are associated with lower acceptance rates. For the continuous predictors, positive coefficients indicate that a higher value on that predictor is associated with a higher probability of accepting the loan offer (e.g., income: higher income customers tend more to accept the offer). Similarly, negative coefficients indicate that a higher value on that predictor is associated with a lower probability of accepting the loan offer (e.g., Age: older customers are less likely to accept the offer).

If we want to talk about the *odds* of offer acceptance, we can use the last column (entitled "odds") to obtain the following equation:

$$\text{Odds(Personal Loan = Yes)} = e^{-13.201}(0.956)^{\text{Age}}\ (1.058)^{Experience}\ (1.068)^{\text{Income}}$$
$$\times (1.771)^{\text{Family}}\ (1.206)^{\text{CCAvg}}\ (1.002)^{\text{Mortgage}}$$
$$\times (0.425)^{\text{Securities}}\ (32.105)^{\text{CD}}\ (0.430)^{\text{Online}}$$
$$\times (0.381)^{\text{CreditCard}}(98.405)^{\text{EducGrad}}\ (92.086)^{\text{EducProf}}.$$

$$(10.10)$$

Notice how positive coefficients in the logit model translate into coefficients larger than 1 in the odds model, and negative positive coefficients in the logit translate into coefficients smaller than 1 in the odds.

A third option is to look directly at an equation for the probability of acceptance, using equation (10.2). This is useful for estimating the probability of accepting the offer for a customer with given values of the 12 predictors.[4]

Interpreting Results in Terms of Odds

Recall that the odds are given by

$$\text{Odds} \ = e^{\beta_0+\beta_1 x_1+\beta_2 x_2+\cdots+\beta_k x_k}.$$

At first let us return to the single predictor example, where we model a customer's acceptance of a personal loan offer as a function of his/her income:

$$\text{Odds} \ (\text{Personal Loan} = \text{Yes}) = e^{\beta_0+\beta_1\cdot Income}.$$

We can think of the model as a multiplicative model of odds. The odds that a customer with income zero will accept the loan is estimated by $e^{-6.535+(0.039)(0)} = 0.0017$. These are the *base-case odds*. In this example it is obviously economically meaningless to talk about a zero income; the value zero and the corresponding base-case odds could be meaningful, however, in the context of other predictors. The odds of accepting the loan with an income of \$100K will increase by a multiplicative factor of $e^{(0.039)(100)} = 50.5$ over the base case, so the odds that such a customer will accept the offer are $e^{-6.535+(0.039)(100)} = 0.088$.

To generalize this to the multiple-predictor case, consider the 12 predictors in the personal loan offer example. The odds of a customer accepting the offer as a function of the 12 predictors are given in (10.10).

Suppose that the value of Income, or in general x_1, is increased by one unit from x_1 to $x_1 + 1$, while the other predictors (denoted $x_2, \ldots, x_{12}$) are held at their current value. We get the odds ratio

$$\frac{\text{odds}(x_1 + 1, x_2, \ldots, x_{12})}{\text{odds}(x_1, \ldots x_{12})} = \frac{e^{\beta_0+\beta_1 (x_1+1)+\beta_2 x_2+\cdots+\beta_{12}x_{12}}}{e^{\beta_0+\beta_1 x_1+\beta_2 x_2+\cdots+\beta_{12}x_{12}}} = e^{\beta_1}.$$

This tells us that a single unit increase in x_1, holding $x_2, \ldots, x_{12}$ constant, is associated with an increase in the odds that a customer accepts the offer by a factor of e^{β_1}. In other words, β_1 is the multiplicative factor by which the odds (of belonging to class 1) increase when the value of x_1 is increased by 1 unit, *holding all other predictors constant*. If $\beta_1 < 0$, an increase in x_1 is associated with a decrease in the odds of belonging to class 1, whereas a positive value of β_1 is associated with an increase in the odds.

---

[4] If all q predictors are categorical, each having m_q categories, we need not compute probabilities/odds for each of the n observations. The number of different probabilities/odds is exactly $m_1 \times m_2 \times \cdots \times m_q$.

When a predictor is a dummy variable, the interpretation is technically the same but has a different practical meaning. For instance, the coefficient for CD was estimated from the data to be 3.469. Recall that the reference group is customers not holding a CD account. We interpret this coefficient as follows: $e^{3.469} = 32.105$ are the odds that a customer who has a CD account will accept the offer relative to a customer who does not have a CD account, holding all other factors constant. This means that customers who have CD accounts in Universal Bank are more likely to accept the offer than customers without a CD account (holding all other variables constant).

The advantage of reporting results in odds as opposed to probabilities is that statements such as those above are true for any value of x_1. Unless x_1 is a dummy variable, we cannot apply such statements about the effect of increasing x_1 by a single unit to probabilities. This is because the result depends on the actual value of x_1. So if we increase x_1 from, say, 3 to 4, the effect on p, the probability of belonging to class 1, will be different than if we increase x_1 from 30 to 31. In short, the change in the probability, p, for a unit increase in a particular predictor variable, while holding all other predictors constant, is not a constant—it depends on the specific values of the predictor variables. We therefore talk about probabilities only in the context of specific observations.

ODDS AND ODDS RATIOS

A common confusion is between odds and odds ratios. Since the odds are in fact a ratio (between the probability of belonging to class 1 and the probability of belonging to class 0), they are sometimes termed, erroneously, "odds ratios." However, odds ratios refer to the ratio of two odds! These are used to compare different classes of observations. For a categorical predictor, odds ratios are used to compare two categories. For example, we could compare loan offer acceptance for customers with professional education versus graduate education by looking at the ratio of odds of loan acceptance for customers with professional education divided by the odds of acceptance for customers with graduate education. This would yield an *odds ratio*. Ratios above 1 would indicate that the odds of acceptance for professionally educated customers are higher than for customers with graduate-level education.

10.3   EVALUATING CLASSIFICATION PERFORMANCE

The general measures of performance that were described in Chapter 5 are used to assess how well the logistic model does. Recall that there are several performance measures, the most popular being those based on the classification matrix (accuracy alone or combined with costs) and the lift chart. As in other classification methods, the goal is to find a model that accurately classifies observations to their class, using only the predictor information. A variant of this goal is to find a model that does a superior job of identifying the members of a particular class of interest (which might come at some cost to overall accuracy). Since the training data are used for selecting the model, we expect the model to perform quite well for those data, and therefore prefer to test its performance on the validation set. Recall that the data in the validation set were not involved in the model building, and thus we can use them to test the model's ability to classify data that it has not "seen" before.

To obtain the classification matrix from a logistic regression analysis, we use the estimated equation to predict the probability of class membership for each observation in the validation set, and use the cutoff value to decide on the class assignment of these observations. We then compare these classifications to the actual class memberships of these observations. In the Universal Bank case we use the estimated model in equation (10.9) to predict the probability of adoption in a validation set that contains 2000 customers (these data were not used in the modeling step). Technically, this is done by predicting the logit using the estimated model in equation (10.9) and then obtaining the probabilities p through the relation $p = e^{\text{logit}}/1 + e^{\text{logit}}$. We then compare these probabilities to our chosen cutoff value in order to classify each of the 2000 validation observations as acceptors or nonacceptors. XLMiner created the validation classification matrix automatically, and it is possible to obtain the detailed probabilities and classification for each observation. For example, Figure 10.4 shows a partial XLMiner output of scoring the validation set. It can be seen that the first four customers have a probability of accepting the offer that is lower than the cutoff of 0.5, and therefore they are classified as nonacceptors (0). The fifth customer's probability of acceptance is estimated by the model to exceed 0.5, and he or she is therefore classified as an acceptor (1), which in fact is a misclassification.

Another useful tool for assessing model classification performance is the lift (gains) chart (see Chapter 5). Figure 10.5(*a*) illustrates the lift chart obtained for the personal loan offer model using the validation set. The "lift" over the base curve indicates for a given number of cases (read on the *x* axis), the additional responders that you can identify by using the model. The same information is portrayed in in Figure 10.5(*b*): Taking the 10% of the records that are ranked by the model as "most probable 1's" yields 7.7 times as many 1's as would simply selecting 10% of the records at random.

Variable Selection

The next step includes searching for alternative models. As with multiple linear regression, we can build more complex models that reflect interactions between independent variables by including factors that are calculated from the interacting factors. For example, if we hypothesize that there is an interactive effect between income and family size, we should add an interaction

Data range ['Universal Bank.xls']'Data_Partition1'!$C$3019:$Q$5018

Back to Navigator

Cut off Prob.Val. for Success (Updatable)   **0.5**   (Updating the value here will NOT update value in summary report)

Row Id.	Predicted Class	Actual Class	Prob. for 1 (success)	Lcg odds	Age	Experience	Income	Family
2	0	0	2.1351E-05	-10.75439275	45	19	34	3
3	0	0	3.34564E-06	-12.60785033	39	15	11	1
7	0	0	0.015822384	-4.13038073	53	27	72	2
8	0	0	0.000216511	-8.437650808	50	24	22	1
11	1	0	0.567824439	0.272980386	65	39	105	4

FIGURE 10.4   SCORING THE VALIDATION DATA: XLMINER'S OUTPUT FOR THE FIRST FIVE CUSTOMERS OF UNIVERSAL BANK (BASED ON 12 PREDICTORS).

204

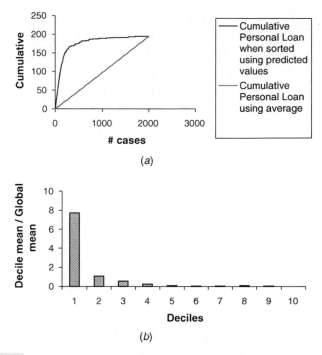

term of the form Income $\times$ Family. The choice among the set of alternative
models is guided primarily by performance on the validation data. For models
that perform roughly equally well, simpler models are generally preferred over
more complex models. Note also that performance on validation data may be
overly optimistic when it comes to predicting performance on data that have not
been exposed to the model at all. This is because when the validation data are used
to select a final model, we are selecting for how well the model performs with
those data and therefore may be incorporating some of the random idiosyncracies
of those data into the judgment about the best model. The model still may be the
best among those considered, but it will probably not do as well with the unseen
data. Therefore, one must consider practical issues such as costs of collecting
variables, error proneness, and model complexity in the selection of the final
model.

Impact of Single Predictors

As in multiple linear regression, for each predictor X_i we have an estimated
coefficient b_i and an associated standard error σ_i. The associated p-value indicates
the statistical significance of the predictor X_i, with very low p-values indicating a
statistically significant relationship between the predictor and the outcome (given

that the other predictors are accounted for), a relationship that is most likely not a result of chance. A statistically significant relationship, however, is not necessarily a *practically significant* one in which the predictor has great impact. If the sample is very large, the *p*-value will be very small simply because the chance uncertainty associated with a small sample is gone. We should also compare the odds of the different predictors, where we can see immediately which predictors have the most impact (given that the other predictors are accounted for) and which have the least impact.

10.4 EXAMPLE OF COMPLETE ANALYSIS: PREDICTING DELAYED FLIGHTS

Predicting flight delays would be useful to a variety of organizations: airport authorities, airlines, aviation authorities. At times, joint task forces have been formed to address the problem. Such an organization, if it were to provide on-going real-time assistance with flight delays, would benefit from some advance notice about flights that are likely to be delayed.

In this simplified illustration, we look at six predictors (see Table 10.1). The outcome of interest is whether the flight is delayed or not (*delayed* means more than 15 minutes late). Our data consist of all flights from the Washington, D.C., area into the New York City area during January 2004. The percent of delayed flights among these 2346 flights is 18%. The data were obtained from the Bureau of Transportation Statistics (available on the Web at www.transtats.bts.gov).

The goal is to predict accurately whether a new flight, not in this dataset, will be delayed or not. Our dependent variable is a binary variable called Delayed, coded as 1 for a delayed flight and 0 otherwise.

Other information that is available on the website, such as distance and arrival time, is irrelevant because we are looking at a certain route (distance, flight time, etc. should be approximately equal). A sample of the data for 20 flights is shown in Table 10.2.

TABLE 10.1	DESCRIPTION OF VARIABLES FOR FLIGHT DELAYS EXAMPLE
Day of Week	Coded as: 1 = Monday, 2 = Tuesday,..., 7 = Sunday
Departure Time	Broken down into 18 intervals between 6 AM and 10 PM
Origin	Three airport codes: DCA (Reagan National), IAD (Dulles), BWI (Baltimore–Washington Int'l)
Destination	Three airport codes: JFK (Kennedy), LGA (LaGuardia), EWR (Newark)
Carrier	Eight airline codes: CO (Continental), DH (Atlantic Coast), DL (Delta), MQ (American Eagle), OH (Comair), RU (Continental Express), UA (United), and US (USAirways)
Weather	Coded as 1 if there was a weather-related delay

TABLE 10.2	SAMPLE OF 20 FLIGHTS

Delayed	Carrier	Day of Week	Departure Time	Destination	Origin	Weather
0	DL	2	728	LGA	DCA	0
1	US	3	1600	LGA	DCA	0
0	DH	5	1242	EWR	IAD	0
0	US	2	2057	LGA	DCA	0
0	DH	3	1603	JFK	IAD	0
0	CO	6	1252	EWR	DCA	0
0	RU	6	1728	EWR	DCA	0
0	DL	5	1031	LGA	DCA	0
0	RU	6	1722	EWR	IAD	0
1	US	1	627	LGA	DCA	0
1	DH	2	1756	JFK	IAD	0
0	MQ	6	1529	JFK	DCA	0
0	US	6	1259	LGA	DCA	0
0	DL	2	1329	LGA	DCA	0
0	RU	2	1453	EWR	BWI	0
0	RU	5	1356	EWR	DCA	0
1	DH	7	2244	LGA	IAD	0
0	US	7	1053	LGA	DCA	0
0	US	2	1057	LGA	DCA	0
0	US	4	632	LGA	DCA	0

The number of flights in each cell for Thursday–Sunday flights is approximately double that of the number of Monday–Wednesday flights. The dataset includes four categorical variables: $X_1 = $ Origin, $X_2 = $ Carrier, $X_3 = $ Day Group (whether the flight was on Monday–Wednesday or Thursday–Sunday), and the response variable $Y = $ Flight Status (delayed or not delayed). In this example we have a binary response variable, or two classes. We start by looking at the pivot table for initial insight into the data (Table 10.3): It appears that more flights departing on Thursday–Sunday are delayed than those leaving on Monday–Wednesday. Also, the worst airport (in term of delays) seems to be IAD. The worst carrier, it

TABLE 10.3	NUMBER OF DELAYED FLIGHTS OUT OF WASHINGTON, D.C. AIRPORTS FOR FOUR CARRIERS BY DAY GROUP[a]

	Carrier				
Airport	Continental	Delta	Northwest	US Airways	Total
BWI	**50** 38	**11** 54	**27** 71	**0** 59	**22** 56
DCA	**46** 47	**22** 74	**43** 57	**18** 54	**26** 60
IAD	**0** 80	**18** 71	**57** 58	**60** 67	**34** 68
Total	**47** 49	**18** 69	**41** 60	**20** 56	**27** 60

[a] Bold numbers are delayed flights on Monday–Wednesday, regular numbers are delayed flights on Thursday–Sunday.

appears, depends on the day group: on Monday–Wedneday Continental seems to have the most delays, whereas on Thursday–Sunday Delta has the most delays.

Our main goal is to find a model that can obtain accurate classifications of new flights based on their predictor information. In some cases we might be interested in finding a certain percentage of flights that are most/least likely to get delayed. In other cases we may be interested in finding out which factors are associated with a delay (not only in this sample but in the entire population of flights on this route), and for those factors we would like to quantify these effects. A logistic regression model can be used for all these goals.

Data Preprocessing

We first create dummy variables for each of the categorical predictors: 2 dummies for the departure airport (with IAD as the reference airport), 2 for the arrival airport (with JFK as the reference), 7 for the carrier (with USAirways as the reference carrier), 6 for the day (with Sunday as the reference group), 15 for the departure hour (hourly intervals between 6 AM and 10 PM), blocked into hours. This yields a total of 33 dummies. In addition, we have a single dummy for weather delays. This is a very large number of predictors. Some initial investigation and knowledge from airline experts led us to aggregate the day of the week in a more compact way: It is known that delays are much more prevalent on this route on Sundays and Mondays. We therefore use a single dummy that signifies whether or not it is a Sunday or a Monday (denoted by 1).

We then partition the data using a 60% : 40% ratio into training and validation sets. We use the training set to fit a model and the validation set to assess the model's performance.

Model Fitting and Estimation

The estimated model with 28 predictors is given in Figure 10.6. Notice how negative coefficients in the logit model (the Coefficient column) translate into odds coefficients lower than 1, and positive logit coefficients translate into odds coefficients larger than 1.

Model Interpretation

The coefficient for Arrival Airport JFK is estimated from the data to be -0.67. Recall that the reference group is LGA. We interpret this coefficient as follows: $e^{-0.67} = 0.51$ are the odds of a flight arriving at JFK being delayed relative to a flight to LGA being delayed (= the base-case odds), holding all other factors constant. This means that flights to LGA are more likely to be delayed than those to JFK (holding everything else constant). If we take into account statistical significance of the coefficients, we see that in general the departure airport is not

Input variables	Coefficient	Std. Error	p-value	Odds
Constant term	-2.76648855	0.60903645	0.00000556	*
Weather	16.94781685	472.3040772	0.97137541	22926812
ORIGIN_BWI	0.31663841	0.407509	0.43715307	1.37250626
ORIGIN_DCA	-0.52621925	0.37920129	0.1652271	0.59083456
DEP_TIME_BLK_0700-0759	0.17635399	0.52038968	0.73469388	1.19286025
DEP_TIME_BLK_0800-0859	0.37122276	0.4879483	0.44678667	1.44950593
DEP_TIME_BLK_0900-0959	-0.2891154	0.61024719	0.6356656	0.74892575
DEP_TIME_BLK_1000-1059	-0.84254718	0.65849793	0.20072155	0.4306123
DEP_TIME_BLK_1100-1159	0.26919952	0.62188113	0.66510242	1.30891633
DEP_TIME_BLK_1200-1259	0.39577994	0.47712085	0.40681183	1.48554242
DEP_TIME_BLK_1300-1359	0.23689635	0.49711299	0.63368666	1.26730978
DEP_TIME_BLK_1400-1459	0.94953001	0.4257178	0.02571949	2.58449459
DEP_TIME_BLK_1500-1559	0.81428736	0.47320139	0.08528619	2.25756645
DEP_TIME_BLK_1600-1659	0.73656398	0.46096623	0.11007198	2.08874631
DEP_TIME_BLK_1700-1759	0.80683631	0.42013136	0.05480258	2.24080753
DEP_TIME_BLK_1800-1859	0.65816337	0.56922781	0.2475834	1.93124211
DEP_TIME_BLK_1900-1959	1.40413988	0.47974923	0.00342446	4.07202291
DEP_TIME_BLK_2000-2059	0.94785261	0.63308424	0.1343417	2.580163
DEP_TIME_BLK_2100-2159	0.76115495	0.45146817	0.09180449	2.14074731
DEST_EWR	-0.33785093	0.31752595	0.28732395	0.7133016
DEST_JFK	-0.66931868	0.2657896	0.01179471	0.5120573
CARRIER_CO	1.81500936	0.53502011	0.0006928	6.14113379
CARRIER_DH	1.25616693	0.52265555	0.016242	3.51193428
CARRIER_DL	0.41380161	0.33544913	0.21736139	1.51255703
CARRIER_MQ	1.73093832	0.32989427	0.00000015	5.64594936
CARRIER_OH	0.15529965	0.85175836	0.8553251	1.16800785
CARRIER_RU	1.27398086	0.51098496	0.01266023	3.57505608
CARRIER_UA	-0.59911883	1.17384589	0.60977846	0.54929543
Sun-Mon	0.53890741	0.16421914	0.00103207	1.71413302

FIGURE 10.6   **ESTIMATED LOGISTIC REGRESSION MODEL FOR DELAYED FLIGHTS (BASED ON THE TRAINING SET)**

associated with the chance of delays. For carriers, it appears that four carriers are significantly different from the base carrier (USAirways), with odds of 3.5–6.6 of delays relative to the other airlines. Weather has an enormous coefficient, which is not statistically significant. This is due to the fact that weather delays occurred only on two days (January 26 and 27), and those affected only some of the flights. Flights leaving on Sunday or Monday have, on average, odds of 1.7 of delays relative to other days of the week. Also, odds of delays appear to change over the course of the day, with the most noticeable difference between 7 and 8 PM and the reference category, 6–7 AM.

Model Performance

How should we measure the performance of models? One possible measure is "percent of flights correctly classified." Accurate classification can be obtained from the classification matrix for the validation data. The classification matrix gives a sense of the classification accuracy and what type of misclassification is more frequent. From the classification matrix and error rates in Figure 10.7 it can be seen that the model does better in classifying nondelayed flights correctly and is less accurate in classifying flights that were delayed. (*Note*: The same pattern appears in the classification matrix for the training data, so it is not surprising to see it emerge for new data.) If there is a nonsymmetric cost structure such that one type of misclassification is more costly than the other, the cutoff value can be selected to minimize the cost. Of course, this tweaking should be carried out on the training data and assessed only using the validation data.

In most conceivable situations, it is likely that the purpose of the model will be to identify those flights most likely to be delayed so that resources can be directed toward either reducing the delay or mitigating its effects. Air traffic controllers might work to open up additional air routes, or allocate more controllers to a specific area for a short time. Airlines might bring on personnel to rebook passengers and to activate standby flight crews and aircraft. Hotels might allocate space for stranded travellers. In all cases, the resources available are going to be limited and might vary over time and from organization to organization. In this situation, the most useful model would provide an ordering of flights by their probability of delay, letting the model users decide how far down that list to go in taking action. Therefore, model lift is a useful measure of performance— as you move down that list of flights, ordered by their delay probability, how much better does the model do in predicting delay than would a naive model which is simply the average delay rate for all flights? From the lift curve for the validation data (Figure 10.7) we see that our model is superior to the baseline (simple random selection of flights).

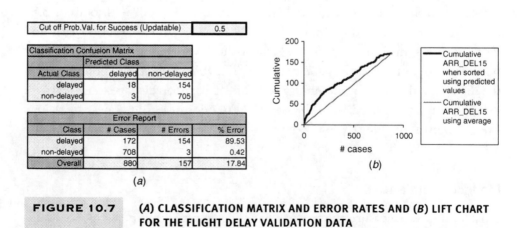

(a)

(b)

FIGURE 10.7   **(*A*) CLASSIFICATION MATRIX AND ERROR RATES AND (*B*) LIFT CHART FOR THE FLIGHT DELAY VALIDATION DATA**

Variable Selection

From the coefficient table for the flights delay model, it appears that several of the variables might be dropped or coded differently. We further explore alternative models by examining pivot tables and charts and using variable selection procedures. First, we find that most carriers depart from a single airport: For those that depart from all three airports, the delay rates are similar regardless of airport. This means that there are multiple combinations of carrier and departure airport that do not include any flights. We therefore drop the departure airport distinction and find that the model performance and fit is not harmed. We also drop the destination airport for a practical reason: Not all carriers fly to all airports. Our model would then be invalid for prediction in nonexistent combinations of carrier and destination airport. We also try regrouping the carriers and hour of day into fewer categories that are more distinguishable with respect to delays. Finally, we apply subset selection. Our final model includes only seven predictors and has the advantage of being more parsimonious. It does, however, include coefficients that are not statistically significant because our goal is prediction accuracy rather than model fit. Also, some of these variables have a practical importance (e.g., weather) and are therefore retained. Figure 10.8 displays the estimated model, with its goodness-of-fit measures, the training and validation classification matrices and error rates, and the lift charts. It can be seen that this model competes well with the larger model in terms of accurate classification and lift.

We therefore conclude with a seven-predictor model that required only the knowledge of the carrier, the day of week, the hour of the day, and whether it is likely that there will be a delay due to weather. The last piece of information is of course not known in advance, but we kept it in our model for purposes of interpretation. The impact of the other factors is estimated while holding weather constant [i.e., (approximately) comparing days with weather delays to days without weather delays]. If the aim is to predict in advance whether a particular flight will be delayed, a model without Weather should be used. To conclude, we can summarize that the highest chance of a nondelayed flight from DC to New York, based on the data from January 2004, would be a flight on Monday–Friday during the late morning hours, on Delta, United, USAirways, or Atlantic Coast Airlines. And clearly, good weather is advantageous!

10.5 APPENDIX: LOGISTIC REGRESSION FOR PROFILING

The presentation of logistic regression in this chapter has been primarily from a data mining perspective, where classification is the goal and performance is evaluated by reviewing results with a validation sample. For reference, some key concepts of a classical statistical perspective, are included below.

The Regression Model

Input variables	Coefficient	Std. Error	p-value	Odds
Constant term	-1.76942575	0.11373349	0	*
Weather	16.77862358	479.4146118	0.97208124	19358154
DEP_TIME_BLK_0600-0659	-0.62896502	0.36761174	0.08709048	0.53314334
DEP_TIME_BLK_0900-0959	-1.26741421	0.47863296	0.00809724	0.28155872
DEP_TIME_BLK_1000-1059	-1.37123489	0.52464402	0.00895813	0.25379336
DEP_TIME_BLK_1300-1359	-0.6303032	0.3188065	0.04803356	0.53243035
Sun-Mon	0.52237105	0.15871418	0.00099736	1.68602061
Carrier_CO_OH_MQ_RU	0.68775123	0.15049717	0.00000488	1.98923719

Residual df	1313
Std. Dev. Estimate	1186.54834
% Success in training data	19.37925814
# Iterations used	16
Multiple R-squared	0.08657298

Training Data Scoring - Summary Report

Cut off Prob.Val. for Success (Updatable)	0.5

Classification Confusion Matrix		
	Predicted Class	
Actual Class	1	0
1	19	237
0	0	1065

Error Report			
Class	# Cases	# Errors	% Error
1	256	237	92.58
0	1065	0	0.00
Overall	1321	237	17.94

Lift Chart (training dataset)

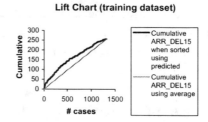

Validation Data Scoring - Summary Report

Cut off Prob.Val. for Success (Updatable)	0.5

Classification Confusion Matrix		
	Predicted Class	
Actual Class	1	0
1	13	159
0	0	708

Error Report			
Class	# Cases	# Errors	% Error
1	172	159	92.44
0	708	0	0.00
Overall	880	159	18.07

Lift Chart (validation dataset)

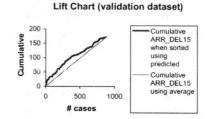

FIGURE 10.8   OUTPUT FOR LOGISTIC REGRESSION MODEL WITH ONLY SEVEN PREDICTORS.

Appendix A: Why Linear Regression Is Inappropriate for a Categorical Response

Now that you have seen how logistic regression works, we explain why linear regression is not suitable. Technically, one can apply a multiple linear regression model to this problem, treating the dependent variable Y as continuous. Of course, Y must be coded numerically (e.g., 1 for customers who did accept the loan offer and 0 for customers who did not accept it). Although software will yield an output that at first glance may seem usual (e.g., Figure 10.9), a closer look will reveal several anomalies:

1. Using the model to predict Y for each of the observations (or classify them) yields predictions that are not necessarily 0 or 1.

The Regression Model

Input variables	Coefficient	Std. Error	p-value	SS
Constant term	-0.23462872	0.01328709	0	27.26533127
Income	0.00318939	0.00009888	0	67.95861816
Family	0.03294198	0.00383914	0	4.53180361
CD Account	0.27016363	0.01788521	0	13.18045044

ANOVA

Source	df	SS	MS	F-statistic	p-value
Regression	3	85.67087221	28.5569574	494.364771	5.9883E-261
Error	2996	173.063797	0.057764952		
Total	2999	258.7346692			

FIGURE 10.9 **OUTPUT FOR MULTIPLE LINEAR REGRESSION MODEL OF PERSONAL LOAN ON THREE PREDICTORS.**

2. A look at the histogram or probability plot of the residuals reveals that the assumption that the dependent variable (or residuals) follows a normal distribution is violated. Clearly, if Y takes only the values 0 and 1, it cannot be normally distributed. In fact, a more appropriate distribution for the number of 1's in the dataset is the binomial distribution with $p = P(Y = 1)$.

3. The assumption that the variance of Y is constant across all classes is violated. Since Y follows a binomial distribution, its variance is $np(1 - p)$. This means that the variance will be higher for classes where the probability of adoption, p, is near 0.5 than where it is near 0 or 1.

Below you will find partial output from running a multiple linear regression of Personal Loan (PL, coded as PL = 1 for customers who accepted the loan offer and PL = 0 otherwise) on three of the predictors.
The estimated model is

$$\widehat{PL} = -0.2346 + 0.0032 \text{ Income} + 0.0329 \text{ Family} + 0.27016363 \text{ CD.}$$

To predict whether a new customer will accept the personal loan offer (PL = 1) or not (PL = 0), we input the information on its values for these three predictors. For example, we would predict the loan offer acceptance of a customer with an annual income of \$50K with two family members who does not hold CD accounts in Universal Bank to be $-0.2346 + (0.0032)(50) + (0.0329)(2) = -0.009$. Clearly, this is not a valid "loan acceptance" value. Furthermore, the histogram of the residuals (Figure 10.10) reveals that the residuals are probably not normally distributed. Therefore, our estimated model is based on violated assumptions.

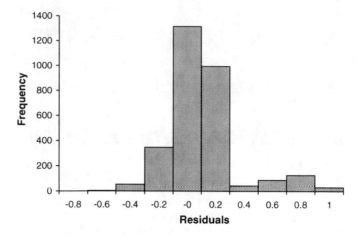

FIGURE 10.10 HISTOGRAM OF RESIDUALS FROM A MULTIPLE LINEAR REGRESSION MODEL OF LOAN ACCEPTANCE ON THE THREE PREDICTORS. THIS SHOWS THAT THE RESIDUALS DO NOT FOLLOW THE NORMAL DISTRIBUTION THAT THE MODEL ASSUMES.

Appendix B: Evaluating Goodness of Fit

When the purpose of the analysis is profiling (i.e., explaining the differences between the classes in terms of predictor values) we want to go beyond simply assessing how well the model classifies new data, and also assess how well the model fits the data it was trained on. For example, if we are interested in characterizing loan offer acceptors versus nonacceptors in terms of income, education, and so on, we want to find a model that fits the data best. However, since overfitting is a major danger in classification, a "too good" fit of the model to the training data should raise suspicions. In addition, questions regarding the usefulness of specific predictors can arise even in the context of classification models. We therefore mention some of the popular measures that are used to assess how well the model fits the data. Clearly, we look at the training set in order to evaluate goodness of fit.

Overall Fit As in multiple linear regression, we first evaluate the overall fit of the model to the data before looking at single predictors. We ask: Is this group of predictors better than a simple naive model for explaining the different classes[5]?

The deviance D is a statistic that measures overall goodness of fit. It is similar to the concept of sum of squared errors (SSE) in the case of least-squares estimation (used in linear regression). We compare the deviance of our model, D (called Std Dev Estimate in XLMiner, e.g., in Figure 10.11), to the deviance

---

[5] In a naive model, no explanatory variables exist and each observation is classified as belonging to the majority class.

Residual df	2987
Std. Dev. Estimate	652.5175781
% Success in training data	9.533333333
# Iterations used	11
Multiple R-squared	0.65443069

FIGURE 10.11   **MEASURES OF GOODNESS OF FIT FOR UNIVERSAL BANK TRAINING DATA WITH A 12-PREDICTOR MODEL**

of the naive model, D_0. If the reduction in deviance is statistically significant (as indicated by a low p-value[6] or in XLMiner by a high *multiple R^2*), we consider our model to provide a good overall fit. XLMiner's *Multiple-R-Squared* measure is computed as $(D_0 - D)/D_0$. Given the model deviance and the multiple R^2, we can compute the null deviance by $D_0 = D/(1 - R^2)$.

Finally, the classification matrix and lift chart for the *training data* (Figure 10.12) give a sense of how accurately the model classifies the data. If the model fits the data well, we expect it to classify these data accurately into their actual classes.

Appendix C: Logistic Regression for More Than Two Classes

The logistic model for a binary response can be extended for more than two classes. Suppose that there are m classes. Using a logistic regression model, for each observation we would have m probabilities of belonging to each of the m classes. Since the m probabilities must add up to 1, we need estimate only $m - 1$ probabilities.

Ordinal Classes   Ordinal classes are classes that have a meaningful order. For example, in stock recommendations, the three classes *buy*, *hold*, and *sell* can be treated as ordered. As a simple rule, if classes can be numbered in a meaningful way, we consider them ordinal. When the number of classes is large (typically, more than 5), we can treat the dependent variable as continuous and perform multiple linear regression. When $m = 2$, the logistic model described above is used. We therefore need an extension of the logistic regression for a small number of ordinal classes ($3 \leq m \leq 5$). There are several ways to extend the binary class case. Here we describe the *proportional odds* or *cumulative logit method*. For other methods, see Hosmer and Lemeshow (2000).

---

[6] The difference between the deviance of a naive model and deviance of the model at hand approximately follows a chi-squared distribution with k degrees of freedom, where k is the number of predictors in the model at hand. Therefore, to get the p-value, compute the difference between the deviances (d) and then look up the probability that a chi-squared variable with k degrees of freedom is larger than d. This can be done using =CHIDIST(d, k) in Excel.

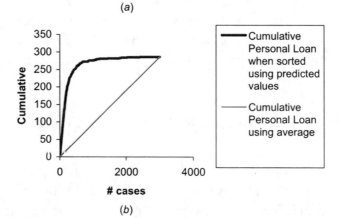

Cut off Prob.Val. for Success (Updatable)	0.5

Classification Confusion Matrix

	Predicted Class	
Actual Class	1	0
1	201	85
0	25	2689

Error Report

Class	# Cases	# Errors	% Error
1	286	85	29.72
0	2714	25	0.92
Overall	3000	110	3.67

(a)

(b)

FIGURE 10.12 **(A) CLASSIFICATION MATRIX AND (B) LIFT CHART FOR TRAINING DATA FOR UNIVERSAL BANK TRAINING DATA WITH 12 PREDICTORS**

For simplicity of interpretation and computation, we look at *cumulative* probabilities of class membership. For example, in the stock recommendations we have $m = 3$ classes. Let us denote them by $1 =$ buy, $2 =$ hold, and $3 =$ sell. The probabilities that are estimated by the model are $P(Y \leq 1)$, (the probability of a buy recommendation) and $P(Y \leq 2)$ (the probability of a buy or hold recommendation). The three noncumulative probabilities of class membership can easily be recovered from the two cumulative probabilities:

$$P(Y = 1) = P(Y \leq 1),$$

$$P(Y = 2) = P(Y \leq 2) - P(Y \leq 1),$$

$$P(Y = 3) = 1 - P(Y \leq 2).$$

Next, we want to model each logit as a function of the predictors. Corresponding to each of the $m - 1$ cumulative probabilities is a logit. In our example we would have

$$\text{logit(buy)} = \log \frac{P(Y \leq 1)}{1 - P(Y \leq 1)},$$

$$\text{logit(buy or hold)} = \log \frac{P(Y \leq 2)}{1 - P(Y \leq 2)}.$$

Each of the logits is then modeled as a linear function of the predictors (as in the two-class case). If in the stock recommendations we have a single predictor x, we have two equations:

$$\text{logit(buy)} = \alpha_0 + \beta_1 x,$$

$$\text{logit(buy or hold)} = \beta_0 + \beta_1 x.$$

This means that both lines have the same slope (β_1) but different intercepts. Once the coefficients $\alpha_0, \beta_0, \beta_1$ are estimated, we can compute the class membership probabilities by rewriting the logit equations in terms of probabilities. For the three-class case, for example, we would have

$$P(Y = 1) = P(Y \leq 1) = \frac{1}{1 + e^{-(a_0 + b_1 x)}},$$

$$P(Y = 2) = P(Y \leq 2) - P(Y \leq 1) = \frac{1}{1 + e^{-(b_0 + b_1 x)}} - \frac{1}{1 + e^{-(a_0 + b_1 x)}},$$

$$P(Y = 3) = 1 - P(Y \leq 2) = 1 - \frac{1}{1 + e^{-(b_0 + b_1 x)}},$$

where a_0, b_0, and b_1 are the estimates obtained from the training set.

For each observation we now have the estimated probabilities that it belongs to each of the classes. In our example, each stock would have three probabilities: for a buy recommendation, a hold recommendation, and a sell recommendation. The last step is to classify the observation into one of the classes. This is done by assigning it to the class with the highest membership probability. So if a stock had estimated probabilities $P(Y = 1) = 0.2$, $P(Y = 2) = 0.3$, and $P(Y = 3) = 0.5$, we would classify it as getting a sell recommendation.

This procedure is currently not implemented in XLMiner. Other non-Excel-based packages that do have such an implementation are Minitab and SAS.

Nominal Classes   When the classes cannot be ordered and are simply different from one another, we are in the case of nominal classes. An example is the choice between several brands of cereal. A simple way to verify that the classes are nominal is when it makes sense to tag them as A, B, C, ..., and the assignment of letters to classes does not matter. For simplicity, let us assume that there are $m = 3$ brands of cereal that consumers can choose from (assuming that each consumer chooses one). Then we estimate the probabilities $P(Y = A)$, $P(Y = B)$, and $P(Y = C)$. As before, if we know two of the probabilities, the third probability is determined. We therefore use one of the classes as the reference class. Let us use C as the reference brand.

The goal, once again, is to model the class membership as a function of predictors. So in the cereals example we might want to predict which cereal will be chosen if we know the cereal's price, x.

Next, we form $m - 1$ pseudologit equations that are linear in the predictors. In our example we would have

$$\text{logit}(A) = \log \frac{P(Y = A)}{P(Y = C)} = \alpha_0 + \alpha_1 x,$$

$$\text{logit}(B) = \log \frac{P(Y = B)}{P(Y = C)} = \beta_0 + \beta_1 x.$$

Once the four coefficients are estimated from the training set, we can estimate the class membership probabilities[7]:

$$P(Y = A) = \frac{e^{a_0 + a_1 x}}{1 + e^{a_0 + a_1 x} + e^{b_0 + b_1 x}},$$

$$P(Y = B) = \frac{e^{b_0 + b_1 x}}{1 + e^{a_0 + a_1 x} + e^{b_0 + b_1 x}},$$

$$P(Y = C) = 1 - P(Y = A) - P(Y = B),$$

where a_0, a_1, b_0, and b_1 are the coefficient estimates obtained from the training set. Finally, an observation is assigned to the class that has the highest probability.

---

[7] From the two logit equations we see that $\begin{aligned} P(Y = A) &= P(Y = C)e^{a_0 + a_1 x}, \\ P(Y = B) &= P(Y = C)e^{b_0 + b_1 x}, \end{aligned}$ and since $P(Y = A) +$
$P(Y = B) + P(Y = C) = 1$, we have $\begin{aligned} P(Y = C) &= 1 - P(Y = C)e^{a_0 + a_1 x} - P(Y = C)e^{b_0 + b_1 x} \\ &> P(Y = C) = \frac{1}{e^{a_0 + a_1 x} + e^{b_0 + b_1 x}}. \end{aligned}$
By plugging this form into the two equations above it, we also obtain the membership probabilities in classes A and B.

PROBLEMS ▨▨▨▨▨▨▨▨▨▨▨▨▨▨▨▨▨▨▨▨▨▨▨▨▨ ▪

10.1 Financial Condition of Banks. The file Banks.xls includes data on a sample of 20 banks. The Financial Condition column records the judgment of an expert on the financial condition of each bank. This dependent variable takes one of two possible values—*weak* or *strong*—according to the financial condition of the bank. The predictors are two ratios used in the financial analysis of banks: TotLns&Lses/Assets is the ratio of total loans and leases to total assets and TotExp/Assets is the ratio of total expenses to total assets. The target is to use the two ratios for classifying the financial condition of a new bank.

Run a logistic regression model (on the entire dataset) that models the status of a bank as a function of the two financial measures provided. Specify the *success* class as weak (this is similar to creating a dummy that is 1 for financially weak banks and 0 otherwise), and use the default cutoff value of 0.5.

a. Write the estimated equation that associates the financial condition of a bank with its two predictors in three formats:

i. The logit as a function of the predictors

ii. The odds as a function of the predictors

iii. The probability as a function of the predictors

b. Consider a new bank whose total loans and leases/assets ratio = 0.6 and total expenses/assets ratio = 0.11. From your logistic regression model, estimate the following four quantities for this bank (use Excel to do all the intermediate calculations; show your final answers to four decimal places): the logit, the odds, the probability of being financially weak, and the classification of the bank.

c. The cutoff value of 0.5 is used in conjunction with the probability of being financially weak. Compute the threshold that should be used if we want to make a classification based on the odds of being financially weak, and the threshold for the corresponding logit.

d. Interpret the estimated coefficient for the total loans & leases to total assets ratio (TotLns&Lses/Assets) in terms of the odds of being financially weak.

e. When a bank that is in poor financial condition is misclassified as financially strong, the misclassification cost is much higher than when a financially strong bank is misclassified as weak. To minimize the expected cost of misclassification, should the cutoff value for classification (which is currently at 0.5) be increased or decreased?

10.2 Identifying Good System Administrators. A management consultant is studying the roles played by experience and training in a system administrator's ability to complete a set of tasks in a specified amount of time. In particular, she is interested in discriminating between administrators who are able to complete given tasks within a specified time and those who are not. Data are collected on the performance of 75 randomly selected administrators. They are stored in the file SystemAdministrators.xls.

The variable Experience measures months of full-time system administrator experience, while Training measures the number of relevant training credits. The dependent variable Completed is either Yes or No, according to whether or not the administrator completed the tasks.

a. Create a scatterplot of Experience versus Training using color or symbol to differentiate programmers who complete the task from those who did not complete it. Which predictor(s) appear(s) potentially useful for classifying task completion?

b. Run a logistic regression model with both predictors using the entire dataset as training data. Among those who complete the task, what is the percentage of programmers who are incorrectly classified as failing to complete the task?

c. To decrease the percentage in part (c), should the cutoff probability be increased or decreased?

d. How much experience must be accumulated by a programmer with 4 years of training before his or her estimated probability of completing the task exceeds 50%?

10.3 **Sales of Riding Mowers.** A company that manufactures riding mowers wants to identify the best sales prospects for an intensive sales campaign. In particular, the manufacturer is interested in classifying households as prospective owners or nonowners on the basis of Income (in $1000s) and Lot Size (in 1000 ft^2). The marketing expert looked at a random sample of 24 households, given in the file RidingMowers.xls. Use all the data to fit a logistic regression of ownership on the two predictors.

a. What percentage of households in the study were owners of a riding mower?

b. Create a scatterplot of Income versus Lot Size using color or symbol to differentiate owners from nonowners. From the scatterplot, which class seems to have the higher average income, owners or nonowners?

c. Among nonowners, what is the percentage of households classified correctly?

d. To increase the percentage of correctly classified nonowners, should the cutoff probability be increased or decreased?

e. What are the odds that a household with a $60K income and a lot size of 20,000 ft^2 is an owner?

f. What is the classification of a household with a $60K income and a lot size of 20,000 ft^2?

g. What is the minimum income that a household with 16,000 ft^2 lot size should have before it is classified as an owner?

10.4 **Competitive Auctions on eBay.com.** The file eBayAuctions.xls contains information on 1972 auctions transacted on eBay.com during May–June 2004. The goal is to use these data to build a model that will distinguish competitive auctions from noncompetitive ones. A competitive auction is defined as an auction with at least two bids placed on the item being auctioned. The data include variables that describe the item (auction category), the seller (his or her eBay rating), and the auction terms that the seller selected (auction duration, opening price, currency, day of week of auction close). In addition, we have the price at which the auction closed. The goal is to predict whether or not the auction will be competitive.

Data Preprocessing. Create dummy variables for the categorical predictors. These include Category (18 categories), Currency (USD, GBP, euro), EndDay (Monday–Sunday), and Duration (1, 3, 5, 7, or 10 days). Split the data into training and validation datasets using a 60% : 40% ratio.

a. Create pivot tables for the average of the binary dependent variable (Competitive?) as a function of the various categorical variables (use the original variables, not the dummies). Use the information in the tables to reduce the number of dummies that will be used in the model. For example, categories that appear most similar with respect to the distribution of competitive auctions could be combined.

b. Run a logistic model with all predictors with a cutoff of 0.5. To remain within the limitation of 30 predictors, combine some of the categories of categorical predictors.

c. If we want to predict at the start of an auction whether it will be competitive, we cannot use the information on the closing price. Run a logistic model with all predictors as above, excluding price. How does this model compare to the full model with respect to accurate prediction?

d. Interpret the meaning of the coefficient for closing price. Does closing price have a practical significance? Is it statistically significant for predicting competitiveness of auctions? (Use a 10% significance level.)

e. Use stepwise selection and an exhaustive search to find the model with the best fit to the training data. Which predictors are used?

f. Use stepwise selection and an exhaustive search to find the model with the lowest predictive error rate (use the validation data). Which predictors are used?

g. What is the danger in the best predictive model that you found?

h. Explain why the best-fitting model and the best predictive models are the same or different.

i. If the major objective is accurate classification, what cutoff value should be used?

j. Based on these data, what auction settings set by the seller (duration, opening price, ending day, currency) would you recommend as being most likely to lead to a competitive auction?

CHAPTER 13

Association Rules

In this chapter we describe the unsupervised learning methods of association rules (also called "affinity analysis"), where the goal is to identify item clusterings in transaction-type databases. Association rule discovery is popular in marketing, where it is called "market basket analysis" and is aimed at discovering which groups of products tend to be purchased together. We describe the two-stage process of rule generation and then assessment of rule strength to choose a subset. We describe the popular rule-generating Apriori algorithm and then criteria for judging the strength of rules. We also discuss issues related to the required data format and nonautomated methods for condensing the list of generated rules. The entire process is illustrated in a numerical example.

13.1 INTRODUCTION

Put simply, association rules, or *affinity analysis*, constitute a study of "what goes with what." For example, a medical researcher wants to learn what symptoms go with what confirmed diagnoses. This method is also called *market basket analysis* because it originated with the study of customer transactions databases to determine dependencies between purchases of different items.

13.2 DISCOVERING ASSOCIATION RULES IN TRANSACTION DATABASES

The availability of detailed information on customer transactions has led to the development of techniques that automatically look for associations between items

Data Mining for Business Intelligence, By Galit Shmueli, Nitin R. Patel, and Peter C. Bruce
Copyright © 2010 John Wiley & Sons Inc.

263

that are stored in the database. An example is data collected using bar code scanners in supermarkets. Such *market basket databases* consist of a large number of transaction records. Each record lists all items bought by a customer on a single-purchase transaction. Managers would be interested to know if certain groups of items are consistently purchased together. They could use these data for store layouts to place items optimally with respect to each other, or they could use such information for cross selling, for promotions, for catalog design, and to identify customer segments based on buying patterns. Association rules provide information of this type in the form of "if–then" statements. These rules are computed from the data; unlike the if–then rules of logic, association rules are probabilistic in nature.

Such rules are commonly encountered in online *recommendation systems* (or *recommender systems*), where customers examining an item or items for possible purchase are shown other items that are often purchased in conjunction with the first item(s). The display from Amazon.com's online shopping system illustrates the application of rules such as this. In the example shown in Figure 13.1, a

Bound Away
Last Train Home
★★★★★   (2 customer reviews)
More about this product

- -

List Price: $16.98
   Price: $16.98 & eligible for **FREE Super Saver Shipping** on orders over $25. Details

Availability: In Stock.
To ensure delivery by December 22, choose FREE Super Saver Shipping. See more on holiday shipping. Ships from and sold by **Amazon.com**. Gift-wrap available.

Want it delivered Tuesday, December 5?   Order it in the next 9 hours and 5 minutes, and choose **One-Day Shipping** at checkout. See details

44 used & new available from $8.99

See larger image
Share your own customer images

Better Together

Buy this album with Time and Water ~ Last Train Home today!
Buy Together Today: $33.96

 +    Buy both now!

FIGURE 13.1   **RECOMMENDATIONS BASED ON ASSOCIATION RULES**

TABLE 13.1   **TRANSACTIONS FOR PURCHASES OF DIFFERENT-COLORED CELLULAR PHONE FACEPLATES**

Transaction	Faceplate	Colors	Purchased
1	red	white	green
2	white	orange	
3	white	blue	
4	red	white	orange
5	red	blue	
6	white	blue	
7	white	orange	
8	red	white	blue	green
9	red	white	blue	
10	yellow		

purchaser of Last Train Home's *Bound Away* audio CD is shown the other CDs most frequently purchased by other Amazon purchasers of this CD.

We introduce a simple artificial example and use it throughout the chapter to demonstrate the concepts, computations, and steps of affinity analysis. We end by applying affinity analysis to a more realistic example of book purchases.

Example 1: Synthetic Data on Purchases of Phone Faceplates

A store that sells accessories for cellular phones runs a promotion on faceplates. Customers who purchase multiple faceplates from a choice of six different colors get a discount. The store managers, who would like to know what colors of faceplates customers are likely to purchase together, collected the transaction database as shown in Table 13.1.

13.3 GENERATING CANDIDATE RULES

The idea behind association rules is to examine all possible rules between items in an if–then format and select only those that are most likely to be indicators of true dependence. We use the term *antecedent* to describe the "if" part, and *consequent* to describe the "then" part. In association analysis, the antecedent and consequent are sets of items (called *item sets*) that are disjoint (do not have any items in common).

Returning to the phone faceplate purchase example, one example of a possible rule is "if red, then white," meaning that if a red faceplate is purchased, a white one is, too. Here the antecedent is *red* and the consequent is *white*. The antecedent and consequent each contain a single item in this case. Another possible rule is "if red and white, then green." Here the antecedent includes the item set {*red, white*} and the consequent is {*green*}.

The first step in affinity analysis is to generate all the rules that would be candidates for indicating associations between items. Ideally, we might want to look at all possible combinations of items in a database with p distinct items (in the phone faceplate example, $p = 6$). This means finding all combinations of single items, pairs of items, triplets of items, and so on in the transactions database. However, generating all these combinations requires a long computation time that grows exponentially in k. A practical solution is to consider only combinations that occur with higher frequency in the database. These are called *frequent item sets*.

Determining what consists of a frequent item set is related to the concept of *support*. The support of a rule is simply the number of transactions that include both the antecedent and consequent item sets. It is called a support because it measures the degree to which the data "support" the validity of the rule. The support is sometimes expressed as a percentage of the total number of records in the database. For example, the support for the item set {red,white} in the phone faceplate example is 4 ($100 \times \frac{4}{10} = 40\%$).

What constitutes a frequent item set is therefore defined as an item set that has a support that exceeds a selected minimum support, determined by the user.

The Apriori Algorithm

Several algorithms have been proposed for generating frequent item sets, but the classic algorithm is the *Apriori algorithm* of Agrawal et al. (1993). The key idea of the algorithm is to begin by generating frequent item sets with just one item (one-item sets) and to recursively generate frequent item sets with two items, then with three items, and so on until we have generated frequent item sets of all sizes.

It is easy to generate frequent one-item sets. All we need to do is to count, for each item, how many transactions in the database include the item. These transaction counts are the supports for the one-item sets. We drop one-item sets that have support below the desired minimum support to create a list of the frequent one-item sets.

To generate frequent two-item sets, we use the frequent one-item sets. The reasoning is that if a certain one-item set did not exceed the minimum support, any larger size item set that includes it will not exceed the minimum support. In general, generating k-item sets uses the frequent $(k - 1)$-item sets that were generated in the preceding step. Each step requires a single run through the database, and therefore the Apriori algorithm is very fast even for a large number of unique items in a database.

13.4 SELECTING STRONG RULES

From the abundance of rules generated, the goal is to find only the rules that indicate a strong dependence between the antecedent and consequent item sets. To measure the strength of association implied by a rule, we use the measures of *confidence* and *lift ratio*, as described below.

Support and Confidence

In addition to support, which we described earlier, there is another measure that expresses the degree of uncertainty about the if–then rule. This is known as the *confidence*[1] of the rule. This measure compares the co-occurrence of the antecedent and consequent item sets in the database to the occurrence of the antecedent item sets. Confidence is defined as the ratio of the number of transactions that include all antecedent and consequent item sets (namely, the support) to the number of transactions that include all the antecedent item sets:

$$\text{Confidence} = \frac{\text{no. transactions with both antecedent and consequent item sets}}{\text{no. transactions with antecedent item set}}.$$

For example, suppose that a supermarket database has 100,000 point-of-sale transactions. Of these transactions, 2000 include both orange juice and (over-the-counter) flu medication, and 800 of these include soup purchases. The association rule "IF orange juice and flu medication are purchased THEN soup is purchased on the same trip" has a support of 800 transactions (alternatively, $0.8\% = 800/100{,}000$) and a confidence of 40% ($= 800/2000$).

To see the relationship between support and confidence, let us think about what each is measuring (estimating). One way to think of support is that it is the (estimated) probability that a transaction selected randomly from the database will contain all items in the antecedent and the consequent:

$$P(\text{antecedent AND consequent}).$$

In comparison, the confidence is the (estimated) *conditional probability* that a transaction selected randomly will include all the items in the consequent *given* that the transaction includes all the items in the antecedent:

$$\frac{P(\text{antecedent AND consequent})}{P(\text{antecedent})} = P(\text{consequent} \mid \text{antecedent}).$$

A high value of confidence suggests a strong association rule (in which we are highly confident). However, this can be deceptive because if the antecedent

---

[1] The concept of confidence is different from and unrelated to the ideas of confidence intervals and confidence levels used in statistical inference.

and/or the consequent has a high level of support, we can have a high value for confidence even when the antecedent and consequent are independent! For example, if nearly all customers buy bananas and nearly all customers buy ice cream, the confidence level will be high regardless of whether there is an association between the items.

Lift Ratio

A better way to judge the strength of an association rule is to compare the confidence of the rule with a benchmark value, where we assume that the occurrence of the consequent item set in a transaction is independent of the occurrence of the antecedent for each rule. In other words, if the antecedent and consequent item sets are independent, what confidence values would we expect to see? Under independence, the support would be

$$P(\text{antecedent AND consequent}) = P(\text{antecedent}) \times P(\text{consequent}),$$

and the benchmark confidence would be

$$\frac{P(\text{antecedent}) \times P(\text{consequent})}{P(\text{antecedent})} = P(\text{consequent}).$$

The estimate of this benchmark from the data, called the *benchmark confidence value* for a rule, is computed by

$$\text{Benchmark confidence} = \frac{\text{no. transactions with consequent item set}}{\text{no. transactions in database}}.$$

We compare the confidence to the benchmark confidence by looking at their ratio: This is called the *lift ratio* of a rule. The lift ratio is the confidence of the rule divided by the confidence, assuming independence of consequent from antecedent:

$$\text{Lift ratio} = \frac{\text{confidence}}{\text{benchmark confidence}}.$$

A lift ratio greater than 1.0 suggests that there is some usefulness to the rule. In other words, the level of association between the antecedent and consequent item sets is higher than would be expected if they were independent. The larger the lift ratio, the greater the strength of the association.

To illustrate the computation of support, confidence, and lift ratio for the cellular phone faceplate example, we introduce a presentation of the data better suited to this purpose.

Data Format

Transaction data are usually displayed in one of two formats: a list of items purchased (each row representing a transaction), or a binary matrix in which columns are items, rows again represent transactions, and each cell has either a 1 or a 0, indicating the presence or absence of an item in the transaction. For example, Table 13.1 displays the data for the cellular faceplate purchases in item list format. We translate these into binary matrix format in Table 13.2.

Now suppose that we want association rules between items for this database that have a support count of at least 2 (equivalent to a percentage support of $2/10 = 20\%$): in other words, rules based on items that were purchased together in at least 20% of the transactions. By enumeration, we can see that only the item sets listed in Table 13.3 have a count of at least 2.

TABLE 13.2 **PHONE FACEPLATE DATA IN BINARY MATRIX FORMAT**

Transaction	Red	White	Blue	Orange	Green	Yellow
1	1	1	0	0	1	0
2	0	1	0	1	0	0
3	0	1	1	0	0	0
4	1	1	0	1	0	0
5	1	0	1	0	0	0
6	0	1	1	0	0	0
7	1	0	1	0	0	0
8	1	1	1	0	1	0
9	1	1	1	0	0	0
10	0	0	0	0	0	1

TABLE 13.3 **ITEM SETS WITH SUPPORT COUNT OF AT LEAST TWO**

Item Set	Support (Count)
{red}	6
{white}	7
{blue}	6
{orange}	2
{green}	2
{red, white}	4
{red, blue}	4
{red, green}	2
{white, blue}	4
{white, orange}	2
{white, green}	2
{red, white, blue}	2
{red, white, green}	2

The first item set {red} has a support of 6 because six of the transactions included a red faceplate. Similarly, the last item set {red, white, green} has a support of 2 because only two transactions included red, white, and green faceplates.

In XLMiner the user can choose to input data using the *Affinity > Association Rules* facility in either item list format or binary matrix format.

Process of Rule Selection

The process of selecting strong rules is based on generating all association rules that meet stipulated support and confidence requirements. This is done in two stages. The first stage, described in Section 13.3, consists of finding all "frequent" item sets, those item sets that have a requisite support. In the second stage we generate, from the frequent item sets, association rules that meet a confidence requirement. The first step is aimed at removing item combinations that are rare in the database. The second stage then filters the remaining rules and selects only those with high confidence. For most association analysis data, the computational challenge is the first stage, as described in the discussion of the Apriori algorithm.

The computation of confidence in the second stage is simple. Since any subset (e.g., {red} in the phone faceplate example) must occur at least as frequently as the set it belongs to (e.g., {red, white}), each subset will also be in the list. It is then straightforward to compute the confidence as the ratio of the support for the item set to the support for each subset of the item set. We retain the corresponding association rule only if it exceeds the desired cutoff value for confidence. For example, from the item set {red, white, green} in the phone faceplate purchases, we get the following association rules:

Rule 1: {red, white} $\Rightarrow$ {green} with confidence
$$= \frac{\text{support of } \{\text{red, white, green}\}}{\text{support of } \{\text{red, white}\}} = 2/4 = 50\%.$$

Rule 2: {red, green} $\Rightarrow$ {white} with confidence
$$= \frac{\text{support of } \{\text{red, white, green}\}}{\text{support of } \{\text{red, green}\}} = 2/2 = 100\%.$$

Rule 3: {white, green} $\Rightarrow$ {red} with confidence
$$= \frac{\text{support of } \{\text{red, white, green}\}}{\text{support of } \{\text{white, green}\}} = 2/2 = 100\%.$$

Rule 4: { red} $\Rightarrow$ { white, green} with confidence
$$= \frac{\text{support of } \{\text{red, white, green}\}}{\text{support of } \{\text{red}\}} = 2/6 = 33\%.$$

Data	
Input Data	Faceplates!$B$1:$G$11
Data Format	Binary Matrix
Minimum Support	2
Minimum Confidence %	70
# Rules	6
Overall Time (secs)	2

Place the cursor on a cell in the rules table to read a rule.
Use up / down arrow keys to browse through the rules.

Rule #	Conf. %	Antecedent (a)	Consequent (c)	Support(a)	Support(c)	Support(a ∪ c)	Lift Ratio
1	100	green=>	red, white	2	4	2	2.5
2	100	green=>	red	2	6	2	1.666667
3	100	green, white=>	red	2	6	2	1.666667
4	100	green=>	white	2	7	2	1.428571
5	100	green, red=>	white	2	7	2	1.428571
6	100	orange=>	white	2	7	2	1.428571

FIGURE 13.2   **ASSOCIATION RULES FOR PHONE FACEPLATE TRANSACTIONS: XLMINER OUTPUT**

Rule 5: $\{\text{white}\} \Rightarrow \{\text{red, green}\}$ with confidence
$$= \frac{\text{support of } \{\text{red, white, green}\}}{\text{support of } \{\text{white}\}} = 2/7 = 29\%.$$

Rule 6: $\{\text{green}\} \Rightarrow \{\text{red, white}\}$ with confidence
$$= \frac{\text{support of } \{\text{red, white, green}\}}{\text{support of } \{\text{green}\}} = 2/2 = 100\%.$$

If the desired minimum confidence is 70%, we would report only the second, third, and last rules.

We can generate association rules in XLMiner by specifying the minimum support count (2) and minimum confidence level percentage (70%). Figure 13.2 shows the output. Note that here we consider all possible item sets, not just {red, white, green} as above.

The output includes information on the support of the antecedent, the support of the consequent, and the support of the combined set [denoted by Support $(a \cup c)$]. It also gives the confidence of the rule (in percent) and the lift ratio. In addition, XLMiner has an *interpreter* that translates the rule from a certain row into English. In the snapshot shown in Figure 13.2, the first rule is highlighted (by clicking), and the corresponding English rule appears in the yellow box:

Rule 1: If item(s) green= is/are purchased, then this implies item(s) red, white is/are also purchased. This rule has confidence of 100%.

Interpreting the Results

In interpreting results, it is useful to look at the various measures. The support for the rule indicates its impact in terms of overall size: What proportion of transactions is affected? If only a small number of transactions are affected, the rule may be of little use (unless the consequent is very valuable and/or the rule is very efficient in finding it).

The lift ratio indicates how efficient the rule is in finding consequents, compared to random selection. A very efficient rule is preferred to an inefficient rule, but we must still consider support: A very efficient rule that has very low support may not be as desirable as a less efficient rule with much greater support.

The confidence tells us at what rate consequents will be found and is useful in determining the business or operational usefulness of a rule: A rule with low confidence may find consequents at too low a rate to be worth the cost of (say) promoting the consequent in all the transactions that involve the antecedent.

Statistical Significance of Rules

What about confidence in the nontechnical sense? How sure can we be that the rules we develop are meaningful? Considering the matter from a statistical perspective, we can ask: Are we finding associations that are really just chance occurrences?

Let us examine the output from an application of this algorithm to a small database of 50 transactions, where each of the 9 items is assigned randomly to each transaction. The data are shown in Table 13.4, and the association rules generated are shown in Table 13.5.

In this example, the lift ratios highlight rule 6 as most interesting, as it suggests that purchase of item 4 is almost five times as likely when items 3 and 8 are purchased than if item 4 was not associated with the item set {3,8}. Yet we know

TABLE 13.4   **FIFTY TRANSACTIONS OF RANDOMLY ASSIGNED ITEMS**

Transaction	Items					Transaction	Items				Transaction	Items			
1	8					18	8				35	3	4	6	8
2	3	4	8			19					36	1	4	8	
3	8					20	9				37	4	7	8	
4	3	9				21	2	5	6	8	38	8	9		
5	9					22	4	6	9		39	4	5	7	9
6	1	8				23	4	9			40	2	8	9	
7	6	9				24	8	9			41	2	5	9	
8	3	5	7	9		25	6	8			42	1	2	7	9
9	8					26	1	6	8		43	5	8		
10						27	5	8			44	1	7	8	
11	1	7	9			28	4	8	9		45	8			
12	1	4	5	8	9	29	9				46	2	7	9	
13	5	7	9			30	8				47	4	6	9	
14	6	7	8			31	1	5	8		48	9			
15	3	7	9			32	3	6	9		49	9			
16	1	4	9			33	7	9			50	6	7	8	
17	6	7	8			34	7	8	9						

TABLE 13.5	ASSOCIATION RULES OUTPUT FOR RANDOM DATA

Input Data: $A$5:$E$54
Min. Support: 2 = 4%
Min. Conf. % :   70

Rule	Confidence (%)	Anteced,, a		Conseq., c	Support (a)	Support (c)	Support $(a \cup c)$	Confidence If $P(c\|a)=$ $P(c)$ (%)	Lift Ratio (conf./ prev. col.)
1	80	2	⇒	9	5	27	4	54	1.5
2	100	5, 7	⇒	9	3	27	3	54	1.9
3	100	6, 7	⇒	8	3	29	3	58	1.7
4	100	1, 5	⇒	8	2	29	2	58	1.7
5	100	2, 7	⇒	9	2	27	2	54	1.9
6	100	3, 8	⇒	4	2	11	2	22	4.5
7	100	3, 4	⇒	8	2	29	2	58	1.7
8	100	3, 7	⇒	9	2	27	2	547	1.9
9	100	4, 5	⇒	9	2	27	2	54	1.9

there is no fundamental association underlying these data—they were generated randomly.

Two principles can guide us in assessing rules for possible spuriousness due to chance effects:

1. The more records the rule is based on, the more solid the conclusion. The key evaluative statistics are based on ratios and proportions, and we can look to statistical confidence intervals on proportions, such as political polls, for a rough preliminary idea of how variable rules might be owing to chance sampling variation. Polls based on 1500 respondents, for example, yield margins of error in the range of ±1.5%.

2. The more distinct rules we consider seriously (perhaps consolidating multiple rules that deal with the same items), the more likely it is that at least some will be based on chance sampling results. For one person to toss a coin 10 times and get 10 heads would be quite surprising. If 1000 people toss a coin 10 times apiece, it would not be nearly so surprising to have one get 10 heads. Formal adjustment of "statistical significance" when multiple comparisons are made is a complex subject in its own right and beyond the scope of this book. A reasonable approach is to consider rules from the top down in terms of business or operational applicability and not consider more than can reasonably be incorporated in a human decision-making process. This will impose a rough constraint on the dangers that arise from an automated

review of hundreds or thousands of rules in search of "something interesting."

We now consider a more realistic example, using a larger database and real transactional data.

Example 2: Rules for Similar Book Purchases

The following example (drawn from the Charles Book Club case) examines associations among transactions involving various types of books. The database includes 2000 transactions, and there are 11 different types of books. The data, in binary matrix form, are shown in Figure 13.3. For instance, the first transaction included YouthBks (youth books), DoItYBks (do-it-yourself books), and GeogBks (geography books). Figure 13.4 shows (part of) the rules generated by XLMiner's *Association Rules* on these data. We specified a minimal support of 200 transactions and a minimal confidence of 50%. This resulted in 49 rules (the first 26 rules are shown in Figure 13.4).

In reviewing these rules, we can see that the information can be compressed. First, rule 1, which appears from the confidence level to be a very promising rule, is probably meaningless. It says: "If Italian cooking books have been purchased, then cookbooks are purchased." It seems likely that Italian cooking books are simply a subset of cookbooks. Rules 2 and 7 involve the same trio of books, with different antecedents and consequents. The same is true of rules 14 and 15 and rules 9 and 10. (Pairs and groups like this are easy to track down by looking for rows that share the same support.) This does not mean that the rules are not useful. On the contrary, it can reduce the number of item sets to be considered for possible action from a business perspective.

ChildBks	YouthBks	CookBks	DoItYBks	RefBks	ArtBks	GeogBks	ItalCook	ItalAtlas	ItalArt	Florence
0	1	0	1	0	0	1	0	0	0	0
1	0	0	0	0	0	0	0	0	0	0
0	0	0	0	0	0	0	0	0	0	0
1	1	1	0	1	0	1	0	0	0	0
0	0	1	0	0	0	1	0	0	0	0
1	0	0	0	0	1	0	0	0	0	1
0	1	0	0	0	0	0	0	0	0	0
0	1	0	0	1	0	0	0	0	0	0
1	0	0	1	0	0	0	0	0	0	0
1	1	1	0	0	0	1	0	0	0	0
0	0	0	0	0	0	0	0	0	0	0

FIGURE 13.3   **SUBSET OF BOOK PURCHASE TRANSACTIONS IN BINARY MATRIX FORMAT**

Data	
Input Data	Books! $A$1:$K$2001
Data Format	Binary Matrix
Minimum Support	200
Minimum Confidence %	50
# Rules	49
Overall Time (secs)	1

Rule 1: If item(s) ItalCook= is / are purchased, then this implies item(s) CookBks is / are also purchased. This rule has confidence of 100%.

Rule #	Conf. %	Antecedent (a)	Consequent (c)	Support(a)	Support(c)	Support(a U c)	Lift Ratio
1	100	ItalCook=>	CookBks	227	862	227	2.320186
2	62.77	ArtBks, ChildBks=>	GeogBks	325	552	204	2.274247
3	54.13	CookBks, DoItYBks=>	ArtBks	375	482	203	2.246196
4	61.98	ArtBks, CookBks=>	GeogBks	334	552	207	2.245509
5	53.77	CookBks, GeogBks=>	ArtBks	385	482	207	2.230964
6	57.11	RefBks=>	ChildBks, CookBks	429	512	245	2.230842
7	52.31	ChildBks, GeogBks=>	ArtBks	390	482	204	2.170444
8	60.78	ArtBks, CookBks=>	DoItYBks	334	564	203	2.155264
9	58.4	ChildBks, CookBks=>	GeogBks	512	552	299	2.115885
10	54.17	GeogBks=>	ChildBks, CookBks	552	512	299	2.115885
11	57.87	CookBks, DoItYBks=>	GeogBks	375	552	217	2.096618
12	56.79	ChildBks, DoItYBks=>	GeogBks	368	552	209	2.057735
13	52.49	ArtBks=>	ChildBks, CookBks	482	512	253	2.050376
14	52.12	YouthBks=>	ChildBks, CookBks	495	512	258	2.035985
15	50.39	ChildBks, CookBks=>	YouthBks	512	495	258	2.035985
16	57.03	ChildBks, CookBks=>	DoItYBks	512	564	292	2.022385
17	51.77	DoItYBks=>	ChildBks, CookBks	564	512	292	2.022385
18	56.36	CookBks, GeogBks=>	DoItYBks	385	564	217	1.998711
19	52.9	ArtBks=>	GeogBks	482	552	255	1.916832
20	82.19	ArtBks, DoItYBks=>	CookBks	247	862	203	1.906873
21	53.59	ChildBks, GeogBks=>	DoItYBks	390	564	209	1.900346
22	81.89	DoItYBks, GeogBks=>	CookBks	265	862	217	1.899926
23	80.33	CookBks, RefBks=>	ChildBks	305	846	245	1.899004
24	80	ArtBks, GeogBks=>	ChildBks	255	846	204	1.891253
25	81.18	ArtBks, GeogBks=>	CookBks	255	862	207	1.883445
26	79.63	CookBks, YouthBks=>	ChildBks	324	846	258	1.882497

FIGURE 13.4 **ASSOCIATION RULES FOR BOOK PURCHASE TRANSACTIONS: XLMINER OUTPUT**

13.5 SUMMARY

Affinity analysis (also called market basket analysis) is a method for deducing rules on associations between purchased items from databases of transactions. The main advantage of this method is that it generates clear, simple rules of the form "IF X is purchased THEN Y is also likely to be purchased." The method is very transparent and easy to understand.

The process of creating association rules is two staged. First, a set of candidate rules based on frequent item sets is generated (the Apriori algorithm being the most popular rule-generating algorithm). Then from these candidate rules, the rules that indicate the strongest association between items are selected. We use the measures of support and confidence to evaluate the uncertainty in a rule. The user also specifies minimal support and confidence values to be used in the rule generation and selection process. A third measure, the lift ratio, compares the efficiency of the rule to detect a real association compared to a random combination.

One shortcoming of association rules is the profusion of rules that are generated. There is therefore a need for ways to reduce these to a small set of useful and strong rules. An important nonautomated method to condense the information involves examining the rules for noninformative and trivial rules as well as for rules that share the same support.

Another issue that needs to be kept in mind is that rare combinations tend to be ignored because they do not meet the minimum support requirement. For this reason it is better to have items that are approximately equally frequent in the data. This can be achieved by using higher level hierarchies as the items. An example is to use types of audio CDs rather than names of individual audio CDs in deriving association rules from a database of music store transactions.

PROBLEMS

13.1 Satellite Radio Customers. An analyst at a subscription-based satellite radio company has been given a sample of data from their customer database, with the goal of finding groups of customers that are associated with one another. The data consist of company data, together with purchased demographic data that are mapped to the company data (see Figure 13.5). The analyst decides to apply association rules to learn more about the associations between customers. Comment on this approach.

13.2 Online Statistics Courses. Consider the data in the file CourseTopics.xls, the first few rows of which are shown in Figure 13.6. These data are for purchases of online statistics courses at statistics.com. Each row represents the courses attended by a single customer.

The firm wishes to assess alternative sequencings and combinations of courses. Use association rules to analyze these data and interpret several of the resulting rules.

13.3 Cosmetics Purchases. The data shown in Figure 13.7 are a subset of a dataset on cosmetic purchases given in binary matrix form. The complete dataset (in the file Cosmetics.xls) contains data on the purchases of different cosmetic items at a large chain drugstore. The store wants to analyze associations among purchases of these items for purposes of

Row Id.	zipconvert_2	zipconvert_3	zipconvert_4	zipconvert_5	homeowner dummy	NUMCHLD	INCOME	gender dummy	WEALTH
17	0	1	0	0	1	1	5	1	9
25	1	0	0	0	1	1	1	0	7
29	0	0	0	1	0	2	5	1	8
38	0	0	0	1	1	1	3	0	4
40	0	1	0	0	1	1	4	0	8
53	0	1	0	0	1	1	4	1	8
58	0	0	0	1	1	1	4	1	8
61	1	0	0	0	1	1	1	0	7
71	0	0	1	0	1	1	4	0	5
87	1	0	0	0	1	1	4	1	8
100	0	0	0	1	1	1	4	1	8
104	1	0	0	0	1	1	1	1	5
121	0	0	1	0	1	1	4	1	5
142	1	0	0	0	0	1	5	0	8

FIGURE 13.5 **SAMPLE OF DATA ON SATELLITE RADIO CUSTOMERS**

Course Topics

Intro	Data Mining	Survey	Cat Data	Regression	Forecast	DOE	SW
1	1	0	0	0	0	0	0
0	0	1	0	0	0	0	0
0	1	0	1	1	0	0	1
1	0	0	0	0	0	0	0
1	1	0	0	0	0	0	0
0	1	0	0	0	0	0	0
1	0	0	0	0	0	0	0
0	0	0	1	0	1	1	1
1	0	0	0	0	0	0	0
0	0	0	1	0	0	0	0
1	0	0	0	0	0	0	0

FIGURE 13.6 **DATA ON PURCHASES OF ONLINE STATISTICS COURSES**

Trans. #	Bag	Blush	Nail Polish	Brushes	Concealer	Eyebrow Pencils	Bronzer
1	0	1	1	1	1	0	1
2	0	0	1	0	1	0	1
3	0	1	0	0	1	1	1
4	0	0	1	1	1	0	1
5	0	1	0	0	1	0	1
6	0	0	0	0	1	0	0
7	0	1	1	1	1	0	1
8	0	0	1	1	0	0	1
9	0	0	0	0	1	0	0
10	1	1	1	0	0	0	0
11	0	0	1	0	0	0	1
12	0	0	1	1	1	0	1

FIGURE 13.7   DATA ON COSMETICS PURCHASES IN BINARY MATRIX FORM

point-of-sale display, guidance to sales personnel in promoting cross sales, and guidance for piloting an eventual time-of-purchase electronic recommender system to boost cross sales. Consider first only the subset shown in Figure 13.7.

a. Select several values in the matrix and explain their meaning.

b. Consider the results of the association rules analysis shown in Figure 13.8 and:

   i. For the first row, explain the "Conf. %" output and how it is calculated.

   ii. For the first row, explain the "Support(a)," "Support(c)," and "Support($a \cup c$)" output and how it is calculated.

   iii. For the first row, explain the "Lift Ratio" and how it is calculated.

   iv. For the first row, explain the rule that is represented there in words.
Now, use the complete dataset on the cosmetics purchases (in the file Cosmetics.xls).

   v. Using XLMiner, apply association rules to these data.

   vi. Interpret the first three rules in the output in words.

   vii. Reviewing the first couple of dozen rules, comment on their redundancy and how you would assess their utility.

Rule #	Conf. %	Antecedent (a)	Consequent (c)	Support(a)	Support(c)	Support(a ∪ c)	Lift Ratio
2	60.19	Bronzer, Nail Polish=>	Brushes, Concealer	103	77	62	3.909
1	80.52	Brushes, Concealer=>	Bronzer, Nail Polish	77	103	62	3.909
4	56.36	Brushes=>	Bronzer, Concealer, Nail Polish	110	76	62	3.708
3	81.58	Bronzer, Concealer, Nail Polish	Brushes	76	110	62	3.708
6	76.36	Brushes=>	Bronzer, Nail Polish	110	103	84	3.707
5	81.55	Bronzer, Nail Polish=>	Brushes	103	110	84	3.707
8	56.88	Concealer, Nail Polish=>	Bronzer, Brushes	109	84	62	3.386
7	73.81	Bronzer, Brushes=>	Concealer, Nail Polish	84	109	62	3.386
10	70	Brushes=>	Concealer, Nail Polish	110	109	77	3.211
9	70.64	Concealer, Nail Polish=>	Brushes	109	110	77	3.211
12	50	Brushes=>	Blush, Nail Polish	110	82	55	3.049
11	67.07	Blush, Nail Polish=>	Brushes	82	110	55	3.049

FIGURE 13.8   ASSOCIATION RULES FOR COSMETICS PURCHASES DATA

CHAPTER

4

Statistics 101: What You Should Know About Data

For statisticians (and economists too), the term *data mining* once had a pejorative meaning. Instead of "to find useful patterns in large volumes of data," data mining had the connotation of searching for data to fit preconceived ideas. This definition is much like what politicians do around election time — search for data to show the success of their deeds. It is certainly not what the authors mean by data mining!

This chapter is intended to bridge some of the gaps between traditional statistics and data mining. The two disciplines are very similar. Statisticians and data miners commonly use many of the same techniques, and statistical software vendors now include many of the techniques described throughout this book in their software packages. Data miners should have a foundation of knowledge in statistics.

A fact that will perhaps surprise some readers is that statistics developed as a discipline distinct from mathematics over the past century and a half to help scientists make sense of observations and design experiments that yield the reproducible and accurate results associated with the scientific method. Because statistics is intimately tied to scientific understanding of the world, applying it to the scientific understanding of business is natural.

For almost all of this period, the issue was not too much data, but too little. Scientists had to figure out how to understand the world using data collected by hand in notebooks. These quantities were sometimes mistakenly recorded, illegible due to fading and smudged ink, difficult to copy, and painful to manipulate (especially by the standards of modern spreadsheets). Early statisticians

101

were practical people who invented techniques to handle whatever problem was at hand. Quite a few of the techniques mentioned in this book date back to the 1950s and 1960s when computers first appeared at universities — and statistics departments were some of the first groups to take advantage of those newfangled machines.

What is remarkable and a testament to the founders of modern statistics is that techniques developed long ago on tiny amounts of data in a world of hand calculations have survived and still prove their utility. These techniques have proven their worth not only in the original domains but also in virtually all areas where data is collected, from agriculture to psychology to astronomy and even to business.

Perhaps the greatest statistician of the twentieth century was R. A. Fisher, considered by many to be the father of modern statistics. In the 1920s, long before the invention of modern computers, he devised methods for designing and analyzing experiments. For two years, while living on a farm outside London, he collected various measurements of crop yields along with potential explanatory variables — amount of rain and sun and fertilizer, for instance. To understand what has an effect on crop yields, he invented new techniques (such as *analysis of variance* — ANOVA) and performed perhaps a million calculations on the data he collected. Although twenty-first-century computer chips easily handle many millions of calculations in a second, each of Fisher's calculations required pulling a lever on a manual calculating machine. Results emerged slowly over weeks and months, along with sore hands and calluses. (In fact, he did not do the calculations himself; many of his "calculators" were women studying statistics.)

The advent of computing power has clearly simplified some aspects of analysis, although its bigger effect is the wealth of available data. The goal in data mining is no longer to extract every last iota of possible information from each rare datum. The goal is instead to make sense of quantities of data so large that they are beyond the ability of human brains to comprehend in their raw format.

The purpose of this chapter is to present some key ideas from statistics that have proven to be useful tools for data mining. This chapter is intended to be neither a thorough nor a comprehensive introduction to statistics; rather, it is an introduction to a handful of useful statistical techniques and ideas. These tools are shown by demonstration, rather than through mathematical proof.

The chapter starts with an introduction to what is probably the most important aspect of applied statistics — a skeptical attitude. It then discusses looking at data through a statistician's eye, introducing important concepts and terminology along the way. Examples of this skepticism are sprinkled through the chapter, especially in the discussion of confidence intervals and the chi-square test. One example, using the chi-square test to understand geography and channel, is an unusual application of the ideas presented in the chapter. Another case study applies the ideas to A/B tests, as a way to determine the best recommendations to make to online customers. The chapter ends with a brief discussion of some of the differences between data miners and statisticians — differences that are more a matter of degree than of substance.

Occam's Razor

William of Occam was a Franciscan monk born in a small English town in 1280 — not only before modern statistics was invented, but also before the Renaissance and the printing press. (The English village, now spelled Ockham, is about 25 miles southwest of London.) William of Occam was an influential philosopher, theologian, and professor who expounded many ideas about many things, including church politics. As a monk, he was an ascetic who took his vow of poverty very seriously. He was also a fervent advocate of the power of reason, denying the existence of universal truths and espousing a modern philosophy that was quite different from the views of most of his contemporaries living in the Middle Ages.

What does William of Occam have to do with data mining? His name has become associated with a very simple idea. He himself explained it in Latin (the language of learning, even among the English, at the time), *"Entia non sunt multiplicanda praeter necessitatem."* In more familiar English, one would say "The simpler explanation is the preferable one" or, more colloquially, "Keep it simple, stupid." Any explanation should strive to reduce the number of causes to the bare minimum sufficient for explaining the phenomenon. This line of reasoning is referred to as Occam's razor and is his gift to data analysis.

The story of William of Occam has an interesting ending. Perhaps because of his focus on the power of reason, he also believed that the powers of the church should be separate from the powers of the state — that the church should be confined to religious matters. This resulted in his opposition to the meddling of Pope John XXII in politics and eventually to his own excommunication. He died in Munich during an outbreak of the plague in 1349, leaving a legacy of clear and critical thinking for future generations.

Skepticism and Simpson's Paradox

The flip side of Occam's razor is that explanations should not be oversimplified. Oversimplification is as bad as overcomplication, when it impedes one's ability to understand what is really happening. As an example, oversimplification can occur when looking at summary statistics, because underlying factors — that affect the summaries — may be hidden.

One of the authors has family in Minnesota and Iowa. There is a joke in Minnesota that goes something like, "Did you hear about the guy who moved from Minnesota to Iowa and raised the average IQ of both states?" The first reaction is that this is impossible. After all, the combined population of the two states remains the same, as does the average IQ of the combined population, regardless of who moves back and forth. How could the average of each state be lower before the move and higher afterwards?

More careful thought reveals how the joke can be true. If the average IQ in Iowa is less than the average IQ in Minnesota, then someone who lives in Minnesota with a higher IQ than the Iowa average but lower than the Minnesota average can move to the adjoining state, raising the average IQ of both states. This type of paradox has a name — Simpson's paradox (named after the statistician Edward Simpson, not the fictional character Homer Simpson).

Simpson's paradox occurs when underlying factors are hidden by summary statistics. In the case of the joke, the average IQs of the two states change, but so does their population. The weighted average remains the same, even though the averages for each group increase. Statisticians have a name for such phenomena; variables that affect the outcome but are not seen in the data are examples of *unobserved heterogeneity*.

A case study later in this chapter was inspired by a version of Simpson's paradox. The metrics used to judge a recommendation engine showed that it was successful; that is, all the metrics except the final bottom-line result.

The Null Hypothesis

Occam's razor is very important for data mining and statistics, although statistics expresses the idea a bit differently. The *null hypothesis* is the assumption that differences among observations are due simply to chance. To give an example, consider a presidential poll that gives Candidate A 45 percent and Candidate B 47 percent. The goal, of course, is to estimate the preference for each candidate in the general population (or perhaps more importantly among people who are going to vote). Because this data is from a poll, there are several sources of error. The values are only approximate estimates of the popularity of each candidate among the larger population. The layperson is inclined to ask, "Is one candidate more popular than the other?" The statistician phrases the question slightly differently, "What is the probability that the two candidates are equally popular, given the difference in their polling numbers?"

Although the two questions are very similar, the statistician's has a bit of an attitude. This attitude is that the difference observed in the polling numbers may have no significance at all, an attitude inspired by the null hypothesis. Just to be clear, there is an observed difference of 2 percent based on the poll. However, the observed polling numbers may be explained by the particular sample of people included in the polling population. Another poll using the exact same methodology might have a difference of 2 percent in the other direction, or a difference of 0 percent, or some other value. All may be reasonably likely results. Of course, if the preferences differed by 20 percent, then sampling variation is much less likely to be the cause. Such a large difference would greatly improve the confidence that one candidate is more popular than the other among the larger population, and greatly reduce the probability of the null hypothesis being true.

> **TIP** The simplest explanation is usually the best one — even (or especially) if it does not prove the hypothesis you want to prove.

This skeptical attitude is very valuable for both statisticians and data miners. Our goal as data miners is to demonstrate results that work, and to discount the null hypothesis. One difference between data miners and statisticians is the volume of data that data miners work with. This is often sufficiently large that worrying about the mechanics of calculating the probability of something being due to sample variation is unnecessary.

P-Values

The null hypothesis is not merely an approach to analysis; it can also be quantified. The *p-value* is the probability of observing a difference as large as the observed difference given that the null hypothesis is true. Remember, when the null hypothesis is true, nothing interesting is really happening, because differences are due to chance (strictly speaking, sampling variation). Much of statistics is devoted to determining bounds for the p-value under different circumstances.

For the previous example of the presidential poll, assume that the p-value is calculated to be 60 percent (more on how this is done later in this chapter). Such a p-value means that when support for the two candidates is in fact equal, then 60 percent of the time a poll of this type will find a difference of at least 2 percent. This is a large value, which provides little evidence to reject the null hypothesis. There is little support for the notion that the two candidates differ in popularity.

Suppose the p-value is 5 percent, instead. This is a relatively small number. It means that if the two candidates have equal popularity, then only 5 percent of the time would a difference as large as 2 percent show up in the poll. In this case, there is little support for the null hypothesis. A common way to phrase this is that you are at least 95 percent *confident* that the null hypothesis is false, hence 95 percent confident that the candidates differ in popularity, with Candidate B doing better than Candidate A. This rephrasing is not strictly accurate, as explained in the sidebar "A Common Misunderstanding."

Confidence, sometimes called the *q-value*, is the flip side of the p-value. Generally, the goal is to aim for a confidence level of at least 90 percent, if not 95 percent or more (meaning that the corresponding p-value is less than 10 percent, or 5 percent, respectively).

A COMMON MISUNDERSTANDING

The definition of the p-value is often shortened to "the probability that the null hypothesis is true." This shorthand is not technically correct, but it does reflect how the value gets used in practice. The p-value really measures the probability of observing a value at least as unlikely as the observed value, given that the null hypothesis is true. As a consequence, when the p-value is small, little evidence exists that the null hypothesis is true, but how little?

There are two scenarios for any test:

▪ The null hypothesis is actually true.

▪ The null hypothesis is actually false.

For any given test, you do not know which of these is true, or the probabilities of one versus the other. The definition of the p-value makes no claim in the second case, only in the first case. When the null hypothesis is actually true, then the p-value measures how often rejecting it is incorrect based on a particular observation. It does not measure how often the null hypothesis is itself true or false. This is a subtle but important distinction.

With respect to the question, "How often is the null hypothesis true?" the p-value is overly conservative, but you cannot say by how much. Why is it overly conservative? Go back to the two cases. The p-value provides a measure in the first case of being wrong when rejecting the null hypothesis. In the second case, rejecting the null hypothesis is never wrong. In the real world, the null hypothesis is sometimes true and sometimes false; however, you just do not know the probability in any given situation.

In other words, when rejecting the null hypothesis, you are wrong between never (in the second case) and the p-value (the first case). The actual probability of being correct in rejecting the statement, "The null hypothesis is true," is therefore between zero and the p-value.

These ideas — the null hypothesis, p-value, and confidence — are three basic ideas in statistics. The next section carries these ideas further and introduces the statistical concept of distributions, with particular attention to the normal distribution.

Looking At and Measuring Data

A *statistic* refers to a measure taken on a sample of data. Statistics is the study of these measures and the samples they are measured on. This section describes various different methods for exploring data.

Categorical Values

Much of the data used in data mining is categorical, rather than numeric. Categorical data shows up to describe products, channels, regions, and other aspects of businesses. This section discusses ways of looking at and analyzing categorical fields.

Histograms

The most basic descriptive statistic for categorical variables is the number of times different values occur. Figure 4-1 shows a *histogram* of stop reason codes during a period of time. A histogram shows how often each value occurs in the data and can have either absolute quantities (204 times) or percentage (14.6 percent). Often, too many values exist to show in a single histogram, such as in this case where dozens of additional codes are grouped into the "other" category.

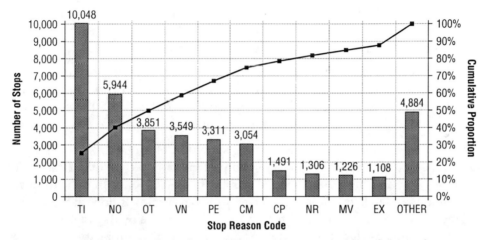

Figure 4-1: This example shows both a histogram (as a vertical bar chart) and cumulative proportion (as a line) on the same chart for stop reasons associated with a particular marketing effort.

In addition to the values for each category, this histogram also shows the cumulative proportion of stops, whose scale is shown on the left side. Through the cumulative histogram, you can see that the top three codes account for about 50 percent of stops, and the top 10, almost 90 percent. As an aesthetic note, the grid lines intersect both the left and right scales at reasonable points on the scale, making it easier to read the values on both vertical axes.

> **TIP** When making charts that have two vertical axes, use grid lines and make the grid lines match the ticks on both axes (this may require playing with the maximum values and tick mark intervals on one or both axes).

Time Series

Histograms are quite useful and easily made with a spreadsheet such as Excel or any statistics package. However, histograms describe a single moment. Data mining is often concerned with what is happening over time. A key question is whether the frequency of values is constant or changing over time.

Answering this question uses a rudimentary form of time series analysis. The first step is deciding on an appropriate time frame for the data; this includes choosing not only the units of time, but also when to start counting from. Some different time frames are the beginning of a customer relationship, when a customer requests a stop, the actual stop date, and so on. Different fields may have different time frames. For example:

- Fields describing the beginning of a customer relationship — such as original product, original channel, or original market — should be looked at by the customer's original start date.

- Fields describing the end of a customer relationship — such as last product, stop reason, or stop channel — should be looked at by the customer's stop date or the customer's tenure at that point in time.

- Fields describing events during the customer relationship — such as product upgrade or downgrade, response to a promotion, or a late payment — should be looked at by the date of the event, the customer's tenure at that point in time, or the relative time since some other event.

The next step is to plot the time series as shown in Figure 4-2, which has two series for stops by stop date. One shows a particular stop type over time (price increase stops) and the other, the total number of stops. Notice that the units for the time axis are in days. Although much business reporting is done at the weekly and monthly level, the authors often prefer to look at data by day in order to see important patterns that might emerge at a fine level of granularity — patterns that might be obscured by summarization.

This chart shows some interesting patterns. One is a weekly pattern in the overall stops, which is evident because of the four or five spikes during each month (additional work is needed to confirm that the peaks are, indeed, exactly one week apart). A big change also occurs between the first four months, which have higher stops, and the subsequent dates. The lighter line, for price increase–related stops, has a very large jump at the end of January. The cause, of course, was an increase in price that went into effect at that time.

> **TIP** When looking at field values over time, look at the data by day to get a feel for the data at the most granular level.

A time series chart has a wealth of information. For example, fitting a line to the data makes it possible to see and quantify long-term trends, as shown in Figure 4-2. Be careful when doing this, because of seasonality. Partial years might introduce inadvertent trends, so try to include entire years when using a best-fit line. The likely correlation between the number of stops and the number of customers suggests that a better measure would be the stop rate, rather than the raw number of stops.

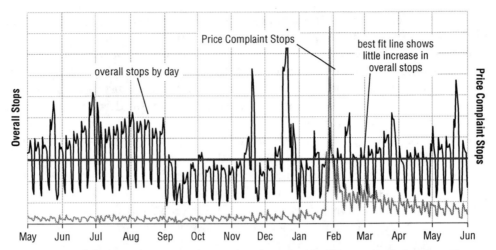

Figure 4-2: This chart shows two time series plotted with different vertical scales. The dark line is for overall stops; the light line for pricing related stops shows the impact of a change in pricing strategy at the end of January.

Standardized Values (Z-Scores)

A time series chart provides useful information. However, it does not give an idea as to whether the changes over time are expected or unexpected. For this, let's borrow some tools from statistics.

One way of looking at a time series is as a bunch of samples of all the data, with a small sample on each day. Remember the null hypothesis: The statistician wants to be a skeptic and ask the question: "Is it possible that the differences seen on each day are strictly due to chance?" The p-value answers this question; recall it is the probability that the observed variation among values would be seen if each day were just a random sample.

Statisticians have been studying this fundamental question for more than a century. Fortunately, they have also devised some techniques for answering it. This is a question about *sample variation*. Each day represents a sample of stops from all the stops that occurred during the period. The variation in stops observed on different days might simply be due to an expected variation in taking random samples.

A basic theorem in statistics, called the *central limit theorem*, says the following:

As more and more random samples are taken from a population, the distribution of the averages of the samples (or any similar statistic) follows the normal distribution. As the number of samples grows, the average of the average values of the samples comes closer and closer to the average of the entire population.

The central limit theorem is actually a very complex idea whose proof is quite interesting to those with an affinity for advanced mathematics. More importantly for everyone else, the central limit theorem is useful. In the case of discrete variables, such as the number of customers who stop on each day, the same idea holds. The statistic used for this example is the count of the number of stops on each day, as shown earlier in Figure 4-2. (Strictly speaking, using a proportion, such as the ratio of stops to the number of customers, would probably make this clearer; the two are equivalent under the assumption that the number of customers is constant over the period.)

How is the central limit theorem used? The idea is easy. If the samples (daily totals) are indeed randomly drawn from all the stops, then the values on each day will follow a normal distribution. As mathematicians might say, the contra-positive is true as well. That is, if the distribution of the values does *not* follow a normal distribution, then it is highly unlikely that the original values were drawn randomly. And, if they weren't drawn randomly, some other process is at work, indicating a likely dependency on time. This comparison does not say what the dependency is, just that a dependency is likely to exist.

The normal distribution is described by two parameters: the average and the standard deviation. The standard deviation measures the extent to which values tend to cluster around the average and is explained more fully later in the chapter; for now, using a function such as STDEV() in Excel or STDDEV() in SQL is sufficient. For the time series, the standard deviation is the standard deviation of the daily counts. Assuming that the values for each day are taken randomly from the stops for the entire period, the set of counts should follow a normal distribution. If they don't, then something besides chance is affecting the values. In this case, the simplest explanation, differences due to sampling, is insufficient to explain the variation in the number of stops from day to day.

Because of their relation to the normal distribution, standard deviations are quite useful. One way to incorporate them directly into data analysis is to convert values in a particular variable into the number of standard deviations from the average. This process, called *standardizing* values, is quite simple for a time series:

1. Calculate the average value for all days.

2. Calculate the standard deviation for all days.

3. For each value, subtract the average and divide by the standard deviation to get the number of standard deviations from the average.

Standardized values, also called *z-scores*, make observing information pertinent to the null hypothesis easier. One property of standardized values is that the sum is always zero.

When the null hypothesis is true, the standardized values should follow the normal distribution (with an average of 0 and a standard deviation of 1). In this case, the standardized value should take on negative values and positive values with about equal frequency. Also, when standardized, about two-thirds (68.4 percent) of the values should be between –1 and 1. A bit more than 95 percent of the values should be between –2 and 2. Values more than 3 or less than –3 should be very, very rare — probably not visible in the data. Of course, "should" here means that the values follow the normal distribution and the null hypothesis need not be rejected (that is, that sample variation is sufficient to explain time-related effects). When the null hypothesis does not hold, it is often apparent from the standardized values. The sidebar, "A Question of Terminology," talks a bit more about distributions, normal and otherwise.

Figure 4-3 shows the standardized values for the data in Figure 4-2. The first thing to notice is that the shape of each standardized curve is very similar to the shape of the original data; what has changed is the scale on the vertical dimension. In the previous figure, overall stops were much larger than pricing stops, so the two were shown using different scales. In this figure, though, the curve for the standardized pricing stops towers over the standardized overall stops in February, even though both are on the same scale.

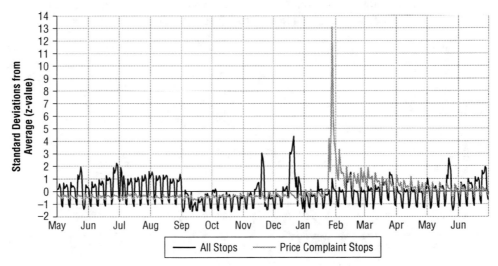

Figure 4-3: Standardized values allow you to compare different groups on the same chart using the same scale; this chart shows overall stops and price increase–related stops.

The overall stops in Figure 4-3 are normal, with the following caveats. A large peak occurs at the end of December, which probably needs to be explained because the value is more than four standard deviations away from the average. Also, there is a strong weekly pattern. To average out the intraweek variation, construct the chart using weekly stops instead of daily stops. Finally, the first four months of stops are consistently on the high side.

A QUESTION OF TERMINOLOGY

A very important idea in statistics is the idea of a *distribution*. For a categorical variable, a distribution is a lot like a histogram — it tells how often a given value occurs as a probability between 0 and 1. For instance, a uniform distribution says that all values are equally represented. An example of a uniform distribution would occur in a business where customers pay by credit card and equal numbers of customers pay with American Express, MasterCard, and Visa.

The normal distribution, which plays a very special role in statistics, is an example of a distribution for a continuous variable. The following figure shows the normal (sometimes called Gaussian or bell-shaped) distribution with an average of 0 and a standard deviation of 1. The way to read this curve is to look at areas between two points. For a value that follows the normal distribution, the probability that the value falls between two values — for example, between 0 and 1 — is the area under the curve. For the values of 0 and 1, the probability is 34.1 percent, meaning that 34.1 percent of the time a variable that follows a normal distribution will take on a value within one standard deviation above the average. Because the curve is symmetric, there is an additional 34.1 percent probability of being one standard deviation below the average, and hence 68.2 percent probability of being within one standard deviation of the average.

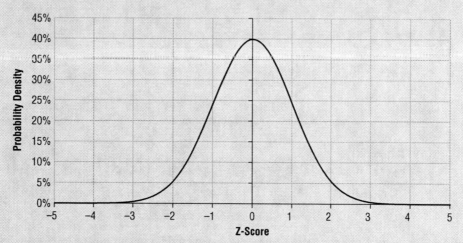

The probability density function for the normal distribution looks like the familiar bell-shaped curve.

The preceding figure shows a picture of a bell-shaped curve and calls it the normal distribution. Actually, the correct terminology is *density function* (or *probability density function*). Although this terminology derives from advanced mathematical probability theory, it makes sense. The density function gives a flavor for how "dense" a variable is for different values. You use a density function by measuring the area under the curve between two points, rather than by reading the individual values themselves. In the case of the normal distribution, the values are densest around 0 and less dense as you move away.

The following figure shows the curve that is more properly called the normal distribution. This form, where the curve starts at 0 on the left and rises to 1 on the right, is also called a *cumulative distribution function*. Mathematically, the distribution function for a value *X* is defined as the probability that the variable takes on a value less than or equal to *X*. Because of the "less than or equal to" characteristic, this function always starts near 0, climbs upward, and ends up close to 1. In general, the density function provides more visual clues about what is going on with a distribution. Because density functions provide more information, they are often referred to as distributions, although that is technically inaccurate.

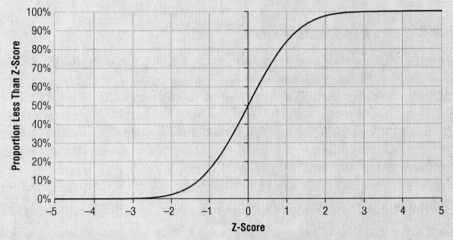

The (cumulative) distribution function for the normal distribution has an S-shape.

Finally, there is one very important point about understanding distributions. People tend to look at the "bulge" in the distribution, coming to the conclusion that a distribution that has a big hump "looks" like a normal distribution. In fact, what makes a distribution normal is what happens in the tails of the distribution as the values get further from the center. The normal distribution has very well-defined tails, and it is extremely unlikely to observe values more than three or four standard deviations from the average.

The lighter line showing the pricing-related stops clearly does not follow the normal distribution. Many more values are negative than positive. The peak is more than 13 — which is way, way too high for a normal distribution. The negative peaks, on the other hand, are never less than –2, so the distribution is highly asymmetric in terms of positive and negative values. The sum of the standardized value is 0, so a few large positive values often result in many small negative ones.

This example uses z-scores to look at values over time to see whether they look like random samples whose variation could be explained as a by-product of sampling itself. Days when the z-score is relatively high or low are suspicious.

Some other factor might be affecting the stops. The high peak in pricing stops can be explained by a change in pricing — a price increase, in fact. This effect is quite evident in the daily z-score.

The z-score is useful for other reasons as well. It is one way of taking several variables and converting them to similar ranges using the same units. That is, different columns, such as amount spent, interest rate, tenure, and so on can all be converted from dollars, percents, and days into a common unit — standard deviations from the average. This can be useful for several data mining techniques, such as clustering and neural networks. Other uses of z-scores are covered in Chapter 19, which covers data transformations.

From Z-Scores to Probabilities

Assuming that a set of standardized values follows the normal distribution allows you to calculate the probability that any given value would have occurred by chance. Actually, there is about a zero percent probability of any particular value exactly occurring. So, the p-value measures the probability that something as far as or farther from the average would have occurred (assuming the null hypothesis). Probabilities are defined on ranges of z-scores as the area under the normal curve between two points.

Calculating something farther from the average might mean one of two things:

- The probability of being more than z standard deviations from the average
- The probability of being z standard deviations greater than the average (or separately z standard deviations less than the average)

The first is called a two-tailed test and the second is called a one-tailed test. Figure 4-4 perhaps makes the terminology a bit clearer. The two-tailed probability is always twice as large as the one-tailed probability for z-scores. The two tests measure different things. The two-tailed tests measure the probability of observing a difference this large between A and B (under the null hypothesis). The one-tailed test measures the probability of observing such a difference *and A is the winner*. The two-tailed p-value is more pessimistic than the one-tailed one, in the sense that it is more likely to assume that the null hypothesis is true. If the one-tailed says the probability of the null hypothesis is 10 percent, then the two-tailed says it is 20 percent.

The two-tailed p-value can be calculated conveniently in Excel, using the function called `NORMSDIST()`, which calculates the cumulative normal distribution. Using this function, the two-tailed p-value is `2 * NORMSDIST(-ABS(z))`. For a value of 2, the result is 4.6 percent, indicating a 4.6 percent chance of observing a value more than two standard deviations from the average — plus or minus. Or, put another way, there is a 95.4 percent confidence that a value falling outside two standard deviations is due to something besides chance. For a precise 95 percent confidence, a bound of 1.96 can be used instead of 2. For 99 percent confidence, the limit is 2.58. The following shows the limits on the z-score for some common confidence levels:

- 90% confidence → z-score > 1.64

- 95% confidence → z-score > 1.96

- 99% confidence → z-score > 2.58

- 99.5% confidence → z-score > 2.81

- 99.9% confidence → z-score > 3.29

- 99.99% confidence → z-score > 3.89

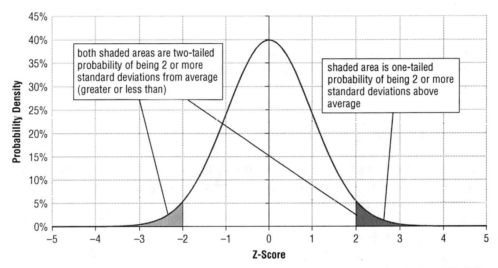

Figure 4-4: The tail of the normal distribution answers the question: "What is the probability of getting a value of z or greater?"

Confidence is the opposite of the p-value. When confidence is close to 100 percent, the value is unlikely to be due to chance; when it is close to 0 the value is likely to be due to chance. The signed confidence adds information about whether the value is too low or too high. When the observed value is less than the average, the signed confidence is negative.

Figure 4-5 shows the signed confidence for the data shown in Figures 4-2 and 4-3, using the two-tailed probability. The shape of the signed confidence is different from the earlier shapes. The confidence of the stop count bounces around, usually remaining within reasonable bounds — that is, the confidence does not hover around 0. The pricing-related stops show a very distinct pattern, being too low for a long time, then peaking and descending. The signed confidence levels are bounded by 100 percent and –100 percent. In this chart, the extreme values are near 100 percent or –100 percent, and telling the difference between 99.9 percent and 99.99999 percent is difficult. To distinguish values near the extremes, the z-scores in Figure 4-3 are better than the signed confidence.

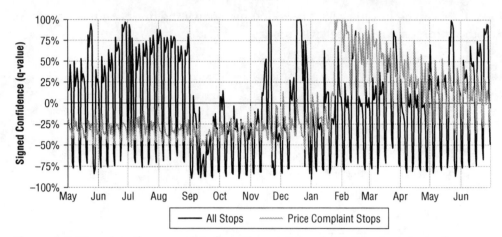

Figure 4-5: Based on the same data from Figures 4-2 and 4-3, this chart shows the signed confidence (q-values) of the observed value based on the average and standard deviation. This sign is positive when the observed value is too high, negative when it is too low.

Cross-Tabulations

Time series are an example of cross-tabulation — looking at the values of two or more variables at one time. For time series, the second variable is the time or date when something occurred.

Table 4-1 shows an example used later in this chapter. The cross-tabulation shows the number of new customers from counties in southeastern New York State by three channels: telemarketing, direct mail, and other. This table shows both the raw counts and the relative frequencies.

Table 4-1: Cross-tabulation of Starts by County and Channel

	COUNTS				FREQUENCIES			
COUNTY	TM	DM	OTHER	TOTAL	TM	DM	OTHER	TOTAL
Bronx	3,212	413	2,936	**6,561**	2.5%	0.3%	2.3%	5.1%
Kings	9,773	1,393	11,025	**22,191**	7.7%	1.1%	8.6%	17.4%
Nassau	3,135	1,573	10,367	**15,075**	2.5%	1.2%	8.1%	11.8%
New York	7,194	2,867	28,965	**39,026**	5.6%	2.2%	22.7%	30.6%
Queens	6,266	1,380	10,954	**18,600**	4.9%	1.1%	8.6%	14.6%
Richmond	784	277	1,772	**2,833**	0.6%	0.2%	1.4%	2.2%
Suffolk	2,911	1,042	7,159	**11,112**	2.3%	0.8%	5.6%	8.7%
Westchester	2,711	1,230	8,271	**12,212**	2.1%	1.0%	6.5%	9.6%
Total	**35,986**	**10,175**	**81,449**	**127,610**	28.2%	8.0%	63.8%	100.0%

Visualizing cross-tabulations is challenging because there is a lot of data to present, and some people do not easily interpret complicated pictures. Figure 4-6 shows a three-dimensional column chart for the counts shown in the table. This chart shows that the "OTHER" channel is quite high for Manhattan (New York County).

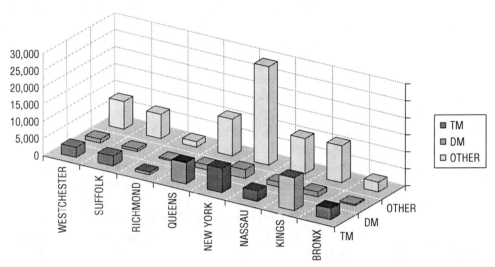

Figure 4-6: A surface plot provides a visual interface for cross-tabulated data.

Numeric Variables

Statistics was originally developed to understand the data collected by scientists, most of which took the form of numeric measurements. In data mining, not all variables are numeric, because of a wealth of descriptive data as well. This section talks about such data from the perspective of descriptive statistics.

Statistical Measures for Continuous Variables

The most basic statistical measures describe a set of data with just a single value. The most commonly used statistic is the arithmetic average value, which statisticians call the *mean*. Some other important values are:

- **Range.** The range is the difference between the smallest and largest observation in the sample. The range is often looked at along with the minimum and maximum values themselves.

- **Average.** The sum of all the values divided by the number of values.

- **Median.** The median value is the one that splits the observations into two equally sized groups, one having values smaller than the median and the other having values larger than the median.

- **Mode.** This is the value that occurs most often.

The median can be used in some situations where calculating the average is impossible, such as when incomes are reported in ranges of $10,000 dollars with a final category "over $100,000" (the Census provides several informative demographic variables in this manner). The number of observations is known for each range, but not the actual values within the range. In addition, the median is less affected by a few observations that are out of line with the others. For instance, if Bill Gates or Carlos Slim Helú moves onto your block, the average net worth of the neighborhood will dramatically increase. However, the median net worth may not change at all.

In addition, various ways of characterizing the range are useful. The range itself is defined by the minimum and maximum value. Looking at percentile information, such as the 25th and 75th percentile, is often valuable for understanding the limits of the middle half of the values as well.

Figure 4-7 shows a chart where the range and average are displayed for order amount by day. This chart uses a logarithmic (log) scale for the vertical axis, because the minimum order is less than $10 and the maximum is more than $1,000. In fact, the daily minimum is consistently around $10, the daily average around $70, and the daily maximum around $1,000. As with categorical variables, it is valuable to use a time chart for continuous values to see when unexpected things are happening.

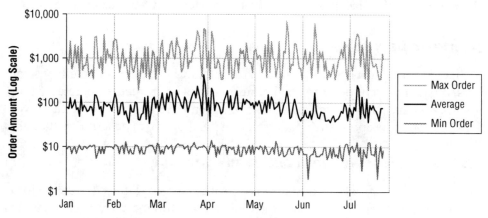

Figure 4-7: A time chart can also be used for continuous values; this one shows the range and average for order amounts each day.

Interesting Properties of the Average and Median

The definition of the average as the sum of all values divided by the number of values is a common definition familiar to most readers. Averages have another property which is also quite interesting, and probably more unfamiliar. The average value is the value that minimizes the sum of the squares of the differences from all other points. For a set of numbers, these definitions are equivalent. However, for computational purposes, computing the sum is much easier than figuring out the value from the other property.

The median has a similar definition. It is the value that minimizes the sum of the absolute differences from all other values. In practice, calculating the median is more computationally difficult than calculating the average, because you basically need to sort the list rather than just summing the values.

Why are these properties important? For more complicated data than just numbers, the common definitions can't be applied. How do you "sum up" points on a scatter plot? How do you "sort" them to find the middle value? In fact, these ideas become quite important in Chapter 13 when describing the various flavors of k-means clustering.

In fact, you don't need to do this. To find the average of a set of points, you can apply the second definition — and it turns out that taking the average along each dimension is the right thing to do. To calculate the median, you can apply the second definition, although the calculations are a bit more cumbersome.

Variance and Standard Deviation

Variance is a measure of the dispersion of data values. Another way of saying this is that variance measures how closely the values cluster around their average. A low variance means that the values stay near the average; a high variance means the opposite. Range is not a good measure of dispersion because it takes only two values into account — the extremes. Removing one extreme can, sometimes, dramatically change the range (indicating an outlier in the data). The variance, on the other hand, takes every value into account. The difference between a given observation and the average of the sample is called its *deviation*. The variance is defined as the average of the squares of the deviations.

Standard deviation, the square root of the variance, is the most frequently used measure of dispersion. It is more convenient than variance because it is expressed in the same units as the values themselves rather than in terms of those units squared. The z-score, introduced earlier, is an observation's distance from the average measured in standard deviations; the calculation makes sense because the data value, the average, and the standard deviation are all measured in the same units. The z-score allows different variables, measured in different units, to be converted to the same unit — distance from the average measured in standard deviations. Assuming the normal distribution, the z-score can be converted to a probability or confidence value.

A Couple More Statistical Ideas

The *Pearson correlation* coefficient (often the "Pearson" is dropped) measures the extent to which a change in one variable is related to a change in another. Correlation, which is called *r*, ranges from –1 to 1. A correlation of 0 means that two variables are not related at all. A correlation of 1 is perfect correlation, meaning that as the first variable changes, the second is guaranteed to change in the same direction, though not necessarily by the same amount. A correlation of –1 simply means that the two variables are totally correlated, except as one goes up the other goes down.

Another measure of correlation is the R^2 value, which is the correlation squared. R^2 goes from 0 (no relationship) to 1 (complete relationship). For instance, the radius and the circumference of a circle are perfectly correlated, although the latter has larger values than the former. A negative correlation means that the two variables move in opposite directions. For example, altitude is negatively correlated with air pressure.

Regression is the process of using the value of one of a pair of variables in order to predict the value of the second. The most common form of regression is ordinary least squares linear regression, so called because it attempts to fit a straight line through the observed *X* and *Y* pairs in a sample. After the line has been established, it can be used to predict a value for *Y* given any *X* and for *X* given any *Y*. Chapter 6 covers the topic of regression in more detail.

Measuring Response

This section looks at statistical ideas in the context of a marketing campaign. The champion-challenger approach to marketing tries out different ideas against business as usual. For instance, assume that a company sends out a million billing inserts each month to entice existing customers to do something. They have settled on one approach to the bill inserts, which is the *champion* offer. Another offer is a *challenger* to this offer. Their approach to comparing these is:

- Send the champion offer to 900,000 customers.
- Send the challenger offer to 100,000 customers, chosen randomly.
- Determine which is better.

Business Analytics

The question is how do you tell when one offer is better than the other? This section introduces the idea of the confidence interval to understand this approach in more detail.

Standard Error of a Proportion

The approach to answering this question uses the idea of a confidence interval. The challenger offer, in the preceding scenario, is sent to a random subset of customers. Based on the response in this subset, what is the expected response for this offer for the entire population?

Assume that 50,000 people in the original population would have responded to the challenger offer if they had received it. Then about 5,000 would be expected to respond in the 10 percent of the population that received it. If exactly this number did respond, then the sample response rate and the population response rate would both be 5.0 percent.

On the other hand, it is possible (though highly, highly unlikely) that all 50,000 responders are in the sample that receives the challenger offer; this would yield a response rate of 50 percent. It is also possible (and is also highly, highly unlikely) that none of the 50,000 are in the sample chosen, for a response rate of 0 percent. In any sample of one-tenth the population, the observed response rate might be as low as 0 percent or as high as 50 percent. These are the extreme values, of course; the actual value is much more likely to be close to 5 percent. "How close?," is the question.

Many different samples can be pulled from the population, with widely varying response rates. Now flip the situation around and say that the sample has 5,000 responders. What does this tell you about the entire population? Once again, it is possible that these are all the responders in the population, so the low-end estimate is 0.5 percent. On the other hand, it is also possible that everyone else was a responder and the sample was very, very unlucky. The high end would then be 90.5 percent.

That is, there is a 100 percent confidence that the actual response rate on the population is between 0.5 percent and 90.5 percent. Having a high confidence is good; however, the range is too broad to be useful. One should be willing to settle for a lower confidence level. Often, 95 or 99 percent confidence is quite sufficient for marketing purposes.

The distribution for the response values follows something called the binomial distribution. Happily, the binomial distribution is very similar to the normal distribution whenever the population is larger than a few hundred people. In Figure 4-8, the jagged line is the binomial distribution and the smooth line is the corresponding normal distribution; they are practically identical.

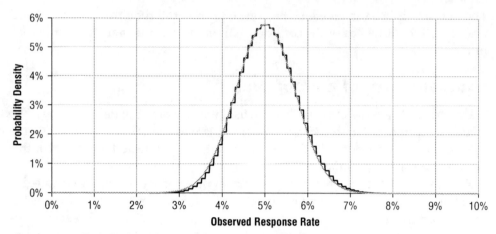

Figure 4-8: Statistics has proven that actual response rate on a population is very close to a normal distribution whose average is the measured response on a sample and whose standard deviation is the standard error of proportion (SEP).

The challenge is to determine the corresponding normal distribution given that a sample with a size of 100,000 has a response rate of 5 percent. As mentioned earlier, the normal distribution has two parameters: the average and standard deviation. The average is the observed average (5 percent) in the sample. To calculate the standard deviation, a formula is needed, and statisticians have figured out the relationship between the standard deviation of a proportion on the one hand (strictly speaking, this is the standard error but the two are similar enough for this discussion) and the average value and sample size on the other. This is called the standard error of a proportion (SEP) and has the formula:

$$SEP = \sqrt{\left(\frac{p * (1 - p)}{N} \right)}$$

In this formula, p is the average value and N is the size of the population. So, the corresponding normal distribution has a standard deviation equal to the square root of the product of the observed response times one minus the observed response divided by the total number of samples.

As discussed earlier in this chapter, about 68 percent of data following a normal distribution lies within one standard deviation of the average value. For the sample size of 100,000, the formula SQRT(5% * 95% / 100,000) is about 0.07 percent, indicating 68 percent confidence that the actual response is between 4.93 percent and 5.07 percent. A bit more than 95 percent is within two standard deviations; so the range of 4.86 percent and 5.14 percent is just over 95 percent confident. So, a 5 percent response rate for the challenger offer implies 95 percent confidence that the response rate on the whole population would have been between 4.86 percent and 5.14 percent. Note that this conclusion depends very much on the fact that people who got the challenger offer were selected randomly from the entire population.

Comparing Results Using Confidence Bounds

The previous section discussed confidence intervals as applied to the response rate of one group who received the challenger offer. In a champion-challenger test, there are actually two response rates, one for the champion and one for the challenger. Are these response rates different? Notice that the observed rates could be different (say 5.000 percent and 5.001 percent), and yet so close that they are effectively the same. One way to compare results is to look at the confidence interval for each response rate and see whether they overlap. If the intervals do not overlap, then the difference in response rates is *statistically significant*.

This example investigates a range of response rates from 4.5 percent to 5.5 percent for the champion model. In practice, a single response rate would be known. However, investigating a range shows what happens as the rate varies from much lower (4.5 percent) to the same (5.0 percent) to much larger (5.5 percent).

The 95 percent confidence bounds is 1.96 standard deviations from the average, so the lower value is the average minus this 1.96 standard deviations, and the upper is the average plus 1.96 standard deviations. Table 4-2 shows the lower and upper bounds for a range of response rates for the champion model going from 4.5 percent to 5.5 percent.

Table 4-2: The 95 Percent Confidence Interval Bounds for the Champion Group for Different Response Rates

RESPONSE	SIZE	SEP	95% CONF	95% CONF * SEP	LOWER	UPPER
4.5%	900,000	0.0219%	1.96	0.0219%*1.96=0.0429%	4.46%	4.54%
4.6%	900,000	0.0221%	1.96	0.0221%*1.96=0.0433%	4.56%	4.64%
4.7%	900,000	0.0223%	1.96	0.0223%*1.96=0.0437%	4.66%	4.74%
4.8%	900,000	0.0225%	1.96	0.0225%*1.96=0.0441%	4.76%	4.84%
4.9%	900,000	0.0228%	1.96	0.0228%*1.96=0.0447%	4.86%	4.94%
5.0%	900,000	0.0230%	1.96	0.0230%*1.96=0.0451%	4.95%	5.05%
5.1%	900,000	0.0232%	1.96	0.0232%*1.96=0.0455%	5.05%	5.15%
5.2%	900,000	0.0234%	1.96	0.0234%*1.96=0.0459%	5.15%	5.25%
5.3%	900,000	0.0236%	1.96	0.0236%*1.96=0.0463%	5.25%	5.35%
5.4%	900,000	0.0238%	1.96	0.0238%*1.96=0.0466%	5.35%	5.45%
5.5%	900,000	0.0240%	1.96	0.0240%*1.96=0.0470%	5.45%	5.55%

Response rates vary from 4.5% to 5.5%. The bounds for the 95% confidence level are calculated using 1.96 standard deviations from the average.

You can determine whether the confidence bounds overlap based on these response rates. The 95 percent confidence bounds for the challenger model vary from about 4.86 percent to 5.14 percent. These bounds overlap the confidence bounds for the champion model when its response rates are 4.9 percent, 5.0 percent, or 5.1 percent. For instance, the confidence interval for a response rate of 4.9 percent goes from 4.86 percent to 4.94 percent; this overlaps 4.86 percent–5.14 percent. Using the overlapping bounds method, these are considered statistically equivalent.

Comparing Results Using Difference of Proportions

The overlapping bounds method is easy but its results are a bit pessimistic. Even when the confidence intervals overlap, the observed *difference* between the values may be significant with some given level of confidence. This suggests another approach, which is to ask whether the difference between the response rates is statistically different from zero. Specifically, the question is: Does the confidence interval for the difference of the values include zero?

Just as a formula exists for the standard error of a proportion, a formula exists for the standard error of the difference of proportions (SEDP):

$$\text{SEDP} = \sqrt{\left(\frac{P_1 * (1 - P_1)}{N_1} + \frac{P_2 * (1 - P_2)}{N_2} \right)}$$

This formula is a lot like the formula for the standard error of a proportion, except the part in the square root is repeated for each group. Table 4-3 shows this formula applied to the champion-challenger problem with response rates varying between 4.5 percent and 5.5 percent for the champion group.

Based on the difference of proportions, three response rates on the champion have confidences under 95 percent (that is, the p-value exceeds 5 percent). If the challenger response rate is 5.0 percent and the champion is 5.1 percent, then the difference in response rates might be due to chance. However, if the champion has a response rate of 5.2 percent, then the likelihood of the difference being due to chance falls to under 1 percent. These results are very similar to the overlapping confidence intervals approach.

WARNING   Confidence intervals only measure the likelihood that sampling affects the result. Many other factors may need to be taken into consideration to determine whether two offers are significantly different.

Table 4-3: Z-scores and P-values for Difference Between Champion and Challenger Response Rates, with 900,000 contacts for Champion and 100,000 for Challenger

RESPONSE			DIFFERENCE OF PROPORTIONS		
CHAMPION	CHALLENGER	DIFFERENCE	SEDP	Z-VALUE	P-VALUE
5.0%	4.5%	0.5%	0.07%	6.9	0.0%
5.0%	4.6%	0.4%	0.07%	5.5	0.0%
5.0%	4.7%	0.3%	0.07%	4.1	0.0%
5.0%	4.8%	0.2%	0.07%	2.8	0.6%
5.0%	4.9%	0.1%	0.07%	1.4	16.8%
5.0%	5.0%	0.0%	0.07%	0.0	100.0%
5.0%	5.1%	-0.1%	0.07%	-1.4	16.9%
5.0%	5.2%	-0.2%	0.07%	-2.7	0.6%
5.0%	5.3%	-0.3%	0.07%	-4.1	0.0%
5.0%	5.4%	-0.4%	0.07%	-5.5	0.0%
5.0%	5.5%	-0.5%	0.07%	-6.9	0.0%

Size of Sample

The formulas for the standard error of a proportion and for the standard error of a difference of proportions both include the sample size. An inverse relationship exists between the sample size and the size of the confidence interval: the more data, the narrower the confidence interval. So, to have more confidence in results, use larger samples.

Table 4-4 shows the confidence interval for different sizes of the challenger group, assuming the challenger response rate is observed to be 5 percent. For very small sizes, the confidence interval is very wide, often too wide to be useful. The normal distribution is an approximation for estimating the actual response rate; with small sample sizes, the estimates are not very good. Statistics has several methods for handling such small sample sizes. However, these are generally not of much interest to data miners because data mining samples are much larger.

Table 4-4: The 95 Percent Confidence Interval for Difference Sizes of the Challenger Group

RESPONSE	SIZE	SEP	95% CONF	LOWER	UPPER	WIDTH
5.0%	1,000	0.6892%	1.96	3.65%	6.35%	2.70%
5.0%	5,000	0.3082%	1.96	4.40%	5.60%	1.21%
5.0%	10,000	0.2179%	1.96	4.57%	5.43%	0.85%
5.0%	20,000	0.1541%	1.96	4.70%	5.30%	0.60%
5.0%	40,000	0.1090%	1.96	4.79%	5.21%	0.43%
5.0%	60,000	0.0890%	1.96	4.83%	5.17%	0.35%
5.0%	80,000	0.0771%	1.96	4.85%	5.15%	0.30%
5.0%	100,000	0.0689%	1.96	4.86%	5.14%	0.27%
5.0%	120,000	0.0629%	1.96	4.88%	5.12%	0.25%
5.0%	140,000	0.0582%	1.96	4.89%	5.11%	0.23%
5.0%	160,000	0.0545%	1.96	4.89%	5.11%	0.21%
5.0%	180,000	0.0514%	1.96	4.90%	5.10%	0.20%
5.0%	200,000	0.0487%	1.96	4.90%	5.10%	0.19%
5.0%	500,000	0.0308%	1.96	4.94%	5.06%	0.12%
5.0%	1,000,000	0.0218%	1.96	4.96%	5.04%	0.09%

What the Confidence Interval Really Means

The confidence interval is a measure of only one thing, the dispersion of the sample estimate with respect to the overall population estimate. Assuming that everything else remains the same, it measures the amount of inaccuracy introduced by the process of sampling. The confidence interval also rests on the assumption that the sampling process itself is random — that is, that any of the one million customers could have been offered the challenger with an equal likelihood. Random means random. The following examples are not random:

- Use customers in California for the challenger and everyone else for the champion.

- Use the 5 percent lowest and 5 percent highest value customers for the challenger, and everyone else for the champion.

- Use the 10 percent most recent customers for the challenger, and everyone else for the champion.

- Use the customers with telephone numbers for the telemarketing campaign; everyone else for the direct mail campaign.

All of these are biased ways of splitting the population into groups, and it is quite possible that the criterion for the split (California, customer value, customer tenure, presence of a phone number) are correlated with the outcome of the marketing test. The previous results all assume no such systematic bias. When there is systematic bias, the formulas for the confidence intervals are not correct.

Bias creeps in in many different ways. For instance, consider a champion model that predicts the likelihood of customers responding to the champion offer. If this model were used to select recipients, then the challenger sample would no longer be a random sample. It would consist of the leftover customers from the champion model, introducing another form of bias.

Or, perhaps the challenger model is only available to customers in certain markets or with certain products. This introduces other forms of bias. In such cases, similar constraints should be used to select recipients for the champion offer. Another form of bias might come from the method of response. The challenger may only accept responses via telephone, but the champion may accept them by telephone or on the Web. In such a case, the challenger response may be dampened because of the lack of a Web channel. Or, there might need to be special training for the inbound telephone service reps to handle the challenger offer. Having a smaller, specially trained group for the challenge offer might increase wait times, another form of bias.

The confidence interval is simply a statement about statistics and dispersion. It does not address all the other forms of bias that might affect results, and these forms of bias are often more damaging than sample variation. The next section talks about setting up a test and control experiment in marketing, diving into these issues in more detail.

Size of Test and Control for an Experiment

The champion-challenger model is an example of a two-way test, where a new method (the challenger) is compared to business-as-usual activity (the champion). This section talks about ensuring that the test and control are large enough to make an informed determination of which, if either, is better. The previous section explained how to calculate the confidence interval for the sample response rate. This section turns this logic inside out. Instead of starting with the size of the groups, instead consider sizes from the perspective of test design. This requires knowing several things:

- Estimated response rate p for one of the groups
- Difference in response rates d that the test should be able to detect with the specified confidence (acuity of the test)
- Confidence interval (say 95 percent)

These three factors provide enough information to determine the size of the samples needed for the test and control. For instance, suppose that the business as usual has a response rate of 5 percent (*p*) and the goal is to measure with 95 percent confidence a difference of 0.2 percent (*d*). This means that if the response of the test group is greater than 5.2 percent, then the experiment can detect the difference with a 95 percent confidence level.

For a problem of this type, the first step is to determine the value of SEDP. What is the standard error associated with a 0.2 percent difference at a 95 percent confidence level? A confidence of 95 percent corresponds to 1.96 standard deviations from the average. The calculation is simple: 1.96 times the standard error is 0.2, meaning that the standard error is 0.102 percent. More generally, the process is to convert the p-value (95 percent) to a z-score (which can be done using the Excel function NORMSINV()) and then divide the desired confidence by this value.

The next step is to plug these values into the formula for SEDP. For this, assume that the test and control are the same size:

$$\frac{0.2\%}{1.96} = \sqrt{\left(\frac{p * (1 - p)}{N} + \frac{(p + d) * (1 - p - d)}{N}\right)}$$

Plugging in the values just described (*p* is 5% and *d* is 0.2%) results in:

$$0.102\% = \sqrt{\left(\frac{5\% * 95\%}{N} + \frac{5.2\% * (94.8\%)}{N}\right)} - \sqrt{\left(\frac{0.0963}{N}\right)}$$

$$N = \frac{((5\%*95\%) + (5.2\%*94.8\%))}{(0.00102)^2}$$

$$= \frac{0.096796}{(0.00102)^2} = 92,963$$

So, having equal-sized groups of 92,963 provides sufficient acuity for measuring a 0.2 percent difference in response rates with 95 percent confidence. Of course, this does not guarantee that the results will differ by at least 0.2 percent. It merely says that with control and test groups of at least this size, a difference in response rates of 0.2 percent should be measurable and statistically significant.

The size of the test and control groups affects how the results can be interpreted. However, this effect can be determined in advance, before the test. Determine the acuity of the test and control groups before running marketing tests to be sure that the test can produce useful results.

TIP Before running a marketing test, determine the acuity of the test by calculating the difference in response rates that can be measured with a high confidence (such as 95 percent).

Multiple Comparisons

The discussion has so far used examples with only one comparison, such as the difference between two presidential candidates or between a test and control group. Often, there are multiple tests at the same time. For instance, there might be three different challenger messages to determine whether one of these produces better results than the business-as-usual message. Handling multiple tests affects the underlying statistics, so understanding what happens is important.

The Confidence Level with Multiple Comparisons

Consider two groups that have been tested. You are told that the difference between the responses in the two groups is 95 percent certain to be due to factors other than sampling variation. A reasonable conclusion is that the two groups are different. In a well-designed test, the most likely reason would the difference in message, offer, or treatment.

Now consider the same situation, except that you are now told that there were actually 20 groups tested, and you were shown only the pair with the greatest difference. Now you might reach a very different conclusion. If 20 groups are tested, you should expect one of them to exceed the 95 percent confidence bound due only to chance, because 95 percent means 19 times out of 20. You can no longer conclude that the difference is due to the testing parameters. Instead, because it is likely that the difference is due to sampling variation, this is the simplest explanation.

The calculation of the confidence level is based on only one comparison. With multiple comparisons, the confidence as calculated previously is not quite sufficient.

Bonferroni's Correction

Fortunately, there is a simple way to fix this problem, developed by the Italian mathematician Carlo Bonferroni. Consider the following conclusions with two challengers, instead of one:

- Champion is better than Challenger X with a confidence of 95%.
- Champion is better than Challenger Y with a confidence of 95%.

Bonferroni calculated the probability that both of these are true. Another way to look at it is to determine the probability that one or the other is false, which is actually easier to calculate. The probability that the first is false is 5 percent, as is the probability of the second being false. The probability that either is false is the sum, 10 percent, minus the probability that both are false at the same time (0.25 percent). So, the probability that both statements are true is about 90 percent (actually 90.25 percent).

Looking at this from the p-value perspective says that the p-value of both statements together (10 percent) is approximated by the sum of the p-values of the two statements separately. This is not a coincidence. Using this estimate, to get a 95 percent confidence for two tests, each would have to be 97.5 percent confident (which corresponds to 2.24 standard deviations from the average).

In fact, a reasonable estimate of the p-value of any number of statements is the sum of the p-values of each one. If there were eight test results with a 95 percent confidence, then the expectation is that all eight would be in their ranges 60 percent at any given time (because 8 * 5% is a p-value of 40%).

Bonferroni applied this observation in reverse. If there are eight tests and the goal is an overall 95 percent confidence, then the bound for the p-value must be 5% / 8 = 0.625%. That is, each observation must be at least 99.375 percent confident, corresponding to a z-score of 2.734. The Bonferroni correction is to divide the desired bound for the p-value by the number of comparisons being made, in order to get a confidence of 1 − p for all comparisons together.

Chi-Square Test

The difference of proportions method is a very powerful method for estimating the effectiveness of campaigns and for other similar situations. However, another statistical test can also be used. This test, the chi-square test, is designed specifically for multiple tests having at least two discrete outcomes (such as response and non-response).

The appeal of the chi-square test is that it readily adapts to multiple test groups and multiple outcomes, as long as the different groups are distinct from each other. In fact, this is about the only important rule when using the chi-square test. As described in Chapter 7, the chi-square test is also the basis for an important type of decision tree.

Expected Values

The place to start with chi-square is to lay data out in a table, as in Table 4-5. This is an example of a simple 2×2 table, which represents a champion-challenger test with two outcomes, say response and non-response. This table also shows the total values for each column and row; that is, the total number of responders and non-responders (each column) and the total number in the test and control groups (each row). The response rate column is added for reference; it is not part of the calculation.

Table 4-5: The Champion-Challenger Data Laid Out for the Chi-Square Test

GROUP	RESPONDERS	NON-RESPONDERS	TOTAL	RESPONSE RATE
Champion	43,200	856,800	900,000	4.80%
Challenger	5,000	95,000	100,000	5.00%
Total	48,200	951,800	1,000,000	4.82%

What if the data were broken up among these groups in a completely unbiased way? That is, what if there really were no differences between the columns and rows in the table? This is a completely reasonable question. The goal is to calculate the expected values in each cell. The expected value assumes that the response rate is the same for both groups and the overall response rate remains the same.

To calculate the expected values, multiply the overall response rate by the sizes of each group to get the expected champion responders and the expected challenger responders. Do the same calculation for the non-responders (using 1 minus the response rate). Table 4-6 shows the expected values for each of the four cells.

Table 4-6: Calculating the Expected Values and Deviations from Expected for the Data in Table 4-5

	ACTUAL RESPONSE			EXPECTED RESPONSE		DEVIATION	
	YES	NO	TOTAL	YES	NO	YES	NO
Champion	43,200	856,800	900,000	43,380	856,620	−180	180
Challenger	5,000	95,000	100,000	4,820	95,180	180	−180
Total	48,200	951,800	1,000,000	48,200	951,800		
Overall Proportion	4.82%	95.18%					

The expected value shows how the data would break up if there were no difference between the champion and challenger. Notice that the expected value is measured in the same units as each cell, typically a customer count, so it actually has a meaning. Also, the sum of the expected values is the same as the sum of all the cells in the original table. The sums of the rows and the sums of the columns are also the same as in the original table.

The table also includes the deviation, which is the difference between the observed value and the expected value. In this case, the deviations all have the same value, but with different signs. This is because the original data has two rows and two columns. Later in the chapter you see examples using larger tables where the deviations are different. However, the deviations in each row and each column always cancel out, so the sum of the deviations in each row and each column is always 0.

Chi-Square Value

The deviation is a good tool for looking at values. However, it does not provide information as to whether the deviation is expected or not expected. Doing this requires another tool from statistics, namely the chi-square distribution developed by the English statistician Karl Pearson in 1900.

The chi-square value for each cell is simply the calculation:

$$\text{Chi-square}(x) = \frac{(x - \text{expected}(x))^2}{\text{expected}(x)}$$

The chi-square value for the entire table is the sum of the chi-square values of all the cells in the table. Notice that the chi-square value is always 0 or positive. Also, when the values in the table match the expected value, then the overall chi-square is 0. This is the smallest possible chi-square value. As the deviations from the expected values get larger in magnitude, the chi-square value also gets larger.

Unfortunately, chi-square values do not follow a normal distribution. This is actually obvious, because the value is always positive, and the normal distribution is symmetric, having both positive and negative values. The good news is that chi-square values follow another distribution, which is also well understood. The chi-square distribution depends not only on the value itself but also on the size of the table. Figure 4-9 shows the density functions for several chi-square distributions.

What the chi-square really depends on is the degrees of freedom, which is easier to calculate than to explain. The number of degrees of freedom of a table is calculated by subtracting 1 from the number of rows and the number of columns and multiplying them together. The 2×2 table in the previous example has 1 degree of freedom. A 5×7 table would have 24 (4 * 6) degrees of freedom. The sidebar "Degrees of Freedom" explains the concept in a bit more detail.

DEGREES OF FREEDOM

The idea behind the degrees of freedom is how many different variables are needed to describe the table of expected values. This is a measure of how constrained the data is in the table.

If the table has r rows and c columns, then there are $r * c$ cells in the table. With no constraints on the table, this is the number of variables that would be needed to describe it. However, the calculation of the expected values has imposed some constraints. In particular, the sum of the values in each row is the same for the expected values as for the original table. That is, if one value were missing, you could recalculate it by taking the constraint into account. The unknown value would be the total sum of the row minus the sum of the values that are present. This suggests that the degrees of freedom is $r * c - r$. The same situation exists for the columns, yielding an estimate of $r * c - r - c$.

However, there is one additional constraint. The sum of all the row sums and the sum of all the column sums must be the same. It turns out that the constraints have been overcounted by one. The degrees of freedom are really $r * c - r - c + 1$. Another way of writing this is $(r - 1) * (c - 1)$.

WARNING   The chi-square test does not work when the expected value in any cell is less than 5 (and more is better). Although not an issue for large data mining problems, it can be an issue when analyzing results from a small test.

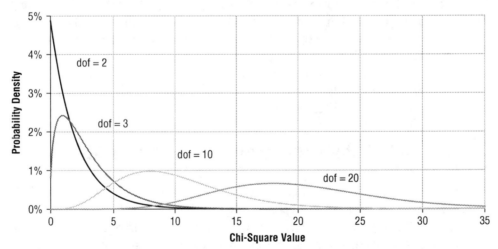

Figure 4-9: The chi-square distribution depends on the degrees of freedom. In general, though, it starts low, peaks early, and gradually descends.

The process for using the chi-square test is:

1. Set up the results as a contingency table.

2. Calculate the expected values.

3. Calculate the deviations from the expected values.

4. Calculate the chi-square (square the deviations and divide by the expected).

5. Sum for an overall chi-square value for the table.

6. Calculate the probability that a chi-square value as large as the observed value would occur when the null hypothesis is true (in Excel, you can use the CHIDIST() function).

The result is the probability that the distribution of values in the table would occur under the null hypothesis (that champion and challenger produce the same results). As Occam's razor suggests, the simplest explanation is that the various factors have no influence on the results; that observed differences from expected values are entirely within the range of expectation. Low chi-square values support the null hypothesis; high values support the opposite, that the factors do make a difference.

Comparison of Chi-Square to Difference of Proportions

Chi-square and difference of proportions can be applied to the same problems. Although the results are not exactly the same, they are similar enough for comfort. Table 4-4 earlier in the chapter shows the likelihood of champion and challenger results being the same using the difference of proportions method for a range of champion response rates. Table 4-7 repeats this using the chi-square calculation instead of the difference of proportions. The results from the chi-square test are very similar to the results from the difference of proportions — a remarkable result considering how different the two methods are.

An Example: Chi-Square for Regions and Starts

A large consumer-oriented company has been running acquisition campaigns in the New York City area. The purpose of this analysis is to look at its acquisition channels to try to gain an understanding of different parts of the market area. For the purposes of this analysis, three channels are of interest:

- **Telemarketing.** Customers who are acquired through outbound telemarketing calls.

- **Direct mail.** Customers who are acquired through direct mail pieces.

- **Other.** Customers who come in through other means.

Table 4-7: Chi-Square Calculation for Difference of Proportions Example in Table 4-4

CHALLENGER		CHAMPION			CHALLENGER EXP.		CHAMPION EXP.	
RESP	NON-RESP	RESP	NON-RESP	OVERALL RESP	RESP	NON-RESP	RESP	NON-RESP
5,000	95,000	40,500	859,500	4.55%	4,550	95,450	40,950	859,050
5,000	95,000	41,400	858,600	4.64%	4,640	95,360	41,760	858,240
5,000	95,000	42,300	857,700	4.73%	4,730	95,270	42,570	857,430
5,000	95,000	43,200	856,800	4.82%	4,820	95,180	43,380	856,620
5,000	95,000	44,100	855,900	4.91%	4,910	95,090	44,190	855,810
5,000	95,000	45,000	855,000	5.00%	5,000	95,000	45,000	855,000
5,000	95,000	45,900	854,100	5.09%	5,090	94,910	45,810	854,190
5,000	95,000	46,800	853,200	5.18%	5,180	94,820	46,620	853,380
5,000	95,000	47,700	852,300	5.27%	5,270	94,730	47,430	852,570
5,000	95,000	48,600	851,400	5.36%	5,360	94,640	48,240	851,760
5,000	95,000	49,500	850,500	5.45%	5,450	94,550	49,050	850,950

CHALLENGER		CHALLENGER CHI-SQUARE		CHAMPION CHI-SQUARE		CHI-SQUARE		DIFF. PROP.
RESP	NON-RESP	RESP	NON RESP	RESP	NON RESP	VALUE	P-VALUE	P-VALUE
5,000	95,000	44.51	2.12	4.95	0.24	51.81	0.00%	0.00%
5,000	95,000	27.93	1.36	3.10	0.15	32.54	0.00%	0.00%
5,000	95,000	15.41	0.77	1.71	0.09	17.97	0.00%	0.00%
5,000	95,000	6.72	0.34	0.75	0.04	7.85	0.51%	0.58%
5,000	95,000	1.65	0.09	0.18	0.01	1.93	16.50%	16.83%
5,000	95,000	0.00	0.00	0.00	0.00	0.00	100.00%	100.00%
5,000	95,000	1.59	0.09	0.18	0.01	1.86	17.23%	16. 91%
5,000	95,000	6.25	0.34	0.69	0.04	7.33	0.68%	0.60%
5,000	95,000	13.83	0.77	1.54	0.09	16.23	0.01%	0.00%
5,000	95,000	24.18	1.37	2.69	0.15	28.39	0.00%	0.00%
5,000	95,000	37.16	2.14	4.13	0.24	43.66	0.00%	0.00%

The area of interest consists of eight counties in New York State. Five of these counties are the boroughs of New York City, two others (Nassau and Suffolk counties) are on Long Island, and one (Westchester) lies just north of the city. This data was shown earlier in Table 4-1. The purpose of this analysis is to determine whether the breakdown of starts by channel and county is due to chance or whether some other factors might be at work.

This problem is particularly suitable for chi-square because the data can be laid out in rows and columns, with no customer being counted in more than one cell. Table 4-8 shows the deviation, expected values, and chi-square values for each combination in the table. Notice that the chi-square values are often quite large in this example. The overall chi-square score for the table is 7,200, which is very large; the probability that the overall score is due to chance is basically zero. That is, the variation among starts by channel and by region is not due to sample variation. Other factors are at work.

Table 4-8: Chi-Square Calculation for Counties and Channels Example

COUNTY	EXPECTED			DEVIATION			CHI-SQUARE		
	TM	DM	OTHER	TM	DM	OTHER	TM	DM	OTHER
Bronx	1,850.2	523.1	4,187.7	1,362	−110	−1,252	1,002.3	23.2	374.1
Kings	6,257.9	1,769.4	14,163.7	3,515	−376	−3,139	1,974.5	80.1	695.6
Nassau	4,251.1	1,202.0	9,621.8	−1,116	371	745	293.0	114.5	57.7
New York	11,005.3	3,111.7	24,908.9	−3,811	−245	4,056	1,319.9	19.2	660.5
Queens	5,245.2	1,483.1	11,871.7	1,021	−103	−918	198.7	7.2	70.9
Richmond	798.9	225.9	1,808.2	−15	51	−36	0.3	11.6	0.7
Suffolk	3,133.6	886.0	7,092.4	−223	156	67	15.8	27.5	0.6
Westchester	3,443.8	973.7	7,794.5	−733	256	477	155.9	67.4	29.1

The next step is to determine which of the values are too high and too low and with what probability. Converting each chi-square value in each cell into a probability, using the degrees of freedom for the table, is tempting. The table is 8×3, so it has 14 degrees of freedom. However, this approach is not correct. The chi-square result is for the entire table; inverting the individual scores to get a probability does not necessarily produce valid probabilities at the cell level (although the results are directionally correct).

An alternative approach proves more accurate. The idea is to compare each cell to everything else. The result is a table that has two columns and two rows, as shown in Table 4-9. One column is the column of the original cell; the other column is everything else. One row is the row of the original cell; the other row is everything else.

Table 4-9: Chi-Square Calculation for Bronx and TM

COUNTY	EXPECTED		DEVIATION		CHI-SQUARE	
	TM	NOT_TM	TM	NOT_TM	TM	NOT_TM
Bronx	1,850.2	4,710.8	1,361.8	−1,361.8	1,002.3	393.7
Not Bronx	34,135.8	86,913.2	−1,361.8	1,361.8	54.3	21.3

The result is a set of chi-square values for the Bronx-TM combination, in a table with 1 degree of freedom. This process can be repeated to estimate the effect of each combination of variables. The result is a table that has a set of p-values that a given cell in the original table is caused by chance, as shown in Table 4-10.

Table 4-10: Estimated P-Value for Each Combination of County and Channel, without Correcting for Number of Comparisons

COUNTY	TM	DM	OTHER
Bronx	0.00%	0.00%	0.00%
Kings	0.00%	0.00%	0.00%
Nassau	0.00%	0.00%	0.00%
New York	0.00%	0.00%	0.00%
Queens	0.00%	0.74%	0.00%
Richmond	59.79%	0.07%	39.45%
Suffolk	0.01%	0.00%	42.91%
Westchester	0.00%	0.00%	0.00%

A second correction must still be made because many comparisons are taking place at the same time. Bonferroni's adjustment takes care of this by multiplying each p-value by the number of comparisons — which is the number of cells in the table. For final presentation purposes, convert the p-values to their opposite, the confidence, and multiply by the sign of the deviation to get a signed confidence. Figure 4-10 illustrates the result.

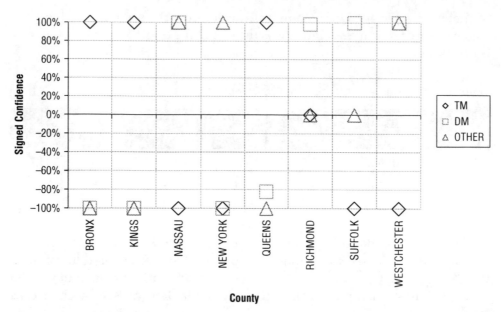

Figure 4-10: This chart shows the signed confidence values for each county and region combination; the preponderance of values near 100% and −100% indicate that observed differences are statistically significant.

The result is interesting. Almost all the values are near 100 percent or −100 percent, meaning that statistically significant differences exist among the counties. In fact, telemarketing (the diamond) and direct mail (the square) are almost always at opposite ends. A direct inverse relationship exists between the two. Direct mail response is high and telemarketing is low in three counties — Manhattan, Nassau, and Suffolk. Many wealthy areas are in these counties, possibly suggesting that wealthy customers are more likely to respond to direct mail than telemarketing. Of course, this could also mean that direct mail campaigns are directed to these areas, and telemarketing to other areas, so the geography was determined by the business operations, rather than the responders. To determine which of these possibilities is correct requires knowing who was contacted as well as who responded.

Case Study: Comparing Two Recommendation Systems with an A/B Test

This case study involves MyBuys, a company that serves up recommendations on the websites of its clients, who are online retailers. On a website that incorporates recommendations from MyBuys, every product page contains recommendations for other products that might also interest the shopper. MyBuys generates recommendations automatically using software that analyzes website behavior and shopping carts.

There are three different types of recommendations. A recommendation might be a *cross sell* — something that the shopper might want to buy in addition to the main item on the product page. It might be an *up sell* — a higher-end version of the main product on the page. A recommendation can also be a *substitution*, an alternative product that is no more expensive, but that might have a better chance of ending up in the shopping cart and being paid for. In all cases, the goal is to get the shopper to spend more money. Figure 4-11 shows the product page for a particular skirt that features four recommendations. Three are cross sells for tops and boots that might go with the skirt. One suggests a different skirt in a similar style.

Figure 4-11: This screen shot shows an example of a site using MyBuys recommendations.

MyBuys did not invent the idea of using recommendations to increase order sizes; online retailers typically do that. MyBuys needs to prove to its prospective clients that the recommendations it delivers are better than the ones the retailers are already using.

MyBuys can (and does) describe the sophisticated profiles built for each shopper and the patented algorithms used to generate recommendations based on those profiles. Its most persuasive sales tool is an A/B test: its challenger against the client's champion, which is typically a system based on rules developed by the client's own merchandisers who are quite knowledgeable about the products and customers.

What constitutes a convincing win? This case study looks at several different ways of analyzing the results from the test. This case highlights the challenges in choosing a metric, as well as the ways to determine which side, if either, is doing better.

First Metric: Participating Sessions

Shoppers have an opportunity to click on recommendations on nearly every page. After a shopper has clicked on any recommendation, the session is called *participating*, because the shopper has shown interest in a recommendation. This understanding of shopper behavior suggests four types of sessions:

- Sessions exposed to MyBuys recommendations that have attracted a click
- Sessions exposed to MyBuys recommendations that have not attracted a click
- Sessions exposed to client recommendations that have attracted a click
- Sessions exposed to client recommendations that have not attracted a click

Participating sessions (the first and third) are known to produce more revenue than non-participating sessions. In most A/B comparisons, the MyBuys recommendation system results in more participating sessions.

Is participating sessions (or more directly, number of clicks) a good metric? Perhaps surprisingly, the answer is no. There are two reasons. One is Simpson's paradox. Even though participating sessions always do better on both sides of an A/B test, the side with more participating sessions can actually produce less revenue if the relationship between revenue and clicks also differs between the two sides. This could happen if, for example, one side specialized in high-value cross-sell recommendations that are less likely to be accepted, but more valuable when they are, and the other side specializes in recommendations for minor upgrades that are often accepted, but worth little.

The second reason that counting clicks is not a good metric is that clicks, in and of themselves, are not valuable. If the goal were to collect clicks, it would be easy to win by recommending fabulous items at ridiculously low prices. But that would be losing sight of the business goal, which is to increase revenue.

Second Metric: Daily Revenue Per Session

The next metric considered was daily revenue per session, regardless of whether shoppers clicked on the recommendations or not. What this means is the average revenue for shoppers on either side of the A/B test — for all shoppers, not just purchasers. Using average dollars per session rather than the total revenue works even when the sizes of the "A" and "B" sides are different.

Figure 4-12 shows the daily revenue standardized over the entire population (so the same average and standard deviation is used for both sides of the tests). This chart also shows the 95 percent confidence bounds, so seeing when a particular day's pattern exceeds thresholds is easy. Using standardized values with such boundaries quickly shows outliers and unusual behavior. However, neither side seems to be consistently doing better than the other, at least by visual inspection of the chart.

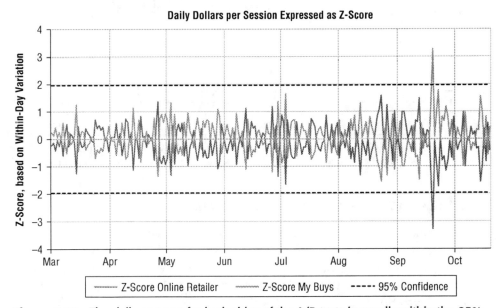

Figure 4-12: The daily revenue for both sides of the A/B tests is usually within the 95% confidence bounds and does not obviously favor one side of the test over the other.

> **TIP** A control chart that shows daily fluctuations conveys more information when confidence bounds are included on the chart.

The chart is highly symmetric because the average and standard deviation are calculated separately for each day, for all sessions on that day. There are only two types of sessions (one for the "A" side and one for the "B" side), so one will tend to be above the overall average and the other below it. Figure 4-13 illustrates similar data for a shorter time-period, but with the vertical axis being the total dollar value of all orders each day. Notice that the first version of the chart takes into account all the inter-day variation; the second version gives a better feel for what happens from one day to the next in terms of dollar volume.

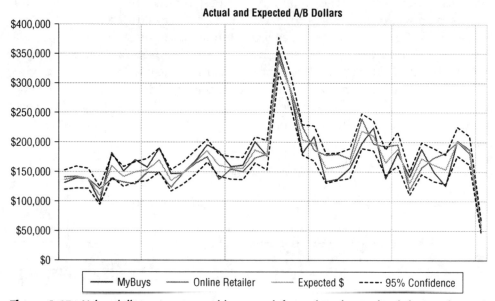

Figure 4-13: Using dollar amounts provides more information about what is happening over time, in terms of sales. The data here is similar to Figure 4-12, but for a shorter time frame.

Third Metric: Who Wins on Each Day?

The previous two figures suggest yet another way of measuring success. Consider the A/B tests as a competition on each day: Which side wins more often? The example has data for 233 days. The score for these days is: MyBuys, 126; client, 107. MyBuys is winning, but is this a significant effect? Or, is it within the realm of sample variation?

This type of question goes far back into history to the 1600s, to the work of the mathematician Jacob Bernoulli, one of several prominent mathematicians in the Bernoulli family. Before there was data mining, there was statistics. Before statistics, probability. Before probability, gambling. Jacob Bernoulli studied games of chance in the 1600s. In doing so, he invented the binomial distribution, which was mentioned earlier in this chapter. This distribution can answer questions such as: "How often will a fair coin land on heads seven or more times in ten coin tosses?"

The particular mathematics are beyond the scope of this book. However, the exact same ideas can be applied — centuries later — to an A/B test run on 233 days to ask: "How often would one side win 126 or more times, assuming there is no difference between the two sides?" The "or more" is generally added because any particular value of wins is highly unlikely; instead the question becomes one about doing "at least as well as 126 wins."

What is the probability that one side wins at least 126 times, assuming no difference between the two sides? The calculation can be done in Excel, using the formula 1-BINOMDIST(126,233,0.5,1). The answer is, about 9.5 percent.

This means that 90.5 percent of the time, in a run of 233 days, neither side wins 126 times. So the MyBuys win record is a bit unusual, but such an outcome is expected about 10 percent of the time. The traditional (although admittedly arbitrary) cutoff for statistical significance is 5%, so, although suggestive, the results are not conclusive. Running the test for more days could resolve this issue, but 233 days is already almost eight months.

Fourth Metric: Average Revenue Per Session

Yet another measure is perhaps the simplest. Instead of breaking out the A/B test by day, just consider the average revenue per session:

- The overall average for 45,213 sessions is $6.01.
- The average for the 22,640 sessions on the MyBuys side of the test is $6.52.
- The average for the 22,573 sessions using the client approach is $5.51.

These numbers suggest that the recommendation software is doing better, with an improvement of $1.01. However, "suggest" is quite different from statistical significance.

Earlier, this chapter introduced the notion of standard error of a proportion to determine whether two proportions are the same or different. The same idea applies to averages, where the notion of standard error of a mean (SEM) has a simple formula:

$$\text{SEM} = \frac{\text{standard deviation}}{\sqrt{\text{sample size}}}$$

In this case, the standard deviation is calculated as 158 and the sample size is 45,213, resulting in a standard error of 0.734. The difference of $1.01 is then 1.36 standard errors above the average. This is a largish number, but statistical significance is usually at the 5% threshold, which implies a value larger than 1.96.

Comparing averages, once again, produces a suggestive result in favor of MyBuys, but not a result that is statistically significant.

Fifth Metric: Incremental Revenue Per Customer

All the measures so far have hinted that the automatic recommendations do a better job than the client's recommendations. However, none are conclusive. After pondering this problem and discussing the issues with the marketing group at MyBuys, the authors realized that a shortcoming exists in all these methods: They focus on sessions rather than customers.

What if a shopper sees a recommendation, then ponders it, and comes back *later* and makes the purchase? None of the metrics discussed so far benefit from this effect, because they measure only what happens in the session containing the particular recommendation.

Instead of looking at sessions on a daily basis, a better approach is to put customers in two groups: the "A" group that sees the MyBuys recommendations and the "B" group that sees the client's. These groups can then be tracked over time. In particular, the total customer revenue can be measured over time for both groups. Does one group have more revenue per customer than the other group?

> **TIP** Metrics focused on the customer often come closer to what the business needs. However, gathering the appropriate data at the customer level may be harder.

Implementing this test required changing the testing methodology. Instead of sessions being assigned to a particular group (A or B) at the beginning of a visit, shoppers are assigned to a particular group and remain in that group for the duration of the test.

This method has several advantages over the other approaches. One is its focus on incremental revenue per customer which, ultimately, is what any retailer wants to improve. If the recommendations encourage customers to return to the site, then this customer-focused metric captures that improvement.

Another is that it allows for the tests to accumulate data over longer periods of time. The test can start, and each day's information accumulates until the numbers are significant. This accumulation typically occurs much more quickly than the "which side won on a particular day" method.

A third advantage is that the results from the tests are impressive and understandable, because they are measured in dollars. Using a 28-day period for testing, the MyBuys recommendations generated more than 15 percent more revenue than the client recommendations. This result had a confidence of more than 99 percent. Furthermore, this metric is more closely aligned with what the retailers want to do, demonstrating the value of the MyBuys recommendation system much more clearly than other metrics.

Data Mining and Statistics

Many data mining techniques were invented by statisticians or have now been integrated into statistical software; they are now extensions of standard statistics. Although data miners and statisticians use similar techniques to solve similar problems, the data mining approach differs from the standard statistical approach in several areas:

- Data miners tend to ignore measurement error in raw data.
- Data miners assume the availability of more than enough data and processing power.
- Data mining assumes dependency on time everywhere.
- Designing experiments in the business world can be hard.
- Data is truncated and censored.

These are differences of approach and emphasis, rather than fundamental differences. As such, they shed some light on how the business problems addressed by data miners differ from the scientific problems that spurred the development of statistics.

No Measurement Error in Basic Data

Statistics originally derived from measuring scientific quantities, such as the width of skulls or the brightness of stars. These measurements are quantitative and the precise measured value depends on extraneous factors such as the type of measuring device and the ambient temperature. In particular, two people taking the same measurement at the same time are going to produce slightly different results. The results might differ by 5 percent or 0.05 percent, but the results are very likely to differ. Traditionally, statistics looks at observed measurements as falling into a confidence interval.

On the other hand, the amount of money a customer paid last January is quite well understood — down to the last penny. The definition of customer may be a little bit fuzzy; the definition of January may be fuzzy (consider 5-4-4 accounting cycles). However, after these are defined, the amount of the payment is precise. There is no measurement error.

There are other sources of error in business data. Of particular concern is operational error, which can cause systematic bias in the data being collected. For instance, clock skew may mean that two events that seem to happen in one sequence may have actually occurred in the opposite order (this is a particular problem when time zone information gets dropped from date and time stamps). A database record may have a Tuesday update date, when it really was updated on Monday, because the updating process runs just after midnight. Such forms of bias are systematic, and potentially represent spurious patterns that might be picked up by data mining algorithms.

One major difference between business data and scientific data is that the latter has many numeric values and the former has many categorical values. Even monetary amounts are discrete — two values can differ only by multiples of pennies (or some similar amount) — even though the values might be represented by real numbers.

A Lot of Data

Traditionally, statistics has been applied to smallish data sets (at most a few thousand rows) with few columns (fewer than a dozen). The goal has been to squeeze as much information as possible out of the data. This is still important in problems where collecting data is expensive or arduous — such as market research, crash testing cars, or testing the chemical composition of Martian soil.

Business data, on the other hand, is very voluminous. The challenge is understanding *anything* about what is happening, rather than *every possible thing*. Fortunately, enough computing power is now available to handle the large volumes of data.

Sampling theory is an important part of statistics. The discipline explains how results on a subset of data (a *sample*) relate to the whole. This is very important when planning to do a poll, because asking everyone a question is not possible; rather, pollsters ask a very small sample in order to derive overall opinion. However, sampling is much less important when all the data is available along with the computing power to process it. Usually, using all the data available produces better results than using a small subset.

There are a few cases when this is not necessarily true. There might simply be too much data. Instead of building models on tens of millions of customers, build models on hundreds of thousands — at least to learn how to build better models. Another reason is to get an intentionally *unrepresentative* sample. Such a sample, for instance, might have an equal number of responders and non-responders, although the original data had different proportions, because many data mining algorithms work better on a balanced sample. However, using more data rather than sampling down and using less is generally better, unless you have a good reason for sampling down.

Time Dependency Pops Up Everywhere

Almost all data used in data mining has a time dependency associated with it. Customers' reactions to marketing efforts change over time. Prospects' reactions to competitive offers change over time. A marketing campaign run this year is rarely going to produce the same results as the same campaign run last year. You should expect the results to change.

On the other hand, scientific experiments should yield similar results regardless of when the experiment takes place. The laws of science are considered immutable; they do not change over time. By contrast, the business climate changes daily. Statistics often considers repeated observations to be independent observations. That is, one observation does not influence another. Data mining, on the other hand, must often consider the time component of the data.

Experimentation Is Hard

Data mining has to work within the constraints of existing business practices. This can make it difficult to set up experiments, for several reasons:

- Businesses may not be willing to invest in efforts that reduce short-term gain for long-term learning.
- Business processes may interfere with well-designed experimental methodologies.
- Factors that may affect the outcome of the experiment may not be obvious.
- Timing plays a critical role and may render results useless.

Of these, the first two are the most difficult. The first simply says that tests do not get done. Or, they are done so poorly that the results are useless. The second poses the problem that a seemingly well-designed experiment may not be executed correctly. There are always hitches when planning a test; sometimes these hitches make reading the results impossible.

Data Is Censored and Truncated

The data used for data mining is often incomplete in one of two special ways. *Censored* values are incomplete because whatever is being measured is not complete. One example is customer tenure. The final tenure of active customers is greater than the current tenure; however, which customers are going to stop tomorrow and which are going to stop 10 years from now? The actual tenure is greater than the observed value and cannot be known until the customer actually stops at some unknown point in the future.

Figure 4-14 shows another situation that illustrates the challenge with censored data. This curve shows sales and inventory for one product at a retailer. Sales are always less than or equal to the available inventory. On the days with the Xs, though, the inventory sold out. What is the demand on these days? The potential sales are greater than or equal to the observed sales — however the full potential is not known.

Truncated data poses another problem in terms of biasing samples. Truncated records are not included in the database, often because they are too old. For instance, when Company A purchases Company B, their systems are merged. Often, data about the active customers from Company B are moved into the data warehouse for Company A. That is, all customers active on a given date are moved over. Customers who had stopped the day before are not moved over (in extreme cases). This is an example of left truncation, and it pops up throughout corporate databases, usually with no warning (unless the documentation is very, very good about saying what is not in the database as well as what is). This can cause confusion when looking at tenures by customer start date — and discovering that all customers who started five years before the merger were mysteriously active for at least five years. This is not due to a miraculous acquisition program. This is because all the ones who stopped earlier were excluded.

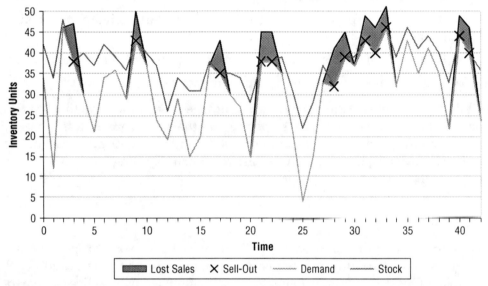

Figure 4-14: A time series of product sales and inventory illustrates the problem of censored data.

Lessons Learned

This chapter covers some basic statistical methods that are useful for analyzing data. When looking at data, it is useful to look at histograms and cumulative histograms to see what values are most common. More important, though, is looking at values over time.

One of the big questions addressed by statistics is whether observed values are expected or not. For this, the number of standard deviations from the average (z-score) can be used to calculate the probability of the value being due to chance, assuming the null hypothesis (the p-value). High p-values mean that the null hypothesis is probably true; that is, nothing interesting is happening. Low p-values are suggestive that other factors may be influencing the results. Converting z-scores to p-values depends on the normal distribution.

Business problems often require analyzing data expressed as proportions. Fortunately, these behave similarly to normal distributions. The formula for the standard error for proportions (SEP) defines a confidence interval on a proportion such as a response rate. The standard error for the difference of proportions (SEDP) helps determine whether two values are similar. This works by defining a confidence interval for the difference between two values.

When designing marketing tests, the SEP and SEDP can be used for sizing test and control groups. In particular, these groups should be large enough to measure differences in response with a high enough confidence. Tests that have more than two groups need to take into account an adjustment, called Bonferroni's correction, when setting the group sizes.

The chi-square test is another statistical method that is often useful. This method directly calculates the estimated values for data laid out in rows and columns. Based on these estimates, the chi-square test can determine whether the results are likely or unlikely. As shown in an example, the chi-square test and SEDP methods produce similar results.

Statisticians and data miners solve similar problems. However, because of historical differences and differences in the nature of the problems, there are some differences in emphasis. Data miners generally have a lot of data with few measurement errors. This data changes over time, and values are sometimes incomplete. The data miner has to be particularly suspicious about bias introduced into the data by business processes.

The rest of the book dives into more detail about modern techniques for building models and understanding data. Many of these techniques have been adopted by statisticians and build on centuries of work in this area. Directed data mining techniques, the subject of the next section of this book, rely heavily on the statistical ideas presented in this chapter. The next chapter starts the discussion on this important class of data mining techniques.

CHAPTER 13

Finding Islands of Similarity: Automatic Cluster Detection

This is the first of two chapters about finding islands of similarity in complex data sets. This chapter focuses on the most general of the automatic clustering techniques, k-means clustering, and focuses on practical applications. The next chapter dives into more detail on several other techniques.

Why is cluster detection useful? The patterns found by data mining are not always immediately forthcoming. Sometimes this is because there are no patterns to be found. Other times, the problem is not the lack of patterns, but the excess. The data may contain so much complex structure that even the best data mining techniques are unable to coax out meaningful patterns. When mining such data for the answer to a specific question, competing explanations might cancel each other out. As with radio reception, too many competing signals add up to noise. Low prices stimulate purchases in one customer segment, but make the product seem less appealing to another. In these situations, cluster detection — an undirected technique — can be of assistance. Cluster detection provides a way to learn about the structure of complex data; to break up the cacophony of competing signals into simpler components.

When human beings try to make sense of complex questions, our natural tendency is to break the subject into smaller pieces, each of which can be explained more simply. What do trees look like? It is a hard question to answer, not because you haven't seen any trees, but because you have seen so many. Not all trees look alike, so you start looking for organizing principles. By narrowing the focus to particular clusters defined by these attributes, the question becomes easier to answer.

459

When clusters have been defined, finding simple patterns within each cluster is often possible. If you happen to define two clusters based on whether trees have broad leaves or whether they have needles, you will notice certain things that members of each cluster have in common with each other and things (other than the defining foliage type) that differ between the clusters. For example, trees in one cluster change color with the seasons; trees in the other do not. A different choice of cluster defining variables might not yield a color pattern, but might reveal some other useful pattern involving timber value or resistance to infestation by beetles.

This is an example of a very noisy dataset being decomposed into a number of better-behaved clusters. The question is: How can these better behaved groups be found? This is where techniques for automatic cluster detection come in — to help see the forest without getting lost in the trees.

This chapter begins with a discussion of customer segmentation and the role that clustering can play in it. This is followed by several examples of the usefulness of clustering in fields as diverse as banking and clothing design. The examples seem very different, but they all share the central idea of cluster detection — finding groups of records that are close to each other and far from records in other clusters. This notion of closeness or similarity is the same idea used to find nearest neighbors for memory-based reasoning, so all the distance and similarity measures introduced in Chapter 9 can also be used for finding clusters.

K-means clustering, which is among the most popular techniques for cluster detection, is used for the examples in this chapter. The next chapter introduces several more clustering techniques. K-means relies on a geometric interpretation of data as points in space. The distance between two data points depends on their representation, so cluster detection has data preparation requirements similar to those for memory-based reasoning.

Whatever technique is used to find them, clusters must be evaluated and, for many applications, interpreted. Several approaches to cluster evaluation and interpretation are described. Occasionally, cluster interpretation leads to new insights that have business value. One of the case studies in this chapter describes a bank that, inspired by results from clustering, changes the way it markets home equity loans. Another case study shows how automatic cluster detection was used to evaluate and propose changes to the boundaries used to define editorial zones for the *Boston Globe*, a daily newspaper.

Clustering can be a preliminary step for directed data mining. Records that have been scored by a cluster model have a field indicating which cluster they belong to. This can be an important input to predictive models. Clusters or segments are also often useful as a dimension for producing reports and cross-tabulations.

The chapter ends with some variations on the k-means algorithm — soft k-means, k-medians, and k-medoids. It also provides some discussion of data preparation issues that are important for clustering.

Searching for Islands of Simplicity

Automatic cluster detection is a tool for undirected data mining, because the automatic cluster detection techniques find patterns in the data without regard to any target variable. Directed data mining starts out with a preclassified model set. In clustering, the model set is not preclassified, or at least the target variable is not used. Instead, clustering algorithms search for groups of records that are similar to each other and different from other records. It is up to you to determine whether the resulting groups of similar records represent something of interest to the business or something inexplicable and perhaps unimportant. Finding clusters is rarely an end in itself. After clusters have been detected, they may become objects of study, or a reporting dimension in an OLAP cube, or the cluster assignments may become inputs to other models, or clusters may be monitored over time to see when and how customers migrate among them.

Clustering does produce data mining models that can be used to produce scores. A cluster model can produce the same kinds of scores as a decision tree. Just as a single decision tree can produce scores as either a class label indicating the most likely class or a list of probability estimates for each of several classes, a cluster model can make "hard" or "soft" cluster assignments. Hard clustering assigns each record to a single cluster. Soft clustering associates each record with several clusters with varying degrees of strength. What distinguishes clustering from other classification techniques is that the classes are detected automatically instead of being provided in the form of a categorical target.

> **TIP** As with other modeling techniques, clustering algorithms find patterns in the model set that can be expressed as rules or formulas that can, in turn, be applied to other data sets to produce scores. The scores produced by cluster models are cluster assignments, which may be a single cluster label, or estimates of probability of membership in each cluster.

Although clustering is undirected in a technical sense, it is often part of a directed activity in the business sense because clusters are sought for some business purpose. In marketing and customer relationship management, clusters are usually called "segments," and customer segmentation is a popular application of clustering.

Customer Segmentation and Clustering

For a variety of marketing purposes, many companies find that segmenting their customer base into groups that are expected to behave similarly is useful. These customer segments may be used for targeting cross-sell offers, for focusing retention efforts, for customizing messaging, or for a myriad of other purposes. The expectation is that by focusing on groups of similar customers, these efforts will be more effective than a one-size-fits-all approach.

Customer segmentation is a business in its own right. It is possible to append commercially available segment labels to ZIP codes, census tracts, and even individual households. The sidebar "Clustering Americans by Demographics and Behavior" describes one such scheme.

CLUSTERING AMERICANS BY DEMOGRAPHICS AND BEHAVIOR

A company called Claritas (now part of Nielsen) divides the United States population into 66 segments. You can go to the Claritas website to look up which segments predominate in your favorite U.S. ZIP codes.

The segments combine demographic data from the U.S. Census with behavioral data gleaned from multiple sources such as magazine subscriptions, product registrations, automobile registrations, and the like. Each segment is a cell in a matrix defined by social groups with catchy names, such as "Urban Uptown" or "City Centers," and lifestage groups with catchy names, such as "Young Achievers" or "Conservative Classics." The segments, called PRIZM codes, are made available at several levels of a geographic hierarchy, including the individual household, the ZIP+4 (the finest granularity postal code in the U.S., which may be a floor in an apartment building or a small group of houses), and ZIP code (an entire town or village, or a neighborhood in a larger city).

According to Claritas, one author's neighbors belong predominantly to these segments:

29	American Dreams
16	Bohemian Mix
07	Money & Brains
31	Urban Achievers
04	Young Digerati

The other author's neighbors belong to these segments:

29	American Dreams
16	Bohemian Mix
07	Money & Brains
26	The Cosmopolitans
04	Young Digerati

Pretty similar. The only difference is that one has Urban Achievers where the other has Cosmopolitans. Urban Achievers, as described by Claritas, are:

Concentrated in the nation's port cities, Urban Achievers is often the first stop for up-and-coming immigrants from Asia, South America, and Europe. These young singles, couples, and families are typically college-educated and ethnically diverse: about a third are foreign-born, and even more speak a language other than English.

Cosmopolitans are:

Educated, upper-midscale, and ethnically diverse, the Cosmopolitans are urbane couples in America's fast-growing cities. Concentrated in a handful of metros — such as Las Vegas, Miami, and Albuquerque — these households feature older, empty-nesting homeowners. A vibrant social scene surrounds their older homes and apartments, and residents love the nightlife and enjoy leisure-intensive lifestyles.

It is debatable whether segment names like these reveal more than they obscure. A name tends to highlight one or two features of a cluster that may be defined by many more factors. The raw data for the authors' two neighborhoods would reveal that their populations are not really as similar as the cluster names suggest. Another way to characterize a cluster is to look at a typical member and then ask which features of the typical member are most different from the overall population.

Customers are often assigned to segments based on geography, product usage, length of relationship, revenue, demographics, or attitudes expressed to market researchers through surveys. After segments have been defined, products or services can be developed with them in mind. Segments can also be used the same way that RFM cells (from Chapter 6) are used — as a way to test and measure the effects of marketing campaigns and to track customers as they move from segment to segment.

There are several approaches to defining customer segments. This section describes various ways that data mining techniques can be made part of the process.

Similarity Clusters

Chapter 6 describes how you can use similarity models to score customers based on their distance from a prototypical or ideal customer. In that example, newspaper subscribers are compared to the reader profile that the newspaper offers to advertisers. You can use the same approach to assign customers to segments. Each segment is represented by a prototype. Customers are assigned to clusters based on their similarity to the segment prototypes.

In another example, in a case the authors described in an earlier book, *Mastering Data Mining*, a credit card issuer defined three profitable customer segments:

- High-balance revolvers
- High-volume transactors
- Convenience users

High-balance revolvers are profitable because they maintain a high balance and pay interest and finance charges on it every month. High-volume transactors are profitable because they make many transactions and the card issuer receives a percentage of each one. Convenience users are profitable because of their occasional large purchases that take months to be paid off.

The bank created a prototype for each of these segments and then gave cardholders three scores based on their distance from each prototype. Cardholders were assigned to a customer segment based on these scores.

A variation on this approach uses clustering to form the initial segments. The prototype for each segment is the cluster centroid. That is how subscribers were assigned to segments in the following example of cluster-based segmentation of newspaper subscribers.

Tracking Campaigns by Cluster-Based Segments

The authors were once asked to use clustering to build customer segments for a newspaper using k-means clustering. For clients to recommend a particular data mining algorithm is unusual. In this case, the client was intrigued by the notion that naturally occurring clusters of customers might reveal segments that would otherwise be missed. The client was especially interested in finding segments with particularly good customer retention, so the project is an example of using an undirected data mining technique for a directed goal.

The clusters found in this project did have different retention characteristics, as hoped, but when a target variable can be identified, a decision tree produces segments chosen to maximize differences in the target. A better approach for finding retention clusters would be to use retention as a target variable for a decision tree, and then to keep the leaf size quite large so only a few leaves are created. Each leaf is a cluster that comes with a built-in description in the form of a rule.

WARNING It is not usually a good idea for business people to select a data mining technique. Business people should concentrate on properly defining the business problem and let a data mining expert decide how best to attack it.

In any clustering project, one of the first questions is what variables should be used to define the clusters. In this case, previous directed models for the same subscriber base provided guidance. The directed models were built for a variety of purposes, such as predicting voluntary cancellation, failure to pay, and the purchase of ancillary products.

Any variable that had proved to be predictive for one of these models was deemed suitable for clustering. These were a mixture of customer behaviors measured and demographic variables measured at the level of the census tract of the subscriber's address. Following is a list of the demographic variables:

- Tenure in the current subscription period
- Number of previous subscriptions, prior to the current one
- Total tenure over all subscriptions
- Original acquisition channel
- Original offer
- Billing frequency
- Original payment type
- Current payment type
- Subscription change rate
- Complaint rate
- Proportion of vacation days to all days in subscription
- Census income per capita
- Census percent white
- Census percent foreign born
- Census percent single household
- Census percent private school
- Census percent management and professional
- Census percent college educated

A few of the variables require explanation. The ones with names ending in "rate" are based on counts of various kinds of events such as complaints, vacation suspensions, and changes to the subscription. In order to allow comparison between subscribers with different tenures, these counts are expressed as events per year even for subscribers with less than a full year of tenure. So, a subscriber with six months of tenure and two complaints has a complaint rate of four per year.

Of the variables on the list, tenure was considered so important that it was used for an initial segmentation, one for new subscriptions with less than a year of tenure and one for established subscriptions. Within each tenure segment, an automatic cluster detection algorithm was used to find four clusters.

The next step is to try to understand the clusters. Several meetings were held to try to come up with descriptive names for them. These meetings considered the average member of each cluster and the variables whose value in the cluster was most different from the population average. The naming effort was eventually abandoned and the names New A, B, C, and D and Tenured A, B, C, and D were adopted. The problem was that any name short enough to be catchy left out too many factors that were important for defining cluster membership. A name such as "Old and Wealthy" leaves out important information, but "Old, Wealthy, Suburban, Married, with few complaints, and few changes in subscription" is not very catchy.

Despite the difficulty in naming the clusters, the cluster-based segments proved their usefulness the first month they were in use. The newspaper conducted an upgrade campaign trying to persuade people who received only the Sunday paper to subscribe to the daily paper as well. Overall, the campaign was not a success. When telemarketers reached the Sunday subscribers, instead of accepting the upgrade offer, some took the opportunity to cancel their subscriptions completely! When the results were analyzed by segment, however, there turned out to be a couple of segments where the campaign had worked quite well. Rather than giving up on the upgrade campaign, future efforts could concentrate on the segments where it was effective.

TIP Lurking inside failed marketing campaigns may be customer segments where the campaign actually worked. Finding these segments can powerfully improve subsequent campaigns.

Clustering Reveals an Overlooked Market Segment

In the previous story, the clusters proved useful because of the differential response to marketing campaigns. The clusters themselves did not provide much insight. In this story, the principal reward of a clustering effort was the insight a marketing analyst gained by examining the clusters.

Back in the 1990s, Bank of America's National Consumer Assets Group in San Francisco embarked on a data mining program that resulted in increased adoption rates for home equity loans. Before the project, home equity loan marketing targeted two groups: parents of college-age children, and people with high but variable incomes. Marketing materials and outbound call lists reflected this focus.

The data mining effort included both directed data mining in the form of propensity models for various products, including home equity lines, and undirected data mining to explore new ways of segmenting customers. While doing the analysis, fourteen clusters were discovered. Many of these were hard to interpret and the clusters did not prove useful as an overall customer segmentation scheme. The effort to interpret them revealed something interesting.

The analysts at the bank tried to understand the clusters by looking at how the propensity scores varied across them. One cluster stood out because it had a high proportion of customers who either had a home equity line of credit or had a high propensity score for that product. Although the cluster included only about 7 percent of customers, it had more than a quarter of the customers with the highest home equity propensity scores.

Clusters can be characterized by what members have in common and by what separates members from the customer population as a whole. Members of this cluster tended to be middle aged, married home owners with teenage children. In addition to the unusually high density of home equity lines, the cluster was notable because 30 percent of cluster members had both personal and business-oriented banking products under the same tax ID. Because only small, sole proprietorships use the owner's Social Security number as a tax ID, the cluster clearly included many small business owners.

A survey of branch managers confirmed that the small business owners and the home equity line customers were often one and the same. Apparently, people were borrowing against their home equity to fund the startup of a small business. None of the bank's marketing material had been oriented that way. A new campaign based on this idea got dramatically better response than the previous campaign, which had focused on using home equity to pay for college tuition.

Fitting the Troops

Cluster detection has even been applied to the field of clothing design — not for shows in New York, Paris, or Milan, but for the U.S. Army. In the 1990s, the army commissioned a study on how to redesign the sizing of uniforms for female soldiers. The army's goal was to reduce the number of different sizes that have to be kept in inventory, while still providing each soldier with well-fitting uniforms. Maintaining inventory and supply lines is a major expense and logistical problem for any army.

As anyone who has ever shopped for women's clothing is aware, there is already a surfeit of classification systems (odd sizes, even sizes, plus sizes, junior sizes, petite sizes, and so on) for categorizing garments. None of these systems was designed with the needs of the U.S. military in mind. Susan Ashdown and Beatrix Paal, researchers at Cornell University's College of Human Ecology, went back to the basics; they designed a new set of sizes based on the actual shapes of women. All soldiers, when they enter the army, are subject to physical exams that take many measurements of body size. This is the data that Professor Ashdown used for her research.

Unlike the traditional clothing size systems, the one Ashdown and Paal came up with is not an ordered set of graduated sizes where all dimensions increase together. Instead, they came up with sizes that fit particular body types. Each body type corresponds to a cluster of records in a database of body measurements. The database contained more than 100 measurements for each of nearly 3,000 women. The clustering technique employed was the k-means algorithm, described in the next section.

Of course, the army has not changed the method of sizing women's uniforms. Although it is heartening to know that there is a more sensible sizing system for women's clothes, history shows that when the military does things differently than the rest of the world, the "mil spec" versions tend to be considerably more costly than civilian alternatives. There is a multi-trillion dollar fashion industry based on the current sizing system. The inertia of the market precludes making big changes to women's sizing, even to a saner system.

The K-Means Clustering Algorithm

The k-means algorithm is one of the most commonly used clustering algorithms. The "k" in its name refers to the fact that the algorithm looks for a fixed number of clusters. K is specified by the user. The version described here was first published by J. B. MacQueen in 1967, but the idea goes back to the 1950s. For ease of explaining, the technique is illustrated using two-dimensional diagrams. Keep in mind that there are usually more than two input variables. However, limiting the example to two dimensions makes it possible to use simple scatter plots to illustrate the procedure, which works the same way in higher dimensions.

Each record is considered a point in a scatter plot, which in turn implies that all the input variables are numeric. The data can be pictured as clouds on the scatter plot. The goal of the clustering algorithm is to find k points that make good cluster centers. The cluster centers define the clusters: Each record is assigned to the cluster defined by its nearest cluster center.

Clearly, good cluster centers should be in the densest parts of the data cloud. The *best* assignment of cluster centers could be defined as the one that minimizes the sum of the distance from every data point to its nearest cluster center (or perhaps the distance squared). Finding that optimal solution is difficult, and the k-means algorithm does not attempt to do so. Instead, it starts with an initial guess and uses a series of steps to improve upon it.

Two Steps of the K-Means Algorithm

After initial cluster seeds have been chosen, the algorithm alternates between two steps known as the *assignment* step and the *update* step. In Figure 13-1, three initial cluster seeds have been chosen randomly. There are several possible approaches to choosing the cluster seeds, and these are explained in a later section. For this illustration three of the data points have been selected arbitrarily to be cluster seeds.

The next step is to assign each record to its closest cluster seed to form initial clusters, as shown in Figure 13-2. This figure also shows the lines that separate the clusters. The cluster boundaries form a "Y" shape with one cluster on the left, one on the right, and one on the top. Drawing the boundaries between clusters is useful for showing the process geometrically. In practice, though, the algorithm only needs to calculate the distance from each record to each seed to assign all records to the closest seed. The assignment step can be performed without actually determining the cluster boundaries.

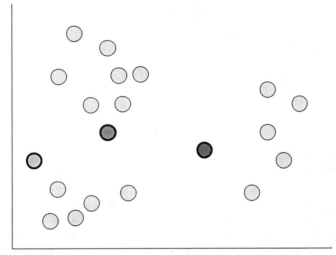

Figure 13-1: Three data points have been chosen as cluster seeds.

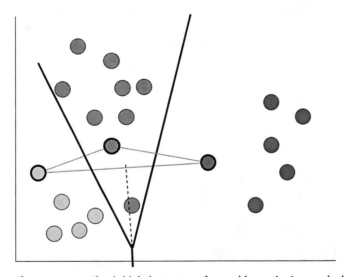

Figure 13-2: The initial clusters are formed by assigning each data point to the closest seed.

In the update step, the *centroid* of each cluster is calculated. The centroid is simply the average position of cluster members in each dimension. Figure 13-3 illustrates the update step.

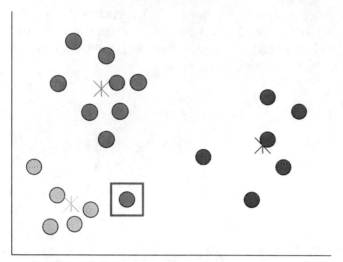

Figure 13-3: In the update step, the cluster centroid is calculated as the average value of the cluster members.

In the assignment step, each data point is assigned to the cluster whose centroid is closest to it. In this example, the highlighted data point is assigned to a new cluster. When the assignment step changes cluster membership, it causes the update step to be executed again. The algorithm continues alternating between update and assignment until no new assignments are made. Although designing pathological datasets in which this process takes exponential time is possible, in practice the algorithm converges quite quickly. Figure 13-4 shows the final clusters after the highlighted record has been reassigned and the new centroids have been calculated.

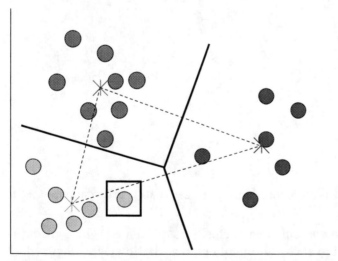

Figure 13-4: The k-means algorithm terminates when no records are reassigned following the latest relocation of the centroids.

Voronoi Diagrams and K-Means Clusters

In the k-means clustering algorithm, the cluster centers can be used to define a *Voronoi diagram*, a diagram whose lines mark the points that are equidistant from the two nearest seeds. The result is that each region on a Voronoi diagram consists of all the points closest to one of the cluster centers, making Voronoi diagrams a good way to visualize the k-means clustering algorithm. One thing that the diagram makes clear is that some clusters are unbounded; clusters that are at the edge of a collection of clusters have no borders in directions where there are no neighbors. See the sidebar for some history and applications of this visualization tool.

Recalling a lesson from high-school geometry makes finding the Voronoi cells easier than it sounds: Given any two points, A and B, all points that are equidistant from A and B fall along a line (called the *perpendicular bisector*) that is perpendicular to the line connecting A and B and halfway between them.

K-means can be defined as successive refinements to a Voronoi diagram. Figure 13-2 shown earlier has light lines connecting the initial seeds; the resulting cluster boundaries are shown with solid lines. Using these lines as guides, it is obvious which records are closest to which seeds. In three dimensions, these boundaries would be planes; in N dimensions they would be hyperplanes of dimension $N - 1$.

After defining the diagram for the initial seeds, the next step in the k-means algorithms is to calculate the average of all the records in a given cell. This average defines a new cluster center. The Voronoi diagram is created based on these new centers. The process continues until the cluster centers no longer move. The result is the same k-means clustering algorithm described in the previous section.

VORONOI DIAGRAMS

Voronoi diagrams are named after Russian mathematician Georgy Voronoi who defined them in 1908. The idea actually goes back much further. The philosopher-mathematician René Descartes used the idea in 1644.

One of the most famous uses of what was not yet called a Voronoi diagram was by the English physician John Snow, who lived from 1813 to 1858. Dr. Snow was an early advocate for the use of anesthetics such as ether and chloroform in surgery. He is also considered a founder of epidemiology because of his work linking a London cholera outbreak of 1854 to a particular water pump on Broad Street in Soho. He drew a map showing that almost all the people who died lived closer to the Broad Street pump than to any other water source.

The illustration for this sidebar was generated using an applet available at `www.cs.cornell.edu/home/chew/Delaunay.html`. The points in the Voronoi diagram pictured here could represent metro stations, in which case the cells indicate each station's natural catchment area.

Continued

VORONOI DIAGRAMS *(continued)*

The points in this diagram could represent stations on two metro lines that cross near the center of the map.

Voronoi diagrams facilitate nearest neighbor queries such as the location of the closest metro station, cell phone tower, or Starbucks to a given address. Answering such a question requires determining which Voronoi cell the questioner is in. Fortunately, determining the cell containing a given point requires considerably less computation than calculating the distance from that point to each of the stations, towers, or coffee shops.

Voronoi diagrams are equally useful for finding a spot far away from others. If the points generating the Voronoi diagram represent land mines, or something else to be avoided, the edges of the diagram are paths that give the widest berth to the known dangers. This technique is used by autonomous robots to navigate between obstacles.

The vertexes in the diagram also have an interpretation. Each of the intersecting lines is as far as possible from some pair of points, so the point where two intersect is as far as possible from both pairs. If you want to dump some hazardous waste as far away as possible from drinking water wells, look at the vertices of the Voronoi diagram defined by the wells. Each vertex is the point that is farthest from some group of wells. Find the vertex which is farthest from its closest neighbor, and create your hazardous waste site there.

Choosing the Cluster Seeds

Different choices for the initial cluster seeds can lead to different final clusters. Designing examples where some choices lead to clearly sub-optimal clusters is easy. Figure 13-5 is one example.

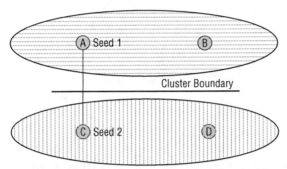

Figure 13-5: With K=2, choosing A and C as the cluster seeds leads to one cluster containing A and B and another containing C and D, which is clearly not the best pair of clusters.

In this diagram, A is closest to C and B is closest to D, but if A and C are chosen as the initial seeds, B is closest to A, and D is closest to C, which leads to the clusters shown.

Because of examples like this, researchers have developed a variety of algorithms for choosing good positions for the initial seeds. As a practical matter, however, if different choices of initial seed positions yield radically different clusters, then the k-means algorithm is not finding stable clusters. This could be because there are no good clusters to be found, or because a different choice for k is needed, or it could be because clusters are present but the k-means algorithm is unable to detect them.

> **TIP** You can try different choices of initial seeds, even for the same value of k. This may result in different clusters, and some may be more useful than others.

Choosing K

How many clusters should you look for? In many cases, the answer to that question is supplied by the business purpose. If the point of customer segmentation is to design different offerings for each segment, k is determined by the number of segments the business can reasonably support. Often, however, the needs of the business do not dictate a precise value for k; there is a range of acceptable values.

When a range of acceptable values exists, the best way to choose is to build clusters using each value of *k* and then evaluate the resulting clusters. The evaluation may be subjective, "these segments make sense to me," or it may be based on technical criteria such as the ratio of the average intra-cluster distance to the average inter-cluster distance, or the cluster silhouette, a measure of cluster goodness, described later in the chapter.

Mathematical measures of cluster goodness provide some guidance, but the clusters must also be evaluated on a more subjective basis to determine their usefulness for a given application. Consider a deck of playing cards that has four suits, two red and two black. You might look for two clusters in it, and come up with one cluster of the red suits and one cluster of the black suits. Or, you might look for four clusters, and come up with a separate cluster for each suit. And there are other possibilities even for these values. Two clusters might differentiate face cards from number cards. Four clusters might separate red face cards, black face cards, red number cards, and black number cards. Different values of *k* may lead to very different clusterings that are equally good mathematically speaking. Figure 13-6 shows two ways of clustering a deck of playing cards. Is one better than the other? The answer to that requires human judgment.

Figure 13-6: These examples of clusters of size 2 and 4 in a deck of playing cards illustrate that there is no one correct clustering.

Using K-Means to Detect Outliers

When screening for a very rare defect, there may not be enough data to train a directed data mining model to detect it. One example is testing electric motors at the factory that makes them. Cluster detection methods can be used on a sample containing only good motors to determine the shape of the "usual" cluster or clusters. When a motor comes along that falls outside the usual clusters for any reason, it is suspect. For this to work, "outside" should be defined as beyond some threshold distance from the cluster as measured by single linkage — the distance to the nearest cluster member. The single linkage distance metric takes into account the fact that the "usual" cluster may have a highly irregular shape. Measuring distance to the centroid would not be appropriate because it assumes spherical clusters.

The "outside the usual clusters" approach has been used successfully in medicine to detect the presence of abnormal cells in tissue samples, and in telecommunications to detect calling patterns indicative of fraud.

This method depends on the notion that clusters have a maximum diameter even when its Voronoi diagram does not impose one because it has no neighbors. This maximum may be defined by various attributes of the cluster, such as some function of the average distance from members to the cluster center.

Semi-Directed Clustering

Many applications of automatic cluster detection are directed in the sense that the goal is to discover clusters that have different distributions of one or (more likely) several targets. Unlike a true directed technique, the clustering targets have no direct influence on the clusters discovered. Instead, they are used to profile the clusters as part of the process of evaluating them. Clusters that do not produce the desired variance in the targets are rejected. This rejection of candidate solutions based on the target turns undirected clustering into semi-directed clustering.

Semi-directed clustering is a good option when there is more than one target. (With a single target, decision trees, a fully directed approach, is usually more effective.) This chapter includes a case study from the *Boston Globe* newspaper, which is a good example of semi-directed clustering.

Interpreting Clusters

In marketing applications of clustering, especially customer segmentation, the interpretation of the clusters as meaningful customer segments is quite important. As discussed earlier, giving customer segments catchy names can sometimes be useful to provide a shorthand reminder of key features of the segment. You would typically do this by finding typical members of the segment and brainstorming to come up with names that capture their essence. The same approach works when clustering any kind of data, but it is especially popular among marketing people viewing the clusters as market segments.

There are drawbacks to this idea. One is that the catchy name tends to focus attention on just one or two of the many things that define the cluster. The other is that some clusters just don't seem to lend themselves to catchy names.

Two factors can help when interpreting clusters. The first is what cluster members have in common with each other. The second is what distinguishes each cluster from the others.

WARNING Customer segments discovered through clustering may not have obvious interpretations of the kind that suggest descriptive names. When understanding segments is an important goal, a more directed approach may be called for.

Characterizing Clusters by Their Centroids

The centroid provides one convenient definition of a cluster's typical member — the one who has the average value in each of the cluster dimensions. Of course, no actual family has 1.86 children and 2.4 cars, so the typical member of a cluster may not exist, but if it did, the typical member would be at the center. K-medoids, a variant of k-means described later, produces clusters with the property that the cluster centers are data points that actually exist in the model set.

The centroids also provide one good way to visualize clusters. The chart in Figure 13-7 is a parallel coordinates plot. The variables used to define the clusters are arranged horizontally. The order is not important. For the clusters shown here, each dimension is a department in a catalog, such as kitchen products and gardening products. The vertical axis is the percent of shoppers in the cluster who have made a purchase in the department. So, everyone in Cluster 2 has made a purchase in Department 22; and everyone in Cluster 3 has made a purchase in Department 23.

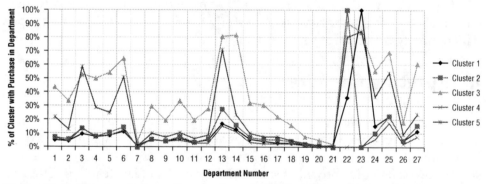

Figure 13-7: This parallel coordinates chart shows five clusters with the percentage of shoppers who have made a purchase in each department.

The vertical axis is on the same scale for all dimensions. Because the clustering process itself works best under these circumstances, that is easy to arrange. In this case the values are percentages, so they range from 0 to 100. Another common approach is to use z-scores, to put all variables on the same scale.

The dimensions for clustering are the 27 departments in the store. An individual shopper has a value of 1 or 0 for each department indicating whether or not he or she has made a purchase in that department. The average value for a cluster is therefore the percentage of shoppers in the cluster who have made a purchase in each department.

Parallel coordinate plots are very handy for seeing where clusters are similar and where they differ. You can clearly see from the chart that some departments are more important than others for distinguishing clusters from each other. For example, Department 7 is equally unpopular in all clusters. Department 23, on the other hand, is very popular with members of Cluster 1, but never visited by members of Cluster 2.

Characterizing Clusters by What Differentiates Them

The parallel dimension plot provides a lot of information about the clusters. However, it does not say which variables are most important for distinguishing one cluster from the others. Some cases are obvious. For instance, Departments 7 and 21 probably do not distinguish any of the clusters, because so few purchases are made in these departments. Which variables are most important for defining which clusters?

A good approach for answering this question is to take the average value of each variable within a particular cluster and compare it to the average of the same variable in the overall population. Represent this difference as a z-score, by dividing the difference by the standard deviation in the overall population. This is a measure of how different the distribution of each variable is in each cluster from the overall population.

In each cluster, order the variables by the magnitude of the z-score. The variables that show the largest difference between the cluster and the rest of the database do a good job of explaining what makes each cluster special. Figure 13-8 shows the results from the Segment Profile node in SAS Enterprise Miner, which essentially takes this approach to determine which variables stand out from the crowd for each cluster.

The two rows of bar charts in Figure 13-8 represent Clusters 2 and 5 from the parallel coordinates chart in Figure 13-7. The bar charts are ordered from the most important variable to the least import. So, for Cluster 2, only two variables are deemed important. Cluster 5 has seven such variables.

The first bar chart on the upper left says that Cluster 2 is most distinguishable from other clusters because of purchases in the Household department. For each customer, the household variable takes on the value 0, indicating no purchase in the department, or 1 indicating a purchase. The solid fill represents the distribution for the cluster; the hollow lines show the overall distribution in the data. The solid fill indicates that everyone in Cluster 2 made a purchase in this department, versus about 40 percent of customers overall.

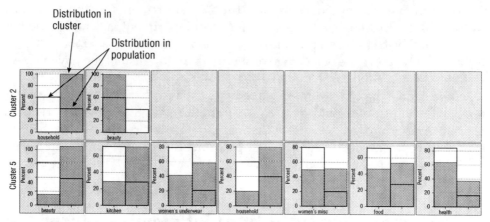

Figure 13-8: This chart compares the distribution of purchasers and non-purchasers in two clusters with the distribution in the overall population.

The situation for the Beauty department is exactly the opposite. What distinguishes Cluster 2 from the overall population is that all customers in this cluster make purchases from Household and none make purchases from Beauty. In the other 25 departments, their behavior is close to average so nothing is shown.

Cluster 5 differs from the population by being more likely than the population as a whole to make purchases in seven departments. There is no department where Cluster 5 makes significantly fewer purchases than average.

Using Decision Trees to Describe Clusters

One way of thinking about decision trees is that they produce directed clusters. Every split in a decision tree increases the purity of its children in terms of the target. The path from the root of the decision tree to one of its leaves is a rule describing that leaf.

When the decision tree's target is a cluster assignment, the result is a set of rules describing the clusters. These rules can be illustrated geometrically, as shown in Figure 13-9. This figure shows both the cluster boundaries discovered by k-means and the leaf boundaries created by a decision tree trained using the same input variables and the k-means cluster assignment as the target.

Quite interestingly, the clusters themselves and the decision trees can both be described geometrically. In fact, this underlines a remarkable similarity in the results from the techniques. There is one important difference, though. The boundaries of the decision tree leaves are always parallel to an axis, because each split on a numeric input is in the form *If X is greater than or equal to n, go left. Otherwise, go right.* Each split is governed by the value of a single X. In contrast, the boundaries of k-means clusters can be at any angle.

A decision tree can do a very good job of explaining the k-means clusters. Several leaves may be needed for a single cluster because the cluster boundaries are at arbitrary angles and the decision tree boundaries are parallel to an axis. Because of the geometric interpretation of the clusters and the associated decision tree, the tree typically does an excellent job of explaining the clusters. Often,there is perfect agreement between the two techniques on a given collection of records to be classified.

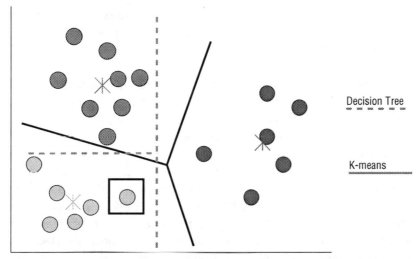

Figure 13-9: The directed clusters found by decision trees have boundaries that are parallel to the axes.

Evaluating Clusters

In general terms, clusters should have members that have a high degree of similarity — or, in geometric terms, that are close to each other — and the clusters themselves should be widely spaced. For many applications, including customer segmentation, clusters should have roughly the same number of members. An exception to this rule is when clustering is used for detecting fraud or other anomalies. There may be a small number of compact, but populous clusters representing the most usual cases and a few less-populous clusters of unusual cases that merit further investigation.

A general-purpose measure that works with any form of cluster detection is to take whatever similarity measure or distance metric is used to form the clusters and use it to compare the average distance between members of a cluster and its centroid to the average distance between cluster centroids. This can be done for each cluster individually and for the entire collection of clusters.

Cluster Measurements and Terminology

Which is bigger: Oklahoma City or New York City? If you answered Oklahoma City, you're right. Oklahoma City covers more than 600 square miles; New York City's five boroughs occupy only 304.8. If you said New York City, you are also right. New York's population of more than 8 million is almost 16 times that of Oklahoma City.

Similarly, depending on context, a small cluster might be one with few members, or one with low variance, or one with a small diameter. A requirement for clusters of similar sizes might refer to the need to create customer segments with similar numbers of members or the need to site warehouses such that they have similar maximum delivery trip lengths.

Because of this potential for confusion, using unambiguous adjectives such as "compact" or "populous" in preference to "small" or "large" is a good idea. For describing how much space a cluster takes up and, and how tight or dispersed it is, the technical terms *cluster diameter* and *cluster variance* have precise definitions.

A cluster's *diameter* is the maximum distance between any two records in the same cluster. Note that, in general, this is not the same as twice the distance from the centroid to the record farthest from the centroid. A cluster's variance is the sum of the squared distance from the centroid of cluster members. A cluster whose members are all close to the centroid has low variance. The square root of the variance also makes a useful measure, because it is in the same units as the distance. Another measure of a cluster's dispersion is its *silhouette*, described in the next section.

Cluster Silhouettes

A cluster's silhouette is a measure of cluster goodness first described by Peter Rousseeuw in 1986. It has some nice properties, but does require a lot of calculation if the clusters have many members. For the benefit of readers who would like to try out the calculations for themselves, Figure 13-10 gives the (x,y) coordinates of the points used in the examples.

To calculate a cluster's silhouette, first calculate the average distance within the cluster. Each cluster member has its own average distance from all other members of the same cluster. The average of these averages is the *dissimilarity* score for the cluster.

Figure 13-11 shows how the dissimilarity score for one record is calculated. Cluster members with low dissimilarity are comfortably within the cluster to which they have been assigned. The average dissimilarity for the cluster is a measure of how compact it is.

Next calculate the dissimilarity of each cluster member from the members of its next nearest cluster. Note that two members of the same cluster may have different neighboring clusters. For points that are close to the boundary between two clusters, the two dissimilarity scores may be nearly equal. Points far from a boundary should be much more similar to other members of their own cluster than they are to members of the neighboring cluster.

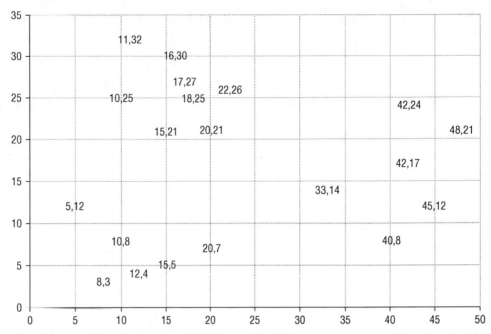

Figure 13-10: The distances used to illustrate the silhouette measure are based on the (x,y) coordinates shown here.

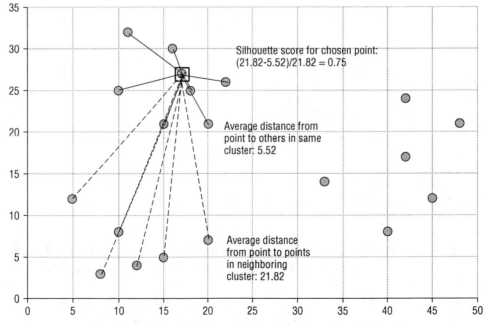

Figure 13-11: The dissimilarity score for a point depends on its distance from members of its own cluster and its distance from members of its neighboring cluster.

Finally, each point is given a score that is the difference between its average dissimilarity with members of its own cluster and its average dissimilarity with members of its neighboring cluster divided by the latter. This is the *silhouette* score. The typical range of the score is from zero when a record is right on the boundary of two clusters to one when it is identical to the other records in its own cluster. Figure 13-12 shows the silhouette scores for the records and clusters from Figure 13-10.

In theory, the silhouette score can go from negative one to one. A negative value means that the record is more similar to the records of its neighboring cluster than to other members of its own cluster. This could potentially happen because the k-means algorithm assigns records based on which cluster centroid they are nearest which, in unusual cases, could be different from the most similar cluster according to the silhouette measure. A cluster's silhouette is the average of these scores.

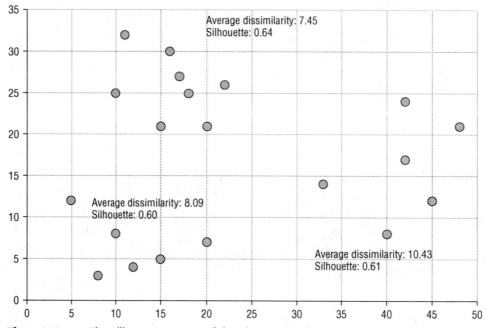

Figure 13-12: The silhouette scores of the cluster members are averaged to obtain the cluster silhouette.

The silhouette score for an entire cluster is calculated as the average of the silhouette scores of its members. This measures the degree of similarity of cluster members.

The silhouette of the entire dataset is the average of the silhouette scores of all the individual records. This is a measure of how appropriately the data has been clustered. What is nice about this measure is that it can be applied at the level of the dataset to determine which clusters are not very good and at the level of a cluster to determine which members do not fit in very well. The silhouette can be used to choose an appropriate value for k in k-means by trying each value of k in the acceptable range and choosing the one that yields the best silhouette. It can also be used to compare clusters produced by different random seeds.

> **TIP** Strong clusters can be identified by their silhouettes.

One way to use silhouettes is to evaluate the strength of clusters. If there are one or two good clusters along with a number of weaker ones, it may be possible to improve results by removing all members of the strong clusters. The strong clusters are worthy of further analysis anyway, and removing their strong pull may allow new clusters to be detected in the records left behind. When doing this, it is important to assign a maximum diameter to the stronger clusters. When scoring, first apply the strong clusters. Then, for records that are not close enough to those, apply the weaker clusters.

Limiting Cluster Diameter for Scoring

Any measurement of a cluster's diameter, variance, or silhouette is actually a measure of a particular set of cluster members. When a new batch of records is scored and given cluster assignments, these measurements can change. If the clusters truly reflect the population from which the new elements are drawn, the cluster measurements should change very little.

What should happen when the cluster model is used to score inappropriate data that includes records far removed from the training data used to create the model? The Voronoi diagram is open at its edges, so all records get assigned to a cluster. As shown in Figure 13-13, even a very distant point is marginally closer to one cluster centroid than all the rest.

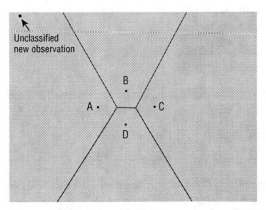

Figure 13-13: Should the new record really be assigned to Cluster A?

The rule that a record should be assigned to the closest cluster allows the clusters to grow literally without bound. Imposing a maximum diameter on all clusters by incorporating it into the cluster model is therefore prudent. Data points that fall outside the maximum diameter of all clusters are classified as unclusterable. This means that reporting systems and other consumers of cluster labels must be prepared to swallow one more case than the actual number of clusters.

WARNING Even points that are very far from any cluster centroid will be assigned to some cluster unless business rules are imposed to require all cluster members to be within some pre-determined distance of the cluster centroid.

Case Study: Clustering Towns

The *Boston Globe* is one of two major dailies serving Boston and the surrounding area of eastern Massachusetts and southern New Hampshire. As with many newspapers, the *Globe* faces declining readership in its core Boston market and strong competition from local papers in the suburban markets where many of its readers have migrated (as well as from other channels such as the Web). In 2003 the *Globe* introduced geographically distinct versions of the paper with specialized editorial content for each of 12 geographically defined zones.

Two days a week, readers are treated to a few pages of local coverage for their area. The editorial zones were drawn up using data available to the *Globe*, common sense, and a map, but no formal statistical analysis. Some constraints on the composition of the editorial zones included:

- The zones had to be geographically contiguous so that the trucks carrying the localized editions from the central printing plant in Boston could take sensible routes.

- The zones had to be reasonably compact and contain sufficient population to justify specialized editorial content.

- The editorial zones had to be closely aligned with the geographic zones used to sell advertising.

Within these constraints, the *Globe* wanted to design editorial zones that would group similar towns together. Sounds sensible, but which towns are similar?

Creating Town Signatures

Before deciding which towns belonged together, there needed to be a way of describing the 200 or so towns that comprise the *Globe*'s home market — a town signature with a column for every feature that might be useful for characterizing a town and comparing it with its neighbors. As it happened, an earlier project to find towns with good prospects for future circulation growth had already defined town signatures. Those signatures, which had been developed for a regression model to predict *Globe* home delivery penetration, turned out to be equally useful for undirected clustering.

This is a fairly common occurrence; after a useful set of descriptive attributes has been collected it can be used for all sorts of things. In another example, a long-distance company developed customer signatures based on call detail data in order to predict fraud and later found that the same variables were useful for distinguishing between business and residential users.

TIP Although the time and effort needed to create a good customer signature can seem daunting, the effort is repaid over time because the same attributes can often be used for many different models. The oft-quoted maxim that 80 percent of the time spent on a data mining project goes into data preparation becomes less true when the data preparation effort can be amortized over several data mining efforts.

The town signatures were derived from several sources, with most of the variables coming from town-level U.S. Census data. The census data provides counts of the number of residents by age, race, ethnic group, occupation, income, home value, average commute time, and many other interesting variables. In addition, the *Globe* had household-level data on its subscribers supplied by an outside data vendor as well as circulation figures for each town and subscriber-level information on discount plans, complaint calls, and type of subscription (daily, Sunday, or both).

The first step in turning this data into a town signature was to aggregate everything to the town level. For example, the subscriber data was aggregated to produce the total number of subscribers and median subscriber household income for each town.

The next step was to transform counts into percentages. Most of the demographic information was in the form of counts. Even things like income, home value, and number of children are reported as counts of the number of people in predefined bins. Transforming all counts into percentages of the town population is an example of normalizing data across towns with widely varying populations. The fact that in the 2000 census data, there were 27,573 people with four-year college degrees residing in Brookline, Massachusetts, is not nearly as interesting as the fact that they represented 47.5 percent of that well-educated town. Even more interesting is the fact that the much larger number of people with similar degrees in Boston proper make up only 19.4 percent of the population there.

Each of the scores of variables in the census data was available for two different years 10 years apart. Historical data is interesting because you can use it to look at trends. Is a town gaining or losing population? School-age population? Hispanic population? Trends like these affect the feel and character of a town so they should be represented in the signature. For certain factors, such as total population, the absolute trend is interesting, so the ratio of the population count in 2000 to the count in 1990 was used. For other factors such as a town's mix of renters and home owners, the change in the proportion of home owners in the population is more interesting, so the ratio of the 2000 home ownership percentage to the percentage in 1990 was used. In all cases, the resulting value is an index that is larger than 1 for anything that has increased over time and less than 1 for anything that has decreased over time.

Finally, to capture important attributes of a town that were not readily discernable from variables already in the signature, additional variables were derived. Both distance and direction from Boston seemed likely to be important in forming town clusters. These are calculated from the latitude and longitude of the gold-domed State House on Boston's Beacon Hill. The distance and direction from the town to Boston could then be calculated from the latitude and longitude.

Creating Clusters

The first attempt to build clusters used signatures that describe the towns in terms of both demographics and geography. Clusters built this way could not be used directly to create editorial zones because of the geographic constraint that editorial zones must comprise contiguous towns. Because towns with similar demographics are not necessarily close to one another, clusters based on the signatures include towns literally all over the map.

Weighting could be used to increase the importance of the geographic variables in cluster formation, but the result would be to cause the nongeographic variables to be ignored completely. Because the goal was to find similarities based mainly on demographic data, the idea of *geographic* clusters was abandoned in favor of *demographic* clusters. The demographic clusters could then be used as one factor in designing editorial zones, along with the geographic constraints.

Determining the Right Number of Clusters

There were business reasons for wanting about a dozen editorial zones. There was no guarantee that a dozen good clusters would be found. This raises the general issue of how to determine the right number of clusters.

The data mining tool used to perform the clustering provided an interesting approach by repeatedly applying k-means clustering. First, decide on a lower bound k for the number of clusters. Build k clusters using the ordinary k-means algorithm. Using a fitness measure (such as the variance, the average distance from the cluster center, or the silhouette measure), determine the worst cluster. Then, using the data only from this cluster, split it to form two clusters. Repeat this process until some upper bound is reached. After each iteration, remember some measure of the overall fitness of the collection of clusters. For this project, the values were two and ten.

The clusters that resulted from each round of splitting were profiled using target variables that were not part of the cluster definitions. The clusters were created based on demographic variables, but evaluated based on customer behavior; in particular, household penetration and average tenure. The cluster tree shown in Figure 13-14 was selected because the four clusters had very different values for these targets.

TIP The variables used to evaluate clusters are generally different from the ones used to create them.

Evaluating the Clusters

The most important fitness measure for clusters is one that is hard to quantify — the usefulness of the clusters for business purposes. In the cluster tree shown in Figure 13-14, the next iteration of the cluster tree algorithm created five clusters by splitting Cluster 2. The resulting clusters 2A and 2B had well-defined differences in demographic terms, but they did not behave differently according to the targets of interest to the *Globe*. Figure 13-14 shows the final cluster tree and lists some statistics about each of the four clusters at the leaves.

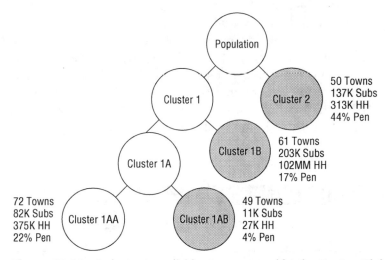

Figure 13-14: A cluster tree divides towns served by the *Boston Globe* into four distinct groups.

Cluster 2 contains 50 towns with 313,000 households, 137,000 of which subscribed to the daily or Sunday *Globe*. This level of home delivery penetration makes Cluster 2 far and away the best cluster. The variables that best distinguish Cluster 2 from the other clusters are home value and education. This cluster has the highest proportion of any cluster of home values in the top two bins; the highest proportion of people with four-year college degrees, the highest average years of education, and the lowest proportion of people in blue-collar jobs.

The next best cluster from the point of view of home delivery penetration is Cluster 1AA, which is distinguished by its ordinariness. Its average values for the most important variables, which in this case are home value and household income, are very close to the overall population averages.

Cluster 1B is characterized by some of the lowest household incomes, the oldest subscribers, and proximity to Boston. Cluster 1AB is most easily characterized by geography even though geographic variables were not used for clustering. These are towns far from Boston. Not surprisingly, home delivery penetration is very low. Cluster 1AB has the lowest home values of any cluster, but incomes are average. You might infer that people in Cluster 1AB have chosen to live far from the city because they want to own homes and real estate is less expensive on the outer fringes of the metro area. Figure 13-15 shows how the demographic clusters are distributed on a map of eastern Massachusetts and southern New Hampshire.

Using Demographic Clusters to Adjust Zone Boundaries

The goal of the clustering project was to validate and improve editorial zones that already existed. Each editorial zone consisted of a set of towns assigned one of the four clusters described earlier. The next step was to manually increase each zone's purity by swapping towns with adjacent zones.

Table 13-1 shows the assignments for ten towns west of Boston, belonging to two zones, the City Zone and West 1. At first glance, the split between the City and West 1 zones seems reasonable. Boston, Brookline, Cambridge, and Somerville are all adjacent to each other. All have universities, and all are connected by the MBTA, the local mass transit system. The other towns are a bit farther out, and are generally accessed by car or bus.

Table 13-1: Towns in the *City* and *West 1* Editorial Zones

TOWN	EDITORIAL ZONE	CLUSTER ASSIGNMENT
Boston	City	1B
Brookline	City	2
Cambridge	City	1B
Somerville	City	1B
Needham	West 1	2
Newton	West 1	2
Waltham	West 1	1B
Watertown	West 1	1B
Wellesley	West 1	2
Weston	West 1	2

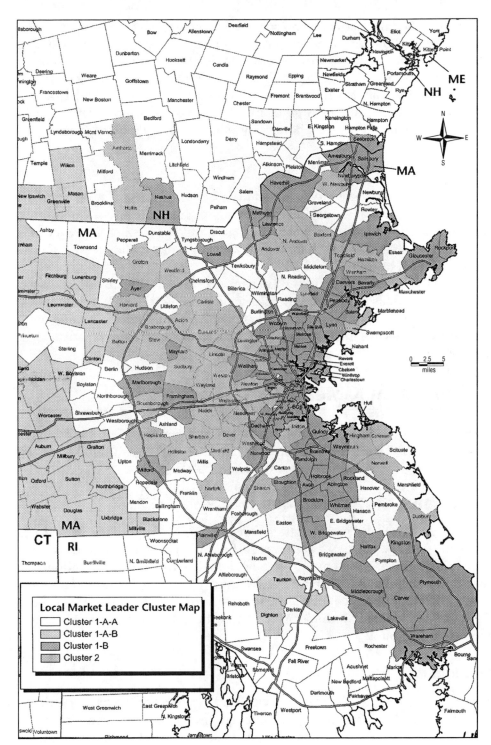

Figure 13-15: The map shows how the demographic clusters are distributed on a map of the *Globe's* coverage area.

However, the cluster assignments suggest that some towns may be in the wrong zone. Although Brookline is geographically surrounded by Boston on three sides, it is also very similar to Newton — a wealthy, leafy suburb more than an urban core town. The demographic cluster assignments hint that Brookline should be in West 1. Similarly, Waltham and Watertown are located even farther west. However, both are demographically more similar to Cambridge and Boston. This suggests placing them in the City zone. The new zones are still geographically contiguous.

Business Success

This clustering is an example of a successful data mining project. The demographic clustering showed that the original zone assignments made sense. On the other hand, it also showed ways in which the zones could be further improved. The *Boston Globe* was sufficiently happy with the results that it allowed the authors to refer to them by name.

Having editorial zones composed of similar towns makes providing sharper editorial focus in its localized content easier for the *Globe*, which should lead to better circulation. More importantly, it allows them to target advertising in the localized editions to similar audiences, which should lead to better advertising sales.

Variations on K-Means

There are many variations on the basic k-means algorithm. One variation has already been discussed, the repeated use of k-means to refine clusters by building a cluster tree. This section discusses other useful variations.

K-Medians, K-Medoids, and K-Modes

Three other closely related variations on k-means are k-medians, k-medoids, and k-modes. Each of these addresses a limitation of k-means and expands the applicability of the technique to new domains. In all these variations, the goal is to minimize the distance between members of a cluster and a central point. Different distance metrics lead to different definitions of centrality. The sidebar "Means, Medians, Modes and their Relationship to Distance" explores this topic.

K-Medians

A median is a statistical measure that is usually defined as the middle value in a list of values. For instance, for the numbers 1, 2, 3, 4, and 5, the middle value is 3 so that is the median. Unlike averages, medians are not sensitive to outliers, so the median of 1, 2, 3, 4, and 999 is still 3.

MEANS, MEDIANS, MODES AND THEIR RELATIONSHIP TO DISTANCE

All the clustering variants described in this chapter attempt to minimize the distance between cluster members and some central point. The location of that central point depends on the function used to measure the distance.

All distance functions follow certain rules:

■ The distance from A to B is always greater than or equal to zero.

■ The distance from A to B is the same as the distance from B to A.

■ The distance from A to itself is zero.

■ The distance from A to B by way of C cannot be less than the distance from A to B without the detour.

Many functions meet these criteria and can be used to measure distance. For simple numerical values, the simplest function is the absolute value of A minus B.

Generalizing this to more dimensions requires figuring out how to combine values along different dimensions. One method is simply to take the sum of the absolute values of distances along each dimension. So, the distance from (3, 0) to (0, 4) is $3 + 4 = 7$. This is called the Manhattan distance.

The more familiar Euclidean distance is the square root of the sum of the squares of the differences in each dimension, and it would yield a value of 5 in this case. This introduces a family of distance functions that can be written as $(|\Delta X_1|^d + |\Delta X_2|^d + \cdots + |\Delta X_n|^d)^{1/d}$. When $d = 1$ this is called the one-norm distance (which is the same as the Manhattan distance). When $d = 2$, it is called the two-norm distance, or the Euclidean distance. In the context of clustering, dispensing with the outer exponent is alright because minimizing the quantity in parentheses also minimizes its root.

Although clustering usually involves multiple dimensions, the effect of different values of d can be seen in one dimension. For concreteness, consider two points at 2 and 4 on a number line. What point minimizes the distance to these two points? When $d = 2$, the distance function is Euclidean and the answer is 3, the average of 2 and 4. This is the answer used by k-means.

When $d = 1$, any value between 2 and 4 works equally well. The closer a point is to 2, the farther it is from 4 and the sum of the two distances is always 2. This is the answer used by k-medians.

When d is less than 1, but greater than 0, the distance is minimized at both 2 and 4. This is the answer used by k-modes. In k-modes, the central point is at the most common value. In this example, there are only two points, so either one of them will do. For this to work in more dimensions, d must be zero. Any non-zero ΔX_i raised to the power of zero is one, so the distance from one point to another in n dimensions is always n wherever it is defined. When some $\Delta X_i = 0$, there is a problem because zero to the power of zero is not defined. But, by definition, the distance from a record to itself is 0, which means that for this purpose zero to the power of zero must be treated as zero. With this definition, the zero norm counts the number of non-zero dimensions.

Continued

MEANS, MEDIANS, MODES AND THEIR RELATIONSHIP TO DISTANCE (*continued*)

The figure graphs the total distance to the points 2 and 4 for a range of values using three different distance functions of the form $|A - B|^d$ with d taking on the values 2, 1, and 0.5.

The relationship between the value of d in the d-norm family of distance functions and three important statistical measures — the mean (which is called average in the rest of the book), median, and mode — sheds light on the relationship between the various clustering methods discussed in this section.

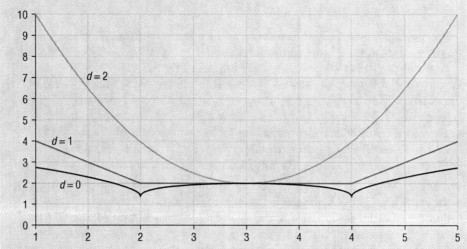

The total distance to the points 2 and 4 is minimized at different points for different values of d using $|A - B|^d$ as the distance function.

Another way of defining the median of a set of numbers exists. It is the value that minimizes the sum of the distances from itself to all members of the set. Unlike the notion of a middle value, this alternative definition works in any number of dimensions, which makes it more useful for the multidimensional data used in data mining.

One variation of the k-means algorithm uses the idea of medians instead of averages. K-medians clustering looks for the set of centroids that minimizes the sum of the distances from cluster members to cluster centroids. Each centroid is the median for the set of records in the cluster. One advantage of k-medians over k-means is that the k-medians algorithm is less sensitive to outliers. The k-means algorithm is sensitive to outliers because a few distant data points can have a large effect on the average but such points have no effect on the median.

The algorithm for k-medians is quite similar to k-means. First, an arbitrary set of cluster centers is chosen. Then, each record is assigned to the nearest cluster. The difference is in the step where the new cluster centroids are calculated. With the k-medians algorithm, the new center is the median along each dimension, rather than the average. The process repeats until the clusters are stable. Medians require more computing power to calculate than an average (essentially, lists have to be sorted rather than summed up for an average), k-medians requires more computing power than k-means.

K-medians clustering is also analogous to the robust regression technique mentioned in Chapter 6. Robust regression finds the line that minimizes the sum of the absolute distance of records from the line, rather than the sum of the squares of the distances (as in ordinary least squares regression). K-medians applies a similar idea to clustering.

As an example of k-medians, pretend that you know where all the coffee drinkers are in a city, and you want to place 100 Starbucks so as to minimize the distance between the coffee drinkers and their nearest Starbucks. The goal of minimizing the distance suggests k-medians, because the minimum is the sum of the absolute values of distances, rather than distances squared. In fact, one major application for k-medians is in the area of siting facilities of one sort or another to minimize such distances. The result is k clusters, each with a facility at its center.

When the choice of cluster centers is limited to the original data points, then the problem is called the facilities location problem. Suppose Starbucks already has 100 sites in a city. It now wants to select six stores where it will bake special coffee cakes and distribute them to the rest of the stores. Which store locations should it use in order to minimize the distance that the coffee cakes need to travel when distributed? The solution to this facilities location problem can be found using k-medians.

K-Medoids

K-means and k-medians are both happy to let centroids fall where they may even when they land somewhere where no actual cluster member could exist. The family with 1.86 children and 2.4 cars comes to mind again. For clustering families, there is no harm in having fractional numbers of children and cars at the centers of clusters. The cluster centers are used as reference points for calculating the distances that determine cluster membership as well as for descriptive purposes, but the cluster center does not have to correspond to an actual record.

For some problems, however, most of the space in which the clusters can form is unusable. For example, the records might describe facilities such as factories, warehouses, and distribution centers that have immovable physical locations. Clustering them involves finding groups of facilities that are close to each other. In such a group, the most central member is called the medoid.

In the k-medoids algorithm, clusters are based on the most representative object, rather than the average. At the start, k objects are chosen at random to be representative objects. These are the cluster seeds. The rest of the objects are then assigned to clusters based on which representative object they are closest to. Next, one by one, cluster members are swapped with the current representative object of their cluster. If the overall variance of the cluster is reduced, there is a new representative object for that cluster. The next round of cluster reassignments is based on the best representative object for each cluster. When things stop changing, the current cluster segments are the cluster medoids.

Because the medoids are actual records, they have actual values for fields not used for clustering. This makes profiling the clusters easy. K-medoids should be used when it is important that cluster centers be actual data points.

The Soft Side of K-Means

Ordinarily, when a hard cluster model is used for scoring, each record is assigned to a cluster based on which centroid it is closest to. To produce soft cluster membership instead, all that is required is a fuzzy membership function. Such a function is actually several functions, one for each cluster centroid.

The authors would like to thank our friend, Dr. Donald Wedding, for introducing us to this approach using the idea of fuzzy membership with k-means clustering. The method starts by creating hard clusters using k-means or any other clustering algorithm that produces cluster centroids.

The fuzzy membership function used by Dr. Wedding was suggested by Dr. James Bezdek. It gives every record a membership score for each of the k clusters based on its distance from that cluster relative to its distance from others. Note that the strength of a records membership in any one cluster depends on its distance from all clusters.

This is best shown by example. Figure 13-16 shows two cluster centroids and a data point to be assigned fuzzy membership in both of them. The record to be scored is distance 3 from Cluster A and distance 2 from Cluster B. By the rules of hard clustering, the record belongs to B, and B alone.

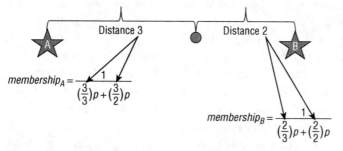

Figure 13-16: The data point shown here is to be assigned fuzzy membership in clusters A and B, which are represented by their centroids.

In this soft variant, the record gets two membership scores, one for each cluster. The scores are calculated by adding up a series of as many fractions as there are clusters and then taking the reciprocal of their sum. To calculate the membership score for this record's membership in Cluster A, the fractions all have the distance to A as the numerator. Each denominator is the distance to a different one of the clusters. There is always a fraction with the value of one because numerator and denominator are the distance to the cluster for which fuzzy membership is being computed.

In this case, the distance to A is 3, so computing fuzzy membership in A involves two fractions with 3 in the numerator. The denominators are 3 and 2 for the distance to A and the distance to B, respectively. Before summing the fractions, each one is raised to a power p, which is a parameter set by the user. If p is 1, the relationship is linear and the membership score for A is the reciprocal of the sum of 3/3 and 3/2, in other words 2/5 or 0.4. Similarly, the membership score for B is the reciprocal of 2/3 + 2/2, which is 3/5 or 0.6.

The parameter p controls the level of fuzziness. As the exponent p gets larger, the fuzzy scores look more and more like the hard clusters. As p goes to zero, the record becomes a member of all clusters equally. A typical value for p is 2. In this example, with $p=2$, the record to be classified gets a membership score for A of about 0.3 and a membership score for B of about 0.7. Table 13-2 shows the fuzzy membership values for this record in both clusters for several different values of p.

Table 13-2: Fuzzy Membership in A and B for Different Values of P

P	MEMBERSHIP IN A	MEMBERSHIP IN B
0	0.50	0.50
1	0.40	0.60
2	0.31	0.69
3	0.23	0.77

Data Preparation for Clustering

The data preparation issues for clustering are similar to those for memory-based reasoning because both rely on the concept of distance. This means that getting everything onto the same scale is especially important. The notions of *scaling* and *weighting* each play important roles in clustering.

Although similar, and often confused with each other, the two notions are not the same. Scaling adjusts the values of variables to take into account the fact that different variables are measured in different units or over different ranges. For instance, household income is measured in tens of thousands of dollars and number of children in single digits. Weighting provides a relative adjustment for a variable, because some variables are more important than others.

Scaling for Consistency

In geometry, all dimensions are equally important. A distance of 1 on the X dimension is the same as a distance of 1 on the Y dimension. It doesn't matter what units X and Y are measured in, as long as they are the same.

Unfortunately, in commercial data mining usually no common scale is available because the different units being used measure quite different things. If variables include plot size, number of children, car ownership, and family income, they cannot all be converted to a common unit. On the other hand, it is misleading that a difference of 20 acres is indistinguishable from a change of $20. As discussed in Chapter 4, the best solution is to convert all the values to z-scores.

> **TIP** Scaling different variables so their values fall roughly into the same range is important. Standardizing the values is a good approach.

Use Weights to Encode Outside Information

Scaling takes care of the problem that changes in one variable appear more significant than changes in another simply because of differences in the magnitudes of the values in the variable. What if you think that two families with the same income have more in common than two families on the same size lot, and you want that to be taken into consideration during clustering? That is where weighting comes in. The purpose of weighting is to encode the information that one variable is more (or less) important than others.

A good place to start is by standardizing all variables so each has a mean of zero and a variance (and standard deviation) of one. That way, all fields contribute equally when the distance between two records is computed.

You can go further. The whole point of automatic cluster detection is to find clusters that make sense to *you*. If, for your purposes, whether people have children is much more important than the number of credit cards they carry, there is no reason not to bias the outcome of the clustering by multiplying the number of children field by a higher weight than the number of credit cards field. After scaling to get rid of bias that is due to the units, use weights to introduce bias based on knowledge of the business context.

Some clustering tools allow the user to attach weights to different dimensions, simplifying the process. Even for tools that don't have such functionality, it is possible to introduce weights by adjusting the scaled values. That is, first scale the values to a common range to eliminate range effects. Then multiply the resulting values by weights to introduce bias based on the business context. Make sure that the tool is not configured to automatically standardize the inputs (which would undo the scaling).

Selecting Variables for Clustering

Before clustering, you must decide which variables will be used to define the clusters. These should be variables that you think ought to be important in defining segments. In semi-directed clustering, the target variables are not usually included among the variables used to define the clusters. Typically, the goal is to understand how targets from one domain, such as customer behavior, are affected by inputs in another domain such as geography or demographics.

There are also technical considerations to keep in mind. When calculating a distance, every dimension is as important as any other and ideally, they should all be linearly independent. Although true independence is hard to achieve, it is important not to include highly correlated variables in the cluster definition. Otherwise, the concept represented by those variables will contribute more than its fair share to the clusters.

Another technical consideration is that finding clusters in two, three, or four dimensions is much easier than in twenty. To be close, records have to have similar values in all dimensions; high-dimensional spaces are very sparse. Chapter 20 discusses variable reduction techniques that you can use to allow a few variables to convey information from many.

Lessons Learned

Automatic cluster detection is an undirected data mining technique that can be used to learn about the structure of complex data. Clustering does not answer any question directly, but studying clusters can lead to valuable insights. One important application of clustering is customer segmentation. Clusters of customers form naturally occurring customer segments of people whose similarities may include similar needs and interests.

Another important application of clustering is breaking complex datasets into simpler clusters to increase the chance of finding patterns that were drowned out in the original data. Automatic cluster detection is a form of modeling. Clusters are detected in training data and the rules governing the clusters are captured in a model, which can be used to score previously unclassified data. Scoring a dataset with a cluster model means assigning a cluster label to each record, or in the case of soft clustering, assigning several scores indicating the probability of membership in various clusters. After cluster labels have been assigned, they often become input to directed data mining models. They may also serve as reporting dimensions.

The k-means cluster detection algorithm creates clusters with boundaries that extend halfway to the neighboring clusters in all directions, even if the neighbor is very far away. In directions where no neighbor exists, a k-means cluster goes on forever. Including a maximum cluster diameter in the cluster scoring model is therefore recommended so distant outliers are declared to be members of no cluster.

Clusters often require interpretation to be useful. The cluster centroid or average cluster member provides one way of thinking about what cluster members have in common. The variables with large z-scores define major differences between a cluster and its neighbors and the population as a whole.

There are various technical measures for evaluating clusters, including cluster variance and silhouettes, but cluster evaluation also requires subjective judgment of usefulness.

The k-means algorithm has a number of variations including soft k-means, k-medians, k-medoids, and k-modes. Each of these extends the usefulness of the technique to new domains.

Clustering is based on distance and similarity so it requires the same sort of data preparation as memory-based reasoning. In addition to standardizing numeric values to put all inputs on a comparable scale, you can use weighting to make sure that variables that are important to the business play a strong part in the definition of the clusters.

K-means and its close relatives are good, general-purpose clustering tools, but there are situations when other cluster detection techniques are more appropriate, as discussed in the next chapter.

## CHAPTER 17

Data Warehousing, OLAP, Analytic Sandboxes, and Data Mining

The final chapters of this book cover the topic of data, a topic that has been present in all the earlier chapters, lurking under the surface of discussions about methodology and techniques. As a bad pun to emphasize the importance of data, one could say that "data" is data mining's first name. This chapter puts data into the larger context of decision support systems. The remaining chapters zoom in for a closer look at methods for transforming data to make records more suitable for data mining, at clever ways for bringing important information to the surface, and at external sources of data.

Since the introduction of computers into data processing centers a few decades ago, just about every operational system in business has been computerized, spewing out large amounts of data along the way, and data mining is one way of making sense out of the deluge of data. Automation has changed how people do business and how we live: online retailing, social networking, automated tellers, adjustable rate mortgages, just-in-time inventory control, credit cards, Google, overnight deliveries, and frequent flier/buyer clubs are a few examples of how computer-based automation has opened new markets and revolutionized existing ones. Automation has also created immense amounts of data at the companies that profit from these activities. Data accumulates, but not information — *and not the right information at the right time*.

Data warehousing is the process of bringing together disparate data from throughout an organization for decision support purposes. A data warehouse serves as a decision-support system of record, making it possible to reconcile

613

311

diverse reports because they have the same underlying source and definitions. Such a system not only reduces the need to explain conflicting results, it also provides consistent views of the business across different organizational units and time. Data warehouses help managers make more informed decisions, and over time more informed decisions should lead to better bottom-line results. As used here, decision support is an intentionally ambiguous and broad term, covering everything from production reports to sophisticated modeling to online recommendation engines.

Data warehousing is a natural ally of data mining, which has a firm requirement for clean and consistent data in the quest for finding actionable patterns. Much of the effort behind data mining endeavors is in the steps of identifying, acquiring, understanding, and cleansing data. A well-designed corporate data warehouse is a valuable ally. Better yet, if the design of the data warehouse includes support for data mining applications, the warehouse facilitates data mining efforts. The two technologies work together to deliver value. Data mining fulfills some of the promise of data warehousing by converting an essentially inert source of clean and consistent data into actionable information.

The relationship between data and data mining also has a technological component. Apart from the ability of users to run multiple jobs at the same time, most software, including data mining and statistical software, does not readily take advantage of the multiple processors, multiple disks, and large memory available on the fastest servers. Relational database management systems (RDBMS), the heart of most data warehouses, are parallel-enabled and readily take advantage of all of a system's resources for processing a single query. Even more importantly, users do not need to be aware of this fact, because the interface, some variant of SQL, remains the same. A database running on a powerful server can be a powerful asset for processing large amounts of data, such as when creating customer signatures for data mining.

As useful as data warehouses are, such systems are not prerequisite for data mining and data analysis. Statisticians, actuaries, and analysts have been using statistical packages for decades — and achieving good results with their analyses — without the benefit of a well-designed centralized data repository. Such analyses often take place on *analytic sandboxes*, special-purpose systems for analyzing data. Nowadays, statistical work uses data mining tools and statistical software packages; reporting uses OLAP tools and Excel; and ad hoc query analysis takes place on the data warehouse itself. Analytic sandboxes are still useful for pushing the envelope of what can be done, for analyzing the ridiculously large volumes of data generated by web servers or for complex statistical methods to simulate aspects of the business, and for other advanced endeavors.

The perspective of this chapter is that data warehouses are part of the virtuous cycle of data mining. They are a valuable and often critical component in supporting all four phases of the cycle: identifying opportunities, analyzing data, applying information, and measuring results. This chapter is not a how-to guide for building a warehouse — many books are already devoted to that subject, and the authors heartily recommend Ralph Kimball's *The Data Warehouse Lifecycle Toolkit* (Wiley, 2008) and Bill Inmon's *Building the Data Warehouse* (Wiley, 2005).

This chapter starts with a discussion of the different types of data that are available, and then discusses data warehousing requirements from the perspective of data mining. It shows a typical data warehousing architecture and variants on this theme. The chapter explains analytic sandboxes, and how they fit into the decision support picture. A discussion about Online Analytic Processing (OLAP), an alternative approach to the normalized data warehouse, follows. The chapter ends with a discussion on the role of data mining in these environments. As with much that has to do with data mining, however, the place to start is with data.

The Architecture of Data

Many different flavors of information are represented on computers. Different levels of data represent different types of abstraction, as shown in Figure 17-1:

- Operational/Transaction data
- Operational summary data
- Decision-support summary data
- Schema
- Metadata
- Business rules

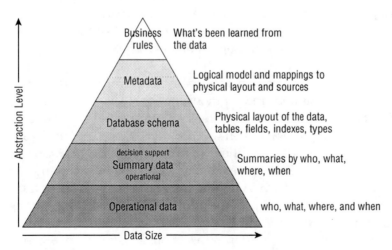

Figure 17-1: A hierarchy of data and its descriptions helps users navigate around a data warehouse. As data gets more abstract, it generally gets less voluminous.

The level of abstraction is an important characteristic of data used in data mining. A well-designed system should allow users to drill down through these levels of abstraction to obtain the base data that supports every summarization and business rule. The lower levels of the pyramid are more voluminous and tend to be the stuff of databases. The upper levels are smaller and tend to be the stuff of spreadsheets and computer code. All these levels are important, because you do not want to analyze the detailed data to merely produce what should already be known.

Transaction Data, the Base Level

Every product purchased by a customer, every bank transaction, every web page visit, every credit card purchase, every flight segment, every delivered package, every telephone call is recorded in at least one operational system. Every time a customer opens an account or clicks on a website or pays a bill or geolocates on a mobile phone, a record of the transaction is stored somewhere, providing information about who, what, where, when, and how much. Such transaction-level data is the raw material for understanding customer behavior. It is the eyes and ears of the enterprise.

Unfortunately, over time operational systems change because of changing business needs. Fields may change their meaning. Important data is rolled off and expunged. Change is constant, in response to the introduction of new products, expanding numbers of customers, acquisitions, reorganizations, and new technology. The fact that operational data changes over time has to be part of any robust data warehousing approach.

> **TIP** Data warehouses need to store data so the information is compatible over time, even when product lines change, when markets change, when customer segments change, and when business organizations change. Otherwise, the data warehouse will have a finite life and quickly become obsolete.

The amount of data gathered from transactional systems can be enormous. A single fast-food restaurant sells hundreds of thousands of meals over the course of a year. A chain of supermarkets can have tens or hundreds of thousands of transactions a day. Big banks process millions of check, credit card, and debit card purchases a day. Large websites have millions of hits each day (in 2009, Google handled more than two billion searches each day). A telephone company has millions of completed calls every hour. A large ad server on the Web keeps track of billions of ad views every day. Even with the price of disk space falling, storing all these transactions requires a significant investment. For reference, remember that a day has 86,400 seconds, so a million transactions a day is an average of about 12 transactions per second all day (and two billion searches amounts to close to 25,000 searches every second!) — with peaks several times higher.

Because of the large data volumes, companies are often reluctant to store transaction-level data in a data warehouse. From the perspective of data mining, this is a shame, because the transactions best describe customer behavior. Analytic sandboxes are an effective alternative for exploring and using transactional data that does not readily fit into the warehouse.

Operational Summary Data

Operational summaries play the same role as transactions; the difference is that operational summaries are derived from transactions. A common example is billing systems, which summarize transactions, usually into monthly bill cycles. These summaries are customer-facing and often result in other transactions, such as bill payments. In some cases, operational summaries may include fields that are summarized to enhance the company's understanding of its customers rather than for operational purposes. For instance, AT&T once used call detail records to calculate a "bizocity" score, measuring the business-like behavior of a telephone number's calling pattern. The records of each call are discarded, but the score is kept up to date.

There is a distinction between operational summary data and transaction data, because summaries are for a period of time and transactions represent events. Consider the amount paid by a subscription customer. In a billing system, amount paid is a summary for the billing period, because it includes all payments during the period. A payment history table instead provides detail on every payment transaction. For most customers, the monthly summary and payment transactions are equivalent. However, two payments might arrive during the same billing period. The more detailed payment information might be useful for insight into customer payment patterns.

Decision-Support Summary Data

Decision-support summary data is the data used for making decisions about the business. The financial data used to run a company provides an example of decision-support summary data; upper levels of management often consider this to be the cleanest information available. Another example is the data warehouses and data marts whose purpose is to provide a decision-support system of record at the customer level.

Generally, it is a bad idea to use the same system for analytic and operational purposes, because operational needs are more important, resulting in a system that is optimized for operations and not decision support. Financial systems are not generally designed for understanding customers, because they are designed for accounting purposes. One of the goals of data warehousing is to provide consistent definitions and layouts so similar reports produce similar results, no matter which business user is producing them or when they are produced.

WARNING   Do not expect customer-level data warehouse information to balance exactly against financial systems (although the two systems should be close). Although theoretically possible, such balancing can prove very difficult and distract from the purpose of the data warehouse.

In one sense, summaries destroy information as they aggregate data together. However, summaries can also bring information to the surface. Point-of-sale transactions may capture every can of sardines that goes over the scanner, but only summaries begin to describe the shopper's behavior in terms of her habits — the time of day when she shops, the proportion of her dollars spent on canned foods, whether organic produce complements the sardines, and so on. In this case, the customer summary seems to be creating information or at least bringing it to the surface, making it visible.

Database Schema/Data Models

The structure of data is also important — what data is stored, where it is stored, what is not stored, and so on. The sidebar "What Is a Relational Database?" explains the key ideas behind relational databases, the most common systems for storing large amounts of data.

No matter how the data is stored, there are at least two ways of describing the layout. The *physical data model* describes the layout in the technical detail needed by the underlying software. An example is the `"CREATE TABLE"` statement in SQL. A *logical data model*, on the other hand, describes the data in a way more accessible to end users. The two are not necessarily the same, nor even similar, as shown in Figure 17-2. Note that the term "data model" means something quite different from "data mining model."

WARNING   The existence of fields in a database does not mean that the data is actually present. It is important to understand every field used for data mining, and not to assume that a field is populated correctly just because it exists. Skepticism is your ally.

An analogy might help to understand the differences between the physical and logical data models. A logical model for a house is analogous to saying that a house is ranch style, with four bedrooms, three baths, and a two-car garage. The physical model goes into more detail about how it is laid out. The foundation is reinforced concrete, 4 feet deep; the slab is 1,500 square feet; the walls are concrete block; and so on. The details of construction, although useful and complete, may not be so helpful for a family looking for the right home.

Logical Data Model

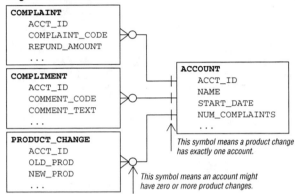

This logical model has four entities for customer generated events and one for accounts.

The logical model is intended to be understood by business users.

Physical Data Model

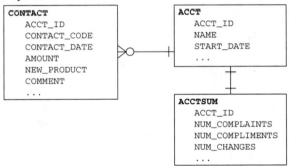

In the physical model, information from three entities is combined into a single CONTACT table, where different types of contacts are distinguished using the CONTACT_TYPE field.

Information about accounts is actually split into two tables, because one is summarized from the CONTACT table.

The physical model also specifies exact types, partitioning, indexes, storage characteristics, degrees of parallels, constraints on values, and many other things not of interest to the business user.

Figure 17-2: The physical and logical data models may not be similar to each other.

WHAT IS A RELATIONAL DATABASE?

One of the most common ways to store data is in a relational database management system (RDBMS). The theoretical foundation of relational databases starts with research by E. F. Codd in the early 1970s on the mathematical properties of a special type of set composed of *tuples* — what you would call rows in tables. His work led to the creation of a relational algebra, consisting of a set of operations that are depicted in the following figure:

Continued

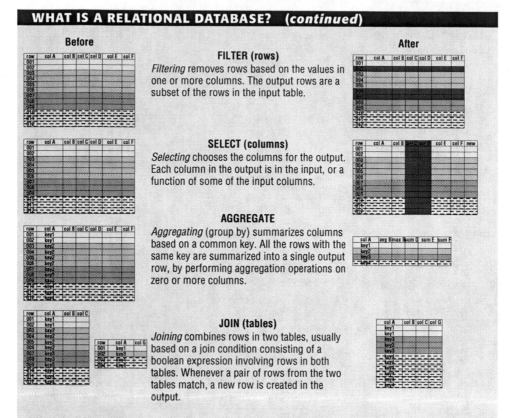

Relational databases have four major querying operations.

> **In nonscientific terminology, these relational operations are:**
>
> > *Filter* **a given set of rows based on the values in the rows.**
>
> > *Select* **a given set of columns and perform functions on the values of the columns in a single row.**
>
> > *Aggregate* **rows together and calculate summary values in the columns.**
>
> > *Join* **two tables together by appending rows together based on rows in the table satisfying a match condition.**

The relational operations do not include sorting, except for output purposes. These operations specify *what* **can be done with tuples, not** *how* **it gets done. Although relational databases often use sorting for grouping and joining operations, there are non-sort-based algorithms for these operations as well.**

   SQL, originally developed by IBM in the 1980s, has become the standard language for accessing relational databases and implements these basic operations. Because SQL supports subqueries (that is, using the results of one query as a data source for another query), it can express some very complex data manipulations. Since SQL was first standardized in 1992, SQL has been extended in many ways; some, such as the addition of window functions and grouping sets, have made it even more useful for complex queries and data analysis.

A common way of representing the database structure is to use an entity-relationship (E-R) diagram. The following figure is a simple E-R diagram with five entities and four relationships among them. In this case, each entity corresponds to a separate table with columns corresponding to the attributes of the entity. In addition, columns represent the relationships between tables in the database; such columns are called *keys* (either foreign or primary keys). Explicitly storing keys in the database tables using a consistent naming convention helps users find their way around the database.

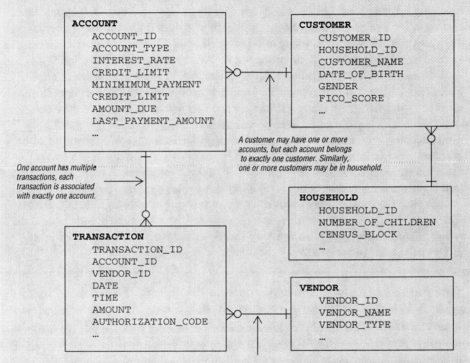

ACCOUNT
 ACCOUNT_ID
 ACCOUNT_TYPE
 INTEREST_RATE
 CREDIT_LIMIT
 MINIMIMUM_PAYMENT
 CREDIT_LIMIT
 AMOUNT_DUE
 LAST_PAYMENT_AMOUNT
 …

CUSTOMER
 CUSTOMER_ID
 HOUSEHOLD_ID
 CUSTOMER_NAME
 DATE_OF_BIRTH
 GENDER
 FICO_SCORE
 …

A customer may have one or more accounts, but each account belongs to exactly one customer. Similarly, one or more customers may be in household.

One account has multiple transactions, each transaction is associated with exactly one account.

HOUSEHOLD
 HOUSEHOLD_ID
 NUMBER_OF_CHILDREN
 CENSUS_BLOCK
 …

TRANSACTION
 TRANSACTION_ID
 ACCOUNT_ID
 VENDOR_ID
 DATE
 TIME
 AMOUNT
 AUTHORIZATION_CODE
 …

VENDOR
 VENDOR_ID
 VENDOR_NAME
 VENDOR_TYPE
 …

A single transaction has exactly one vendor, but a vendor may have multiple transactions.

An ER diagram can be used to show the tables and fields in a relational database. Each box shows a single table and its columns. The lines between the boxes show relationships, such as 1-many, 1-1, and many-to-many. Because each table corresponds to an entity, this is called a physical model.

Sometimes, the physical model of a database is very complicated. For instance, the TRANSACTION table might actually be split into a separate table for each month of transactions, to facilitate backup and restore processes.

An entity relationship diagram describes the layout of data for a simple credit card database.

Relational databases can be designed so that any given data item appears in exactly one place — with no duplication. Such a database is called *normalized*. Knowing exactly where each data item is located is highly efficient for some purposes, because updating any value requires modifying only one row

Continued

WHAT IS A RELATIONAL DATABASE?   (*continued*)

in one table. When a normalized database is well-designed and implemented, there is no redundant data, out-of-date data, or invalid data.

An important idea behind normalization is the creation of reference tables. Each reference table logically corresponds to an entity, and each has a key used for looking up information about the entity. In a normalized database, the "join" operation is used to lookup values in reference tables.

Relational databases are a powerful way of storing and accessing data. However, the focus of their technical implementation is usually to support updating large volumes of data and handling large numbers of transactions. Data mining is interested in combining data together to spot higher-level patterns. Typically, data mining uses many queries, each of which requires several joins, several aggregations, and subqueries — a veritable army of killer queries.

With respect to data mining, relational databases (and SQL) have some limitations. First, they provide little support for time series. This makes it hard to figure out from transaction data such things as the second product purchased, the last three promos a customer responded to, or the most common ordering of a set of events. Another problem is that two operations often eliminate fields inadvertently. When a field contains a missing value (NULL) then it automatically fails any comparison, even "not equals." Also, the default join operation (called an inner join) eliminates rows that do not match, which means that customers may inadvertently be left out of a data pull. The set of functions in SQL is not particularly rich, especially for text data and dates. The result is that every database vendor extends standard SQL to include slightly different sets of functionality.

Data models can also illuminate unusual findings in the data. For instance, the authors once worked with a file of call detail records in the United States that had city and state fields for the destination of every call. The file contained more than 200 state codes — that is a lot of states. What was happening? The city and state fields were never read by operational systems, so their contents were automatically suspicious — data that is not used is not likely to be correct. Instead of the city and state, all location information was derived from ZIP codes. These redundant fields were inaccurate because the state field was written first and the city field, with 14 characters, was written second. Longer city names overwrote the state field next to it. So, "WEST PALM BEACH, FL" ended up putting the "H" in the state field, becoming "WEST PALM BEAC, HL," and "COLORADO SPRINGS, CO" became "COLORADO SPRIN, GS." Understanding the data layout helped us figure out this amusing but admittedly uncommon problem.

Metadata

Metadata goes beyond the data model to let business users know what types of information are stored in the database. This is, in essence, documentation about the system, including information such as:

- The values legally allowed in each field

- A description of the contents of each field (for instance, is the start date the date of the sale or the date of activation?)

- The date when the data was loaded

- An indication of how recently the data has been updated (when after the billing cycle does the billing data land in this system?)

- Mappings to other systems (the status code in table A is the status code field in table B in such-and-such source system)

When available, metadata provides an invaluable service. When not available, this type of information needs to be gleaned, usually from friendly database administrators and analysts — a perhaps inefficient use of everyone's time. For a data warehouse, metadata provides discipline, because changes to the warehouse must be reflected in the metadata to be communicated to users. Overall, a good metadata system helps ensure the success of a data warehouse by making users more aware of and comfortable with the contents. For data miners, metadata provides valuable assistance in tracking down and understanding data.

Business Rules

The highest level of abstraction is business rules. These describe why relationships exist and how they are applied. Some business rules are easy to capture, because they represent the history of the business — what marketing campaigns took place when, what products were available when, and so on. Other types of rules are more difficult to capture and often lie buried deep inside code fragments and old memos. No one may remember why the fraud detection system ignores claims under $500. Presumably there was a good business reason, but the reason, the business rule, may be lost when the rule is embedded in computer code.

Business rules have a close relationship to data mining. Some data mining techniques, such as market basket analysis and decision trees, produce explicit rules. Often, these rules may already be known. A direct mail response model that ends up targeting only wealthy areas may reflect the fact that the historical data used to build the model was focused only on those areas. That is, the model set may only have responders in these areas, because only wealthy people were targeted in the past.

Discovering business rules in the data is both a success and a failure. Finding these rules is a successful demonstration of sophisticated algorithms. However, in data mining, you want actionable patterns and such patterns are not actionable.

A General Architecture for Data Warehousing

The multitiered approach to data warehousing recognizes that data comes in many different forms. It provides a comprehensive system for managing data for decision support. The major components of this architecture (see Figure 17-3) are:

- *Source systems* are where the data comes from.
- Extraction, transformation, and load (ETL) tools move data between different data stores.
- The *central repository* is the main store for the data warehouse.
- The *analytic sandbox* provides an environment for more complex analysis than is possible with SQL queries or data mining tools.
- The *metadata repository* describes what is available and where.
- *Data marts* provide fast, specialized access for end users and applications.
- *Operational feedback* integrates decision support back into the operational systems.
- *End users* are the reason for developing the warehouse in the first place.

One or more of these components exist in virtually every system called a data warehouse. They are the building blocks of decision support throughout an enterprise. The following discussion of these components follows a data-flow approach. The data is like water. It originates in the source systems and flows through the components of the data warehouse ultimately to deliver information and value to end users. These components rest on a technological foundation consisting of hardware, software, and networks; this infrastructure must be sufficiently robust both to meet the needs of end users and to meet growing data and processing requirements.

Source Systems

Data originates in the source systems, typically operational systems and external data feeds. These are designed for operational efficiency, not for decision support, and the data reflects this reality. For instance, transactional data might be rolled off every few months to reduce storage needs. The same information might be represented in multiple ways. For example, one retail point-of-sale source system represented returned merchandise using a "returned item" flag. That is, except when the customer made a new purchase at the same time. In this case, there would be a negative amount in the purchase field. Such anomalies abound in the real world.

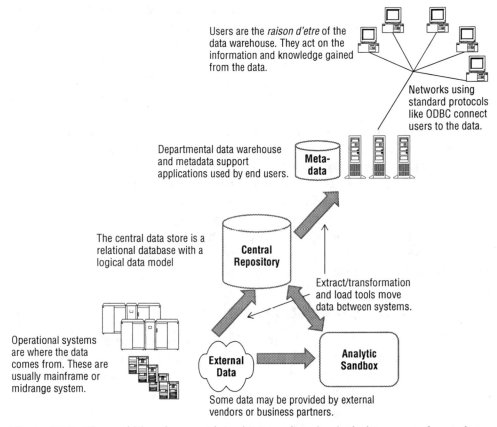

Figure 17-3: The multitiered approach to data warehousing includes a central repository, data marts, analytic sandboxes, end-user tools, and tools that connect all these pieces together.

Often, information of interest for customer relationship management is not gathered as intended. Here, for instance, are six ways that business customers might be distinguished from consumers in a telephone company:

- Customer type indicator: "B" or "C," for business versus consumer.

- Rate plans: Some are only sold to business customers; others to consumers.

- Acquisition channels: Some channels are reserved for business, others for consumers.

- Number of lines: one or two for consumer, more for business.

- Credit class: Businesses have a different set of credit classes from consumers.
- Model score based on businesslike calling patterns.

Needless to say, these definitions do not always agree. One challenge in data warehousing is arriving at a consistent definition that can be used across the business. The key to achieving this is metadata that documents the precise meaning of each field, so everyone using the data warehouse is speaking the same language.

Gathering data for decision support stresses operational systems because these systems were originally designed for transaction processing. Bringing the data together in a consistent format is almost always the most expensive part of implementing a data warehousing solution.

The source systems offer other challenges as well. They generally run on a wide range of hardware, and much of the software is built in-house or highly customized (or they are outsourced and the raw data may be very difficult to get). They sometimes use complicated and proprietary file structures. Mainframe systems are designed for holding and processing data, not for sharing it. Although systems are becoming more open, getting access to the data is always an issue, especially when different systems support very different parts of the organization. And, systems may be geographically dispersed, further contributing to the difficulty of bringing the data together.

Extraction, Transformation, and Load

Extraction, transformation, and load (ETL) tools solve the problem of gathering data from disparate systems by providing the ability to map and move data from source systems to other environments. Traditionally, data movement and cleansing have been the responsibility of programmers, who wrote special-purpose code as the need arose. Such application-specific code becomes brittle as systems multiply and source systems change.

Although programming may still be necessary, products are now available that solve the bulk of the ETL problems. These tools specify source systems and mappings between different tables and files. They provide the ability to verify data, and spit out error reports when loads do not succeed. The tools also support looking up values in tables (so only known product codes, for instance, are loaded into the data warehouse). The goal of these tools is to describe where data comes from and what happens to it — not to write the step-by-step code for pulling data from one system and putting it into another. Standard procedural languages, such as C++, C#, Java, COBOL, and RPG, focus on each step instead of the bigger picture of what needs to be done. ETL tools often provide a metadata interface, so end users can understand what is happening to "their" data during the loading of the central repository.

This genre of tools is often so good at processing data that the authors are surprised that such tools remain embedded in IT departments and are not more generally used by data miners. *Mastering Data Mining* has a case study from 1998 on using one of these tools from Ab Initio for analyzing hundreds of gigabytes of call detail records — a quantity of data that might still pose a challenge even today.

Central Repository

The central repository is the heart of the data warehouse. It is usually a relational database accessed through some variant of SQL.

One of the advantages of relational databases is their ability to run on powerful, scalable machines by taking advantage of multiple processors and multiple disks (see the sidebar "Background on Parallel Technology"). Most statistical and data mining packages, for instance, can run multiple processing threads at the same time. However, each thread represents one task, running on one processor. More hardware does not make any given task run faster (except when other tasks happen to be interfering with it). Relational databases, on the other hand, can take a single query and, in essence, create multiple threads all running at the same time for that one query. As a result, data-intensive applications on powerful computers often run more quickly when using a relational database than when using non-parallel-enabled software — and data mining is a very data-intensive application.

A key component in the central repository is a logical data model, which describes the structure of the data inside a database in terms familiar to business users. As discussed earlier in this chapter, the logical data model differs from the physical data model. The purpose of the physical data model is to maximize performance and facilitate the work of database administrators (DBAs), such as ensuring security, backing up the database, and so on. The physical data model is an implementation of the logical data model, incorporating compromises and choices along the way to optimize performance and to meet other system objectives.

> **TIP** Data warehousing is a process. Be wary of any large database called a data warehouse that does not have a process in place for updating the system to continuously meet end user needs and evolving business requirements. A data warehouse without a change process will eventually fade into disuse, because users' needs evolve.

When embarking on a data warehousing project, many organizations feel compelled to develop a comprehensive, enterprise-wide data model. These efforts are often surprisingly unsuccessful. The logical data model for the data warehouse does not have to be quite as uncompromising as an enterprise-wide model. For instance, a conflict between product codes in the logical data model for the data warehouse can be (but not necessarily should be) resolved by including both product hierarchies — a decision that takes 10 minutes to make. In an enterprise-wide effort, resolving conflicting product codes can require months of investigations and meetings.

Data warehousing is a process for managing the decision-support system of record. A process is something that can adjust to users' needs as they are clarified and change over time. The central repository itself is going to be a brittle, little-used system without the awareness that as users learn about data and about the business, they are going to want changes and enhancements on the time scale of marketing (days and weeks) rather than on the time scale of IT (months).

BACKGROUND ON PARALLEL TECHNOLOGY

Parallel technology is the key to scalable hardware, and it traditionally comes in two flavors: symmetric multiprocessing systems (SMPs) and massively parallel processing systems (MPPs), both of which are shown in the following figure. An SMP machine is centered on a *bus*, a special very local network present in all computers that connects processing units to memory and disk drives. The bus acts as a central communication device, so SMP systems are sometimes called *shared everything*. Every processing unit can access all the memory and all the disk drives. This form of parallelism is quite popular because an SMP box supports the same applications as uniprocessor boxes — and some applications can take advantage of additional hardware with minimal changes to code. However, SMP technology has its limitations because it places a heavy burden on the central bus, which becomes saturated as the processing load increases. Contention for the central bus is often what limits the performance of SMPs. They tend to work best when they have no more than 10 to 20 processing units.

MPPs, on the other hand, behave like separate computers connected by a very high-speed network, and, in fact, MPP is sometimes referred to as *grid computing*. Each processing unit has its own memory and its own disk storage. Some nodes may be specialized for processing and have minimal disk storage, and others may be specialized for storage and have lots of disk capacity. The bus connecting the processing unit to memory and disk drives never gets saturated, because it is not shared among all processors. However, one drawback is that some memory and some disk drives are now local and some are remote — a distinction that can make MPPs harder to program. Programs designed for one processor can always run on one processor in an MPP — but they require modifications to take advantage of all the hardware. MPPs are truly scalable as long as the network connecting the processors can supply more bandwidth, and faster networks are generally easier to design than faster buses. There are MPP-based computers with thousands of nodes and thousands of disks.

Both SMPs and MPPs have their advantages. Recognizing this, the vendors of these computers are making them more similar to each other. SMP vendors are connecting their SMP computers together in clusters that start to resemble MPP boxes. At the same time, MPP vendors are replacing their single-processing units with SMP units, creating a very similar architecture. Newer technologies, such as solid state disks, ultrafast networks, and cheap

memory, are making computers even more powerful with fewer processing bottlenecks. However, regardless of the power of the hardware, software needs to be designed to take advantage of these machines. Fortunately, the largest database vendors have invested years of research into enabling their products to do so.

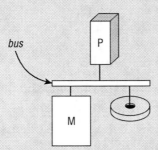

Uniprocessor

A simple computer follows the architecture laid out by Von Neumann. A processing unit communicates to memory and disk over a local bus. (Memory stores both data and the executable program.) The speed of the processor, bus, and memory limits performance and scalability.

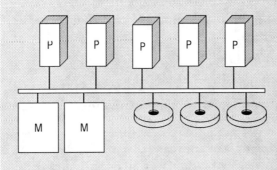

SMP

The symmetric multiprocessor (SMP) has a shared-everything architecture. It expands the capabilities of the bus to support multiple processors, more memory, and a larger disk. The capacity of the bus limits performance and scalability. SMP architecture usually max out with fewer than 20 processing units.

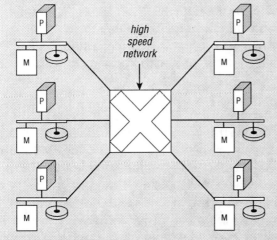

MPP

The massively parallel processor (MMP) has a shared-nothing architecture. It introduces a high-speed network (also called a switch that connects independent processor/memory/disk components. MPP architectures are very scalable but fewer software packages can take advantage of all the hardware.

Parallel computers build on the basic Von Neumann uniprocessor architecture. SMP and MPP systems are scalable because more processing units, disk drives, and memory can be added to the system.

Metadata Repository

Metadata should also be considered a component of the data warehouse, although it is often overlooked. The lowest level of metadata is the database schema, the physical layout of the data. When used correctly, though, metadata is much more. It answers questions posed by end users about the availability of data, gives them tools for browsing through the contents of the data warehouse, and gives everyone more confidence in the data. This confidence is the basis for new applications and an expanded user base.

A good metadata system should include the following:

- The annotated logical data model. The annotations should explain the entities and attributes, including valid values.
- Mapping from the logical data model to the source systems.
- The physical schema.
- Mapping from the logical model to the physical schema.
- Common views and formulas for accessing the data. What is useful to one user may be useful to others.
- Information about loads and updates.
- Security and access information.
- Interfaces for end users and developers, so they share the same description of the database.

In any data warehousing environment, each of these pieces of information is available somewhere — in scripts written by the DBA, in e-mail messages, in documentation, in the system tables in the database, and so on. A metadata repository makes this information available to the users in a format they can readily understand. The key is giving users access so they feel comfortable with the data warehouse, with the data it contains, and with knowing how to use it.

Data Marts

Data warehouses do not actually do anything, except store and retrieve clean, consistent data effectively. Applications are needed to realize value, and these often take the form of data marts. A data mart is a specialized system that brings together the data needed for a department or related applications.

Data marts are often associated with reporting systems and slicing-and-dicing pre-summarized data. Such data marts often use OLAP technology, which is discussed later in this chapter. Another important type of data mart is an exploratory environment used for data mining, which is discussed in more detail in the section on analytic sandboxes.

Not all the data in data marts needs to come from the central repository. Often specific applications have an exclusive need for data. The real estate department, for instance, might be using geographic information in combination with data from the central repository. The marketing department might be combining ZIP code demographics with customer data from the central repository. The central repository only needs to contain data that is likely to be shared among different applications, so it is just one data source — usually the dominant one — for data marts.

Operational Feedback

Operational feedback systems integrate data-driven decisions back into the operational systems. For instance, a large bank may develop cross-sell models to determine what product to offer a customer next. This is a result of a data mining system. To be useful this information needs to go back into the operational systems so customers can get a targeted message in their mailbox, at the ATM, on hold at the call center, as banner ads when they log into online banking, and so on. This requires a connection back from the decision-support infrastructure into the operational infrastructure.

Operational feedback offers the capability to complete the virtuous cycle of data mining very quickly. After a feedback system is set up, intervention is only needed for monitoring and improving it — letting computers do what they do best (repetitive tasks) and letting people do what they do best (spot interesting patterns and come up with ideas). One of the advantages of e-businesses is that they can, in theory, provide such feedback to their operational systems in a fully automated way.

Users and Desktop Tools

The users are the final and most important component in any data warehouse. A system that has no users is not worth building. These end users are analysts looking for information, application developers, and business users who act on the information.

Analysts

Analysts want to access as much data as possible to discern patterns and create ad hoc reports. They use special-purpose tools, such as statistics packages, data mining tools, and spreadsheets. Often, analysts are considered to be the primary audience for data warehouses.

Usually, though, just a few technically sophisticated people fall into this category. Although the work that they do is important, justifying a large investment based on increases in their productivity is difficult. The virtuous cycle of data mining comes into play here. A data warehouse brings together data in a cleansed, meaningful format. The purpose, though, is to spur creativity, a very hard concept to measure.

Analysts have very specific demands on a data warehouse:

- The system has to be responsive. Much of the work of analysts is answering urgent questions using ad hoc analysis or ad hoc queries.

- Data needs to be consistent across the database. That is, if a customer started on a particular date, then the first occurrence of a product, channel, and so on should normally be exactly on that date.

- Data needs to be consistent across time. A field that has a particular meaning now should have the same meaning going back in time. At the very least, differences should be well documented or incorporated into slowly changing dimensions.

- Analysts must be able to drill down to the customer level and preferably to the transaction level detail to verify values in the data warehouse and to develop new summaries of customer behavior.

Analysts place a heavy load on data warehouses, and need access to consistent information in a timely manner.

Application Developers

Data warehouses usually support a wide range of applications (in other words, data marts come in many flavors). To develop stable and robust applications, developers have some specific needs from the data warehouse.

First, the applications need to be shielded from changes in the structure of the data warehouse. New tables, new fields, and reorganizing the structure of existing tables should have a minimal impact on existing applications. Special application-specific views on the data help provide this assurance. Open communication and knowledge about what applications use which attributes and entities can prevent development gridlock.

Second, the developers need access to valid field values and to know what the values mean. This is the purpose of the metadata repository, which provides documentation on the structure of the data. By setting up the application to verify data values against expected values in the metadata, developers can circumvent problems that often appear only after applications have rolled out.

The developers also need to provide feedback on the structure of the data warehouse. This is one of the principle means of improving the warehouse, by identifying new data that needs to be included and by fixing problems with data already loaded. Because real business needs drive the development of applications, understanding the needs of developers is important to ensure that a data warehouse contains the data it needs to deliver business value.

The data warehouse is going to change and applications are going to continue to use it. The key to delivering success is controlling and managing the changes. The applications are for the end users. The data warehouse is there to support their data needs — not vice versa.

Business Users

Business users are the ultimate devourers of information derived from the corporate data warehouse. Their needs drive the development of applications, the architecture of the warehouse, the data it contains, and the priorities for implementation.

Many business users only experience the warehouse through printed reports, simple online reports, or spreadsheets — basically the same way they have been gathering information for a long time. Even these users will experience the power of having a data warehouse as reports become more accurate, more consistent, and easier to produce.

More important, though, are the people who use the computers on their desks for more than just e-mail and Facebook and are able to take advantage of direct access to the data warehousing environment. Typically, these users access intermediate data marts to satisfy the vast majority of their information needs using friendly, graphical tools that run in their familiar desktop environment. These tools include off-the-shelf query generators, custom applications, OLAP interfaces, Excel-driven query tools, and report generation tools. On occasion, business users may drill down into the central repository to explore particularly interesting things they find in the data. More often, they will contact an analyst and have him or her do the heavier analytic work or prepare a data extract for Excel.

Business users also have applications built for specific purposes. These applications may even incorporate some of the data mining techniques discussed in previous chapters. For instance, a resource scheduling application might include an engine that optimizes the schedule using genetic algorithms. A sales forecasting application may have built-in survival analysis models. When embedded in an application, the data mining algorithms are usually quite well hidden from the end users, who care more about the results than the algorithms that produced them.

Analytic Sandboxes

Analytic sandboxes are the environment for the ad hoc data transformations, investigations, and analyses that go beyond the capabilities of the data warehouse and the predefined goals of data marts. The term *sandbox* is intended to convey the idea that these are environments where analysts play with data and tools to achieve interesting results.

Why Are Analytic Sandboxes Needed?

Analytics sandboxes serve several purposes. Data warehouses are powerful systems for *publishing* and sharing data. As with publishing books, the data warehousing process cleans and edits the data to be sure that it is consistent and meets standards. However, situations arise where the data in the warehouse may not be sufficient for some reason. These are the situations where analytic sandboxes are important.

Too Much Data

An obvious need for an analytic sandbox arises when the volume of data is simply too large for a relational database. Some data sources grow by tens of millions, hundreds of millions, or even billions of transactions per day, and are often associated with web and telecommunications applications. When the raw data starts measuring in the hundreds of megabytes or gigabytes of data per day — or more — then more advanced tools are often needed for ad hoc analysis.

The data sources feeding an analytic sandbox are still valuable sources for a data warehouse. However, ad hoc analyses that are outside the scope of the warehouse may be needed.

On one project, for instance, the authors were asked to answer a seemingly simple question for a large media company: "How many unique users visit our website in one month?" The website in question had more than a billion page views per month. A page view includes a lot of data, so this corresponds to more than 200GB of raw data per month. The page view contains URIs (which stands for *uniform resource identifier*, but is more commonly known as a web address) for the page being loaded and for the referring page, information about the browser, various cookie IDs, date and time stamps, and so on.

At the website in question, some users identify themselves by logging in. These identified users can be reliably tracked and counted. Users who remain anonymous pose more of a challenge. The idea was to find some metric, such as number of page views per logged-in user, and then use this to determine the total number of users. The actual metric required first *sessionizing* the data, to determine the number of visits to the site, a visit being a contiguous sequence of page views. The key measure was the average number of sessions an identi-fied (logged-in) user has in a month. Dividing the total number of sessions in a month by this average provides an estimate of the number of unique visitors in a month.

The problem was that the data warehouse that stored all the web data did not maintain all the detail needed for this analysis. Answering the question required an analytic sandbox, in this case, one using cloud computing (specifi-cally, Amazon's Elastic Computing Cloud, EC2) and code written using Hadoop, which is discussed later in this section.

The purpose of this example is not to go into the calculation in detail. Instead, when working with large amounts of data, such as the data in web logs, the features extracted for data warehouse data structures may not include all the information needed for a particular analysis. An analytic sandbox provides the infrastructure for answering such questions.

More Advanced Techniques

Analytic sandboxes can support more advanced techniques than supported in a standard data mart or in reporting systems. Often, statistical tools, such as SAS, SPSS, R, and other programming languages are used in this environment, where statisticians write special-purpose code to develop useful methods for analyzing data.

The range of possible techniques is limitless. Some of the more interesting involve simulations described in Chapter 12. A basic type of simulation is the Monte Carlo simulation, named after the famous casino. Consider a situation where a company wants to make a strategic decision on whether it should enter a new line of business. The business model for this decision might involve a number of variables, such as the number of customers the new business would attract and the amount of money the company would need to invest. Another set of inputs into this type of model involve financial measures, such as the cost of money, which in turn depends on the prevailing interest rate and other economic factors.

Of course, the future values of these variables are not actually known. Instead, the values are assumed to follow some statistical distribution, such as a normal distribution with a particular average and standard deviation. Monte Carlo simulation is the process of testing different scenarios, over and over, by pulling the input variables from their appropriate distributions, and then calculating the possible values for the investment.

Monte Carlo simulation is just one example of many. Another computationally intensive approach that requires advanced statistical knowledge is Bayesian models (not to be confused with the naïve Bayesian models introduced in Chapter 6). What these techniques have in common is that they often require advanced statistical knowledge and special-purpose tools.

Complex Data

The third reason why an analytic sandbox might be necessary is for complex data structures that do not fit neatly into a relational data structure. These include text, images, audio, video, social networks, and so on. Relational databases are not optimized for these sorts of content.

LinkedIn is a popular site for professional networking. One feature of the site is "People You May Know." One of the authors was impressed to find his brother at the top of the list. In telling this story to an acquaintance, he was trumped: LinkedIn suggested that the person might know his wife.

The point of this example is that "People You May Know" is not a SQL function, not even in the most advanced database. Although it is based on link analysis, it requires special-purpose code to implement. LinkedIn used an implementation of a methodology called *MapReduce* (discussed in the next section) to create this feature.

Technology to Support Analytic Sandboxes

There are many different types of analytic sandboxes, because there are so many different ways to use them. This section discusses some of the technology that supports them. In some cases, the analytic sandbox can also be the data warehouse — at a certain cost, however. In such cases, the data warehouse would have to be sized to be able to perform both its duties as a data warehouse (delivering quality data to downstream applications and ad hoc query requests) and as a platform for analysis.

Faster Databases

Relational databases have become even more adept at analysis than their inventor, E. F. Codd, envisioned. Partly, this is due to more functionality in the SQL language, such as window functions (sometimes called analytic functions), grouping sets, better scalar functions, and user-defined functions. Another important factor is improvements in performance.

In the past few years, a new breed of database vendor has emerged that complements the traditional vendors such as Teradata, Oracle, IBM, HP, and Microsoft. These databases are based on open-source code, often on a database called PostGres, originally developed at the University of California, Berkeley in the 1980s. What makes PostGres so popular for these new vendors is its open-source license: Although PostGres itself is free and open-source, a vendor can modify the source code and sell the resulting product, something not allowed by all open-source licenses.

The most common feature added to PostGres is parallel processing to make the database scalable; virtually all vendors who use PostGres as a base for their database have this functionality. The first successful company was Netezza (acquired by IBM in 2010), whose product combines a parallel database with a hardware accelerator. XtremeData is another company following the example of a hardware accelerator, whereas companies such as GreenPlum and Aster Data run on generic platforms, without special hardware.

Vertical partitioning refers to storing each column separately from other columns. Such column-oriented databases have the advantage that when one column is used in a query, then the rest of the columns in the same table do not have to be loaded into memory greatly saving time on reading and writing data. Furthermore, compressing each column independently is usually much more efficient than compressing rows (which consists of different types in different columns), providing further performance improvements. Two leading vendors in this area are ParAccel and Vertica.

Yet another feature is in-memory processing, which significantly speeds up the database by storing everything in memory, eschewing slower disk. ParAccel is a leader with this technology.

As time goes by, the good technology offered by different vendors will converge to create faster and faster databases at all vendors. As today's technology becomes standard, new technologies will emerge. The traditional database vendors are not standing still; they are enhancing their databases with similar features to remain competitive.

Improvements in hardware are also speeding up databases, especially the reduced cost of memory and the increased adoption of solid-state disk drives. Both of these are moving in the same direction — obtaining in-memory performance at accessible prices. As time goes by, standard databases will only become stronger in the area of applying SQL for complex ad hoc analyses.

In Database Analytics

Another trend that is becoming popular is putting more advanced analytic functions directly into the database. Because databases are very good at processing data — and powerful databases take advantage of parallel processing — this is a good way to broaden the functionality of SQL, making it possible to use a data mart or data warehouse as an analytic sandbox.

In the mid-1990s, the data mining software package Clementine started offering "in-database" data mining. This allowed the package to take advantage of databases for some model building and scoring work. The first database to support Clementine was produced by a company called Tandem. Moving ahead several years, Clementine is now part of IBM (ISL, the original creator of Clementine, was purchased by SPSS, which IBM purchased) and Tandem is now part of HP (Tandem became Digital became Compaq became HP), and Clementine still supports in-database processing.

Starting in 2002, Oracle Data Mining software started moving all its data mining functionality directly into the database. This speeds the algorithms both because they can access the data directly through the database engine and also because they can take advantage of its parallel capabilities. Since then, Oracle has greatly expanded the data mining functionality of its software.

Because SAS's software is so widespread, SAS's efforts in this area are also very important. Database vendors are implementing certain SAS primitives in the database, and the range of functionality will only grow in the future. This allows SAS's software — which is generally not parallel-enabled — to take advantage of the power of relational databases.

Another step in this direction is offered by companies such as Fuzzy Logix, which extends databases using user-defined functions. Its package offers a range of statistical and data mining routines that can be called directly from SQL. Of course, these functions are not part of the SQL standard.

Statistical Tools

Another reason for an analytic sandbox is to support processing not available in databases or data mining tools. Statistical programming languages — such as SAS, SPSS, R, and S-plus — support a very large variety of statistical routines and data manipulation functions.

As described in the previous section, such processing may take place in the database, taking advantage of parallel processing. More often, such code may access a data warehouse or data mart to retrieve values , process them into new values, and publish the results back into the data warehouse. However, the intermediate processing is independent of the database.

Hadoop/MapReduce

In the early 1960s, a programming language called APL introduced two important ideas. One, called *scalar extension*, was that any function defined on a scalar (a fancy word for a single value) could be applied to the elements of an array of any shape and number of dimensions. For instance, a function could multiply any value by two, and when applied as a scalar extension to an array, would multiply all the values by two. The second idea was the *reduce operator*, so called because it uses a function such as addition or maximum to reduce an array's number of dimensions by one. Plus reduce (spelled +/) applied to a one-dimensional list returns a scalar by adding up the elements of the list. Applied to a two-dimensional table, it returns a one-dimensional list by adding up the rows or columns. Later, these ideas were picked up by other programming languages, including Lisp, where scalar extension is known as map and reduce kept the name used in APL.

Fast forward several decades. Researchers at Google revisited these Lisp primitives and realized that map and reduce could be implemented on MPP systems to process large quantities of data. That realization — and a lot of hard work building the infrastructure to support grid computing, a parallel file system, and code to implement map and reduce — led to the invention of MapReduce. The most common implementation of MapReduce goes by the name of Hadoop, named by the project's founder Dave Cutter (who then worked at Yahoo!), who named it after his son's favorite toy, a stuffed elephant.

Hadoop is an open-source platform that has become increasingly popular for five reasons. First, it works. Second, it is free. Third, it is available on Amazon's Elastic Cloud computing infrastructure. And fourth, if Google, Amazon, and Yahoo! are all involved, then other companies suddenly become interested. Fifth, companies such as Cloudera offer support with training and documentation. Hadoop supports MapReduce, but it also supports other technologies as well.

The technical details of MapReduce and Hadoop are beyond the scope of this book. They are most useful when the volume of data is very, very large. Typical problems involve web logs, which are text files containing information about every web page visited by millions of users. This information includes the referring web page, information about the browser, cookies, date and time stamps, and so on. Placing such data in databases is cumbersome, because even a relatively small site that gets one million page views per day generates more than 100GB of raw data in a year. And the queries to make sense of the data are quite complicated.

MapReduce and Hadoop can approach these tasks efficiently, using grid computing — arrays of processors that provide an MPP approach to processing. The downside is that they generally require programming in order to perform the work. Increasingly, the Hadoop platform is expanding to include higher-level SQL-like languages such as Hive for manipulating data.

Hadoop is not a requirement for using MapReduce. Other implementations are available. For instance, some database vendors include MapReduce functionality in their databases. The example with LinkedIn suggesting "People You May Know" used GreenPlum's implementation of MapReduce inside its database engine.

Where Does OLAP Fit In?

The business world has been generating automated reports to meet business needs for many decades. Figure 17-4 shows a range of common reporting capabilities. Once upon a time, mainframe computers generated reports on green bar paper or green screens. These mainframe reports automated paper-based methods that preceded computers. More modern interfaces have superseded most of these reports.

Producing such reports is often a primary function of IT departments. Even minor changes to the reports require modifying code that can date back decades at some companies. The result is a lag between a user requesting changes and the user seeing the new information that is measured in weeks and months. This is old technology that organizations are generally trying to move away from, except for the lowest-level reports that summarize specific operational systems.

In the middle are off-the-shelf query generation packages that have become popular for accessing data in the past decade. These generate queries in SQL and can talk to local or remote data sources using a standard protocol, such as the Open Database Connectivity (ODBC) standard. Such reports might be embedded in a spreadsheet, accessed through the Web, or through some other reporting interface. With a day or so of training, business analysts can usually generate the reports that they need. Of course, the report itself is often running as an SQL query on an already-overburdened database, so response times can be measured in minutes or hours, when the queries are even allowed to run to completion. These response times are much faster than the older report-generation packages, but they still make exploiting the data difficult. The goal is to be able to ask a question and still remember the question when the answer comes back.

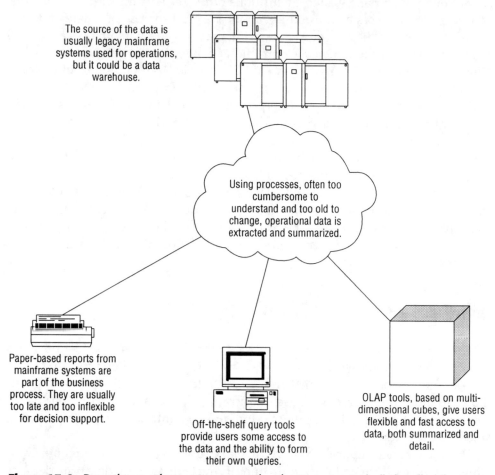

The source of the data is usually legacy mainframe systems used for operations, but it could be a data warehouse.

Using processes, often too cumbersome to understand and too old to change, operational data is extracted and summarized.

Paper-based reports from mainframe systems are part of the business process. They are usually too late and too inflexible for decision support.

Off-the-shelf query tools provide users some access to the data and the ability to form their own queries.

OLAP tools, based on multi-dimensional cubes, give users flexible and fast access to data, both summarized and detail.

Figure 17-4: Reporting requirements on operational systems are typically handled the same way they have been for decades. Is this the best way?

OLAP is a significant improvement over ad hoc query systems, because OLAP systems design the data structure with users and their reporting needs in mind. It starts by defining a set of dimensions (such as month, geography, and product) and storing important measures (such as total sales and total discounts) for each combination of the dimensions. This powerful and efficient representation is called a cube, which is ideally suited for slicing and dicing data. The cube itself is usually stored in a relational database, typically using a star schema. In addition, OLAP tools provide handy analysis functions that are difficult or impossible to express in SQL. If OLAP tools have one downside, it is that business users start to focus only on the dimensions of data represented by the tool. Data mining, on the other hand, is particularly valuable for creative thinking.

Setting up the cube requires analyzing the data and user needs, which is generally done by specialists familiar with the data and the tool, through a process called dimensional modeling. Although designing and loading an OLAP system requires an initial investment, the result provides informative and fast access to users. Response times, after the cube has been built, are almost always measured in seconds, allowing users to explore data and drill down to understand interesting features that they encounter.

TIP Quick response times are important for getting user acceptance of reporting systems. When users have to wait, they may forget the question that they asked. Interactive response times as experienced by users should be in the range of 3–5 seconds.

OLAP is a powerful enhancement to earlier reporting methods. Its power rests on three key features:

- A well-designed OLAP system has a set of relevant dimensions — such as geography, product, and time — understandable to business users. These dimensions often prove important for data mining purposes.

- A well-designed OLAP system has a set of useful measures relevant to the business.

- OLAP systems allow users to slice and dice data, and sometimes to drill down to the customer level.

These capabilities are complementary to data mining, but not a substitute for it. Nevertheless, OLAP is a very important (perhaps even the most important) part of the data warehouse architecture because it has the largest number of users.

What's in a Cube?

A good way to approach OLAP is to think of data as a cube split into subcubes, as shown in Figure 17-5. Although this example uses three dimensions, OLAP can have many more. This example shows a typical retailing cube that has one dimension for time, another for product, and a third for store. Each subcube contains various measures indicating what happened regarding that product in that store on that date, such as:

- Total number of items sold
- Total value of the items
- Total amount of discount on the items
- Inventory cost of the items

The measures are called *facts*. As a general rule, dimensions consist of categorical variables and facts are numeric. As users slice and dice the data, they are aggregating facts from many different subcubes. The dimensions are used to determine exactly which subcubes are used in the query.

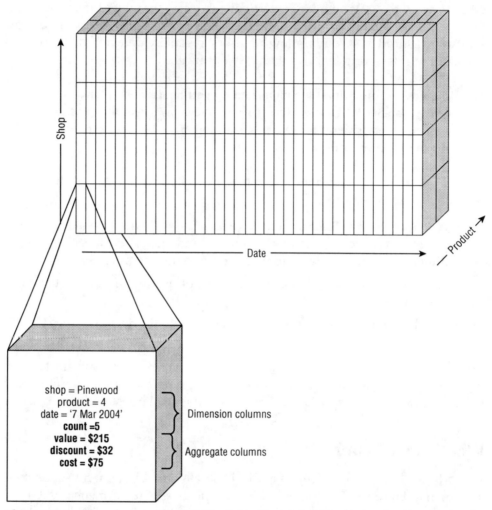

Figure 17-5: The cube used for OLAP is divided into subcubes. Each subcube contains the key for that subcube and summary information for the data falls into that subcube.

Even a simple cube such as the one just described is very powerful. Figure 17-5 shows an example of summarizing data in the cube to answer the question: "On how many days did a particular store not sell a particular product?" Such a question requires using the store and product dimensions to determine which subcubes are used for the query. This question only looks at one fact, the number of items sold, and returns all the dates for which this value is zero. Here are some other questions that can be answered relatively easily:

- What was the total number of items sold in the past year?

- What were the year over year sales, by month, of stores in the Northeast?

- What was the overall margin for each store in November? (Margin being the price paid by the customer minus the inventory cost.)

The ease of getting a report that can answer one of these questions depends on the particular implementation of the reporting interface. However, even for ad hoc reporting, accessing the cube structure can prove much easier than accessing a normalized relational database.

There is one cardinal rule when creating a cube: Any particular item of information should fall into exactly one subcube. When this rule is violated, the cube cannot easily be used to report on the various dimensions. A corollary of this rule is that when an OLAP cube is being loaded, keeping track of any data that has unexpected dimensional values is very important. Every dimension should have an "other" category to guarantee that all data makes it in.

TIP When choosing the dimensions for a cube, be sure that each record lands in exactly one subcube. If you have redundant dimensions — such as one dimension for date and another for day of the week — then the same record will land in two or more subcubes. If this happens, then the summarizations based on the subcubes will no longer be accurate.

Facts

Facts are the measures in each subcube. The most useful facts are *additive*, so they can be combined together across many different subcubes to provide responses to queries at arbitrary levels of summarization. Additive facts can be summarized along any dimension or along several dimensions at one time — which is exactly the purpose of the cube.

Examples of additive facts are:

- Counts

- Counts of variables with a particular value

- Total duration of time (such as spent on a website)

- Total monetary values

The total amount of money spent on a particular product on a particular day is a good example of an additive fact. However, not all facts are additive. Examples include:

- Averages

- Unique counts

- Counts of things shared across different cubes, such as transactions

Averages are an uninteresting example of a nonadditive fact, because an average is a total divided by a count. Because each of these is additive, the average can be derived after combining these facts.

The other examples are more interesting. A common question is how many unique customers did some particular action. Although this number can be stored in a subcube, it is not additive. Consider a retail cube with the date, store, and product dimensions. A single customer may purchase items in more than one store, or purchase more than one item in a store, or make purchases on different days. A field containing the number of unique customers has information about one customer in more than one subcube, violating the cardinal rule of OLAP, so the cube is not going to be able to report on unique customers.

A similar thing happens when trying to count numbers of transactions. The information about the transaction may be stored in several different subcubes, because a single transaction may involve more than one product. So, counts of transactions also violate the cardinal rule. This type of information cannot be gathered at the summary level. On the other hand, counts of transactions can be stored in a separate fact table, using store and time as dimensions, or using store, time, and customer as dimensions.

Another note about facts is that not all numeric data is appropriate as a fact in a cube. For instance, age in years is numeric, but it might be better treated as a dimension rather than a fact. Another example is customer value. Discrete ranges of customer value are useful as dimensions, and in many circumstances more useful than including customer value as a fact.

When designing cubes, there is a temptation to mix facts and dimensions by creating a count or total for a group of related values. For instance:

- Count of active customers of less than one-year tenure, between one and two years, and greater than two years
- Amount credited on weekdays; amount credited on weekends
- Total for each day of the week

Such partial totals suggest the need for another dimension for the cube. The first should have a customer tenure dimension that takes at least three values. The second appeared in a cube where the time dimension was by month. These facts suggest a need for daily summaries, or at least for separating weekdays and weekends along a dimension. The third suggests a need for a date dimension at the granularity of days.

Dimensions and Their Hierarchies

Sometimes, a single column seems appropriate for multiple dimensions. For instance, OLAP is a good tool for visualizing trends over time, such as for sales or financial data. A specific date in this case potentially represents information along several dimensions, as shown in Figure 17-6:

- Day of the week
- Month
- Quarter
- Calendar year

One approach is to represent each of these as a different dimension. In other words, there would be four dimensions, one for the day of the week, one for the month, one for the quarter, and one for the calendar year. The data for January 2004 then would be the subcube where the January dimension intersects the 2004 dimension.

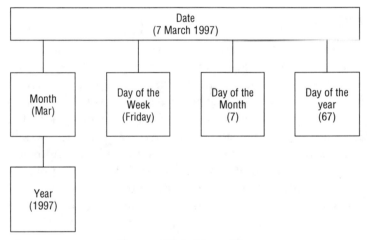

Figure 17-6: Dates have multiple hierarchies.

This is not a good approach. Multidimensional modeling recognizes that time is an important dimension, and that time can have many different attributes. In addition to the attributes described earlier, there are others, such as the week of the year, whether the date is a holiday (which may in turn depend on a particular country), whether the date is a work day, and so on. Such attributes are stored in reference tables, called dimension tables. Dimension tables support changing the attributes of the dimension without changing the underlying fact table.

WARNING Do not take shortcuts when designing the dimensions for an OLAP system. These are the skeleton of the data mart, and a weak skeleton will not last very long.

Dimension tables contain many different attributes describing each value of the dimension. A detailed geography dimension might be built from ZIP codes and include dozens of summary variables about the ZIP codes. These attributes can be used for filtering ("How many customers are in high-income areas?"). These values are stored in the dimension table rather than the fact table, because they cannot be aggregated correctly. If three stores are in a ZIP code, the ZIP code population fact would get added up three times — multiplying the population by three.

Usually, dimension tables are kept up to date with the most recent values for the dimension. So, a store dimension might include the current set of stores with information about the stores, such as layout, square footage, address, and manager name. However, all of these may change over time. Such dimensions are called *slowly changing dimensions*, and are of particular interest to data mining because data mining wants to reconstruct accurate histories of the business at a given point in the past. Slowly changing dimensions are outside the scope of this book. Interested readers should review Ralph Kimball's books.

Conformed Dimensions

As mentioned earlier, data warehouse systems often contain multiple OLAP cubes. Some of the power of OLAP arises from the practice of sharing dimensions across different cubes. These shared dimensions are called conformed dimensions and are shown in Figure 17-7; they help ensure that business results reported through different systems use the same underlying set of business rules.

A good example of a conformed dimension is the calendar dimension, which keeps track of the attributes of each day. A calendar dimension is so important that it should be a part of every data warehouse. However, different components of the warehouse may need different attributes. For instance, a multinational business might include sets of holidays for different countries, so there might be a flag for "United States Holiday," "United Kingdom Holiday," "France Holiday," and so on, instead of an overall holiday flag. January 1st is a holiday in most countries; however, July 4th is mostly celebrated in the United States.

One of the challenges in building OLAP systems is designing the conformed dimensions so that they are suitable for a wide variety of applications. For some purposes geography might be best described by city and state; for another, by county; for another, by census block group; and for another, by ZIP code. Unfortunately, these four descriptions are not fully compatible, because several small towns can be in a ZIP code, and New York City covers five counties. Multidimensional modeling helps resolve such conflicts.

Star Schema

Cubes are easily stored in relational databases, using a denormalized data structure called the *star schema*, developed by Ralph Kimball, a guru of OLAP. One advantage of the star schema is its use of standard database technology to achieve the power of OLAP.

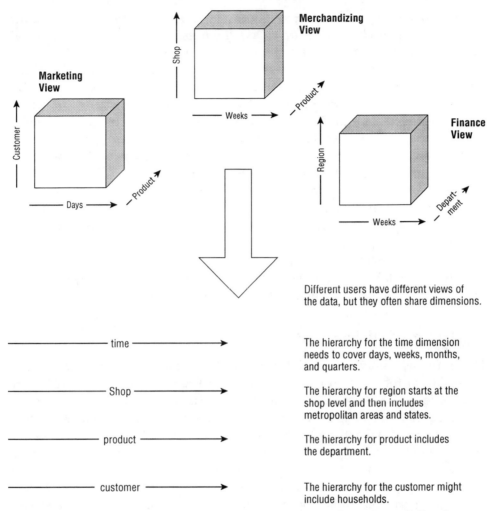

Figure 17-7: Different views of the data often share common dimensions. Finding the common dimensions and their base units is critical to making data warehousing work well across an organization.

A star schema starts with a *central fact table* that corresponds to facts about a business. These can be at the transaction level (for an event cube), although they are more often low-level summaries of transactions. For retail sales, the central fact table might contain daily summaries of sales for each product in each store (shop-SKU-time). For a credit card company, a fact table might contain rows for each transaction by each customer or summaries of spending by product (based on card type and credit limit), customer segment, merchant type, customer geography, and month. For a diesel engine manufacturer interested in repair histories, it might contain each repair made on each engine or a daily summary of repairs at each shop by type of repair.

Each row in the central fact table contains some combination of keys that makes it unique. These keys are called *dimensions*. The central fact table also has other columns that typically contain numeric information specific to each row, such as the amount of the transaction, the number of transactions, and so on. Associated with each dimension are auxiliary tables called *dimension tables*, which contain information specific to the dimensions. For instance, the dimension table for date might specify the day of the week for a particular date, its month, year, and whether it is a holiday.

In diagrams, the dimension tables are connected to the central fact table, resulting in a shape that loosely resembles a star, as shown in Figure 17-8.

In practice, star schemas may not be efficient for answering all users' questions, because the central fact table is so large. In such cases, the OLAP systems introduce summary tables at different levels to facilitate query response. Relational database vendors provide lots of support for star schemas. With a typical architecture, any query on the central fact table would require multiple joins back to the dimension tables. By applying standard indexes, and creatively enhancing indexing technology, relational databases can handle these queries quite well.

OLAP and Data Mining

Data mining is about the successful exploitation of data for decision-support purposes. The virtuous cycle of data mining, described in Chapter 1, reminds us that success depends on more than advanced pattern recognition algorithms. The data mining process needs to provide feedback to people and encourage using information gained from data mining to improve business processes. The data mining process should enable people to provide input, in the form of observations, hypotheses, and hunches about what results are important and how to use those results.

In the larger context of data exploitation, OLAP clearly plays an important role as a means of broadening the audience with access to data. Decisions once made based on experience and educated guesses can now be based on data and patterns in the data. Anomalies and outliers can be identified for further investigation and further modeling, sometimes using the most sophisticated data mining techniques. For instance, a user might discover that a particular item sells better at a particular time during the week through the use of an OLAP tool. This might lead to an investigation using market basket analysis to find other items purchased with that item. Market basket analysis might suggest an explanation for the observed behavior — more information and more opportunities for exploiting the information.

Data mining and OLAP have other synergies. One of the characteristics of decision trees discussed in Chapter 7 is their ability to identify the most informative features in the data relative to a particular outcome. That is, if a decision tree is built to predict attrition, then the upper levels of the tree will have the features that are the most important predictors for attrition. Well, these predictors might be a good choice for dimensions using an OLAP tool. Such analysis helps build better, more useful cubes. Another problem when building cubes is determining how to make continuous dimensions discrete. The nodes of a decision tree can help determine the best breaking point for a continuous value. This information can be fed into the OLAP tool to improve the dimension.

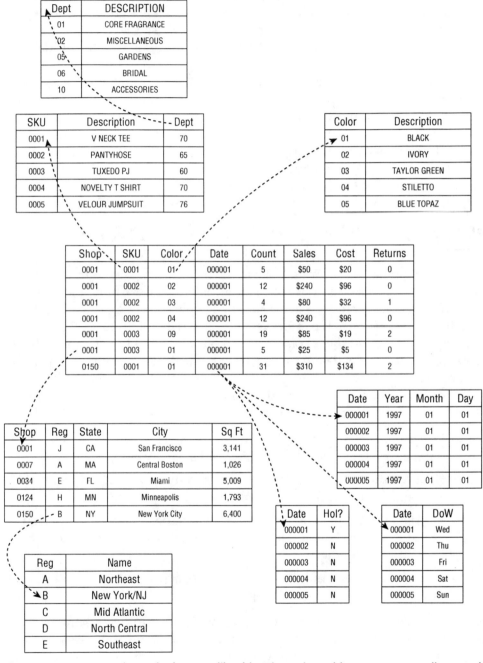

Figure 17-8: A star schema looks more like this. Dimension tables are conceptually nested, with more than one dimension table for a given dimension.

One of the problems with undirected data mining is the difficulty of understanding the results. OLAP to the rescue! Each customer can be assigned his or her cluster, along with other information, such as demographics, purchase history, and so on. This is a good application for a cube. OLAP — with information about the clusters included as a dimension — allows end users to explore the clusters and determining features that distinguish them from each other. The dimensions used for the OLAP cube should include the cluster identifier and other descriptive variables.

As these examples show, OLAP and data mining complement each other. Data mining can help build better cubes by defining appropriate dimensions, and further by determining how to break up continuous values on dimensions. OLAP provides a powerful visualization capability to help users better understand the results of data mining, such as clustering and neural networks. Used together, OLAP and data mining reinforce each other's strengths and provide more opportunities for exploiting data.

Where Data Mining Fits in with Data Warehousing

Data mining plays an important role in the data warehouse environment. The initial value of a data warehouse comes from automating existing processes, such as putting reports online and giving existing applications a clean source of data. The biggest returns are the improved access to data that can spur innovation and creativity — and these come from new ways of looking at and analyzing data. This is the role of data mining — to provide the tools that improve understanding and inspire creativity based on observations in the data.

A good data warehousing environment serves as a catalyst for data mining. The two technologies work together as partners:

- Data mining thrives on large amounts of data and the more detailed the data, the better — data that comes from a data warehouse.

- Data mining thrives on clean and consistent data — capitalizing on the investment in data cleansing tools.

- The data warehouse environment enables hypothesis testing and simplifies efforts to measure the effects of actions taken — enabling the virtuous cycle of data mining.

- Scalable hardware and relational database software can offload the data processing parts of data mining.

However, there is a distinction between the way data mining looks at the world and the way data warehousing does. Normalized data warehouses can store data with time stamps, but it is difficult to do time-related manipulations — such as determining what event happened just before some other event of interest.

OLAP introduces a time dimension. Data mining extends this even further by taking into account the notion of "before" and "after." Data mining learns from data (the "before"), with the purpose of applying these findings to the future (the "after"). For this reason, data mining often puts a heavy load on data warehouses. These are complementary technologies, supporting each other as discussed in the next few sections.

Lots of Data

The traditional approach to data analysis generally starts by reducing the size of the data. The three common ways of doing this are summarizing detailed transactions, taking a subset of the data, and only looking at certain attributes. The reason for reducing the size of the data is to enable analyzing it on the available hardware and software systems (or by hand, in the truly olden days). When properly done, the laws of statistics come into play, allowing you to choose a sample that behaves similarly to the rest of the data.

Data mining, on the other hand, is searching for trends in the data and for valuable anomalies. It is often trying to answer different types of questions from traditional statistical analysis, such as: "What product is this customer most likely to purchase next?" Even if you build a model using a subset of data, you need to deploy the model and score all customers, a process that can be computationally intensive, or score individual customers in real-time (such as on the the Web).

Fortunately, data mining algorithms are often able to take advantage of large amounts of data. When looking for patterns that identify rare events — such as having to write off customers because they failed to pay — having large amounts of data ensures that there is sufficient data for analysis. A subset of the data might be statistically relevant in total, but when you try to decompose it into other segments (by region, by product, by customer segment), there may be too little data to produce statistically meaningful results. Decision trees work very well, even when dozens or hundreds of fields are in each record. Link analysis requires a full complement of the data to create a graph. Neural networks can train on millions of records at a time. And, even though the algorithms often work on summaries of the detailed transactions (especially at the customer level), what gets summarized can change from one run to the next. Prebuilding the summaries and discarding the transaction data locks you into only one view of the business. Often the first result from using such summaries is a request for some variation on them.

Consistent, Clean Data

Data mining algorithms are often applied to gigabytes of data combined from several different sources. Much of the work in looking for actionable information actually takes place when bringing the data together — often 80 percent or more of the time allocated to a data mining project is spent preparing the data — especially when a data warehouse is not available. Subsequent problems, such as matching account numbers, interpreting codes, and assigning accounts to households, further delay analysis. Finding interesting patterns is often an iterative process that requires going back to the data to get additional data elements. Finally, when interesting patterns are found, the process must often be repeated on the most recent data available.

A well-designed and well-built data warehouse helps solve these problems. Data is cleaned once, when it is loaded into the data warehouse. The meaning of fields is well defined and available through the metadata. Incorporating new data into analyses is as easy as finding out what data is available through the metadata and retrieving it from the warehouse. A particular analysis can be reapplied on more recent data, because the warehouse is kept up to date. The end result is that the data is cleaner and more available — and that the analysts can spend more time applying powerful tools and insights instead of moving data and pushing bytes.

Hypothesis Testing and Measurement

The data warehouse (often with the assistance of an analytic sandbox) facilitates two other areas of data mining. Hypothesis testing is the verification of educated guesses about patterns in the data. Do tropical colors really sell better in Florida than elsewhere? Do people really shop during working hours? Are the users of credit cards at restaurants really high-end customers? These questions can be expressed rather easily as queries on the appropriate relational database. Having the data available supports asking such questions and finding out quickly what the answers are.

TIP The ability to test hypotheses and ideas is a very important aspect of data mining. By bringing the data together in one place, data warehouses enable answering in-depth, complicated questions. One caveat is that such queries can be expensive to run, falling into the killer query category.

Measurement is the other area where data warehouses have proven to be very valuable. Often when marketing efforts produce limited feedback on the degree of success achieved, a data warehouse enables you to see the results and to find related effects. Did sales of other products improve? Did customer attrition increase? Did calls to customer service decrease? And so on. Having the data available supports efforts to understand the effects of an action, whether the action was spurred by data mining results or by something else.

Of particular value in terms of measurement is the effect of various marketing actions on the longer-term customer relationship. Often, marketing campaigns are measured in terms of response. Although response is clearly a dimension of interest, it is only one. The longer term behavior of customers is also of interest. Did an acquisition campaign bring in good customers or did the newly acquired customers leave before they even paid? Did an up-sell campaign stick, or did customers return to their previous products? Measurement enables an organization to learn from its mistakes and to build on its successes.

Scalable Hardware and RDBMS Support

The final synergy between data mining and data warehousing is on the systems level. The same scalable hardware and software systems that make storing and querying large databases possible provide a good system for analyzing data. The next chapter talks about building the customer signature. Often, the best place to build the signature is in the central repository or, failing that, in a data mart built off the central repository.

There is also the question of running data mining algorithms in parallel, taking further advantage of the powerful machines. This is often not necessary, because actually building models represents a small part of the time devoted to data mining — preparing the data and understanding the results are much more important. Databases, such as Oracle, Microsoft SQL Server, and the newer generation of PostGres-based databases, are increasingly providing support for data mining algorithms, which enables such algorithms to run in parallel.

Lessons Learned

Data is an integral part of data mining, and data warehousing is a process that can greatly benefit data mining and data analysis efforts. From the perspective of data mining, the most important functionality of data warehouses is the ability to re-create accurate snapshots of history. Another very important facet is support for ad hoc reporting. To learn from data, you need to know what really happened.

A typical data warehousing system contains the following components:

- The source systems provide the input into the data warehouse.

- The extraction, transformation, and load tools clean the data and apply business rules so that new data is compatible with historical data.

- The central repository is a relational database specifically designed to be a decision-support system of record.

- The data marts provide the interface to different varieties of users with different needs.

- One or more analytic sandboxes for handling ad hoc needs, involving larger amounts of data or more sophisticated analyses.

- The metadata repository informs users and developers about what is inside the data warehouse.

One of the challenges in data warehousing is the massive amount of data that must be stored, particularly if the goal is to keep all customer interactions. Fortunately, computers are sufficiently powerful that the question is more about budget than possibility. Relational databases can also take advantage of the most powerful hardware, parallel computers.

Online Analytic Processing (OLAP) is a powerful part of data warehousing. OLAP tools are very good at handling summarized data, allowing users to summarize information along one or several dimensions at one time. Because these systems are optimized for user reporting, they often have interactive response times of less than five seconds.

Any well-designed OLAP system has time as a dimension, in order to see trends over time. Trying to accomplish the same thing on a normalized data warehouse requires very complicated queries that are prone to error. To be most useful, OLAP systems should allow users to drill down to detail data for all reports. This capability ensures that all data is making it into the cubes, as well as giving users the ability to spot important patterns that may not appear in the dimensions.

As pointed out throughout this chapter, OLAP complements rather than replaces data mining. OLAP gives users a better understanding of data and the business. Dimensions developed for OLAP can make data mining results more actionable. However, OLAP does not automatically find patterns in data.

OLAP is a powerful way to distribute information to many end users for advanced reporting needs. It provides the ability to let many more users base their decisions on data, instead of on hunches, educated guesses, and personal experience. OLAP complements undirected data mining techniques such as clustering. OLAP can provide the insight needed to find the business value in the identified clusters. It also provides a good visualization tool to use with other methods, such as decision trees and memory-based reasoning.

Data warehousing and data mining are not the same thing; however, they do complement each other. How data is stored in an organization is just the beginning of the synergies between data mining and data warehousing. The next chapter dives into the complexities of creating customer signatures.

CHAPTER 12

Simple Regression Analysis and Correlation

LEARNING OBJECTIVES

The overall objective of this chapter is to give you an understanding of bivariate linear regression analysis, thereby enabling you to:

1. Calculate the Pearson product-moment correlation coefficient to determine if there is a correlation between two variables.
2. Explain what regression analysis is and the concepts of independent and dependent variable.
3. Calculate the slope and y-intercept of the least squares equation of a regression line and from those, determine the equation of the regression line.
4. Calculate the residuals of a regression line and from those determine the fit of the model, locate outliers, and test the assumptions of the regression model.
5. Calculate the standard error of the estimate using the sum of squares of error, and use the standard error of the estimate to determine the fit of the model.
6. Calculate the coefficient of determination to measure the fit for regression models, and relate it to the coefficient of correlation.
7. Use the t and F tests to test hypotheses for both the slope of the regression model and the overall regression model.
8. Calculate confidence intervals to estimate the conditional mean of the dependent variable and prediction intervals to estimate a single value of the dependent variable.
9. Determine the equation of the trend line to forecast outcomes for time periods in the future, using alternate coding for time periods if necessary.
10. Use a computer to develop a regression analysis, and interpret the output that is associated with it.

© Antonella Carri/Age Fotostock America, Inc.

Predicting International Hourly Wages by the Price of a Big Mac

The McDonald's Corporation is the leading global food-service retailer with more than 30,000 local restaurants serving nearly 50 million people in more than 119 countries each day. This global presence, in addition to its consistency in food offerings and restaurant operations, makes McDonald's a unique and attractive setting for economists to make salary and price comparisons around the world. Because the Big Mac hamburger is a standardized hamburger produced and sold in virtually every McDonald's around the world, the *Economist*, a weekly newspaper focusing on international politics and business news and opinion, as early as 1986 was compiling information about Big Mac prices as an indicator of exchange rates. Building on this idea, researchers Ashenfelter and Jurajda proposed comparing wage rates across countries and the price of a Big Mac hamburger. Shown below are Big Mac prices and net hourly wage figures (in U.S. dollars) for 27 countries. Note that net hourly wages are based on a weighted average of 12 professions.

Country	Big Mac Price (U.S. $)	Net Hourly Wage (U.S. $)
Argentina	1.78	3.30
Australia	3.84	14.00
Brazil	4.91	4.30
Britain	3.48	13.90
Canada	4.00	12.80
Chile	3.34	3.10
China	1.95	3.00
Czech Republic	3.43	5.10
Denmark	4.90	17.70
Hungary	3.33	3.00
Indonesia	2.51	1.30
Japan	3.67	15.70
Malaysia	2.19	3.10
Mexico	2.50	1.80
New Zealand	3.59	8.40

(*continued*)

Country	Big Mac Price (U.S. $)	Net Hourly Wage (U.S. $)
Philippines	2.19	1.40
Poland	2.60	4.10
Russia	2.33	5.90
Singapore	3.08	5.90
South Africa	2.45	5.10
South Korea	2.82	6.10
Sweden	6.56	13.50
Switzerland	6.19	22.60
Thailand	2.17	2.60
Turkey	3.89	4.30
UAE	2.99	10.10
United States	3.73	16.50

Managerial and Statistical Questions

1. Is there a relationship between the price of a Big Mac and the net hourly wages of workers around the world? If so, how strong is the relationship?

2. Is it possible to develop a model to predict or determine the net hourly wage of a worker around the world by the price of a Big Mac hamburger in that country? If so, how good is the model?

3. If a model can be constructed to determine the net hourly wage of a worker around the world by the price of a Big Mac hamburger, what would be the predicted net hourly wage of a worker in a country if the price of a Big Mac hamburger was $3.00?

Sources: McDonald's Web site, at http://www.mcdonalds.com/corp/about.html; Michael R. Pakko and Patricia S. Pollard, "Burgernomics: A Big Mac Guide to Purchasing Power Parity," research publication by the St. Louis Federal Reserve Bank, at http://research.stlouisfed.org/publications/review/03/11/pakko.pdf; Orley Ashenfelter and Stepán Jurajda, "Cross-Country Comparisons of Wage Rates: The Big Mac Index," unpublished manuscript, Princeton University and CERGEEI/Charles University, October 2001; Nicholas Vardy, "The 'Big Mac' Index for 2010," at http://nickvardy.com/2010/07/29/the-big-mac-index-for-2010/; "Prices and Earnings," 2009 edition, UBS, at http://www.ubs.com/1/e/media_overview/media_global/releases?newsId=170250.

In business, the key to decision making often lies in the understanding of the relationships between two or more variables. For example, a company in the distribution business may determine that there is a relationship between the price of crude oil and the company's transportation costs. Financial experts, in studying the behavior of the bond market, might find it useful to know if the interest rates on bonds are related to the prime

471

interest rate set by the Federal Reserve. A marketing executive might want to know how strong the relationship is between advertising dollars and sales dollars for a product or a company.

In this chapter, we will study the concept of correlation and how it can be used to estimate the relationship between two variables. We will also explore simple regression analysis through which mathematical models can be developed to predict one variable by another. We will examine tools for testing the strength and predictability of regression models, and we will learn how to use regression analysis to develop a forecasting trend line.

12.1 CORRELATION

Interactive Applet

TABLE 12.1

Data for the Economics Example

Day	Interest Rate	Futures Index
1	7.43	221
2	7.48	222
3	8.00	226
4	7.75	225
5	7.60	224
6	7.63	223
7	7.68	223
8	7.67	226
9	7.59	226
10	8.07	235
11	8.03	233
12	8.00	241

Correlation is *a measure of the degree of relatedness of variables.* It can help a business researcher determine, for example, whether the stocks of two airlines rise and fall in any related manner. For a sample of pairs of data, correlation analysis can yield a numerical value that represents the degree of relatedness of the two stock prices over time. In the transportation industry, is a correlation evident between the price of transportation and the weight of the object being shipped? If so, how strong are the correlations? In economics, how strong is the correlation between the producer price index and the unemployment rate? In retail sales, are sales related to population density, number of competitors, size of the store, amount of advertising, or other variables?

Several measures of correlation are available, the selection of which depends mostly on the level of data being analyzed. Ideally, researchers would like to solve for ρ, the population coefficient of correlation. However, because researchers virtually always deal with sample data, this section introduces a widely used sample **coefficient of correlation**, r. This measure is applicable only if both variables being analyzed have at least an interval level of data. Chapter 17 presents a correlation measure that can be used when the data are ordinal.

The statistic r is the **Pearson product-moment correlation coefficient**, named after Karl Pearson (1857–1936), an English statistician who developed several coefficients of correlation along with other significant statistical concepts. The term r is a *measure of the linear correlation of two variables.* It is a number that ranges from -1 to 0 to $+1$, representing the strength of the relationship between the variables. An r value of $+1$ denotes a perfect positive relationship between two sets of numbers. An r value of -1 denotes a perfect negative correlation, which indicates an inverse relationship between two variables: as one variable gets larger, the other gets smaller. An r value of 0 means no linear relationship is present between the two variables.

PEARSON PRODUCT-MOMENT CORRELATION COEFFICIENT (12.1)	$$r = \frac{\Sigma(x - \bar{x})(y - \bar{y})}{\sqrt{\Sigma(x - \bar{x})^2 \, \Sigma(y - \bar{y})^2}} = \frac{\Sigma xy - \dfrac{(\Sigma x \, \Sigma y)}{n}}{\sqrt{\left[\Sigma x^2 - \dfrac{(\Sigma x)^2}{n}\right]\left[\Sigma y^2 - \dfrac{(\Sigma y)^2}{n}\right]}}$$

Figure 12.1 depicts five different degrees of correlation: (a) represents strong negative correlation, (b) represents moderate negative correlation, (c) represents moderate positive correlation, (d) represents strong positive correlation, and (e) contains no correlation.

What is the measure of correlation between the interest rate of federal funds and the commodities futures index? With data such as those shown in Table 12.1, which represent the values for interest rates of federal funds and commodities futures indexes for a sample of 12 days, a correlation coefficient, r, can be computed.

FIGURE 12.1

Five Correlations

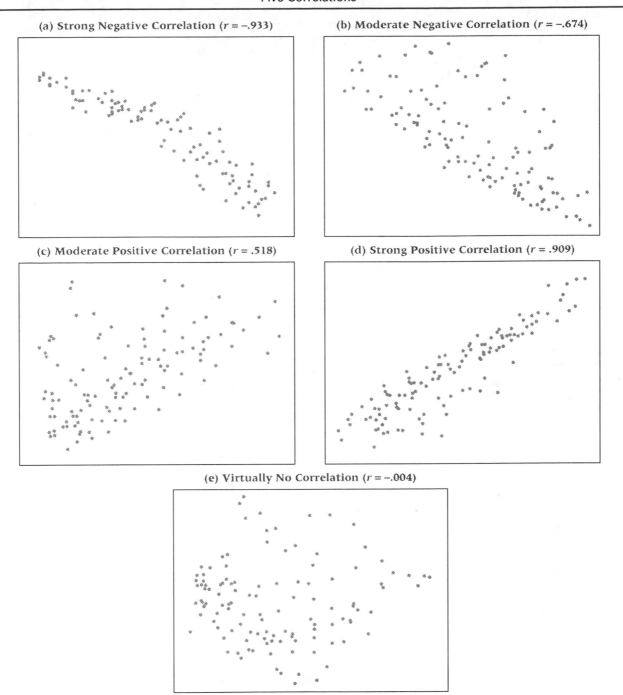

(a) Strong Negative Correlation ($r = -.933$)

(b) Moderate Negative Correlation ($r = -.674$)

(c) Moderate Positive Correlation ($r = .518$)

(d) Strong Positive Correlation ($r = .909$)

(e) Virtually No Correlation ($r = -.004$)

Examination of the formula for computing a Pearson product-moment correlation coefficient (12.1) reveals that the following values must be obtained to compute r: Σx, Σx^2, Σy, Σy^2, Σxy, and n. In correlation analysis, it does not matter which variable is designated x and which is designated y. For this example, the correlation coefficient is computed as shown in Table 12.2. The r value obtained ($r = .815$) represents a relatively strong positive relationship between interest rates and commodities futures index over this 12-day period.

Figure 12.2 shows both Excel and Minitab output for this problem.

TABLE 12.2

Computation of *r* for the Economics Example

Day	Interest Rate x	Futures Index y	x^2	y^2	xy
1	7.43	221	55.205	48,841	1,642.03
2	7.48	222	55.950	49,284	1,660.56
3	8.00	226	64.000	51,076	1,808.00
4	7.75	225	60.063	50,625	1,743.75
5	7.60	224	57.760	50,176	1,702.40
6	7.63	223	58.217	49,729	1,701.49
7	7.68	223	58.982	49,729	1,712.64
8	7.67	226	58.829	51,076	1,733.42
9	7.59	226	57.608	51,076	1,715.34
10	8.07	235	65.125	55,225	1,896.45
11	8.03	233	64.481	54,289	1,870.99
12	8.00	241	64.000	58,081	1,928.00
	$\Sigma x = 92.93$	$\Sigma y = 2{,}725$	$\Sigma x^2 = 720.220$	$\Sigma y^2 = 619{,}207$	$\Sigma xy = 21{,}115.07$

$$r = \frac{(21{,}115.07) - \dfrac{(92.93)(2725)}{12}}{\sqrt{\left[(720.22) - \dfrac{(92.93)^2}{12}\right]\left[(619{,}207) - \dfrac{(2725)^2}{12}\right]}} = .815$$

FIGURE 12.2

Excel and Minitab Output for the Economics Example

Excel Output

	Interest Rate	Futures Index
Interest Rate	1	
Futures Index	0.815	1

Minitab Output

Correlations: Interest Rate, Futures Index
Pearson correlation of Interest Rate and Futures Index = 0.815
p-Value = 0.001

12.1 PROBLEMS

12.1 Determine the value of the coefficient of correlation, *r*, for the following data.

X	4	6	7	11	14	17	21
Y	18	12	13	8	7	7	4

12.2 Determine the value of *r* for the following data.

X	158	296	87	110	436
Y	349	510	301	322	550

12.3 In an effort to determine whether any correlation exists between the price of stocks of airlines, an analyst sampled six days of activity of the stock market. Using the following prices of Delta stock and Southwest stock, compute the coefficient of correlation. Stock prices have been rounded off to the nearest tenth for ease of computation.

Delta	Southwest
47.6	15.1
46.3	15.4
50.6	15.9
52.6	15.6
52.4	16.4
52.7	18.1

12.4 The following data are the claims (in $ millions) for BlueCross BlueShield benefits for nine states, along with the surplus (in $ millions) that the company had in assets in those states.

State	Claims	Surplus
Alabama	$1,425	$277
Colorado	273	100
Florida	915	120
Illinois	1,687	259
Maine	234	40
Montana	142	25
North Dakota	259	57
Oklahoma	258	31
Texas	894	141

Use the data to compute a correlation coefficient, r, to determine the correlation between claims and surplus.

12.5 The National Safety Council released the following data on the incidence rates for fatal or lost-worktime injuries per 100 employees for several industries in three recent years.

Industry	Year 1	Year 2	Year 3
Textile	.46	.48	.69
Chemical	.52	.62	.63
Communication	.90	.72	.81
Machinery	1.50	1.74	2.10
Services	2.89	2.03	2.46
Nonferrous metals	1.80	1.92	2.00
Food	3.29	3.18	3.17
Government	5.73	4.43	4.00

Compute r for each pair of years and determine which years are most highly correlated.

12.2 INTRODUCTION TO SIMPLE REGRESSION ANALYSIS

Regression analysis is *the process of constructing a mathematical model or function that can be used to predict or determine one variable by another variable or other variables.* The most elementary regression model is called **simple regression** or **bivariate regression** involving two variables in which one variable is predicted by another variable. In simple regression, *the variable to be predicted* is called the **dependent variable** and is designated as y. The *predictor* is called the **independent variable**, or *explanatory variable*, and is designated as x. In simple regression analysis, only a straight-line relationship between two variables is examined. Nonlinear relationships and regression models with more than one independent variable can be explored by using multiple regression models, which are presented in Chapters 13 and 14.

Can the cost of flying a commercial airliner be predicted using regression analysis? If so, what variables are related to such cost? A few of the many variables that can potentially contribute are type of plane, distance, number of passengers, amount of luggage/freight, weather conditions, direction of destination, and perhaps even pilot skill. Suppose a study is conducted using only Boeing 737s traveling 500 miles on comparable routes during the same season of the year. Can the number of passengers predict the cost of flying such routes? It seems logical that more passengers result in more weight and more baggage, which could, in turn, result in increased fuel consumption and other costs. Suppose the data displayed in Table 12.3 are the costs and associated number of passengers for twelve 500-mile commercial airline flights using Boeing 737s during the same season of the year. We will use these data to develop a regression model to predict cost by number of passengers.

Usually, the first step in simple regression analysis is to construct a **scatter plot** (or scatter diagram), discussed in Chapter 2. Graphing the data in this way yields preliminary information about the shape and spread of the data. Figure 12.3 is an Excel scatter plot of the data in Table 12.3. Figure 12.4 is a close-up view of the scatter plot produced by

TABLE 12.3

Airline Cost Data

Number of Passengers	Cost ($1,000)
61	4.280
63	4.080
67	4.420
69	4.170
70	4.480
74	4.300
76	4.820
81	4.700
86	5.110
91	5.130
95	5.640
97	5.560

FIGURE 12.3

Excel Scatter Plot of Airline
Cost Data

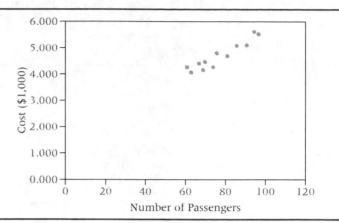

FIGURE 12.4

Close-Up Minitab Scatter Plot
of Airline Cost Data

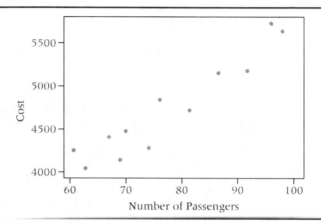

Minitab. Try to imagine a line passing through the points. Is a linear fit possible? Would a curve fit the data better? The scatter plot gives some idea of how well a regression line fits the data. Later in the chapter, we present statistical techniques that can be used to determine more precisely how well a regression line fits the data.

12.3 DETERMINING THE EQUATION OF THE REGRESSION LINE

Interactive Applet

The first step in determining the equation of the regression line that passes through the sample data is to establish the equation's form. Several different types of equations of lines are discussed in algebra, finite math, or analytic geometry courses. Recall that among these equations of a line are the two-point form, the point-slope form, and the slope-intercept form. In regression analysis, researchers use the slope-intercept equation of a line. In math courses, the slope-intercept form of the equation of a line often takes the form

$$y = mx + b$$

where

m = slope of the line

b = y intercept of the line

In statistics, the slope-intercept form of the equation of the regression line through the population points is

$$\hat{y} = \beta_0 + \beta_1 x$$

where

$\hat{y}$ = the predicted value of y

β_0 = the population y intercept

β_1 = the population slope

For any specific dependent variable value, y_i,

$$y_i = \beta_0 + \beta_1 x_i + \epsilon_i$$

where

$x_i =$ the value of the independent variable for the ith value
$y_i =$ the value of the dependent variable for the ith value
$\beta_0 =$ the population y intercept
$\beta_1 =$ the population slope
$\epsilon_i =$ the error of prediction for the ith value

Unless the points being fitted by the regression equation are in perfect alignment, the regression line will miss at least some of the points. In the preceding equation, ϵ_i represents the error of the regression line in fitting these points. If a point is on the regression line, $\epsilon_i = 0$.

These mathematical models can be either deterministic models or probabilistic models. **Deterministic models** are *mathematical models that produce an "exact" output for a given input.* For example, suppose the equation of a regression line is

$$y = 1.68 + 2.40x$$

For a value of $x = 5$, the exact predicted value of y is

$$y = 1.68 + 2.40(5) = 13.68$$

We recognize, however, that most of the time the values of y will not equal exactly the values yielded by the equation. Random error will occur in the prediction of the y values for values of x because it is likely that the variable x does not explain all the variability of the variable y. For example, suppose we are trying to predict the volume of sales (y) for a company through regression analysis by using the annual dollar amount of advertising (x) as the predictor. Although sales are often related to advertising, other factors related to sales are not accounted for by amount of advertising. Hence, a regression model to predict sales volume by amount of advertising probably involves some error. For this reason, in regression, we present the general model as a probabilistic model. A **probabilistic model** is *one that includes an error term that allows for the y values to vary for any given value of x.*

A deterministic regression model is

$$y = \beta_0 + \beta_1 x$$

The probabilistic regression model is

$$y = \beta_0 + \beta_1 x + \epsilon$$

$\beta_0 + \beta_1 x$ is the deterministic portion of the probabilistic model, $\beta_0 + \beta_1 x + \epsilon$. In a deterministic model, all points are assumed to be on the line and in all cases ϵ is zero.

Virtually all regression analyses of business data involve sample data, not population data. As a result, β_0 and β_1 are unattainable and must be estimated by using the sample statistics, b_0 and b_1. Hence the equation of the regression line contains the sample y intercept, b_0, and the sample slope, b_1.

EQUATION OF THE SIMPLE REGRESSION LINE	
	$$\hat{y} = b_0 + b_1 x$$
	where
	$b_0 =$ the sample intercept
	$b_1 =$ the sample slope

To determine the equation of the regression line for a sample of data, the researcher must determine the values for b_0 and b_1. This process is sometimes referred to as least squares analysis. **Least squares analysis** is *a process whereby a regression model is developed by producing the minimum sum of the squared error values.* On the basis of this premise and calculus, a particular set of equations has been developed to produce components of the regression model.*

*Derivation of these formulas is beyond the scope of information being discussed here but is presented in WileyPLUS.

FIGURE 12.5

Minitab Plot of a Regression Line

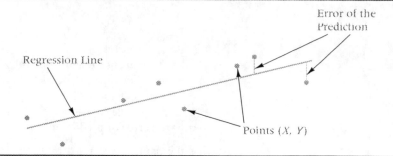

Examine the regression line fit through the points in Figure 12.5. Observe that the line does not actually pass through any of the points. The vertical distance from each point to the line is the error of the prediction. In theory, an infinite number of lines could be constructed to pass through these points in some manner. The least squares regression line is the regression line that results in the smallest sum of errors squared.

Formula 12.2 is an equation for computing the value of the sample slope. Several versions of the equation are given to afford latitude in doing the computations.

SLOPE OF THE REGRESSION LINE (12.2)

$$b_1 = \frac{\Sigma(x - \bar{x})(y - \bar{y})}{\Sigma(x - \bar{x})^2} = \frac{\Sigma xy - n\bar{x}\bar{y}}{\Sigma x^2 - n\bar{x}^2} = \frac{\Sigma xy - \frac{(\Sigma x)(\Sigma y)}{n}}{\Sigma x^2 - \frac{(\Sigma x)^2}{n}}$$

The expression in the numerator of the slope formula 12.2 appears frequently in this chapter and is denoted as SS_{xy}.

$$SS_{xy} = \Sigma(x - \bar{x})(y - \bar{y}) = \Sigma xy - \frac{(\Sigma x)(\Sigma y)}{n}$$

The expression in the denominator of the slope formula 12.2 also appears frequently in this chapter and is denoted as SS_{xx}.

$$SS_{xx} = \Sigma(x - \bar{x})^2 = \Sigma x^2 - \frac{(\Sigma x)^2}{n}$$

With these abbreviations, the equation for the slope can be expressed as in Formula 12.3.

ALTERNATIVE FORMULA FOR SLOPE (12.3)

$$b_1 = \frac{SS_{xy}}{SS_{xx}}$$

Formula 12.4 is used to compute the sample y intercept. The slope must be computed before the y intercept.

---

y INTERCEPT OF THE REGRESSION LINE (12.4)

$$b_0 = \bar{y} - b_1\bar{x} = \frac{\Sigma y}{n} - b_1\frac{(\Sigma x)}{n}$$

Formulas 12.2, 12.3, and 12.4 show that the following data are needed from sample information to compute the slope and intercept: Σx, Σy, Σx^2, and, Σxy, unless sample means are used. Table 12.4 contains the results of solving for the slope and intercept and determining the equation of the regression line for the data in Table 12.3.

The least squares equation of the regression line for this problem is

$$\hat{y} = 1.57 + .0407x$$

TABLE 12.4

Solving for the Slope and the y Intercept of the Regression Line for the Airline Cost Example

Number of Passengers	Cost ($1,000)		
x	y	x^2	xy
61	4.280	3,721	261.080
63	4.080	3,969	257.040
67	4.420	4,489	296.140
69	4.170	4,761	287.730
70	4.480	4,900	313.600
74	4.300	5,476	318.200
76	4.820	5,776	366.320
81	4.700	6,561	380.700
86	5.110	7,396	439.460
91	5.130	8,281	466.830
95	5.640	9,025	535.800
97	5.560	9,409	539.320
$\Sigma x = 930$	$\Sigma y = 56.690$	$\Sigma x^2 = 73,764$	$\Sigma xy = 4462.220$

$$SS_{xy} = \Sigma xy - \frac{(\Sigma x)(\Sigma y)}{n} = 4462.22 - \frac{(930)(56.69)}{12} = 68.745$$

$$SS_{xx} = \Sigma x^2 - \frac{(\Sigma x)^2}{n} = 73,764 - \frac{(930)^2}{12} = 1689$$

$$b_1 = \frac{SS_{xy}}{SS_{xx}} = \frac{68.745}{1689} = .0407$$

$$b_0 = \frac{\Sigma y}{n} - b_1 \frac{\Sigma x}{n} = \frac{56.69}{12} - (.0407)\frac{930}{12} = 1.57$$

$$\hat{y} = 1.57 + .0407x$$

The slope of this regression line is .0407. Because the x values were recoded for the ease of computation and are actually in $1,000 denominations, the slope is actually $40.70. One interpretation of the slope in this problem is that for every unit increase in x (every person added to the flight of the airplane), there is a $40.70 increase in the cost of the flight. The y-intercept is the point where the line crosses the y-axis (where x is zero). Sometimes in regression analysis, the y-intercept is meaningless in terms of the variables studied. However, in this problem, one interpretation of the y-intercept, which is 1.570 or $1,570, is that even if there were no passengers on the commercial flight, it would still cost $1,570. In other words, there are costs associated with a flight that carries no passengers.

Superimposing the line representing the least squares equation for this problem on the scatter plot indicates how well the regression line fits the data points, as shown in the Excel graph in Figure 12.6. The next several sections explore mathematical ways of testing how well the regression line fits the points.

FIGURE 12.6

Excel Graph of Regression Line for the Airline Cost Example

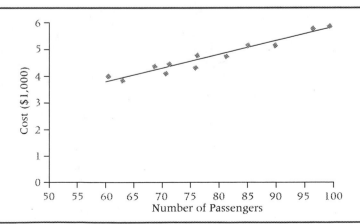

DEMONSTRATION PROBLEM 12.1

A specialist in hospital administration stated that the number of FTEs (full-time employees) in a hospital can be estimated by counting the number of beds in the hospital (a common measure of hospital size). A healthcare business researcher decided to develop a regression model in an attempt to predict the number of FTEs of a hospital by the number of beds. She surveyed 12 hospitals and obtained the following data. The data are presented in sequence, according to the number of beds.

Number of Beds	FTEs	Number of Beds	FTEs
23	69	50	138
29	95	54	178
29	102	64	156
35	118	66	184
42	126	76	176
46	125	78	225

Solution

The following Minitab graph is a scatter plot of these data. Note the linear appearance of the data.

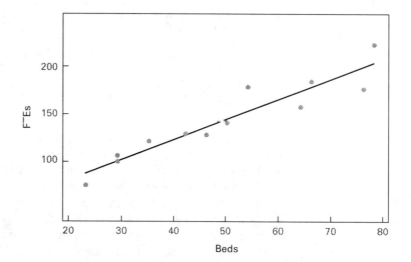

Next, the researcher determined the values of Σx, Σy, Σx^2, and Σxy.

Hospital	Number of Beds x	FTEs y	x^2	xy
1	23	69	529	1,587
2	29	95	841	2,755
3	29	102	841	2,958
4	35	118	1,225	4,130
5	42	126	1,764	5,292
6	46	125	2,116	5,750
7	50	138	2,500	6,900
8	54	178	2,916	9,612
9	64	156	4,096	9,984
10	66	184	4,356	12,144
11	76	176	5,776	13,376
12	78	225	6,084	17,550
	$\Sigma x = 592$	$\Sigma y = 1,692$	$\Sigma x^2 = 33,044$	$\Sigma xy = 92,038$

Using these values, the researcher solved for the sample slope (b_1) and the sample y-intercept (b_0).

$$SS_{xy} = \Sigma xy - \frac{(\Sigma x)(\Sigma y)}{n} = 92{,}038 - \frac{(592)(1692)}{12} = 8566$$

$$SS_{xx} = \Sigma x^2 - \frac{(\Sigma x)^2}{n} = 33{,}044 - \frac{(592)^2}{12} = 3838.667$$

$$b_1 = \frac{SS_{xy}}{SS_{xx}} = \frac{8566}{3838.667} = 2.232$$

$$b_0 = \frac{\Sigma y}{n} - b_1\frac{\Sigma x}{12} = \frac{1692}{12} - (2.232)\frac{592}{12} = 30.888$$

The least squares equation of the regression line is

$$\hat{y} = 30.888 + 2.232x$$

The slope of the line, $b_1 = 2.232$, means that for every unit increase of x (every bed), y (number of FTEs) is predicted to increase by 2.232. Even though the y-intercept helps the researcher sketch the graph of the line by being one of the points on the line (0, 30.888), it has limited usefulness in terms of this solution because $x = 0$ denotes a hospital with no beds. On the other hand, it could be interpreted that a hospital has to have at least 31 FTEs to open its doors even with no patients—a sort of "fixed cost" of personnel.

12.3 PROBLEMS

12.6 Sketch a scatter plot from the following data, and determine the equation of the regression line.

x	12	21	28	8	20
y	17	15	22	19	24

12.7 Sketch a scatter plot from the following data, and determine the equation of the regression line.

x	140	119	103	91	65	29	24
y	25	29	46	70	88	112	128

12.8 A corporation owns several companies. The strategic planner for the corporation believes dollars spent on advertising can to some extent be a predictor of total sales dollars. As an aid in long-term planning, she gathers the following sales and advertising information from several of the companies for 2011 ($ millions).

Advertising	Sales
12.5	148
3.7	55
21.6	338
60.0	994
37.6	541
6.1	89
16.8	126
41.2	379

Develop the equation of the simple regression line to predict sales from advertising expenditures using these data.

12.9 Investment analysts generally believe the interest rate on bonds is inversely related to the prime interest rate for loans; that is, bonds perform well when lending rates are down and perform poorly when interest rates are up. Can the bond rate be predicted by the prime interest rate? Use the following data to construct a least squares regression line to predict bond rates by the prime interest rate.

Bond Rate	Prime Interest Rate
5%	16%
12	6
9	8
15	4
7	7

12.10 Is it possible to predict the annual number of business bankruptcies by the number of firm births (business starts) in the United States? The following data published by the U.S. Small Business Administration, Office of Advocacy, are pairs of the number of business bankruptcies (1000s) and the number of firm births (10,000s) for a six-year period. Use these data to develop the equation of the regression model to predict the number of business bankruptcies by the number of firm births. Discuss the meaning of the slope.

Business Bankruptcies (1000)	Firm Births (10,000)
34.3	58.1
35.0	55.4
38.5	57.0
40.1	58.5
35.5	57.4
37.9	58.0

12.11 It appears that over the past 45 years, the number of farms in the United States declined while the average size of farms increased. The following data provided by the U.S. Department of Agriculture show five-year interval data for U.S. farms. Use these data to develop the equation of a regression line to predict the average size of a farm by the number of farms. Discuss the slope and y-intercept of the model.

Year	Number of Farms (millions)	Average Size (acres)
1950	5.65	213
1955	4.65	258
1960	3.96	297
1965	3.36	340
1970	2.95	374
1975	2.52	420
1980	2.44	426
1985	2.29	441
1990	2.15	460
1995	2.07	469
2000	2.17	434
2005	2.10	444

12.12 Can the annual new orders for manufacturing in the United States be predicted by the raw steel production in the United States? Shown on the next page are the annual new orders for 10 years according to the U.S. Census Bureau and the raw steel production for the same 10 years as published by the American Iron & Steel Institute. Use these data to develop a regression model to predict annual new orders by raw steel production. Construct a scatter plot and draw the regression line through the points.

Raw Steel Production (100,000s of net tons)	New Orders ($ trillions)
99.9	2.74
97.9	2.87
98.9	2.93
87.9	2.87
92.9	2.98
97.9	3.09
100.6	3.36
104.9	3.61
105.3	3.75
108.6	3.95

12.4 RESIDUAL ANALYSIS

How does a business researcher test a regression line to determine whether the line is a good fit of the data other than by observing the fitted line plot (regression line fit through a scatter plot of the data)? One particularly popular approach is to use the *historical data* (x and y values used to construct the regression model) to test the model. With this approach, the values of the independent variable (x values) are inserted into the regression model and a predicted value ($\hat{y}$) is obtained for each x value. These predicted values ($\hat{y}$) are then compared to the actual y values to determine how much error the equation of the regression line produced. *Each difference between the actual y values and the predicted y values is the error of the regression line at a given point, y − ŷ*, and is referred to as the **residual**. It is the sum of squares of these residuals that is minimized to find the least squares line.

Table 12.5 shows $\hat{y}$ values and the residuals for each pair of data for the airline cost regression model developed in Section 12.3. The predicted values are calculated by inserting an x value into the equation of the regression line and solving for $\hat{y}$. For example, when $x = 61$, $\hat{y} = 1.57 + .0407(61) = 4.053$, as displayed in column 3 of the table. Each of these predicted y values is subtracted from the actual y value to determine the error, or residual. For example, the first y value listed in the table is 4.280 and the first predicted value is 4.053, resulting in a residual of $4.280 - 4.053 = .227$. The residuals for this problem are given in column 4 of the table.

Note that the sum of the residuals is approximately zero. Except for rounding error, the sum of the residuals is *always zero*. The reason is that a residual is geometrically the vertical distance from the regression line to a data point. The equations used to solve for the slope

TABLE 12.5

Predicted Values and Residuals for the Airline Cost Example

Number of Passengers x	Cost ($1,000) y	Predicted Value ŷ	Residual y − ŷ
61	4.280	4.053	.227
63	4.080	4.134	−.054
67	4.420	4.297	.123
69	4.170	4.378	−.208
70	4.480	4.419	.061
74	4.300	4.582	−.282
76	4.820	4.663	.157
81	4.700	4.867	−.167
86	5.110	5.070	.040
91	5.130	5.274	−.144
95	5.640	5.436	.204
97	5.560	5.518	.042

$$\Sigma(y - \hat{y}) = -.001$$

FIGURE 12.7

Close-Up Minitab Scatter Plot
with Residuals for the Airline
Cost Example

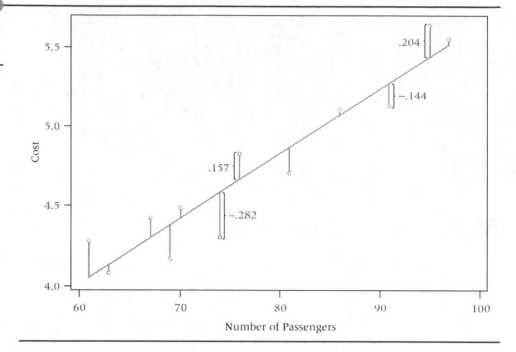

and intercept place the line geometrically in the middle of all points. Therefore, vertical distances from the line to the points will cancel each other and sum to zero. Figure 12.7 is a Minitab-produced scatter plot of the data and the residuals for the airline cost example.

An examination of the residuals may give the researcher an idea of how well the regression line fits the historical data points. The largest residual for the airline cost example is −.282, and the smallest is .040. Because the objective of the regression analysis was to predict the cost of flight in $1,000s, the regression line produces an error of $282 when there are 74 passengers and an error of only $40 when there are 86 passengers. This result presents the *best* and *worst* cases for the residuals. The researcher must examine other residuals to determine how well the regression model fits other data points.

Sometimes residuals are used to locate outliers. **Outliers** are *data points that lie apart from the rest of the points.* Outliers can produce residuals with large magnitudes and are usually easy to identify on scatter plots. Outliers can be the result of misrecorded or miscoded data, or they may simply be data points that do not conform to the general trend. The equation of the regression line is influenced by every data point used in its calculation in a manner similar to the arithmetic mean. Therefore, outliers sometimes can unduly influence the regression line by "pulling" the line toward the outliers. The origin of outliers must be investigated to determine whether they should be retained or whether the regression equation should be recomputed without them.

Residuals are usually plotted against the *x*-axis, which reveals a view of the residuals as *x* increases. Figure 12.8 shows the residuals plotted by Excel against the *x*-axis for the airline cost example.

FIGURE 12.8

Excel Graph of Residuals for
the Airline Cost Example

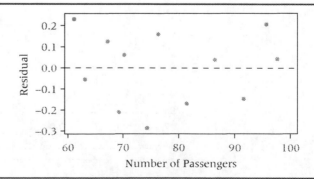

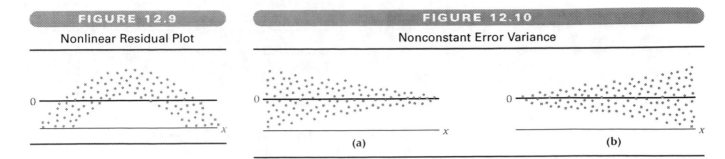

FIGURE 12.9

Nonlinear Residual Plot

FIGURE 12.10

Nonconstant Error Variance

(a)

(b)

Using Residuals to Test the Assumptions of the Regression Model

One of the major uses of residual analysis is to test some of the assumptions underlying regression. The following are the assumptions of simple regression analysis.

1. The model is linear.
2. The error terms have constant variances.
3. The error terms are independent.
4. The error terms are normally distributed.

A particular method for studying the behavior of residuals is the residual plot. The **residual plot** is *a type of graph in which the residuals for a particular regression model are plotted along with their associated value of x as an ordered pair (x, y − ŷ)*. Information about how well the regression assumptions are met by the particular regression model can be gleaned by examining the plots. Residual plots are more meaningful with larger sample sizes. For small sample sizes, residual plot analyses can be problematic and subject to over-interpretation. Hence, because the airline cost example is constructed from only 12 pairs of data, one should be cautious in reaching conclusions from Figure 12.8. The residual plots in Figures 12.9, 12.10, and 12.11, however, represent large numbers of data points and therefore are more likely to depict overall trends accurately.

If a residual plot such as the one in Figure 12.9 appears, the assumption that the model is linear does not hold. Note that the residuals are negative for low and high values of *x* and are positive for middle values of *x*. The graph of these residuals is parabolic, not linear. The residual plot does not have to be shaped in this manner for a nonlinear relationship to exist. Any significant deviation from an approximately linear residual plot may mean that a nonlinear relationship exists between the two variables.

The assumption of *constant error variance* sometimes is called **homoscedasticity**. If *the error variances are not constant* (called **heteroscedasticity**), the residual plots might look like one of the two plots in Figure 12.10. Note in Figure 12.10(a) that the error variance is greater for small values of *x* and smaller for large values of *x*. The situation is reversed in Figure 12.10(b).

If the error terms are not independent, the residual plots could look like one of the graphs in Figure 12.11. According to these graphs, instead of each error term being independent of the one next to it, the value of the residual is a function of the residual value next to it. For example, a large positive residual is next to a large positive residual and a small negative residual is next to a small negative residual.

The graph of the residuals from a regression analysis that meets the assumptions—a *healthy residual graph*—might look like the graph in Figure 12.12. The plot is relatively linear; the variances of the errors are about equal for each value of *x*, and the error terms do not appear to be related to adjacent terms.

FIGURE 12.11

Graphs of Nonindependent Error Terms

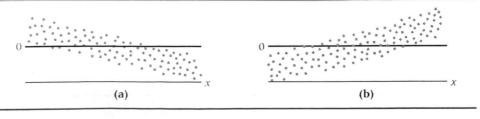

(a)

(b)

FIGURE 12.12

Healthy Residual Graph

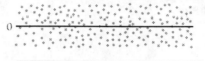

Using the Computer for Residual Analysis

Some computer programs contain mechanisms for analyzing residuals for violations of the regression assumptions. Minitab has the capability of providing graphical analysis of residuals. Figure 12.13 displays Minitab's residual graphic analyses for a regression model developed to predict the production of carrots in the United States per month by the total production of sweet corn. The data were gathered over a time period of 168 consecutive months (see WileyPLUS for the agricultural database).

These Minitab residual model diagnostics consist of three different plots. The graph on the upper right is a plot of the residuals versus the fits. Note that this residual plot "flares-out" as x gets larger. This pattern is an indication of heteroscedasticity, which is a violation of the assumption of constant variance for error terms. The graph in the upper left is a normal probability plot of the residuals. A straight line indicates that the residuals are normally distributed. Observe that this normal plot is relatively close to being a straight line, indicating that the residuals are nearly normal in shape. This normal distribution is confirmed by the graph on the lower left, which is a histogram of the residuals. The histogram groups residuals in classes so the researcher can observe where groups of the residuals lie without having to rely on the residual plot and to validate the notion that the residuals are approximately normally distributed. In this problem, the pattern is indicative of at least a mound-shaped distribution of residuals.

FIGURE 12.13

Minitab Residual Analyses

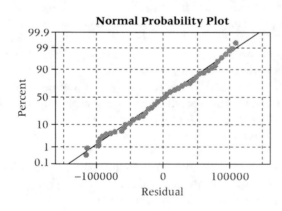

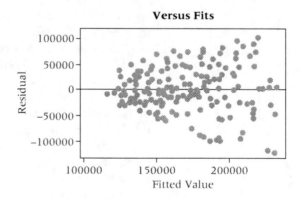

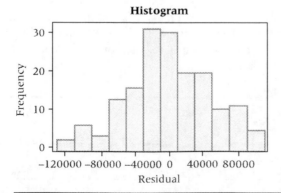

DEMONSTRATION PROBLEM 12.2

Compute the residuals for Demonstration Problem 12.1 in which a regression model was developed to predict the number of full-time equivalent workers (FTEs) by the number of beds in a hospital. Analyze the residuals by using Minitab graphic diagnostics.

Solution

The data and computed residuals are shown in the following table.

Hospital	Number of Beds x	FTES y	Predicted Value $\hat{y}$	Residuals $y - \hat{y}$
1	23	69	82.22	−13.22
2	29	95	95.62	−.62
3	29	102	95.62	6.38
4	35	118	109.01	8.99
5	42	126	124.63	1.37
6	46	125	133.56	−8.56
7	50	138	142.49	−4.49
8	54	178	151.42	26.58
9	64	156	173.74	−17.74
10	66	184	178.20	5.80
11	76	176	200.52	−24.52
12	78	225	204.98	20.02

$$\Sigma(y - \hat{y}) = -.01$$

Note that the regression model fits these particular data well for hospitals 2 and 5, as indicated by residuals of −.62 and 1.37 FTEs, respectively. For hospitals 1, 8, 9, 11, and 12, the residuals are relatively large, indicating that the regression model does

Residual Plots for FTEs

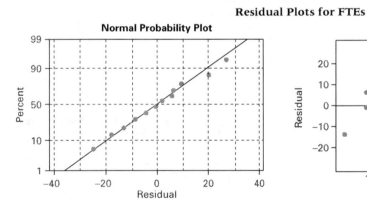

Normal Probability Plot

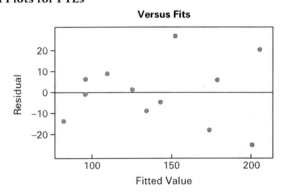

Versus Fits

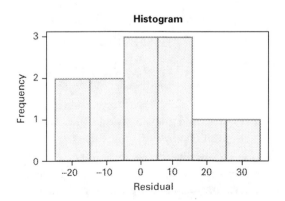

Histogram

not fit the data for these hospitals well. The Residuals Versus the Fitted Values graph indicates that the residuals seem to increase as x increases, indicating a potential problem with heteroscedasticity. The normal plot of residuals indicates that the residuals are nearly normally distributed. The histogram of residuals shows that the residuals pile up in the middle, but are somewhat skewed toward the larger positive values.

12.4 PROBLEMS

12.13 Determine the equation of the regression line for the following data, and compute the residuals.

x	15	8	19	12	5
y	47	36	56	44	21

12.14 Solve for the predicted values of y and the residuals for the data in Problem 12.6. The data are provided here again:

x	12	21	28	8	20
y	17	15	22	19	24

12.15 Solve for the predicted values of y and the residuals for the data in Problem 12.7. The data are provided here again:

x	140	119	103	91	65	29	24
y	25	29	46	70	88	112	128

12.16 Solve for the predicted values of y and the residuals for the data in Problem 12.8. The data are provided here again:

Advertising	12.5	3.7	21.6	60.0	37.6	6.1	16.8	41.2
Sales	148	55	338	994	541	89	126	379

12.17 Solve for the predicted values of y and the residuals for the data in Problem 12.9. The data are provided here again:

Bond Rate	5%	12%	9%	15%	7%
Prime Interest Rate	16%	6%	8%	4%	7%

12.18 In problem 12.10, you were asked to develop the equation of a regression model to predict the number of business bankruptcies by the number of firm births. Using this regression model and the data given in problem 12.10 (and provided here again), solve for the predicted values of y and the residuals. Comment on the size of the residuals.

Business Bankruptcies (1,000)	Firm Births (10,000)
34.3	58.1
35.0	55.4
38.5	57.0
40.1	58.5
35.5	57.4
37.9	58.0

12.19 The equation of a regression line is

$$\hat{y} = 50.506 - 1.646x$$

and the data are as follows.

x	5	7	11	12	19	25
y	47	38	32	24	22	10

Solve for the residuals and graph a residual plot. Do these data seem to violate any of the assumptions of regression?

12.20 Wisconsin is an important milk-producing state. Some people might argue that because of transportation costs, the cost of milk increases with the distance of markets from Wisconsin. Suppose the milk prices in eight cities are as follows.

Cost of Milk (per gallon)	Distance from Madison (miles)
$2.64	1,245
2.31	425
2.45	1,346
2.52	973
2.19	255
2.55	865
2.40	1,080
2.37	296

Use the prices along with the distance of each city from Madison, Wisconsin, to develop a regression line to predict the price of a gallon of milk by the number of miles the city is from Madison. Use the data and the regression equation to compute residuals for this model. Sketch a graph of the residuals in the order of the x values. Comment on the shape of the residual graph.

12.21 Graph the following residuals, and indicate which of the assumptions underlying regression appear to be in jeopardy on the basis of the graph.

x	$y - \hat{y}$
213	−11
216	−5
227	−2
229	−1
237	+6
247	+10
263	+12

12.22 Graph the following residuals, and indicate which of the assumptions underlying regression appear to be in jeopardy on the basis of the graph.

x	$y - \hat{y}$
10	+6
11	+3
12	−1
13	−11
14	−3
15	+2
16	+5
17	+8

12.23 Study the following Minitab Residuals Versus Fits graphic for a simple regression analysis. Comment on the residual evidence of lack of compliance with the regression assumptions.

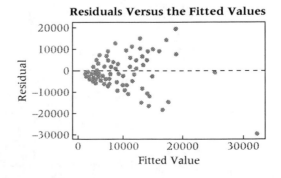

Residuals Versus the Fitted Values

12.5 STANDARD ERROR OF THE ESTIMATE

 Video

 Video

Residuals represent errors of estimation for individual points. With large samples of data, residual computations become laborious. Even with computers, a researcher sometimes has difficulty working through pages of residuals in an effort to understand the error of the regression model. An alternative way of examining the error of the model is the standard error of the estimate, which provides a single measurement of the regression error.

Because the sum of the residuals is zero, attempting to determine the total amount of error by summing the residuals is fruitless. This zero-sum characteristic of residuals can be avoided by squaring the residuals and then summing them.

Table 12.6 contains the airline cost data from Table 12.3, along with the residuals and the residuals squared. The *total of the residuals squared* column is called the **sum of squares of error (SSE)**.

SUM OF SQUARES OF ERROR	$SSE = \Sigma(y - \hat{y})^2$

In theory, infinitely many lines can be fit to a sample of points. However, formulas 12.2 and 12.4 produce a line of best fit for which the SSE is the smallest for any line that can be fit to the sample data. This result is guaranteed, because formulas 12.2 and 12.4 are derived from calculus to minimize SSE. For this reason, the regression process used in this chapter is called *least squares* regression.

A computational version of the equation for computing SSE is less meaningful in terms of interpretation than $\Sigma(y - \hat{y})^2$ but it is usually easier to compute. The computational formula for SSE follows.

COMPUTATIONAL FORMULA FOR SSE	$SSE = \Sigma y^2 - b_0 \Sigma y - b_1 \Sigma xy$

For the airline cost example,

$$\Sigma y^2 = \Sigma[(4.280)^2 + (4.080)^2 + (4.420)^2 + (4.170)^2 + (4.480)^2 + (4.300)^2 + (4.820)^2$$
$$+ (4.700)^2 + (5.110)^2 + (5.130)^2 + (5.640)^2 + (5.560)^2] = 270.9251$$
$$b_0 = 1.5697928$$

TABLE 12.6

Determining SSE for the Airline Cost Example

Number of Passengers x	Cost ($1,000) y	Residual $y - \hat{y}$	$(y - \hat{y})^2$
61	4.280	.227	.05153
63	4.080	−.054	.00292
67	4.420	.123	.01513
69	4.170	−.208	.04326
70	4.480	.061	.00372
74	4.300	−.282	.07952
76	4.820	.157	.02465
81	4.700	−.167	.02789
86	5.110	.040	.00160
91	5.130	−.144	.02074
95	5.640	.204	.04162
97	5.560	.042	.00176
		$\Sigma(y - \hat{y}) = -.001$	$\Sigma(y - \hat{y})^2 = .31434$

Sum of squares of error = SSE = .31434

$$b_1 = .0407016^*$$

$$\Sigma y = 56.69$$

$$\Sigma xy = 4462.22$$

$$SSE = \Sigma y^2 - b_0 \Sigma y - b_1 \Sigma xy$$

$$= 270.9251 - (1.5697928)(56.69) - (.0407016)(4462.22) = .31405$$

The slight discrepancy between this value and the value computed in Table 12.6 is due to rounding error.

The sum of squares error is in part a function of the number of pairs of data being used to compute the sum, which lessens the value of SSE as a measurement of error. A more useful measurement of error is the standard error of the estimate. The **standard error of the estimate**, denoted s_e, is *a standard deviation of the error of the regression model* and has a more practical use than SSE. The standard error of the estimate follows.

STANDARD ERROR OF THE ESTIMATE	$$s_e = \sqrt{\dfrac{SSE}{n - 2}}$$

The standard error of the estimate for the airline cost example is

$$s_e = \sqrt{\frac{SSE}{n - 2}} = \sqrt{\frac{.31434}{10}} = .1773$$

How is the standard error of the estimate used? As previously mentioned, the standard error of the estimate is a standard deviation of error. Recall from Chapter 3 that if data are approximately normally distributed, the empirical rule states that about 68% of all values are within $\mu \pm 1\sigma$ and that about 95% of all values are within $\mu \pm 2\sigma$. One of the assumptions for regression states that for a given x the error terms are normally distributed. Because the error terms are normally distributed, s_e is the standard deviation of error, and the average error is zero, approximately 68% of the error values (residuals) should be within $0 \pm 1s_e$ and 95% of the error values (residuals) should be within $0 \pm 2s_e$. By having knowledge of the variables being studied and by examining the value of s_e, the researcher can often make a judgment about the fit of the regression model to the data by using s_e. How can the s_e value for the airline cost example be interpreted?

The regression model in that example is used to predict airline cost by number of passengers. Note that the range of the airline cost data in Table 12.3 is from 4.08 to 5.64 ($4,080 to $5,640). The regression model for the data yields an s_e of .1773. An interpretation of s_e is that the standard deviation of error for the airline cost example is $177.30. If the error terms were normally distributed about the given values of x, approximately 68% of the error terms would be within $\pm$177.30 and 95% would be within $\pm 2($177.30) = \pm$354.60. Examination of the residuals reveals that 8 out of 12 (67%) of the residuals are within $\pm 1s_e$ and 100% of the residuals are within $2s_e$. The standard error of the estimate provides a single measure of error, which, if the researcher has enough background in the area being analyzed, can be used to understand the magnitude of errors in the model. In addition, some researchers use the standard error of the estimate to identify outliers. They do so by looking for data that are outside $\pm 2s_e$ or $\pm 3s_e$.

DEMONSTRATION PROBLEM 12.3

Compute the sum of squares of error and the standard error of the estimate for Demonstration Problem 12.1, in which a regression model was developed to predict the number of FTEs at a hospital by the number of beds.

*Note: In previous sections, the values of the slope and intercept were rounded off for ease of computation and interpretation. They are shown here with more precision in an effort to reduce rounding error.

Solution

Hospital	Number of Beds x	FTES y	Residuals y − ŷ	(y − ŷ)²
1	23	69	−13.22	174.77
2	29	95	−.62	0.38
3	29	102	6.38	40.70
4	35	118	8.99	80.82
5	42	126	1.37	1.88
6	46	125	−8.56	73.27
7	50	138	−4.49	20.16
8	54	178	26.58	706.50
9	64	156	−17.74	314.71
10	66	184	5.80	33.64
11	76	176	−24.52	601.23
12	78	225	20.02	400.80
	$\Sigma x = 592$	$\Sigma y = 1692$	$\Sigma(y - \hat{y}) = -.01$	$\Sigma(y - \hat{y})^2 = 2448.86$

$$SSE = 2448.86$$

$$S_e = \sqrt{\frac{SSE}{n-2}} = \sqrt{\frac{2448.86}{10}} = 15.65$$

The standard error of the estimate is 15.65 FTEs. An examination of the residuals for this problem reveals that 8 of 12 (67%) are within $\pm 1 s_e$ and 100% are within $\pm 2 s_e$. Is this size of error acceptable? Hospital administrators probably can best answer that question.

12.5 PROBLEMS

12.24 Determine the sum of squares of error (SSE) and the standard error of the estimate (s_e) for Problem 12.6. Determine how many of the residuals computed in Problem 12.14 (for Problem 12.6) are within one standard error of the estimate. If the error terms are normally distributed, approximately how many of these residuals should be within $\pm 1 s_e$?

12.25 Determine the SSE and the s_e for Problem 12.7. Use the residuals computed in Problem 12.15 (for Problem 12.7) and determine how many of them are within $\pm 1 s_e$ and $\pm 2 s_e$. How do these numbers compare with what the empirical rule says should occur if the error terms are normally distributed?

12.26 Determine the SSE and the s_e for Problem 12.8. Think about the variables being analyzed by regression in this problem and comment on the value of s_e.

12.27 Determine the SSE and s_e for Problem 12.9. Examine the variables being analyzed by regression in this problem and comment on the value of s_e.

12.28 In problem 12.10, you were asked to develop the equation of a regression model to predict the number of business bankruptcies by the number of firm births. For this regression model, solve for the standard error of the estimate and comment on it.

12.29 Use the data from problem 12.19 and determine the s_e.

12.30 Determine the SSE and the s_e for Problem 12.20. Comment on the size of s_e for this regression model, which is used to predict the cost of milk.

12.31 Determine the equation of the regression line to predict annual sales of a company from the yearly stock market volume of shares sold in a recent year. Compute the standard error of the estimate for this model. Does volume of shares sold appear to be a good predictor of a company's sales? Why or why not?

Company	Annual Sales ($ billions)	Annual Volume (millions of shares)
Merck	10.5	728.6
Altria	48.1	497.9
IBM	64.8	439.1
Eastman Kodak	20.1	377.9
Bristol-Myers Squibb	11.4	375.5
General Motors	123.8	363.8
Ford Motors	89.0	276.3

12.6 COEFFICIENT OF DETERMINATION

Video

A widely used measure of fit for regression models is the **coefficient of determination**, or r^2. The coefficient of determination is *the proportion of variability of the dependent variable (y) accounted for or explained by the independent variable (x)*.

The coefficient of determination ranges from 0 to 1. An r^2 of zero means that the predictor accounts for none of the variability of the dependent variable and that there is no regression prediction of y by x. An r^2 of 1 means perfect prediction of y by x and that 100% of the variability of y is accounted for by x. Of course, most r^2 values are between the extremes. The researcher must interpret whether a particular r^2 is high or low, depending on the use of the model and the context within which the model was developed.

In exploratory research where the variables are less understood, low values of r^2 are likely to be more acceptable than they are in areas of research where the parameters are more developed and understood. One NASA researcher who uses vehicular weight to predict mission cost searches for the regression models to have an r^2 of .90 or higher. However, a business researcher who is trying to develop a model to predict the motivation level of employees might be pleased to get an r^2 near .50 in the initial research.

The dependent variable, y, being predicted in a regression model has a variation that is measured by the sum of squares of y (SS_{yy}):

$$SS_{yy} = \Sigma(y - \bar{y})^2 = \Sigma y^2 - \frac{(\Sigma y)^2}{n}$$

and is the sum of the squared deviations of the y values from the mean value of y. This variation can be broken into two additive variations: the *explained variation*, measured by the sum of squares of regression (SSR), and the *unexplained variation*, measured by the sum of squares of error (SSE). This relationship can be expressed in equation form as

$$SS_{yy} = SSR + SSE$$

If each term in the equation is divided by SS_{yy}, the resulting equation is

$$1 = \frac{SSR}{SS_{yy}} + \frac{SSE}{SS_{yy}}$$

The term r^2 is the proportion of the y variability that is explained by the regression model and represented here as

$$r^2 = \frac{SSR}{SS_{yy}}$$

Substituting this equation into the preceding relationship gives

$$1 = r^2 + \frac{SSE}{SS_{yy}}$$

Solving for r^2 yields formula 12.5.

COEFFICIENT OF DETERMINATION (12.5)	$$r^2 = 1 - \frac{SSE}{SS_{yy}} = 1 - \frac{SSE}{\Sigma y^2 - \frac{(\Sigma y)^2}{n}}$$
	Note: $0 \le r^2 \le 1$

The value of r^2 for the airline cost example is solved as follows:

$$SSE = .31434$$

$$SS_{yy} = \Sigma y^2 - \frac{(\Sigma y)^2}{n} = 270.9251 - \frac{(56.69)^2}{12} = 3.11209$$

$$r^2 = 1 - \frac{SSE}{SS_{yy}} = 1 - \frac{.31434}{3.11209} = .899$$

That is, 89.9% of the variability of the cost of flying a Boeing 737 airplane on a commercial flight is explained by variations in the number of passengers. This result also means that 11.1% of the variance in airline flight cost, y, is unaccounted for by x or unexplained by the regression model.

The coefficient of determination can be solved for directly by using

$$r^2 = \frac{SSR}{SS_{yy}}$$

It can be shown through algebra that

$$SSR = b_1^2 SS_{xx}$$

From this equation, a computational formula for r^2 can be developed.

COMPUTATIONAL FORMULA FOR r^2	$$r^2 = \frac{b_1^2 SS_{xx}}{SS_{yy}}$$

For the airline cost example, $b_1 = .0407016$, $SS_{xx} = 1689$, and $SS_{yy} = 3.11209$. Using the computational formula for r^2 yields

$$r^2 = \frac{(.0407016)^2 (1689)}{3.11209} = .899$$

DEMONSTRATION PROBLEM 12.4

Compute the coefficient of determination (r^2) for Demonstration Problem 12.1, in which a regression model was developed to predict the number of FTEs of a hospital by the number of beds.

Solution

$$SSE = 2448.86$$

$$SS_{yy} = 260,136 - \frac{(1692)^2}{12} = 21,564$$

$$r^2 = 1 - \frac{SSE}{SS_{yy}} = 1 - \frac{2448.86}{21,564} = .886$$

This regression model accounts for 88.6% of the variance in FTEs, leaving only 11.4% unexplained variance.

Using $SS_{xx} = 3838.667$ and $b_1 = 2.232$ from Demonstration Problem 12.1, we can solve for r^2 with the computational formula:

$$r^2 = \frac{b_1^2 SS_{xx}}{SS_{yy}} = \frac{(2.232)^2 (3838.667)}{21,564} = .886$$

Relationship Between r and r^2

Is r, the coefficient of correlation (introduced in Section 12.1), related to r^2, the coefficient of determination in linear regression? The answer is yes: r^2 equals $(r)^2$. The coefficient of determination is the square of the coefficient of correlation. In Demonstration Problem 12.1, a regression model was developed to predict FTEs by number of hospital beds. The r^2 value for the model was .886. Taking the square root of this value yields $r = .941$, which is the correlation between the sample number of beds and FTEs. A word of caution here: Because r^2 is always positive, solving for r by taking $\sqrt{r^2}$ gives the correct magnitude of r but may give the wrong sign. The researcher must examine the sign of the slope of the regression line to determine whether a positive or negative relationship exists between the variables and then assign the appropriate sign to the correlation value.

12.6 PROBLEMS

12.32 Compute r^2 for Problem 12.24 (Problem 12.6). Discuss the value of r^2 obtained.

12.33 Compute r^2 for Problem 12.25 (Problem 12.7). Discuss the value of r^2 obtained.

12.34 Compute r^2 for Problem 12.26 (Problem 12.8). Discuss the value of r^2 obtained.

12.35 Compute r^2 for Problem 12.27 (Problem 12.9). Discuss the value of r^2 obtained.

12.36 In problem 12.10, you were asked to develop the equation of a regression model to predict the number of business bankruptcies by the number of firm births. For this regression model, solve for the coefficient of determination and comment on it.

12.37 The Conference Board produces a Consumer Confidence Index (CCI) that reflects people's feelings about general business conditions, employment opportunities, and their own income prospects. Some researchers may feel that consumer confidence is a function of the median household income. Shown here are the CCIs for nine years and the median household incomes for the same nine years published by the U.S. Census Bureau. Determine the equation of the regression line to predict the CCI from the median household income. Compute the standard error of the estimate for this model. Compute the value of r^2. Does median household income appear to be a good predictor of the CCI? Why or why not?

CCI	Median Household Income ($1,000)
116.8	37.415
91.5	36.770
68.5	35.501
61.6	35.047
65.9	34.700
90.6	34.942
100.0	35.887
104.6	36.306
125.4	37.005

12.7 HYPOTHESIS TESTS FOR THE SLOPE OF THE REGRESSION MODEL AND TESTING THE OVERALL MODEL

Testing the Slope

A hypothesis test can be conducted on the sample slope of the regression model to determine whether the population slope is significantly different from zero. This test is another way to determine how well a regression model fits the data. Suppose a researcher decides that it is not worth the effort to develop a linear regression model to predict y from x. An alternative approach might be to average the y values and use $\bar{y}$ as the predictor of y for all values of x. For the airline cost example, instead of using number of passengers as the predictor, the researcher would use the average value of airline cost, $\bar{y}$, as the predictor. In this case the average value of y is

$$\bar{y} = \frac{56.69}{12} = 4.7242, \text{ or } \$4,724.20$$

Using this result as a model to predict y, if the number of passengers is 61, 70, or 95—or any other number—the predicted value of y is still 4.7242. Essentially, this approach fits the line of $\bar{y} = 4.7242$ through the data, which is a horizontal line with a slope of zero. Would a regression analysis offer anything more than the $\bar{y}$ model? Using this nonregression model (the $\bar{y}$ model) as a worst case, the researcher can analyze the regression line to determine whether it adds a more significant amount of predictability of y than does the $\bar{y}$ model. Because the slope of the $\bar{y}$ line is zero, one way to determine whether the regression line adds significant predictability is to test the population slope of the regression line to find out whether the slope is different from zero. As the slope of the regression line diverges from zero, the regression model is adding predictability that the $\bar{y}$ line is not generating. For this reason, testing the slope of the regression line to determine whether the slope is different from zero is important. If the slope is not different from zero, the regression line is doing nothing more than the $\bar{y}$ line in predicting y.

How does the researcher go about testing the slope of the regression line? Why not just examine the observed sample slope? For example, the slope of the regression line for the airline cost data is .0407. This value is obviously not zero. The problem is that this slope is obtained from a sample of 12 data points; and if another sample was taken, it is likely that a different slope would be obtained. For this reason, the population slope is statistically tested using the sample slope. The question is: If all the pairs of data points for the population were available, would the slope of that regression line be different from zero? Here the sample slope, b_1, is used as evidence to test whether the population slope is different from zero. The hypotheses for this test follow.

$$H_0: \beta_1 = 0$$
$$H_a: \beta_1 \neq 0$$

Note that this test is two tailed. The null hypothesis can be rejected if the slope is either negative or positive. A negative slope indicates an inverse relationship between x and y. That is, larger values of x are related to smaller values of y, and vice versa. Both negative and positive slopes can be different from zero. To determine whether there is a significant *positive* relationship between two variables, the hypotheses would be one tailed, or

$$H_0: \beta_1 = 0$$
$$H_a: \beta_1 > 0$$

To test for a significant *negative* relationship between two variables, the hypotheses also would be one tailed, or

$$H_0: \beta_1 = 0$$
$$H_a: \beta_1 < 0$$

In each case, testing the null hypothesis involves a t test of the slope.

t TEST OF SLOPE

$$t = \frac{b_1 - \beta_1}{s_b}$$

where

$$s_b = \frac{s_e}{\sqrt{SS_{xx}}}$$

$$s_e = \sqrt{\frac{SSE}{n-2}}$$

$$SS_{xx} = \Sigma x^2 - \frac{(\Sigma x)^2}{n}$$

β_1 = the hypothesized slope
df = $n - 2$

The test of the slope of the regression line for the airline cost regression model for $\alpha = .05$ follows. The regression line derived for the data is

$$\hat{y} = 1.57 + .0407x$$

The sample slope is $.0407 = b_1$. The value of s_e is .1773, $\Sigma x = 930$, $\Sigma x^2 = 73,764$, and $n = 12$. The hypotheses are

$$H_0: \beta_1 = 0$$

$$H_a: \beta_1 \neq 0$$

The df = $n - 2 = 12 - 2 = 10$. As this test is two tailed, $\alpha/2 = .025$. The table t value is $t_{.025,10} = \pm 2.228$. The observed t value for this sample slope is

$$t = \frac{.0407 - 0}{.1773 / \sqrt{73,764 - \frac{(930)^2}{12}}} = 9.43$$

As shown in Figure 12.14, the t value calculated from the sample slope falls in the rejection region and the p-value is .00000014. The null hypothesis that the population slope is zero is rejected. This linear regression model is adding significantly more predictive information to the $\bar{y}$ model (no regression).

It is desirable to reject the null hypothesis in testing the slope of the regression model. In rejecting the null hypothesis of a zero population slope, we are stating that the regression model is adding something to the explanation of the variation of the dependent variable that the average value of y model does not. Failure to reject the null hypothesis in this test causes the researcher to conclude that the regression model has no predictability of the dependent variable, and the model, therefore, has little or no use.

FIGURE 12.14

t Test of Slope from Airline Cost Example

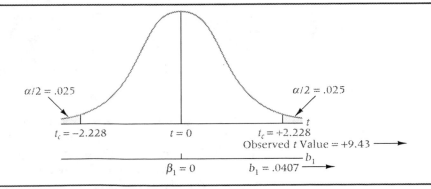

THINKING CRITICALLY ABOUT STATISTICS IN BUSINESS TODAY

Are Facial Characteristics Correlated with CEO Traits?

Researchers John R. Graham, Campbell R. Harvey, and Manju Puri, all of the Fuqua School of Business at Duke, conducted a study using almost 2,000 participants in an effort to determine if facial characteristics are related to various CEO traits. In one experiment of the study, the researchers showed pictures of 138 CEOs to 230 study participants who were asked to rate each CEO picture in terms of four attributes: competence, attractiveness, trustworthiness, and likeability. The results of the study showed that all four traits are positively correlated. That is, if a CEO (based on the picture) was rated as high on competence, he was also rated high on each of attractiveness, trustworthiness, and likeability. The largest correlation was between trustworthiness and likeability, and the smallest correlation was between trustworthiness and attractiveness. These ratings on each of the four traits were also analyzed to determine if there was a correlation with total sales of the CEO's firm and with CEO income. The results showed that there was a small positive correlation between CEO ratings on competence and company sales. There was also a small positive correlation between CEO ratings on competence and their income. In another experiment, 138 CEOs were rated on being "baby-faced." Analysis of the study data showed that there was a positive correlation between CEOs baby-faced rating and likability. That is, the more a CEO appeared to be baby-faced, the higher they were rated in likeability. However, there was a negative correlation between CEOs baby-faced rating and competence.

Things to Ponder

1. Similar studies have been conducted in the area of political science to determine the electability of people running for office. What do you think is the real impact of studies like this in business?

2. The authors of the study suggest that baby-faced people tend to have large, round eyes, high eyebrows and a small chin thereby giving the perception of a baby-faced appearance. In this study, baby-faced CEOs were rated more highly on one attribute and low on another attribute. Based on these results, what advice would you give to a "baby-faced" business manager who aspires to be a CEO?

Source: John R. Graham, Campbell R. Harvey, and Manju Puri. "A Corporate Beauty Contest," working paper (15906) in the NBER Working Paper Series, National Bureau of Economic Research, at http://www.nber.org/papers/w15906, April 2010.

DEMONSTRATION PROBLEM 12.5

Test the slope of the regression model developed in Demonstration Problem 12.1 to predict the number of FTEs in a hospital from the number of beds to determine whether there is a significant positive slope. Use $\alpha = .01$.

Solution

The hypotheses for this problem are

$$H_0: \beta_1 = 0$$
$$H_a: \beta_1 > 0$$

The level of significance is .01. With 12 pairs of data, df = 10. The critical table t value is $t_{.01,10} = 2.764$. The regression line equation for this problem is

$$\hat{y} = 30.888 + 2.232x$$

The sample slope, b_1, is 2.232, and $s_e = 15.65$, $\Sigma x = 592$, $\Sigma x^2 = 33{,}044$, and $n = 12$. The observed t value for the sample slope is

$$t = \frac{2.232 - 0}{15.65 \Big/ \sqrt{33{,}044 - \dfrac{(592)^2}{12}}} = 8.84$$

The observed t value (8.84) is in the rejection region because it is greater than the critical table t value of 2.764 and the p-value is .0000024. The null hypothesis is rejected. The population slope for this regression line is significantly different from zero in the positive direction. This regression model is adding significant predictability over the $\bar{y}$ model.

Testing the Overall Model

It is common in regression analysis to compute an F test to determine the overall significance of the model. Most computer software packages include the F test and its associated ANOVA table as standard regression output. In multiple regression (Chapters 13 and 14), this test determines whether at least one of the regression coefficients (from multiple predictors) is different from zero. Simple regression provides only one predictor and only one regression coefficient to test. Because the regression coefficient is the slope of the regression line, the F test for overall significance is testing the same thing as the t test in simple regression. The hypotheses being tested in simple regression by the F test for overall significance are

$$H_0: \beta_1 = 0$$
$$H_a: \beta_1 \neq 0$$

In the case of simple regression analysis, $F = t^2$. Thus, for the airline cost example, the F value is

$$F = t^2 = (9.43)^2 = 88.92$$

The F value is computed directly by

$$F = \frac{SS_{reg}/df_{reg}}{SS_{err}/df_{err}} = \frac{MS_{reg}}{MS_{err}}$$

where

$$df_{reg} = k$$
$$df_{err} = n - k - 1$$
$$k = \text{the number of independent variables}$$

The values of the sum of squares (SS), degrees of freedom (df), and mean squares (MS) are obtained from the analysis of variance table, which is produced with other regression statistics as standard output from statistical software packages. Shown here is the analysis of variance table produced by Minitab for the airline cost example.

```
Analysis of Variance
Source            DF        SS        MS        F        p
Regression         1    2.7980    2.7980    89.09    0.000
Residual Error    10    0.3141    0.0314
Total             11    3.1121
```

The F value for the airline cost example is calculated from the analysis of variance table information as

$$F = \frac{2.7980/1}{.3141/10} = \frac{2.7980}{.03141} = 89.08$$

The difference between this value (89.08) and the value obtained by squaring the t statistic (88.92) is due to rounding error. The probability of obtaining an F value this large or larger by chance if there is no regression prediction in this model is .000 according to the ANOVA output (the p-value). This output value means it is highly unlikely that the population slope is zero and also unlikely that there is no prediction due to regression from this model given the sample statistics obtained. Hence, it is highly likely that this regression model adds significant predictability of the dependent variable.

Note from the ANOVA table that the degrees of freedom due to regression are equal to 1. Simple regression models have only one independent variable; therefore, $k = 1$. The degrees of freedom error in simple regression analysis is always $n - k - 1 = n - 1 - 1 = n - 2$. With the degrees of freedom due to regression (1) as the numerator degrees of freedom and the degrees of freedom due to error ($n - 2$) as the denominator degrees of freedom, Table A.7 can be used to obtain the critical F value ($F_{\alpha,1,n-2}$) to help make the hypothesis testing decision about the overall regression model if the *p*-value of *F* is not given in the computer output. This critical *F* value is always found in the right tail of the distribution. In simple regression, the relationship between the critical *t* value to test the slope and the critical *F* value of overall significance is

$$t_{\alpha/2,n-2}^2 = F_{\alpha,1,n-2}$$

For the airline cost example with a two-tailed test and $\alpha = .05$, the critical value of $t_{.025,10}$ is ± 2.228 and the critical value of $F_{.05,1,10}$ is 4.96.

$$t_{.025,10}^2 = (\pm 2.228)^2 = 4.96 = F_{.05,1,10}$$

12.7 PROBLEMS

12.38 Test the slope of the regression line determined in Problem 12.6. Use $\alpha = .05$.

12.39 Test the slope of the regression line determined in Problem 12.7. Use $\alpha = .01$.

12.40 Test the slope of the regression line determined in Problem 12.8. Use $\alpha = .10$.

12.41 Test the slope of the regression line determined in Problem 12.9. Use a 5% level of significance.

12.42 Test the slope of the regression line developed in Problem 12.10. Use a 5% level of significance.

12.43 Study the following analysis of variance table, which was generated from a simple regression analysis. Discuss the *F* test of the overall model. Determine the value of *t* and test the slope of the regression line.

```
Analysis of Variance
Source        DF        SS        MS        F        p
Regression     1      116.65    116.65     8.26     0.021
Error          8      112.95     14.12
Total          9      229.60
```

12.8 ESTIMATION

One of the main uses of regression analysis is as a prediction tool. If the regression function is a good model, the researcher can use the regression equation to determine values of the dependent variable from various values of the independent variable. For example, financial brokers would like to have a model with which they could predict the selling price of a stock on a certain day by a variable such as unemployment rate or producer price index. Marketing managers would like to have a site location model with which they could predict the sales volume of a new location by variables such as population density or number of competitors. The airline cost example presents a regression model that has the potential to predict the cost of flying an airplane by the number of passengers.

In simple regression analysis, a point estimate prediction of *y* can be made by substituting the associated value of *x* into the regression equation and solving for *y*. From the airline cost example, if the number of passengers is $x = 73$, the predicted cost of the airline flight can be computed by substituting the *x* value into the regression equation determined in Section 12.3:

$$\hat{y} = 1.57 + .0407x = 1.57 + .0407(73) = 4.5411$$

The point estimate of the predicted cost is 4.5411 or $4,541.10.

Confidence Intervals to Estimate the Conditional Mean of *y*: $\mu_{y|x}$

Although a point estimate is often of interest to the researcher, the regression line is determined by a sample set of points; and if a different sample is taken, a different line will result, yielding a different point estimate. Hence computing a *confidence interval* for the estimation is often useful. Because for any value of x (independent variable) there can be many values of y (dependent variable), one type of **confidence interval** is *an estimate of the average value of y for a given x*. This average value of y is denoted $E(y_x)$—the expected value of y and can be computed using formula (12.6).

CONFIDENCE INTERVAL TO ESTIMATE $E(y_x)$ FOR A GIVEN VALUE OF x (12.6)

$$\hat{y} \pm t_{\alpha/2, n-2} s_e \sqrt{\frac{1}{n} + \frac{(x_0 - \bar{x})^2}{SS_{xx}}}$$

where

$x_0 = $ a particular value of x

$$SS_{xx} = \Sigma x^2 - \frac{(\Sigma x)^2}{n}$$

The application of this formula can be illustrated with construction of a 95% confidence interval to estimate the average value of y (airline cost) for the airline cost example when x (number of passengers) is 73. For a 95% confidence interval, $\alpha = .05$ and $\alpha/2 = .025$. The df $= n - 2 = 12 - 2 = 10$. The table t value is $t_{.025,10} = 2.228$. Other needed values for this problem, which were solved for previously, are

$$s_e = .1773 \quad \Sigma x = 930 \quad \bar{x} = 77.5 \quad \Sigma x^2 = 73,764$$

For $x_0 = 73$, the value of $\hat{y}$ is 4.5411. The computed confidence interval for the average value of y, $E(y_{73})$, is

$$4.5411 \pm (2.228)(.1773) \sqrt{\frac{1}{12} + \frac{(73 - 77.5)^2}{73,764 - \frac{(930)^2}{12}}} = 4.5411 \pm .1220$$

$$4.4191 \leq E(y_{73}) \leq 4.6631$$

That is, with 95% confidence the average value of y for $x = 73$ is between 4.4191 and 4.6631.

Table 12.7 shows confidence intervals computed for the airline cost example for several values of x to estimate the average value of y. Note that as x values get farther from the mean x value (77.5), the confidence intervals get wider; as the x values get closer to the mean, the confidence intervals narrow. The reason is that the numerator of the second term under the radical sign approaches zero as the value of x nears the mean and increases as x departs from the mean.

Prediction Intervals to Estimate a Single Value of y

A second type of interval in regression estimation is a **prediction interval** to *estimate a single value of y for a given value of x*.

TABLE 12.7

Confidence Intervals to Estimate the Average Value of *y* for Some *x* Values in the Airline Cost Example

x	Confidence Interval	
62	$4.0934 \pm .1876$	3.9058 to 4.2810
68	$4.3376 \pm .1461$	4.1915 to 4.4837
73	$4.5411 \pm .1220$	4.4191 to 4.6631
85	$5.0295 \pm .1349$	4.8946 to 5.1644
90	$5.2330 \pm .1656$	5.0674 to 5.3986

PREDICTION INTERVAL TO ESTIMATE y FOR A GIVEN VALUE OF x (12.7)	$$\hat{y} \pm t_{\alpha/2, n-2}\, s_e \sqrt{1 + \frac{1}{n} + \frac{(x_0 - \bar{x})^2}{SS_{xx}}}$$

where

$$x_0 = \text{a particular value of } x$$

$$SS_{xx} = \Sigma x^2 - \frac{(\Sigma x)^2}{n}$$

Formula 12.7 is virtually the same as formula 12.6, except for the additional value of 1 under the radical. This additional value widens the prediction interval to estimate a single value of y from the confidence interval to estimate the average value of y. This result seems logical because the average value of y is toward the middle of a group of y values. Thus the confidence interval to estimate the average need not be as wide as the prediction interval produced by formula 12.7, which takes into account all the y values for a given x.

A 95% prediction interval can be computed to estimate the single value of y for $x = 73$ from the airline cost example by using formula 12.7. The same values used to construct the confidence interval to estimate the average value of y are used here.

$$t_{.025,10} = 2.228,\ s_e = .1773,\ \Sigma x = 930,\ \bar{x} = 77.5,\ \Sigma x^2 = 73{,}764$$

For $x_0 = 73$, the value of $\hat{y} = 4.5411$. The computed prediction interval for the single value of y is

$$4.5411 \pm (2.228)(.1773) \sqrt{1 + \frac{1}{12} + \frac{(73 - 77.5)^2}{73{,}764 - \frac{(930)^2}{12}}} = 4.5411 \pm .4134$$

$$4.1277 \le y \le 4.9545$$

Prediction intervals can be obtained by using the computer. Shown in Figure 12.15 is the computer output for the airline cost example. The output displays the predicted value for $x = 73$ ($\hat{y} = 4.5411$), a 95% confidence interval for the average value of y for $x = 73$, and a 95% prediction interval for a single value of y for $x = 73$. Note that the resulting values are virtually the same as those calculated in this section.

Figure 12.16 displays Minitab confidence intervals for various values of x for the average y value and the prediction intervals for a single y value for the airline example. Note that the intervals flare out toward the ends, as the values of x depart from the average x value. Note also that the intervals for a single y value are always wider than the intervals for the average y value for any given value of x.

An examination of the prediction interval formula to estimate y for a given value of x explains why the intervals flare out.

$$\hat{y} \pm t_{\alpha/2, n-2}\, s_e \sqrt{1 + \frac{1}{n} + \frac{(x_0 - \bar{x})^2}{SS_{xx}}}$$

As we enter different values of x_0 from the regression analysis into the equation, the only thing that changes in the equation is $(x_0 - \bar{x})^2$. This expression increases as individual values of x_0 get farther from the mean, resulting in an increase in the width of the interval. The interval is narrower for values of x_0 nearer $\bar{x}$ and wider for values of x_0 further from $\bar{x}$. A comparison of formulas 12.6 and 12.7 reveals them to be identical except that formula 12.7—to compute a prediction interval to estimate y for a given value of x—contains a 1 under the radical sign. This distinction ensures that formula 12.7 will yield wider intervals than 12.6 for otherwise identical data.

FIGURE 12.15

Minitab Output for Prediction Intervals

Fit	StDev Fit	95.0% CI	95.0 PI
4.5410	0.0547	(4.4191, 4.6629)	(4.1278, 4.9543)

FIGURE 12.16

Minitab Intervals
for Estimation

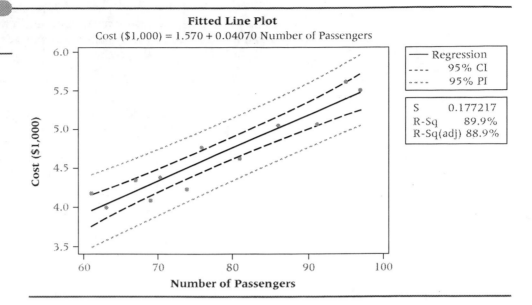

Fitted Line Plot
Cost ($1,000) = 1.570 + 0.04070 Number of Passengers

Caution: *A regression line is determined from a sample of points. The line, the r^2, the s_e, and the confidence intervals change for different sets of sample points. That is, the linear relationship developed for a set of points does not necessarily hold for values of x outside the domain of those used to establish the model. In the airline cost example, the domain of x values (number of passengers) varied from 61 to 97. The regression model developed from these points may not be valid for flights of say 40, 50, or 100 because the regression model was not constructed with x values of those magnitudes. However, decision makers sometimes extrapolate regression results to values of x beyond the domain of those used to develop the formulas (often in time-series sales forecasting). Understanding the limitations of this type of use of regression analysis is essential.*

DEMONSTRATION PROBLEM 12.6

Construct a 95% confidence interval to estimate the average value of y (FTEs) for Demonstration Problem 12.1 when $x = 40$ beds. Then construct a 95% prediction interval to estimate the single value of y for $x = 40$ beds.

Solution

For a 95% confidence interval, $\alpha = .05$ $n = 12$, and df $= 10$. The table t value is $t_{.025,10} = 2.228$; $s_e = 15.65$, $\Sigma x = 592$, $\bar{x} = 49.33$, and $\Sigma x^2 = 33{,}044$. For $x_0 = 40$, $\hat{y} = 120.17$. The computed confidence interval for the average value of y is

$$120.17 \pm (2.228)(15.65)\sqrt{\frac{1}{12} + \frac{(40 - 49.33)^2}{33{,}044 - \frac{(592)^2}{12}}} = 120.17 \pm 11.35$$

$$108.82 \le E(y_{40}) \le 131.52$$

With 95% confidence, the statement can be made that the average number of FTEs for a hospital with 40 beds is between 108.82 and 131.52.

The computed prediction interval for the single value of y is

$$120.17 \pm (2.228)(15.65)\sqrt{1 + \frac{1}{12} + \frac{(40 - 49.33)^2}{33{,}044 - \frac{(592)^2}{12}}} = 120.17 \pm 36.67$$

$$83.5 \le y \le 156.84$$

With 95% confidence, the statement can be made that a single number of FTEs for a hospital with 40 beds is between 83.5 and 156.84. Obviously this interval is much wider than the 95% confidence interval for the average value of y for $x = 40$.

The following Minitab graph depicts the 95% interval bands for both the average y value and the single y values for all 12 x values in this problem. Note once again the flaring out of the bands near the extreme values of x.

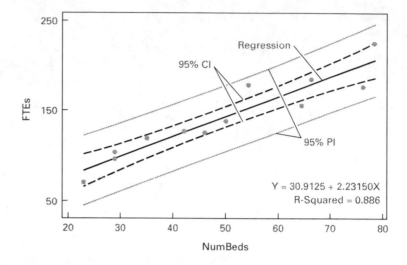

12.8 PROBLEMS

12.44 Construct a 95% confidence interval for the average value of y for Problem 12.6. Use $x = 25$.

12.45 Construct a 90% prediction interval for a single value of y for Problem 12.7; use $x = 100$. Construct a 90% prediction interval for a single value of y for Problem 14.2; use $x = 130$. Compare the results. Which prediction interval is greater? Why?

12.46 Construct a 98% confidence interval for the average value of y for Problem 12.8; use $x = 20$. Construct a 98% prediction interval for a single value of y for Problem 14.3; use $x = 20$. Which is wider? Why?

12.47 Construct a 99% confidence interval for the average bond rate in Problem 12.9 for a prime interest rate of 10%. Discuss the meaning of this confidence interval.

12.9 USING REGRESSION TO DEVELOP A FORECASTING TREND LINE

Business researchers often use historical data with measures taken over time in an effort to forecast what might happen in the future. A particular type of data that often lends itself well to this analysis is **time-series data** defined as *data gathered on a particular characteristic over a period of time at regular intervals*. Some examples of time-series data are 10 years of weekly Dow Jones Industrial Averages, twelve months of daily oil production, or monthly consumption of coffee over a two-year period. To be useful to forecasters, time-series measurements need to be made in regular time intervals and arranged according to time of occurrence. As an example, consider the time-series sales data over a 10-year time period for the Huntsville Chemical Company shown in Table 12.8. Note that the measurements (sales) are taken over time and that the sales figures are given on a yearly basis. Time-series data can also be reported daily, weekly, monthly, quarterly, semi-annually, or for other defined time periods.

TABLE 12.8

Ten-Year Sales Data for
Huntsville Chemicals

Year	Sales ($ millions)
2002	7.84
2003	12.26
2004	13.11
2005	15.78
2006	21.29
2007	25.68
2008	23.80
2009	26.43
2010	29.16
2011	33.06

It is generally believed that time-series data contain any one or combination of four elements: trend, cyclicality, seasonality, and irregularity. While each of these four elements will be discussed in greater deal in Chapter 15, Time-Series Forecasting and Index Numbers, here we examine **trend** and define it as *the long-term general direction of data.* Observing the scatter plot of the Huntsville Chemical Company's sales data shown in Figure 12.17, it is apparent that there is positive trend in the data. That is, there appears to be a long-term upward general direction of sales over time. How can trend be expressed in mathematical terms? In the field of forecasting, it is common to attempt to fit a trend line through time-series data by determining the equation of the trend line and then using the equation of the trend line to predict future data points. How does one go about developing such a line?

Determining the Equation of the Trend Line

Developing the equation of a linear trend line in forecasting is actually a special case of simple regression where the y or dependent variable is the variable of interest that a business analyst wants to forecast and for which a set of measurements has been taken over a period of time. For example, with the Huntsville Chemicals Company data, if company forecasters want to predict sales for the year 2014 using these data, sales would be the dependent variable in the simple regression analysis. In linear trend analysis, the time period is used as the x, the independent or predictor variable, in the analysis to determine the equation of the trend line. In the case of the Huntsville Chemicals Company, the x variable represents the years 2002–2011.

Using sales as the y variable and time (year) as the x variable, the equation of the trend line can be calculated in the usual way as shown in Table 12.9 and is determined to be: $\hat{y} = -5{,}333.91 + 2.6687\, x$. The slope, 2.6687, means that for every yearly increase in time, sales increases by an average of $2.6687 (million). The intercept would represent company sales in the year 0 which, of course, in this problem has no meaning since the Huntsville Chemical Company was not in existence in the year 0. Figure 12.18 is a Minitab display of the Huntsville sales data with the fitted trend line. Note that the output contains the equation of the trend line along with the values of s (standard error of the estimate) and R-Sq (r^2). As is typical with data that have a relatively strong trend, the r^2 value (.963) is quite high.

FIGURE 12.17

Minitab Scatter Plot of
Huntsville Chemicals Data

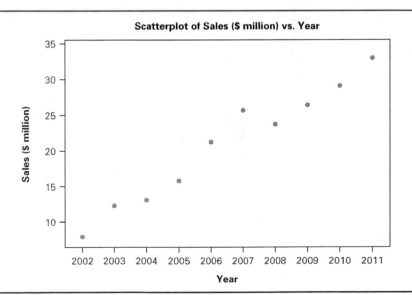

	TABLE 12.9			

Determining the Equation of the Trend Line for the Huntsville Chemical Company Sales Data

Year x	Sales y	x^2	xy
2002	7.84	4,008,004	15,695.68
2003	12.26	4,012,009	24,556.78
2004	13.11	4,016,016	26,272.44
2005	15.78	4,020,025	31,638.90
2006	21.29	4,024,036	42,707.74
2007	25.68	4,028,049	51,539.76
2008	23.80	4,032,064	47,790.40
2009	26.43	4,036,081	53,097.87
2010	29.16	4,040,100	58,611.60
2011	33.06	4,044,121	66,483.66
$\Sigma x = 20,065$	$\Sigma y = 208.41$	$\Sigma x^2 = 40,260,505$	$\Sigma xy = 418,394.83$

$$b_1 = \frac{\Sigma xy - \frac{(\Sigma x)(\Sigma y)}{n}}{\Sigma x^2 - \frac{(\Sigma x)^2}{n}} = \frac{(418,394.83) - \frac{(20,065)(208.41)}{10}}{40,260,505 - \frac{(20,065)^2}{10}} = \frac{220.17}{82.5} = 2.6687$$

$$b_0 = \frac{\Sigma y}{n} - b_1 \frac{\Sigma x}{n} = \frac{208.41}{10} - (2.6687)\frac{20,065}{10} = -5,333.91$$

Equation of the Trend Line: $\hat{y} = -5,333.91 + 2.6687x$

Forecasting Using the Equation of the Trend Line

The main use of the equation of a trend line by business analysts is for forecasting outcomes for time periods in the future. Recall the caution from Section 12.8 that using a regression model to predict y values for x values outside the domain of those used to develop the model may not be valid. Despite this caution and understanding the potential drawbacks, business forecasters nevertheless extrapolate trend lines beyond the most current time periods of the data and attempt to predict outcomes for time periods in the future. To forecast for future time periods using a trend line, insert the time period of interest into the equation of the

	FIGURE 12.18	

Minitab Graph of Huntsville Sales Data with a Fitted Trend Line

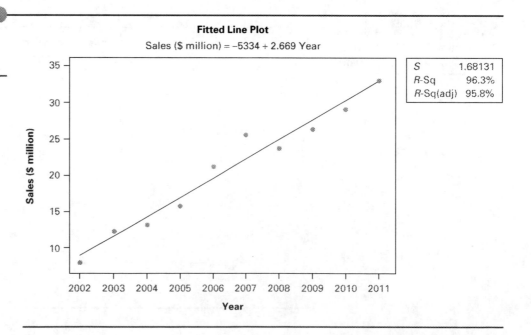

Fitted Line Plot
Sales ($ million) = –5334 + 2.669 Year

S	1.68131
R-Sq	96.3%
R-Sq(adj)	95.8%

FIGURE 12.19

Minitab Output for Trend
Line and Forecasts

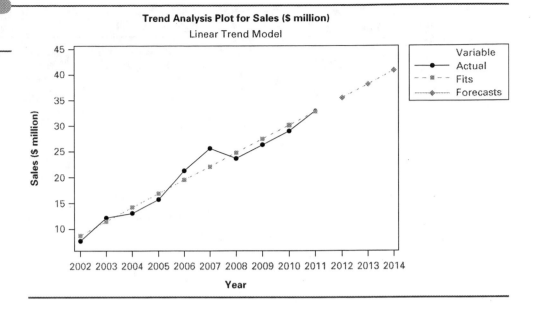

trend line and solve for $\hat{y}$. For example, suppose forecasters for the Huntsville Chemicals Company want to predict sales for the year 2014 using the equation of the trend line developed from their historical time series data. Replacing x in the equation of the sales trend line with 2014, results in a forecast of $40.85 (million):

$$\hat{y}(2014) = -5,333.91 + 2.6687(2014) = 40.85$$

Figure 12.19 shows Minitab output for the Huntsville Chemicals Company data with the trend line through the data and graphical forecasts for the next three periods (2012, 2013, and 2014). Observe from the graph that the forecast for 2014 is about $41 (million).

Alternate Coding for Time Periods

If you manually calculate the equation of a trend line when the time periods are years, you notice that the calculations can get quite large and cumbersome (observe Table 12.9). However, if the years are consecutive, they can be recoded using many different possible schemes and still produce a meaningful trend line equation (albeit a different y intercept value). For example, instead of using the years 2002–2011, suppose we use the years 1 to 10. That is, 2002 = 1 (first year), 2003 = 2, 2004 = 3, and so on, to 2011 = 10. This recoding scheme produces the trend line equation of: $\hat{y} = 6.1632 + 2.6687x$ as shown in Table 12.10. Notice that the slope of the trend line is the same whether the years 2002 through 2011 are used or the recoded years of 1 through 10, but the y intercept (6.1632) is different. This needs to be taken into consideration when using the equation of the trend line for forecasting. Since the new trend equation was derived from recoded data, forecasts will also need to be made using recoded data. For example, using the recoded system of 1 through 10 to represent "years," the year 2014 is recoded as 13 (2011 = 10, 2012 = 11, 2013 = 12, and 2014 = 13). Inserting this value into the trend line equation results in a forecast of $40.86, the same as the value obtained using raw years as time.

$$\hat{y} = 6.1632 + 2.6687x = 6.1632 + 2.6687(13) - \$40.86 \text{ (million)}.$$

Similar time recoding schemes can be used in the calculating of trend line equations when the time variable is something other than years. For example, in the case of monthly time series data, the time periods can be recoded as:

January = 1, February = 2, March = 3, ..., December = 12.

Year x	Sales y	x^2	xy
1	7.84	1	7.84
2	12.26	4	24.52
3	13.11	9	39.33
4	15.78	16	63.12
5	21.29	25	106.45
6	25.68	36	154.08
7	23.80	49	166.60
8	26.43	64	211.44
9	29.16	81	262.44
10	33.06	100	330.60
$\Sigma x = 55$	$\Sigma y = 208.41$	$\Sigma x^2 = 385$	$\Sigma xy = 1{,}366.42$

$$b_1 = \frac{\Sigma xy - \dfrac{(\Sigma x)(\Sigma y)}{n}}{\Sigma x^2 - \dfrac{(\Sigma x)^2}{n}} = \frac{(1{,}366.42) - \dfrac{(55)(208.41)}{10}}{385 - \dfrac{(55)^2}{10}} = \frac{220.165}{82.5} = 2.6687$$

$$b_0 = \frac{\Sigma y}{n} - b_1 \frac{\Sigma x}{n} = \frac{208.41}{10} - (2.6687)\frac{55}{10} = 6.1632$$

Equation of the Trend Line: $\hat{y} = 6.1632 + 2.6687x$

In the case of quarterly data over a two-year period, the time periods can be recoded with a scheme such as:

Time Period		Recoded Time Period
Year 1:	Quarter 1	1
	Quarter 2	2
	Quarter 3	3
	Quarter 4	4
Year 2:	Quarter 1	5
	Quarter 2	6
	Quarter 3	7
	Quarter 4	8

DEMONSTRATION PROBLEM 12.7

Shown below are monthly food and beverage sales in the United States during a recent year over an eight-month period ($ million). Develop the equation of a trend line through these data and use the equation to forecast sales for October.

Month	Sales ($ million)
January	32,569
February	32,274
March	32,583
April	32,304
May	32,149
June	32,077
July	31,989
August	31,977

Solution

Shown here is a Minitab-produced scatter diagram of these time series data:

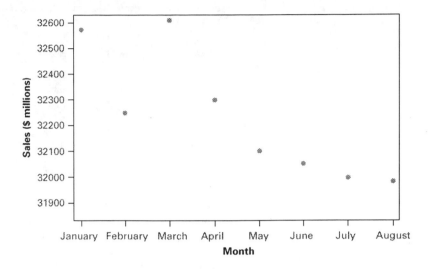

The months of January through August can be coded using the numbers of 1 through 8, respectively. Using these numbers as the time period values (x) and sales as the dependent variable (y), the following output was obtained from Minitab:

```
Regression Analysis: Sales versus Month

The regression equation is
Sales = 32628 - 86.2 Month
Predictor          Coef      SE Coef          T          P
Constant        32628.2         93.3     349.80      0.000
Month            -86.21        18.47      -4.67      0.003
S = 119.708   R-Sq = 78.4%   R-Sq(adj) = 74.8%
```

The equation of the trend line is: $\hat{y} = 32{,}628.2 - 86.21x$. A slope of -86.21 indicates that there is a downward trend of food and beverage sales over this period of time at a rate of \$86.21 (million) per month. The y intercept of 32,628.2 represents what the trend line would estimate the sales to have been in period 0 or December of the previous year. The sales figure for October can be forecast by inserting $x = 10$ into this model and obtaining:

$$\hat{y}(10) = 32{,}628.2 - 86.21(10) = 31{,}766.1.$$

12.9 PROBLEMS

12.48 Determine the equation of the trend line for the data shown below on U.S. exports of fertilizers to Indonesia over a five-year period provided by the U.S Census Bureau. Using the trend line equation, forecast the value for the year 2013.

Year	Fertilizer ($ millions)
2007	11.9
2008	17.9
2009	22.0
2010	21.8
2011	26.0

12.49 Shown below are rental and leasing revenue figures for office machinery and equipment in the United States over a seven-year period according to the U.S. Census Bureau. Use these data to construct a trend line and forecast the rental and leasing revenue for the year 2012 using these data.

Year	Rental and Leasing ($ millions)
2004	5,860
2005	6,632
2006	7,125
2007	6,000
2008	4,380
2009	3,326
2010	2,642

12.50 After a somewhat uncertain start, e-commerce sales in the United States have been growing for the past several years. Shown below are quarterly e-commerce sales figures ($ billions) released by the Census Bureau for the United States over a three-year period. Use these data to determine the equation of a trend line for e-commerce sales during this time and use the trend "model" to forecast e-commerce sales for the third quarter of the year 2012.

Year	Quarter	Sales ($ billions)
2008	1	11.93
	2	12.46
	3	13.28
	4	15.08
2009	1	16.08
	2	16.82
	3	17.60
	4	18.66
2010	1	19.73
	2	21.11
	3	22.21
	4	22.94

12.10 INTERPRETING THE OUTPUT

Although manual computations can be done, most regression problems are analyzed by using a computer. In this section, computer output from both Minitab and Excel will be presented and discussed.

At the top of the Minitab regression output, shown in Figure 12.20, is the regression equation. Next is a table that describes the model in more detail. "Coef" stands for coefficient of the regression terms. The coefficient of Number of Passengers, the x variable, is 0.040702. This value is equal to the slope of the regression line and is reflected in the regression equation. The coefficient shown next to the constant term (1.5698) is the value of the constant, which is the y intercept and also a part of the regression equation. The "T" values are a t test for the slope and a t test for the intercept or constant. (We generally do not interpret the t test for the constant.) The t value for the slope, $t = 9.44$ with an associated probability of .000, is the same as the value obtained manually in section 12.7. Because the probability of the t value is given, the p-value method can be used to interpret the t value.

FIGURE 12.20

Minitab Regression Analysis
of the Airline Cost Example

Regression Analysis: Cost ($1,000) versus Number of Passengers

```
The regression equation is
Cost ($1,000) = 1.57 + 0.0407 Number of Passengers


Predictor                     Coef    SE Coef      T       P
Constant                    1.5698     0.3381    4.64   0.001
Number of Passengers      0.040702   0.004312    9.44   0.000


S = 0.177217  R-Sq = 89.9%    R-Sq(adj) = 88.9%


Analysis of Variance

Source              DF      SS       MS        F       P
Regression           1   2.7980   2.7980    89.09   0.000
Residual Error      10   0.3141   0.0314
Total               11   3.1121


         Number of    Cost
Obs     Passengers  ($1,000)   Fit     SE Fit    Residual
  1        61.0      4.2800   4.0526   0.0876     0.2274
  2        63.0      4.0800   4.1340   0.0808    -0.0540
  3        67.0      4.4200   4.2968   0.0683     0.1232
  4        69.0      4.1700   4.3782   0.0629    -0.2082
  5        70.0      4.4800   4.4189   0.0605     0.0611
  6        74.0      4.3000   4.5817   0.0533    -0.2817
  7        76.0      4.8200   4.6631   0.0516     0.1569
  8        81.0      4.7000   4.8666   0.0533    -0.1666
  9        86.0      5.1100   5.0701   0.0629     0.0399
 10        91.0      5.1300   5.2736   0.0775    -0.1436
 11        95.0      5.6400   5.4364   0.0912     0.2036
 12        97.0      5.5600   5.5178   0.0984     0.0422
```

The next row of output is the standard error of the estimate s_e, S = 0.177217; the coefficient of determination, r^2, R-Sq = 89.9%; and the adjusted value of r^2, R-Sq(adj) = 88.9%. (Adjusted r^2 will be discussed in Chapter 13.) Following these items is the analysis of variance table. Note that the value of $F = 89.09$ is used to test the overall model of the regression line. The final item of the output is the predicted value and the corresponding residual for each pair of points.

Although the Excel regression output, shown in Figure 12.21 for Demonstration Problem 12.1, is somewhat different from the Minitab output, the same essential regression features are present. The regression equation is found under Coefficients at the bottom of ANOVA. The slope or coefficient of x is 2.2315 and the y-intercept is 30.9125. The standard error of the estimate for the hospital problem is given as the fourth statistic under Regression Statistics at the top of the output, Standard Error = 15.6491. The r^2 value is given as 0.886 on the second line. The t test for the slope is found under t Stat near the bottom of the ANOVA section on the "Number of Beds" (x variable) row, $t = 8.83$. Adjacent to the t Stat is the P-value, which is the probability of the t statistic occurring by chance if the null hypothesis is true. For this slope, the probability shown is 0.000005. The ANOVA table is in the middle of the output with the F value having the same probability as the t statistic, 0.000005, and equaling t^2. The predicted values and the residuals are shown in the Residual Output section.

FIGURE 12.21

Excel Regression Output for
Demonstration Problem 12.1

SUMMARY OUTPUT

Regression Statistics

Multiple R	0.942
R Square	0.886
Adjusted R Square	0.875
Standard Error	15.6491
Observations	12

ANOVA

	df	SS	MS	F	Significance F
Regression	1	19115.06322	19115.06	78.05	0.000005
Residual	10	2448.94	244.89		
Total	11	21564			

	Coefficients	Standard Error	t Stat	P-value
Intercept	30.9125	13.2542	2.33	0.041888
Number of Beds	2.2315	0.2526	8.83	0.000005

RESIDUAL OUTPUT

Observation	Predicted FTEs	Residuals
1	82.237	−13.237
2	95.626	−0.626
3	95.626	6.374
4	109.015	8.985
5	124.636	1.364
6	133.562	−8.562
7	142.488	−4.488
8	151.414	26.586
9	173.729	−17.729
10	178.192	5.808
11	200.507	−24.507
12	204.070	20.030

Decision Dilemma SOLVED

Decision Dilemma SOLVED

Predicting International Hourly Wages by the Price of a Big Mac

In the Decision Dilemma, questions were raised about the relationship between the price of a Big Mac hamburger and net hourly wages around the world and if a model could be developed to predict net hourly wages by the price of a Big Mac. Data were given for a sample of 27 countries. In exploring the possibility that there is a relationship between these two variables, a Pearson product-moment correlation coefficient, r, was computed to be .717. This r value indicates that there is a relatively high correlation between the two variables and that developing a regression model to predict one variable by the other has potential. Designating net hourly wages as the y or dependent variable and the price of a Big Mac as the x or predictor variable, the follow-ing regression output was obtained for these data using Excel.

Regression Statistics

Multiple R	0.717
R Square	0.514
Adjusted R Square	0.495
Standard Error	4.213
Observations	27

ANOVA

	df	SS	MS	F	Significance F
Regression	1	469.657	469.657	26.46	0.00003
Residual	25	443.775	17.751		
Total	26	913.432			

	Coefficients	Standard Error	t Stat	P-Value
Intercept	−4.154	2.448	−1.70	.10210
Big Mac Price	3.547	0.690	5.14	.00003

Taken from this output, the regression model is:

Net Hourly Wage = −4.154 + 3.547 (Price of Big Mac)

While the *y*-intercept has virtually no practical meaning in this analysis, the slope indicates that for every dollar increase in the price of a Big Mac, there is an incremental increase of $3.547 in net hourly wages for a country. It is worth underscoring here that just because there is a relationship between two variables, it does not mean there is a cause-and-effect relationship. That is, McDonald's cannot raise net hour wages in a country just by increasing the cost of a Big Mac!

Using this regression model, the net hourly wage for a country with a $3.00 Big Mac can be predicted by substituting *x* = 3 into the model:

Net Hourly Wage = −4.154 + 3.547(3) = $6.49

That is, the model predicts that the net hourly wage for a country is $6.49 when the price of a Big Mac is $3.00.

How good a fit is the regression model to the data? Observe from the Excel output that the *F* value for testing the overall significance of the model (26.46) is highly significant with a *p*-value of .00003, and that the *t* statistic for testing to determine if the slope is significantly different from zero is 5.14 with a *p*-value of .00003. In simple regression, the *t* sta-

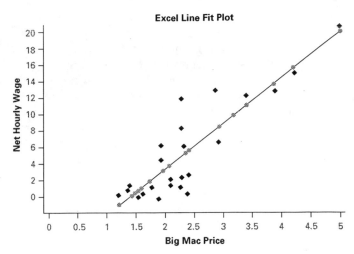

Excel Line Fit Plot

tistic is the square root of the *F* value and these statistics relate essentially the same information—that there are significant regression effects in the model. The r^2 value is 51.4%, indicating that the model has moderate predictability. The standard error of the model, *s* = 4.21, indicates that if the error terms are approximately normally distributed, about 68% of the predicted net hourly wages would fall within ±$4.21.

Shown here is an Excel-produced line fit plot. Note from the plot that there generally appears be a linear relationship between the variables but that many of the data points fall considerably away from the fitted regression line, indicating that the price of a Big Mac only partially accounts for net hourly wages.

ETHICAL CONSIDERATIONS

Regression analysis offers several opportunities for unethical behavior. One way is to present a regression model in isolation from information about the fit of the model. That is, the regression model is represented as a valid tool for prediction without any regard for how well it actually fits the data. While it is true that least squares analysis can produce a line of best fit through virtually any set of points, it does not necessarily follow that the regression model is a good predictor of the dependent variable. For example, sometimes business consultants sell regression models to companies as forecasting tools or market predictors without disclosing to the client that the r^2 value is very low, the slope of the regression line is not significant, the residuals are large, and the standard error of the estimate is large. This is unethical behavior.

Another unethical use of simple regression analysis is stating or implying a cause-and-effect relationship between two variables just because they are highly correlated and produce a high r^2 in regression. The Decision Dilemma presents a good example of this with the regression analysis

of the price of a Big Mac hamburger and the net hourly wages in a country. While the coefficient of determination is 51.4% and there appears to be a modest fit of the regression line to the data, that does not mean that increasing the price of a Big Mac in a given country will increase the country's net hourly wages. Often, two correlated variables are related to a third variable that drives the two of them but is not included in the regression analysis. In the Decision Dilemma example, both Big Mac prices and net hourly wages may be related to exchange rates or a country's economic condition.

A third way that business analysts can act unethically in using regression analysis is to knowingly violate the assumptions underlying regression. Regression analysis requires equal error variance, independent error terms, and error terms that are normally distributed. Through the use of residual plots and other statistical techniques, a business researcher can test these assumptions. To present a regression model as fact when the assumptions underlying it are being grossly violated is unethical behavior.

It is important to remember that since regression models are developed from sample data, when an x value is entered into a simple regression model, the resulting prediction is only a point estimate. While business people do often use regression models as predicting tools, it should be kept in mind that the prediction value is an estimate not a guaranteed outcome. By utilizing or at least pointing out confidence intervals and prediction intervals, such as those presented in Section 12.8, the business researcher places the predicted point estimate within the context of inferential estimation and is thereby acting more ethically.

And lastly, another ethical problem that arises in regression analysis is using the regression model to predict values of the independent variable that are outside the domain of values used to develop the model. The airline cost model used in this chapter was built with between 61 and 97 passengers. A linear relationship appeared to be evident between flight costs and number of passengers over this domain. This model is not guaranteed to fit values outside the domain of 61 to 97 passengers, however. In fact, either a nonlinear relationship or no relationship may be present between flight costs and number of passengers if values from outside this domain are included in the model-building process. It is a mistake and probably unethical behavior to make claims for a regression model outside the perview of the domain of values for which the model was developed.

SUMMARY

Correlation measures the degree of relatedness of variables. The most well-known measure of correlation is the Pearson product-moment coefficient of correlation, r. This value ranges from -1 to 0 to $+1$. An r value of $+1$ is perfect positive correlation and an r value of -1 is perfect negative correlation. Positive correlation means that as one variable increases in value, the other variable tends to increase. Negative correlation means that as one variable increases in value, the other variable tends to decrease. For r values near zero, little or no correlation is present.

Regression is a procedure that produces a mathematical model (function) that can be used to predict one variable by other variables. Simple regression is bivariate (two variables) and linear (only a line fit is attempted). Simple regression analysis produces a model that attempts to predict a y variable, referred to as the dependent variable, by an x variable, referred to as the independent variable. The general form of the equation of the simple regression line is the slope-intercept equation of a line. The equation of the simple regression model consists of a slope of the line as a coefficient of x and a y-intercept value as a constant.

After the equation of the line has been developed, several statistics are available that can be used to determine how well the line fits the data. Using the historical data values of x, predicted values of y (denoted as $\hat{y}$) can be calculated by inserting values of x into the regression equation. The predicted values can then be compared to the actual values of y to determine how well the regression equation fits the known data. The difference between a specific y value and its associated predicted y value is called the residual or error of prediction. Examination of the residuals can offer insight into the magnitude of the errors produced by a model. In addition, residual analysis can be used to help determine whether the assumptions underlying the regression analysis have been met. Specifically, graphs of the residuals can reveal (1) lack of linearity, (2) lack of homogeneity of error variance, and (3) independence of error terms. Geometrically, the residuals are the vertical distances from the y values to the regression line. Because the equation that yields the regression line is derived in such a way that the line is in the geometric middle of the points, the sum of the residuals is zero.

A single value of error measurement called the standard error of the estimate, s_e, can be computed. The standard error of the estimate is the standard deviation of error of a model. The value of s_e can be used as a single guide to the magnitude of the error produced by the regression model as opposed to examining all the residuals.

Another widely used statistic for testing the strength of a regression model is r^2, or the coefficient of determination. The coefficient of determination is the proportion of total variance of the y variable accounted for or predicted by x. The coefficient of determination ranges from 0 to 1. The higher the r^2 is, the stronger is the predictability of the model.

Testing to determine whether the slope of the regression line is different from zero is another way to judge the fit of the regression model to the data. If the population slope of the regression line is not different from zero, the regression model is not adding significant predictability to the dependent variable. A t statistic is used to test the significance of the slope. The overall significance of the regression model can be tested using an F statistic. In simple regression, because only one predictor is present, this test accomplishes the same thing as the t test of the slope and $F = t^2$.

One of the most prevalent uses of a regression model is to predict the values of y for given values of x. Recognizing that the predicted value is often not the same as the actual value, a confidence interval has been developed to yield a range within which the mean y value for a given x should fall. A prediction interval for a single y value for a given x value also is specified. This second interval is wider because it allows for the wide diversity of individual values, whereas the confidence interval for the mean y value reflects only the range of average y values for a given x.

Time-series data are data that are gathered over a period of time at regular intervals. Developing the equation of a forecasting trend line for time-series data is a special case of simple regression analysis where the time factor is the predictor variable. The time variable can be in units of years, months, weeks, quarters, and others.

KEY TERMS

Flash Cards

coefficient of
  determination (r^2)

confidence interval
dependent variable
deterministic model
heteroscedasticity
homoscedasticity
independent variable
least squares analysis

outliers
prediction interval
probabilistic model
regression analysis
residual
residual plot
scatter plot

simple regression
standard error of the
  estimate (s_e)
sum of squares of error
  (SSE)

FORMULAS

Pearson's product-moment correlation coefficient

$$r = \frac{\Sigma(x - \bar{x})(y - \bar{y})}{\sqrt{\Sigma(x - \bar{x})^2 \, \Sigma(y - \bar{y})^2}}$$

$$= \frac{\Sigma xy - \dfrac{(\Sigma x \Sigma y)}{n}}{\sqrt{\left[\Sigma x^2 - \dfrac{(\Sigma x)^2}{n}\right]\left[\Sigma y^2 - \dfrac{(\Sigma y)^2}{n}\right]}}$$

Equation of the simple regression line

$$\hat{y} = \beta_0 + \beta_1 x$$

Sum of squares

$$SS_{xx} = \Sigma x^2 - \frac{(\Sigma x)^2}{n}$$

$$SS_{yy} = \Sigma y^2 - \frac{(\Sigma y)^2}{n}$$

$$SS_{xy} = \Sigma xy - \frac{\Sigma x \Sigma y}{n}$$

Slope of the regression line

$$b_1 = \frac{\Sigma(x - \bar{x})(y - \bar{y})}{\Sigma(x - \bar{x})^2} = \frac{\Sigma xy - n\bar{x}\bar{y}}{\Sigma x^2 - n\bar{x}^2}$$

$$= \frac{\Sigma xy - \dfrac{(\Sigma x)(\Sigma y)}{n}}{\Sigma x^2 - \dfrac{(\Sigma x)^2}{n}}$$

y-intercept of the regression line

$$b_0 = \bar{y} - b_1 \bar{x} = \frac{\Sigma y}{n} - b_1 \frac{(\Sigma x)}{n}$$

Sum of squares of error

$$SSE = \Sigma(y - \hat{y})^2 = \Sigma y^2 - b_0 \Sigma y - b_1 \Sigma xy$$

Standard error of the estimate

$$s_e = \sqrt{\frac{SSE}{n - 2}}$$

Coefficient of determination

$$r^2 = 1 - \frac{SSE}{SS_{yy}} = 1 - \frac{SSE}{\Sigma y^2 - \dfrac{(\Sigma y)^2}{n}}$$

Computational formula for r^2

$$r^2 = \frac{b_1^2 SS_{xx}}{SS_{yy}}$$

t test of slope

$$t = \frac{b_1 - \beta_1}{s_b}$$

$$s_b = \frac{s_e}{\sqrt{SS_{xx}}}$$

Confidence interval to estimate $E(y_x)$ for a given value of x

$$\hat{y} \pm t_{\alpha/2,\, n-2} s_e \sqrt{\frac{1}{n} + \frac{(x_0 - \bar{x})^2}{SS_{xx}}}$$

Prediction interval to estimate y for a given value of x

$$\hat{y} \pm t_{\alpha/2,\, n-2} s_e \sqrt{1 + \frac{1}{n} + \frac{(x_0 - \bar{x})^2}{SS_{xx}}}$$

SUPPLEMENTARY PROBLEMS

CALCULATING THE STATISTICS

12.51 Determine the Pearson product-moment correlation coefficient for the following data.

x	1	10	9	6	5	3	2
y	8	4	4	5	7	7	9

12.52 Use the following data for parts (a) through (f).

x	5	7	3	16	12	9
y	8	9	11	27	15	13

a. Determine the equation of the least squares regression line to predict y by x.

b. Using the x values, solve for the predicted values of y and the residuals.
c. Solve for s_e.
d. Solve for r^2.
e. Test the slope of the regression line. Use $\alpha = .01$.
f. Comment on the results determined in parts (b) through (e), and make a statement about the fit of the line.

12.53 Use the following data for parts (a) through (g).

x	53	47	41	50	58	62	45	60
y	5	5	7	4	10	12	3	11

a. Determine the equation of the simple regression line to predict y from x.
b. Using the x values, solve for the predicted values of y and the residuals.
c. Solve for SSE.
d. Calculate the standard error of the estimate.
e. Determine the coefficient of determination.
f. Test the slope of the regression line. Assume $\alpha = .05$. What do you conclude about the slope?
g. Comment on parts (d) and (e).

12.54 If you were to develop a regression line to predict y by x, what value would the coefficient of determination have?

x	213	196	184	202	221	247
y	76	65	62	68	71	75

12.55 Determine the equation of the least squares regression line to predict y from the following data.

x	47	94	68	73	80	49	52	61
y	14	40	34	31	36	19	20	21

a. Construct a 95% confidence interval to estimate the mean y value for x = 60.
b. Construct a 95% prediction interval to estimate an individual y value for x = 70.
c. Interpret the results obtained in parts (a) and (b).

12.56 Determine the equation of the trend line through the following cost data. Use the equation of the line to forecast cost for year 7.

Year	Cost ($ millions)
1	56
2	54
3	49
4	46
5	45

TESTING YOUR UNDERSTANDING

12.57 A manager of a car dealership believes there is a relationship between the number of salespeople on duty and the number of cars sold. Suppose the following sample is used to develop a simple regression model to predict the

number of cars sold by the number of salespeople. Solve for r^2 and explain what r^2 means in this problem.

Week	Number of Cars Sold	Number of Salespeople
1	79	6
2	64	6
3	49	4
4	23	2
5	52	3

12.58 Executives of a video rental chain want to predict the success of a potential new store. The company's researcher begins by gathering information on number of rentals and average family income from several of the chain's present outlets.

Rentals	Average Family Income ($1,000)
710	65
529	43
314	29
504	47
619	52
428	50
317	46
205	29
468	31
545	43
607	49
694	64

Develop a regression model to predict the number of rentals per day by the average family income. Comment on the output.

12.59 It seems logical that restaurant chains with more units (restaurants) would have greater sales. This assumption is mitigated, however, by several possibilities: some units may be more profitable than others, some units may be larger, some units may serve more meals, some units may serve more expensive meals, and so on. The data shown here were published by Technomic. Perform a simple regression analysis to predict a restaurant chain's sales by its number of units. How strong is the relationship?

Chain	Sales ($ billions)	Number of Units (1000)
McDonald's	17.1	12.4
Burger King	7.9	7.5
Taco Bell	4.8	6.8
Pizza Hut	4.7	8.7
Wendy's	4.6	4.6
KFC	4.0	5.1
Subway	2.9	11.2
Dairy Queen	2.7	5.1
Hardee's	2.7	2.9

12.60 Shown here are the total employment labor force figures for the country of Romania over a 13-year period published in LABORSTA. Develop the equation of a trend line through these data and use the equation to predict the total employment labor force of Romania for the year 2013.

Year	Total Employment (1000s)
1996	10,935
1997	11,050
1998	10,845
1999	10,776
2000	10,764
2001	10,697
2002	9,234
2003	9,223
2004	9,158
2005	9,147
2006	9,313
2007	9,353
2008	9,369

12.61 How strong is the correlation between the inflation rate and 30-year treasury yields? The following data published by Fuji Securities are given as pairs of inflation rates and treasury yields for selected years over a 35-year period.

Inflation Rate	30-Year Treasury Yield
1.57%	3.05%
2.23	3.93
2.17	4.68
4.53	6.57
7.25	8.27
9.25	12.01
5.00	10.27
4.62	8.45

Compute the Pearson product-moment correlation coefficient to determine the strength of the correlation between these two variables. Comment on the strength and direction of the correlation.

12.62 According to the National Marine Fisheries Service, the current landings in millions of pounds of fish by U.S. fleets are more than one and one-half times what they were in the 1970s. In other words, fishing has not faded as an industry. However, the growth of this industry has varied by region as shown in the following data. Some regions have remained relatively constant, the South Atlantic region has dropped in pounds caught, and the Pacific-Alaska region has grown almost threefold.

Fisheries	1977	2009
New England	581	646
Mid-Atlantic	213	200
Chesapeake	668	473
South Atlantic	345	113
Gulf of Mexico	1476	1420
Pacific-Alaska	1776	4972

Develop a simple regression model to predict the 2009 landings by the 1977 landings. According to the model, if a region had 700 landings in 1977, what would the predicted number be for 2009? Construct a confidence interval for the average y value for the 700 landings. Use the t statistic to test to determine whether the slope is significantly different from zero. Use $\alpha = .05$.

12.63 People in the aerospace industry believe the cost of a space project is a function of the weight of the major object being sent into space. Use the following data to develop a regression model to predict the cost of a space project by the weight of the space object. Determine r^2 and s_e.

Weight (tons)	Cost ($ millions)
1.897	$ 53.6
3.019	184.9
0.453	6.4
0.988	23.5
1.058	33.4
2.100	110.4
2.387	104.6

12.64 The following data represent a breakdown of state banks and all savings organizations in the United States every 5 years over a 60-year span according to the Federal Reserve System.

Time Period	State Banks	All Savings
1	1342	2330
2	1864	2667
3	1912	3054
4	1847	3764
5	1641	4423
6	1405	4837
7	1147	4694
8	1046	4407
9	997	4328
10	1070	3626
11	1009	2815
12	1042	2030
13	992	1779

Develop a regression model to predict the total number of state banks by the number of all savings organizations. Comment on the strength of the model. Develop a time-series trend line for All Savings using the time periods given. Forecast All Savings for period 15 using this equation.

12.65 Is the amount of money spent by companies on advertising a function of the total revenue of the company?

Shown are revenue and advertising cost data for seven companies published by *Advertising Age* and *Fortune* magazine.

Company	Advertising ($ millions)	Revenues ($ billions)
Wal-Mart	1,073	408.2
Procter & Gamble	4,898	79.7
AT&T	3,345	123.0
General Motors	3,296	104.6
Verizon	2,822	107.8
Ford Motor	2,577	118.3
Hewlett-Packard	829	114.6

Use the data to develop a regression line to predict the amount of advertising by revenues. Compute s_e and r^2. Assuming $\alpha = .05$, test the slope of the regression line. Comment on the strength of the regression model.

12.66 Can the consumption of water in a city be predicted by air temperature? The following data represent a sample of a day's water consumption and the high temperature for that day.

Water Use (millions of gallons)	Temperature (degrees Fahrenheit)
219	103°
56	39
107	77
129	78
68	50
184	96
150	90
112	75

Develop a least squares regression line to predict the amount of water used in a day in a city by the high temperature for that day. What would be the predicted water usage for a temperature of 100°? Evaluate the regression model by calculating s_e, by calculating r^2, and by testing the slope. Let $\alpha = .01$.

INTERPRETING THE OUTPUT

12.67 Study the following Minitab output from a regression analysis to predict *y* from *x*.
   a. What is the equation of the regression model?
   b. What is the meaning of the coefficient of *x*?
   c. What is the result of the test of the slope of the regression model? Let $\alpha = .10$. Why is the *t* ratio negative?
   d. Comment on r^2 and the standard error of the estimate.
   e. Comment on the relationship of the *F* value to the *t* ratio for *x*.
   f. The correlation coefficient for these two variables is $-.7918$. Is this result surprising to you? Why or why not?

Regression Analysis: Y versus X

The regression equation is
Y = 67.2 - 0.0565 X

Predictor	Coef	SE Coef	T	p
Constant	67.231	5.046	13.32	0.000
X	-0.05650	0.01027	-5.50	0.000

S = 10.32   R-Sq = 62.7%   R-Sq(adj) = 60.6%

Analysis of Variance

Source	DF	SS	MS	F	P
Regression	1	3222.9	3222.9	30.25	0.000
Residual Error	18	1918.0	106.6		
Total	19	5141.0			

12.68 Study the following Excel regression output for an analysis attempting to predict the number of union members in the United States by the size of the labor force for selected years over a 30-year period from data published by the U.S. Bureau of Labor Statistics. Analyze the computer output. Discuss the strength of the model in terms of proportion of variation accounted for, slope, and overall predictability. Using the equation of the regression line, attempt to predict the number of union members when the labor force is 110,000. Note that the model was developed with data already recoded in 1,000 units. Use the data in the model as is.

SUMMARY OUTPUT

Regression Statistics	
Multiple R	0.798
R Square	0.636
Adjusted R Square	0.612
Standard Error	258.632
Observations	17

ANOVA

	df	SS	MS	F	Significance F
Regression	1	1756035.529	1756036	26.25	0.00012
Residual	15	1003354.471	66890.3		
Total	16	2759390			

	Coefficients	Standard Error	t Stat	P-value
Intercept	20704.3805	879.6067	23.54	0.00000
Total Employment	-0.0390	0.0076	-5.12	0.00012

12.69 Study the following Minitab residual diagnostic graphs. Comment on any possible violations of regression assumptions.

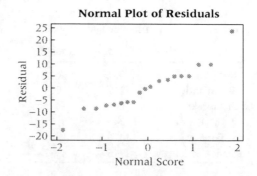

Normal Plot of Residuals

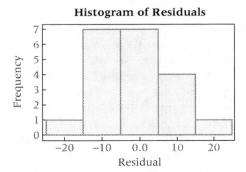

Histogram of Residuals

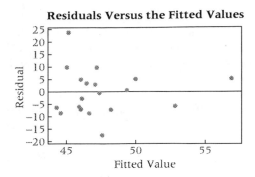

Residuals Versus the Fitted Values

ANALYZING THE DATABASES

see www.wiley.com/college/black and WileyPLUS

Database

1. Develop a regression model from the Consumer Food database to predict Annual Food Spending by Annual Household Income. Discuss the model and its strength on the basis of statistics presented in this chapter. Now develop a regression model to predict Non-Mortgage Household Debt by Annual Household Income. Discuss this model and its strengths. Compare the two models. Does it make sense that Annual Food Spending and Non-Mortgage Household Debt could each be predicted by Annual Household Income? Why or why not?

2. Using the Hospital database, develop a regression model to predict the number of Personnel by the number of Births. Now develop a regression model to predict number of Personnel by number of Beds. Examine the regression output. Which model is stronger in predicting number of Personnel? Explain why, using techniques presented in this chapter. Use the second regression model to predict the number of Personnel in a hospital that has 110 beds.

Construct a 95% confidence interval around this prediction for the average value of y.

3. Analyze all the variables except Type in the Financial database by using a correlation matrix. The seven variables in this database are capable of producing 21 pairs of correlations. Which are most highly correlated? Select the variable that is most highly correlated with P/E ratio and use it as a predictor to develop a regression model to predict P/E ratio. How did the model do?

4. Construct a correlation matrix for the six U.S. and international stock indicators. Describe what you find. That is, what indicators seem to be most strongly related to other indicators? Now focus on the three international stock indicators. Which pair of these stock indicators is most correlated? Develop a regression model to predict the DJIA by the Nikkei 225. How strong is the model? Develop a regression model to predict the DJIA by the Hang Seng. How strong is the model? Develop a regression model to predict the DJIA by the Mexico IPC. How strong is the model? Compare the three models.

CASE

DELTA WIRE USES TRAINING AS A WEAPON

The Delta Wire Corporation was founded in 1978 in Clarksdale, Mississippi. The company manufactures high-carbon specialty steel wire for global markets and at present employs about 100 people. For the past few years, sales increased each year.

A few years ago, however, things did not look as bright for Delta Wire because it was caught in a potentially disastrous bind. With the dollar declining in value, foreign competition was becoming a growing threat to Delta's market position. In addition to the growing foreign competition, industry quality requirements were becoming tougher each year.

Delta officials realized that some conditions, such as the value of the dollar, were beyond their control. However, one

area that they could improve upon was employee education. The company worked with training programs developed by the state of Mississippi and a local community college to set up its own school. Delta employees were introduced to statistical process control and other quality assurance techniques. Delta reassured its customers that the company was working hard on improving quality and staying competitive. Customers were invited to sit in on the educational sessions. Because of this effort, Delta has been able to weather the storm and continues to sustain a leadership position in the highly competitive steel wire industry.

Delta continued its training and education program. In the 1990s, Delta instituted a basic skills training program that eventually led to a decrease in nonconforming material from 6% to 2% and a productivity increase from 70,000 to 90,000 pounds per week. In addition, this initiative resulted in a "best in class" award from Goodyear, its largest customer.

Although acquired by Bekaert of Belgium in January of 2006, the Delta Wire Corporation, a major supplier of bead wire for tire reinforcement and other specialized wire products for the North American market, continues to operate in its current capacity. Bekaert wants to support Delta Wire's market share growth and ensure adequate product availability to its customers.

Discussion

1. Delta Wire prides itself on its efforts in the area of employee education. Employee education can pay off in many ways. Discuss some of them. One payoff can be the renewed interest and excitement generated toward the job and the company. Some people theorize that because of a more positive outlook and interest in implementing things learned, the more education received by a worker, the less likely he or she is to miss work days. Suppose the following data represent the number of days of sick leave taken by 20 workers last year along with the number of contact hours of employee education/training they each received in the past year. Use the techniques learned in this chapter to analyze the data. Include both regression and correlation techniques. Discuss the strength of the relationship and any models that are developed.

Employee	Hours of Education	Sick Days	Employee	Hours of Education	Sick Days
1	24	5	11	8	8
2	16	4	12	60	1
3	48	0	13	0	9
4	120	1	14	28	3
5	36	5	15	15	8
6	10	7	16	88	2
7	65	0	17	120	1
8	36	3	18	15	8
9	0	12	19	48	0
10	12	8	20	5	10

2. Many companies find that the implementation of total quality management eventually results in improved sales. Companies that fail to adopt quality efforts lose market share in many cases or go out of business. One measure of the effect of a company's quality improvement efforts is customer satisfaction. Suppose Delta Wire hired a research firm to measure customer satisfaction each year. The research firm developed a customer satisfaction scale in which totally satisfied customers can award a score as high as 50 and totally unsatisfied

customers can award scores as low as 0. The scores are measured across many different industrial customers and averaged for a yearly mean customer score. Do sales increase with increases in customer satisfaction scores? To study this notion, suppose the average customer satisfaction score each year for Delta Wire is paired with the company's total sales of that year for the last 15 years, and a regression analysis is run on the data. Assume the following Minitab and Excel outputs are the result. Suppose you were asked by Delta Wire to analyze the data and summarize the results. What would you find?

MINITAB OUTPUT

```
Regression Analysis: Sales Versus Satisfaction

The regression equation is
Sales = 1.73 + 0.162 CustSat

Predictor     Coef      StDev       T       p
Constant    1.7332    0.4364     3.97   0.002
CustSat     0.16245   0.01490   10.90   0.000

S = 0.4113    R-Sq = 90.1% R-Sq(adj) = 89.4%

Analysis of Variance

Source          DF   SS       MS       F       p
Regression       1   20.098   20.098   118.80  0.000
Residual Error  13    2.199    0.169
Total           14   22.297
```

EXCEL OUTPUT

SUMMARY OUTPUT

Regression Statistics

Multiple R	0.949
R Square	0.901
Adjusted R Square	0.894
Standard Error	0.411
Observations	15

ANOVA

	df	SS	MS	F	Significance F
Regression	1	20.098	20.098	118.8	0.000
Residual	13	2.199	0.169		
Total	14	22.297			

	Coefficients	Standard Error	t Stat	P-value
Intercept	1.733	0.436	3.97	0.0016
Sick Days	0.162	0.015	10.90	0.0000

3. Delta Wire increased productivity from 70,000 to 90,000 pounds per week during a time when it instituted a basic skills training program. Suppose this program was implemented over an 18-month period and that the following data are the number of total cumulative basic skills hours of training and the per week productivity figures taken once a month over this time. Use techniques from this chapter to analyze the data and make a brief report to Delta about the predictability of productivity from cumulative hours of training.

Cumulative Hours of Training	Productivity (in pounds per week)
0	70,000
100	70,350
250	70,500
375	72,600
525	74,000
750	76,500
875	77,000
1,100	77,400
1,300	77,900
1,450	77,200
1,660	78,900
1,900	81,000
2,300	82,500

Cumulative Hours of Training	Productivity (in pounds per week)
2,600	84,000
2,850	86,500
3,150	87,000
3,500	88,600
4,000	90,000

(continued)

Source: Adapted from "Delta Wire Corporation," *Strengthening America's Competitiveness: Resource Management Insights for Small Business Success.* Published by Warner Books on behalf of Connecticut Mutual Life Insurance Company and the U.S. Chamber of Commerce in association with the Blue Chip Enterprise Initiative, 1991, International Monetary Fund; Terri Bergman, "TRAINING: The Case for Increased Investment," *Employment Relations Today,* Winter 1994–1995, pp. 381–391, available at http://www.ed.psu.edu/nwac/document/train/invest.html. Bekaert Web site, at: http://www.bekaert.com/corporate/press/2006/31-jan-2006.htm.

USING THE COMPUTER

EXCEL

▪ Excel has the capability of doing simple regression analysis. For a more inclusive analysis, use the **Data Analysis** tool. For a more "a la carte" approach, use Excel's **Insert Function**.

▪ To use the **Data Analysis** tool for a more inclusive analysis, begin by selecting the **Data** tab on the Excel worksheet. From the **Analysis** panel at the right top of the **Data** tab worksheet, click on **Data Analysis**. If your Excel worksheet does not show the **Data Analysis** option, then you can load it as an add-in following directions given in Chapter 2. From the **Data Analysis** pulldown menu, select **Regression**. In the **Regression** dialog box, input the location of the y values in **Input $\underline{Y}$ Range**. Input the location of the x values in **Input $\underline{X}$ Range**. Input **Labels** and input **Confidence Level**. To pass the line through the origin, check **Constant is $\underline{Z}$ero**. To print out the raw residuals, check **Residuals**. To print out residuals converted to z scores, check **S$\underline{t}$andardized Residuals**. For a plot of the residuals, check **Resi$\underline{d}$ual Plots**. For a plot of the line through the points, check **L$\underline{i}$ne Fit Plots**. Standard output includes r, r^2, s_e, and an ANOVA table with the F test, the slope and intercept, t statistics with associated p-values, and any optionally requested output such as graphs or residuals.

▪ To use the **Insert Function (f_x)** go to the **Formulas** tab on an Excel worksheet (top center tab). The **Insert Function** is on the far left of the menu bar. In the **Insert Function** dialog box at the top, there is a pulldown menu where it says **Or select a $\underline{c}$ategory**. From the pulldown menu associated with this command, select **Statistical**. Select **INTERCEPT** from the **Insert Function's Statistical** menu to solve for the y-intercept, **RSQ** to solve for r^2, **SLOPE** to

solve for the slope, and **STEYX** to solve for the standard error of the estimate.

MINITAB

▪ Minitab has a relatively thorough capability to perform regression analysis. To begin, select **$\underline{S}$tat** from the menu bar. Select **Regression** from the **$\underline{S}$tat** pulldown menu. Select **Regression** from the **Regression** pulldown menu. Place the column name or column location of the y variable in **Response**. Place the column name or column location of the x variable in **Predictors**. Select **Graphs** for options relating to residual plots. Use this option and check **Four in one** to produce the residual diagnostic plots shown in the chapter. Select **Options** for confidence intervals and prediction intervals. Select **Results** for controlling the regression analysis output. Select **Storage** to store fits and/or residuals.

▪ To obtain a fitted-line plot, select **$\underline{S}$tat** from the menu bar. Select **Regression** from the **$\underline{S}$tat** pulldown menu. Select **Fitted Line Plot** from the **Regression** pulldown menu. In the Fitted Line Plot dialog box, place the column name or column location of the y variable in **Response(Y)**.

Place the column name or column location of the x variable in **Predictor(X)**. Check **Type of Regression Model** as **Linear** (Chapter 12), **Quadratic**, or **Cubic**.

Select **Graphs** for options relating to residual plots. Use this option and check **Four in one** to produce the residual diagnostic plots shown in the chapter.

Select **Options** for confidence intervals and prediction intervals.

Select **Storage** to store fits and/or residuals.

CHAPTER 13

Multiple Regression Analysis

LEARNING OBJECTIVES

This chapter presents the potential of multiple regression analysis as a tool in business decision making and its applications, thereby enabling you to:

1. Explain how, by extending the simple regression model to a multiple regression model with two independent variables, it is possible to determine the multiple regression equation for any number of unknowns.

2. Examine significance tests of both the overall regression model and the regression coefficients.

3. Calculate the residual, standard error of the estimate, coefficient of multiple determination, and adjusted coefficient of multiple determination of a regression model.

4. Use a computer to find and interpret multiple regression outputs.

Michael Krasowitz/Photographer's Choice/Getty Images

Are You Going to Hate Your New Job?

Getting a new job can be an exciting and energizing event in your life.

But what if you discover after a short time on the job that you hate your job? Is there any way to determine ahead of time whether you will love or hate your job? Sue Shellenbarger of *The Wall Street Journal* discusses some of the things to look for when interviewing for a position that may provide clues as to whether you will be happy on that job.

Among other things, work cultures vary from hip, free-wheeling start-ups to old-school organizational-driven domains. Some organizations place pressure on workers to feel tense and to work long hours while others place more emphasis on creativity and the bottom line. Shellenbarger suggests that job interviewees pay close attention to how they are treated in an interview. Are they just another cog in the wheel or are they valued as an individual? Is a work-life balance apparent within the company? Ask what a typical workday is like at that firm. Inquire about the values that undergird the management by asking questions such as "What is your proudest accomplishment?" Ask about flexible schedules and how job training is managed. For example, does the worker have to go to job training on their own time?

A "Work Trends" survey undertaking by the John J. Heldrich Center for Workforce Development at Rutgers University and the Center for Survey Research and Analysis at the University of Connecticut posed several questions to employees in a survey to ascertain their job satisfaction. Some of the themes included in these questions were relationship with your supervisor, overall quality of the work environment, total hours worked each week, and opportunities for advancement at the job.

Suppose another researcher gathered survey data from 19 employees on these questions and also asked the employees to rate their job satisfaction on a scale from 0 to 100 (with 100 being perfectly satisfied). Suppose the following data represent the results of this survey. Assume that relationship

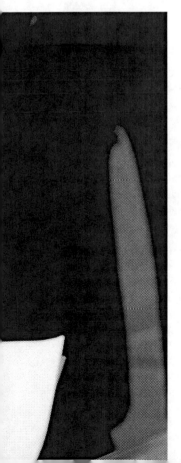

with supervisor is rated on a scale from 0 to 50 (0 represents poor relationship and 50 represents an excellent relationship), overall quality of the work environment is rated on a scale from 0 to 100 (0 represents poor work environment and 100 represents an excellent work environment), and opportunities for advancement is rated on a scale from 0 to 50 (0 represents no opportunities and 50 represents excellent opportunities).

Job Satisfaction	Relationship with Supervisor	Overall Quality of Work Environment	Total Hours Worked per Week	Opportunities for Advancement
55	27	65	50	42
20	12	13	60	28
85	40	79	45	7
65	35	53	65	48
45	29	43	40	32
70	42	62	50	41
35	22	18	75	18
60	34	75	40	32
95	50	84	45	48
65	33	68	60	11
85	40	72	55	33
10	5	10	50	21
75	37	64	45	42
80	42	82	40	46
50	31	46	60	48
90	47	95	55	30
75	36	82	70	39
45	20	42	40	22
65	32	73	55	12

Managerial and Statistical Questions

1. Several variables are presented that may be related to job satisfaction. Which variables are stronger predictors of job satisfaction? Might other variables not mentioned here be related to job satisfaction?

2. Is it possible to develop a mathematical model to predict job satisfaction using the data given? If so, how strong is the model? With four independent variables, will we need to develop four different simple regression models and compare their results?

Source: Adapted from Sue Shellenbarger, "How to Find Out if You're Going to Hate a New Job Before You Agree to Take It," *The Wall Street Journal,* June 13, 2002, p. D1.

Simple regression analysis (discussed in Chapter 12) is bivariate linear regression in which one **dependent variable**, y, is predicted by one **independent variable**, x. Examples of simple regression applications include models to predict retail sales by population density, Dow Jones averages by prime interest rates, crude oil production by energy consumption, and CEO compensation by quarterly sales. However, in many cases, other independent variables, taken in conjunction with these variables, can make the regression model a better fit in predicting the dependent variable. For example, sales could be predicted by the size of store and number of competitors in addition to population density. A model to predict the Dow Jones average of 30 industrials could include, in addition to the prime interest rate, such predictors as yesterday's volume, the bond interest rate, and the producer price index. A model to predict CEO compensation could be developed by using variables such as company earnings per share, age of CEO, and size of company in addition to quarterly sales. A model could perhaps be developed to predict the cost of outsourcing by such variables as unit price, export taxes, cost of money, damage in transit, and other factors. Each of these examples contains only one dependent variable, y, as with simple regression analysis. However, multiple independent variables, x (predictors) are involved. *Regression analysis with two or more independent variables or with at least one nonlinear predictor is called* **multiple regression** analysis.

13.1 THE MULTIPLE REGRESSION MODEL

Multiple regression analysis is similar in principle to simple regression analysis. However, it is more complex conceptually and computationally. Recall from Chapter 12 that the equation of the probabilistic simple regression model is

$$y = \beta_0 + \beta_1 x + \epsilon$$

where

y = the value of the dependent variable
β_0 = the population y intercept
β_1 = the population slope
ϵ = the error of prediction

Extending this notion to multiple regression gives the general equation for the probabilistic multiple regression model.

$$y = \beta_0 + \beta_1 x_1 + \beta_2 x_2 + \beta_3 x_3 + \cdots + \beta_k x_k + \epsilon$$

where

y = the value of the dependent variable
β_0 = the regression constant
β_1 = the partial regression coefficient for independent variable 1
β_2 = the partial regression coefficient for independent variable 2
β_3 = the partial regression coefficient for independent variable 3
β_k = the partial regression coefficient for independent variable k
k = the number of independent variables

In multiple regression analysis, the dependent variable, y, is sometimes referred to as the **response variable**. The **partial regression coefficient** of an independent variable, β_i, *represents the increase that will occur in the value of y from a one-unit increase in that independent variable if all other variables are held constant.* The "full" (versus partial) regression coefficient of an independent variable is a coefficient obtained from the bivariate model (simple regression) in which the independent variable is the sole predictor of y. The partial regression coefficients occur because more than one predictor is included in a model. The partial regression coefficients are analogous to β_1, the slope of the simple regression model in Chapter 12.

In actuality, the partial regression coefficients and the regression constant of a multiple regression model are population values and are unknown. In virtually all research, these values are estimated by using sample information. Shown here is the form of the equation for estimating y with sample information.

$$\hat{y} = b_0 + b_1 x_1 + b_2 x_2 + b_3 x_3 + \cdots + b_k x_k$$

where

$\hat{y}$ = the predicted value of y
b_0 = the estimate of the regression constant
b_1 = the estimate of regression coefficient 1
b_2 = the estimate of regression coefficient 2
b_3 = the estimate of regression coefficient 3
b_k = the estimate of regression coefficient k
k = the number of independent variables

Multiple Regression Model with Two Independent Variables (First-Order)

The simplest multiple regression model is one constructed with two independent variables, where the highest power of either variable is 1 (first-order regression model). The regression model is

$$y = \beta_0 + \beta_1 x_1 + \beta_2 x_2 + \in$$

The constant and coefficients are estimated from sample information, resulting in the following model.

$$\hat{y} = b_0 + b_1 x_1 + b_2 x_2$$

Figure 13.1 is a three-dimensional graph of a series of points (x_1, x_2, y) representing values from three variables used in a multiple regression model to predict the sales price of a house by the number of square feet in the house and the age of the house. Simple regression models yield a line that is fit through data points in the xy plane. In multiple regression analysis, the resulting model produces a **response surface**. In the multiple regression model shown here with two independent first-order variables, the response surface is a **response plane**. The response plane for such a model is fit in a three-dimensional space (x_1, x_2, y).

If such a response plane is fit into the points shown in Figure 13.1, the result is the graph in Figure 13.2. Notice that most of the points are not on the plane. As in simple regression, an error in the fit of the model in multiple regression is usually present. The distances shown in the graph from the points to the response plane are the errors of fit, or residuals $(y - \hat{y})$. Multiple regression models with three or more independent variables involve more than three dimensions and are difficult to depict geometrically.

Observe in Figure 13.2 that the regression model attempts to fit a plane into the three-dimensional plot of points. Notice that the plane intercepts the y axis. Figure 13.2 depicts

FIGURE 13.1

Points in a Sample Space

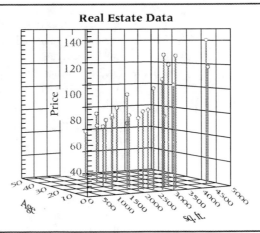

Real Estate Data

FIGURE 13.2

Response Plane for a First-
Order Two-Predictor Multiple
Regression Model

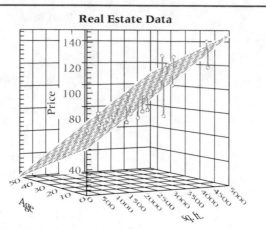

Real Estate Data

some values of y for various values of x_1 and x_2. The error of the response plane ($\in$) in predicting or determining the y values is the distance from the points to the plane.

Determining the Multiple Regression Equation

The simple regression equations for determining the sample slope and intercept given in Chapter 12 are the result of using methods of calculus to minimize the sum of squares of error for the regression model. The procedure for developing these equations involves solving two simultaneous equations with two unknowns, b_0 and b_1. Finding the sample slope and intercept from these formulas requires the values of Σx, Σy, Σxy, and Σx^2.

The procedure for determining formulas to solve for multiple regression coefficients is similar. The formulas are established to meet an objective of *minimizing the sum of squares of error for the model.* Hence, the regression analysis shown here is referred to as **least squares analysis**. Methods of calculus are applied, resulting in $k + 1$ equations with $k + 1$ unknowns (b_0 and k values of b_i) for multiple regression analyses with k independent variables. Thus, a regression model with six independent variables will generate seven simultaneous equations with seven unknowns (b_0, b_1, b_2, b_3, b_4, b_5, b_6).

For multiple regression models with two independent variables, the result is three simultaneous equations with three unknowns (b_0, b_1, and b_2).

$$b_0 n + b_1 \Sigma x_1 + b_2 \Sigma x_2 = \Sigma y$$
$$b_0 \Sigma x_1 + b_1 \Sigma x_1^2 + b_2 \Sigma x_1 x_2 = \Sigma x_1 y$$
$$b_0 \Sigma x_2 + b_1 \Sigma x_1 x_2 + b_2 \Sigma x_2^2 = \Sigma x_2 y$$

The process of solving these equations by hand is tedious and time-consuming. Solving for the regression coefficients and regression constant in a multiple regression model with two independent variables requires Σx_1, Σx_2, Σy, Σx_1^2, Σx_2^2, $\Sigma x_1 x_2$, $\Sigma x_1 y$, and $\Sigma x_2 y$. In actuality, virtually all business researchers use computer statistical software packages to solve for the regression coefficients, the regression constant, and other pertinent information. In this chapter, we will discuss computer output and assume little or no hand calculation. The emphasis will be on the interpretation of the computer output.

A Multiple Regression Model

A real estate study was conducted in a small Louisiana city to determine what variables, if any, are related to the market price of a home. Several variables were explored, including the number of bedrooms, the number of bathrooms, the age of the house, the number of square feet of living space, the total number of square feet of space, and the number of garages. Suppose the researcher wants to develop a regression model to predict the market price of a home by two variables, "total number of square feet in the house" and "the age of the house." Listed in Table 13.1 are the data for these three variables.

TABLE 13.1 Real Estate Data		
Market Price ($1,000)	Total Number of Square Feet	Age of House (Years)
y	x_1	x_2
63.0	1605	35
65.1	2489	45
69.9	1553	20
76.8	2404	32
73.9	1884	25
77.9	1558	14
74.9	1748	8
78.0	3105	10
79.0	1682	28
83.4	2470	30
79.5	1820	2
83.9	2143	6
79.7	2121	14
84.5	2485	9
96.0	2300	19
109.5	2714	4
102.5	2463	5
121.0	3076	7
104.9	3048	3
128.0	3267	6
129.0	3069	10
117.9	4765	11
140.0	4540	8

A number of statistical software packages can perform multiple regression analysis, including Excel and Minitab. The output for the Minitab multiple regression analysis on the real estate data is given in Figure 13.3. (Excel output is shown in Demonstration Problem 13.1.)

The Minitab output for regression analysis begins with "The regression equation is." From Figure 13.3, the regression equation for the real estate data in Table 13.1 is

$$\hat{y} = 57.4 + .0177x_1 - .666x_2$$

The regression constant, 57.4, is the y-intercept. The y-intercept is the value of $\hat{y}$ if both x_1 (number of square feet) and x_2 (age) are zero. In this example, a practical understanding of the y-intercept is meaningless. It makes little sense to say that a house containing no square feet ($x_1 = 0$) and no years of age ($x_2 = 0$) would cost $57,400. Note in Figure 13.2 that the response plane crosses the y-axis (price) at 57.4.

FIGURE 13.3

Minitab Output of Regression for the Real Estate Example

```
Regression Analysis: Price versus Square Feet, Age

The regression equation is
Price = 57.4 + 0.0177 Square Feet - 0.666 Age

Predictor          Coef      SE Coef        T        P
Constant          57.35        10.01     5.73    0.000
Square Feet    0.017718     0.003146     5.63    0.000
Age             -0.6663       0.2280    -2.92    0.008

S = 11.9604   R-Sq = 74.1%      R-Sq(adj) = 71.5%

Analysis of Variance

Source            DF       SS       MS       F       P
Regression         2   8189.7   4094.9   28.63   0.000
Residual Error    20   2861.0    143.1
Total             22  11050.7
```

The coefficient of x_1 (total number of square feet in the house) is .0177, which means that a one-unit increase in square footage would result in a predicted increase of .0177 · ($1,000) — $17.70 in the price of the home if age were held constant. All other variables being held constant, the addition of 1 square foot of space in the house results in a predicted increase of $17.70 in the price of the home.

The coefficient of x_2 (age) is −.666. The negative sign on the coefficient denotes an inverse relationship between the age of a house and the price of the house: the older the house, the lower the price. In this case, if the total number of square feet in the house is kept constant, a one-unit increase in the age of the house (1 year) will result in −.666 · ($1,000) = −$666, a predicted $666 drop in the price.

In examining the regression coefficients, it is important to remember that the independent variables are often measured in different units. It is usually not wise to compare the regression coefficients of predictors in a multiple regression model and decide that the variable with the largest regression coefficient is the best predictor. In this example, the two variables are in different units, square feet and years. Just because x_2 has the larger coefficient (.666) does not necessarily make x_2 the strongest predictor of y.

This regression model can be used to predict the price of a house in this small Louisiana city. If the house has 2500 square feet total and is 12 years old, $x_1 = 2500$ and $x_2 = 12$. Substituting these values into the regression model yields

$$\hat{y} = 57.4 + .0177x_1 - .666x_2$$
$$= 57.4 + .0177(2500) - .666(12) = 93.658$$

The predicted price of the house is $93,658. Figure 13.2 is a graph of these data with the response plane and the residual distances.

DEMONSTRATION PROBLEM 13.1

Demonstration Problem

Since 1980, the prime interest rate in the United States has varied from less than 5% to over 15%. What factor in the U.S. economy seems to be related to the prime interest rate? Two possible predictors of the prime interest rate are the annual unemployment rate and the savings rate in the United States. Shown below are data for the annual prime interest rate for the even-numbered years over a 28-year period in the United States along with the annual unemployment rate and the annual average personal saving (as a percentage of disposable personal income). Use these data to develop a multiple regression model to predict the annual prime interest rate by the unemployment rate and the average personal saving. Determine the predicted prime interest rate if the unemployment rate is 6.5 and the average personal saving is 5.0.

Year	Prime Interest Rate	Unemployment Rate	Personal Saving
1982	14.85	9.7	11.2
1984	12.04	7.5	10.8
1986	8.33	7.0	8.2
1988	9.32	5.5	7.3
1990	10.01	5.6	7.0
1992	6.25	7.5	7.7
1994	7.15	6.1	4.8
1996	8.27	5.4	4.0
1998	8.35	4.5	4.3
2000	9.23	4.0	2.3
2002	4.67	5.8	2.4
2004	4.34	5.5	2.1
2006	7.96	4.6	0.7
2008	5.09	5.8	1.8
2010	3.25	9.6	5.8

Solution

The following output shows the results of analyzing the data by using the regression portion of Excel.

SUMMARY OUTPUT

Regression Statistics	
Multiple R	0.819
R Square	0.671
Adjusted R Square	0.616
Standard Error	1.890
Observations	15

ANOVA

	df	SS	MS	F	Significance F
Regression	2	87.2388	43.6194	12.21	0.0013
Residual	12	42.8539	3.5712		
Total	14	130.0927			

	Coefficients	Standard Error	t Stat	P-value
Intercept	7.4196	1.943	3.82	0.0024
Unemployment Rates	−1.2092	0.425	−2.85	0.0147
Personal Savings	1.3993	0.288	4.86	0.0004

The regression equation is

$$\hat{y} = 7.4196 - 1.2092x_1 + 1.3993x_2$$

where:

$\hat{y}$ = prime interest rate
x_1 = unemployment rate
x_2 = personal saving

The model indicates that for every one-unit (1%) increase in the unemployment rate, the predicted prime interest rate decreases by 1.2092%, if personal saving is held constant. The model also indicates that for every one-unit (1%) increase in personal saving, the predicted prime interest rate increases by 1.3993%, if unemployment is held constant.

If the unemployment rate is 6.5 and the personal saving rate is 5.0, the predicted prime interest rate is 6.56%:

$$\hat{y} = 7.4196 - 1.2092(6.5) + 1.3993(5.0) = 6.56$$

13.1 PROBLEMS

13.1 Use a computer to develop the equation of the regression model for the following data. Comment on the regression coefficients. Determine the predicted value of y for $x_1 = 200$ and $x_2 = 7$.

y	x_1	x_2
12	174	3
18	281	9
31	189	4
28	202	8
52	149	9
47	188	12
38	215	5
22	150	11
36	167	8
17	135	5

13.2 Use a computer to develop the equation of the regression model for the following data. Comment on the regression coefficients. Determine the predicted value of y for $x_1 = 33$, $x_2 = 29$, and $x_3 = 13$.

y	x_1	x_2	x_3
114	21	6	5
94	43	25	8
87	56	42	25
98	19	27	9
101	29	20	12
85	34	45	21
94	40	33	14
107	32	14	11
119	16	4	7
93	18	31	16
108	27	12	10
117	31	3	8

13.3 Using the following data, determine the equation of the regression model. How many independent variables are there? Comment on the meaning of these regression coefficients.

Predictor	Coefficient
Constant	121.62
x_1	−.174
x_2	6.02
x_3	.00026
x_4	.0041

13.4 Use the following data to determine the equation of the multiple regression model. Comment on the regression coefficients.

Predictor	Coefficient
Constant	31,409.5
x_1	.08425
x_2	289.62
x_3	−.0947

13.5 Is there a particular product that is an indicator of per capita personal consumption for countries around the world? Shown on the next page are data on per capita personal consumption, paper consumption, fish consumption, and gasoline consumption for 11 countries. Use the data to develop a multiple regression model to predict per capita personal consumption by paper consumption, fish consumption, and gasoline consumption. Discuss the meaning of the partial regression weights.

Country	Per Capita Personal Consumption ($ U.S.)	Paper Consumption (kg per person)	Fish Consumption (lbs per person)	Gasoline Consumption (liters per person)
Bangladesh	836	1	23	2
Greece	3,145	85	53	394
Italy	21,785	204	48	368
Japan	37,931	250	141	447
Kenya	276	4	12	16
Norway	1,913	156	113	477
Philippines	2,195	19	65	43
Portugal	3,154	116	133	257
United Kingdom	19,539	207	44	460
United States	109,521	308	47	1,624
Venezuela	622	27	40	528

13.6 Jensen, Solberg, and Zorn investigated the relationship of insider ownership, debt, and dividend policies in companies. One of their findings was that firms with high insider ownership choose lower levels of both debt and dividends. Shown here is a sample of data of these three variables for 11 different industries. Use the data to develop the equation of the regression model to predict insider ownership by debt ratio and dividend payout. Comment on the regression coefficients.

Industry	Insider Ownership	Debt Ratio	Dividend Payout
Mining	8.2	14.2	10.4
Food and beverage	18.4	20.8	14.3
Furniture	11.8	18.6	12.1
Publishing	28.0	18.5	11.8
Petroleum refining	7.4	28.2	10.6
Glass and cement	15.4	24.7	12.6
Motor vehicle	15.7	15.6	12.6
Department store	18.4	21.7	7.2
Restaurant	13.4	23.0	11.3
Amusement	18.1	46.7	4.1
Hospital	10.0	35.8	9.0

13.2 SIGNIFICANCE TESTS OF THE REGRESSION MODEL AND ITS COEFFICIENTS

Multiple regression models can be developed to fit almost any data set if the level of measurement is adequate and enough data points are available. Once a model has been constructed, it is important to test the model to determine whether it fits the data well and whether the assumptions underlying regression analysis are met. Assessing the adequacy of the regression model can be done in several ways, including testing the overall significance of the model, studying the significance tests of the regression coefficients, computing the residuals, examining the standard error of the estimate, and observing the coefficient of determination. In this section, we examine significance tests of the regression model and of its coefficients.

Testing the Overall Model

With simple regression, a t test of the slope of the regression line is used to determine whether the population slope of the regression line is different from zero—that is, whether the independent variable contributes significantly in linearly predicting the dependent variable.

The hypotheses for this test, presented in Chapter 12 are

$$H_0: \beta_1 = 0$$
$$H_a: \beta_1 \neq 0$$

For multiple regression, an analogous test makes use of the F statistic. The overall significance of the multiple regression model is tested with the following hypotheses.

$$H_0: \beta_1 = \beta_2 = \beta_3 = \ldots = \beta_k = 0$$

H_a: At least one of the regression coefficeients is $\neq 0$.

If we fail to reject the null hypothesis, we are stating that the regression model has no significant predictability for the dependent variable. A rejection of the null hypothesis indicates that at least one of the independent variables is adding significant predictability for y.

This F test of overall significance is often given as a part of the standard multiple regression output from statistical software packages. The output appears as an analysis of variance (ANOVA) table. Shown here is the ANOVA table for the real estate example taken from the Minitab output in Figure 13.3.

Analysis of Variance

Source	DF	SS	MS	F	p
Regression	2	8189.7	4094.9	28.63	0.000
Residual Error	20	2861.0	143.1		
Total	22	11050.7			

The F value is 28.63; because $p = .000$, the F value is significant at $\alpha = .001$. The null hypothesis is rejected, and there is at least one significant predictor of house price in this analysis.

The F value is calculated by the following equation.

$$F = \frac{MS_{reg}}{MS_{err}} = \frac{SS_{reg}/df_{reg}}{SS_{err}/df_{err}} = \frac{SSR/k}{SSE/(N - k - 1)}$$

where

$$MS = \text{mean square}$$
$$SS = \text{sum of squares}$$
$$df = \text{degrees of freedom}$$
$$k = \text{number of independent variables}$$
$$N = \text{number of observations}$$

Note that in the ANOVA table for the real estate example, $df_{reg} = 2$. The degrees of freedom formula for regression is the number of regression coefficients plus the regression constant minus 1. The net result is the number of regression coefficients, which equals the number of independent variables, k. The real estate example uses two independent variables, so $k = 2$. Degrees of freedom error in multiple regression equals the total number of observations minus the number of regression coefficients minus the regression constant, or $N - k - 1$. For the real estate example, $N = 23$; thus, $df_{err} = 23 - 2 - 1 = 20$.

As shown in Chapter 11, $MS = SS/df$. The F ratio is formed by dividing MS_{reg} by MS_{err}. In using the F distribution table to determine a critical value against which to test the observed F value, the degrees of freedom numerator is df_{reg} and the degrees of freedom denominator is df_{err}. The table F value is obtained in the usual manner, as presented in Chapter 11. With $\alpha = .01$ for the real estate example, the table value is

$$F_{.01,2,20} = 5.85$$

Comparing the observed F of 28.63 to this table value shows that the decision is to reject the null hypothesis. This same conclusion was reached using the p-value method from the computer output.

If a regression model has only one linear independent variable, it is a simple regression model. In that case, the F test for the overall model is the same as the t test for significance of the population slope. The F value displayed in the regression ANOVA table is related to the t test for the slope in the simple regression case as follows.

$$F = t^2$$

In simple regression, the F value and the t value give redundant information about the overall test of the model.

Most researchers who use multiple regression analysis will observe the value of F and its p-value rather early in the process. If F is not significant, then no population regression coefficient is significantly different from zero, and the regression model has no predictability for the dependent variable.

Significance Tests of the Regression Coefficients

In multiple regression, individual significance tests can be computed for each regression coefficient using a t test. Each of these t tests is analogous to the t test for the slope used in Chapter 12 for simple regression analysis. The hypotheses for testing the regression coefficient of each independent variable take the following form:

$$H_0: \beta_1 = 0$$
$$H_a: \beta_1 \neq 0$$

$$H_0: \beta_2 = 0$$
$$H_a: \beta_2 \neq 0$$

$$\vdots$$

$$H_0: \beta_k = 0$$
$$H_a: \beta_k \neq 0$$

Most multiple regression computer packages yield observed t values to test the individual regression coefficients as standard output. Shown here are the t values and their associated probabilities for the real estate example as displayed with the multiple regression output in Figure 13.3.

Variable	T	P
Square feet	5.63	.000
Age	−2.92	.008

At $\alpha = .05$, the null hypothesis is rejected for both variables because the probabilities (p) associated with their t values are less than .05. If the t ratios for any predictor variables are not significant (fail to reject the null hypothesis), the researcher might decide to drop that variable(s) from the analysis as a nonsignificant predictor(s). Other factors can enter into this decision. In Chapter 14, we will explore techniques for model building in which some variable sorting is required.

The degrees of freedom for each of these individual tests of regression coefficients are $n - k - 1$. In this particular example because there are $k = 2$ predictor variables, the degrees of freedom are $23 - 2 - 1 = 20$. With $\alpha = .05$ and a two-tailed test, the critical table t value is

$$t_{.025,20} - \pm 2.086$$

Notice from the t ratios shown here that if this critical table t value had been used as the hypothesis test criterion instead of the p-value method, the results would have been the same. Testing the regression coefficients not only gives the researcher some insight into the fit of the regression model, but it also helps in the evaluation of how worthwhile individual independent variables are in predicting y.

13.2 PROBLEMS

13.7 Examine the Minitab output shown here for a multiple regression analysis. How many predictors were there in this model? Comment on the overall significance of the regression model. Discuss the t ratios of the variables and their significance.

The regression equation is

$$Y = 4.096 - 5.111X_1 + 2.662X_2 + 1.557X_3 + 1.141X_4 + 1.650$$
$$X_5 - 1.248X_6 + 0.436X_7 + 0.962X_8 + 1.289X_9$$

Predictor	Coef	Stdev	T	p
Constant	4.096	1.2884	3.24	.006
X_1	-5.111	1.8700	2.73	.011
X_2	2.662	2.0796	1.28	.212
X_3	1.557	1.2811	1.22	.235
X_4	1.141	1.4712	0.78	.445
X_5	1.650	1.4994	1.10	.281
X_6	-1.248	1.2735	0.98	.336
X_7	0.436	0.3617	1.21	.239
X_8	0.962	1.1896	0.81	.426
X_9	1.289	1.9182	0.67	.508

$S = 3.503$ $R\text{-sq} = 40.8\%$ $R\text{-sq(adj.)} = 20.3\%$

Analysis of Variance

Source	DF	SS	MS	F	p
Regression	9	219.746	24.416	1.99	.0825
Error	26	319.004	12.269		
Total	35	538.750			

13.8 Displayed here is the Minitab output for a multiple regression analysis. Study the ANOVA table and the t ratios and use these to discuss the strengths of the regression model and the predictors. Does this model appear to fit the data well? From the information here, what recommendations would you make about the predictor variables in the model?

The regression equation is

$$Y = 34.7 + 0.0763X_1 + 0.00026X_2 - 1.12X_3$$

Predictor	Coef	Stdev	T	p
Constant	34.672	5.256	6.60	.000
X_1	0.07629	0.02234	3.41	.005
X_2	0.000259	0.001031	0.25	.805
X_3	-1.1212	0.9955	-1.13	.230

$S = 9.722$ $R\text{-sq} = 51.5\%$ $R\text{-sq(adj)} = 40.4\%$

Analysis of Variance

Source	DF	SS	MS	F	p
Regression	3	1306.99	435.66	4.61	.021
Error	13	1228.78	94.52		
Total	16	2535.77			

13.9 Using the data in Problem 13.5, develop a multiple regression model to predict per capita personal consumption by the consumption of paper, fish, and gasoline. Discuss the output and pay particular attention to the F test and the t tests.

13.10 Using the data from Problem 13.6, develop a multiple regression model to predict insider ownership from debt ratio and dividend payout. Comment on the strength of the model and the predictors by examining the ANOVA table and the t tests.

13.11 Develop a multiple regression model to predict y from x_1, x_2, and x_3 using the following data. Discuss the values of F and t.

y	x_1	x_2	x_3
5.3	44	11	401
3.6	24	40	219
5.1	46	13	394
4.9	38	18	362
7.0	61	3	453
6.4	58	5	468
5.2	47	14	386
4.6	36	24	357
2.9	19	52	206
4.0	31	29	301
3.8	24	37	243
3.8	27	36	228
4.8	36	21	342
5.4	50	11	421
5.8	55	9	445

13.12 Use the following data to develop a regression model to predict y from x_1 and x_2. Comment on the output. Develop a regression model to predict y from x_1 only. Compare the results of this model with those of the model using both predictors. What might you conclude by examining the output from both regression models?

y	x_1	x_2
28	12.6	134
43	11.4	126
45	11.5	143
49	11.1	152
57	10.4	143
68	9.6	147
74	9.8	128
81	8.4	119
82	8.8	130
86	8.9	135
101	8.1	141
112	7.6	123
114	7.8	121
119	7.4	129
124	6.4	135

13.13 Study the following Excel multiple regression output. How many predictors are in this model? How many observations? What is the equation of the regression line? Discuss the strength of the model in terms F. Which predictors, if any, are significant? Why or why not? Comment on the overall effectiveness of the model.

SUMMARY OUTPUT

Regression Statistics

Multiple R	0.842
R Square	0.710
Adjusted R Square	0.630
Standard Error	109.430
Observations	15

ANOVA

	df	SS	MS	F	Significance F
Regression	3	321946.82	107315.6	8.96	0.0027
Residual	11	131723.20	11974.8		
Total	14	453670.00			

	Coefficients	Standard Error	t Stat	P-value
Intercept	657.053	167.46	3.92	0.0024
x Variable 1	5.7103	1.792	3.19	0.0087
x Variable 2	−0.4169	0.322	−1.29	0.2222
x Variable 3	−3.4715	1.443	−2.41	0.0349

13.3 RESIDUALS, STANDARD ERROR OF THE ESTIMATE, AND R^2

Three more statistical tools for examining the strength of a regression model are the residuals, the standard error of the estimate, and the coefficient of multiple determination.

Residuals

The **residual**, or error, of the regression model is *the difference between the y value and the predicted value, $\hat{y}$.*

$$\text{Residual} = y - \hat{y}$$

The residuals for a multiple regression model are solved for in the same manner as they are with simple regression. First, a predicted value, $\hat{y}$, is determined by entering the value for each independent variable for a given set of observations into the multiple regression equation and solving for $\hat{y}$. Next, the value of $y - \hat{y}$ is computed for each set of observations. Shown here are the calculations for the residuals of the first set of observations from Table 13.1. The predicted value of y for $x_1 = 1605$ and $x_2 = 35$ is

$$\hat{y} = 57.4 + .0177(1605) - .666(35) = 62.499$$

Actual value of $y = 63.0$
Residual $= y - \hat{y} = 63.0 - 62.499 = 0.501$

All residuals for the real estate data and the regression model displayed in Table 13.1 and Figure 13.3 are displayed in Table 13.2.

An examination of the residuals in Table 13.2 can reveal some information about the fit of the real estate regression model. The business researcher can observe the residuals and decide whether the errors are small enough to support the accuracy of the model. The house price figures are in units of $1,000. Two of the 23 residuals are more than 20.00, or more than $20,000 off in their prediction. On the other hand, two residuals are less than 1, or $1,000 off in their prediction.

Residuals are also helpful in locating outliers. **Outliers** are *data points that are apart, or far, from the mainstream of the other data.* They are sometimes data points that were mistakenly recorded or measured. Because every data point influences the regression model, outliers can exert an overly important influence on the model based on their distance from other points. In examining the residuals in Table 13.2 for outliers, the eighth residual listed

TABLE 13.2

Residuals for the Real Estate Regression Model

y	$\hat{y}$	$y - \hat{y}$
63.0	62.499	.501
65.1	71.485	−6.385
69.9	71.568	−1.668
76.8	78.639	−1.839
73.9	74.097	−.197
77.9	75.653	2.247
74.9	83.012	−8.112
78.0	105.699	−27.699
79.0	68.523	10.477
83.4	81.139	2.261
79.5	88.282	−8.782
83.9	91.335	−7.435
79.7	85.618	−5.918
84.5	95.391	−10.891
96.0	85.456	10.544
109.5	102.774	6.726
102.5	97.665	4.835
121.0	107.183	13.817
104.9	109.352	−4.452
128.0	111.230	16.770
129.0	105.061	23.939
117.9	134.415	−16.515
140.0	132.430	7.570

FIGURE 13.4

Minitab Residual Diagnosis for the Real Estate Example

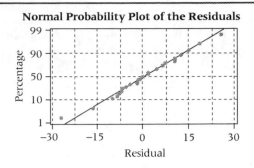

Normal Probability Plot of the Residuals

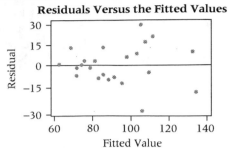

Residuals Versus the Fitted Values

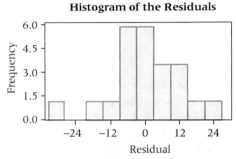

Histogram of the Residuals

is −27.699. This error indicates that the regression model was not nearly as successful in predicting house price on this particular house as it was with others (an error of more than $27,000). For whatever reason, this data point stands somewhat apart from other data points and may be considered an outlier.

Residuals are also useful in testing the assumptions underlying regression analysis. Figure 13.4 displays Minitab diagnostic techniques for the real estate example. In the top right is a graph of the residuals. Notice that residual variance seems to increase in the right half of the plot, indicating potential heteroscedasticity. As discussed in Chapter 12, one of the assumptions underlying regression analysis is that the error terms have homoscedasticity or homogeneous variance. That assumption might be violated in this example. The normal plot of residuals is nearly a straight line, indicating that the assumption of normally distributed error terms probably has not been violated.

SSE and Standard Error of the Estimate

One of the properties of a regression model is that the residuals sum to zero. As pointed out in Chapter 12, this property precludes the possibility of computing an "average" residual as a single measure of error. In an effort to compute a single statistic that can represent the error in a regression analysis, the zero-sum property can be overcome by *squaring the residuals and then summing the squares*. Such an operation produces the sum of squares of error (SSE).

The formula for computing the sum of squares error (SSE) for multiple regression is the same as it is for simple regression.

$$SSE = \Sigma(y - \hat{y})^2$$

For the real estate example, SSE can be computed by squaring and summing the residuals displayed in Table 13.2.

$$\begin{aligned}
SSE = [&(.501)^2 + (-6.385)^2 + (-1.668)^2 + (-1.839)^2 \\
&+ (-.197)^2 + (2.247)^2 + (-8.112)^2 + (-27.699)^2 \\
&+ (10.477)^2 + (2.261)^2 + (-8.782)^2 + (-7.435)^2 \\
&+ (-5.918)^2 + (-10.891)^2 + (10.544)^2 + (6.726)^2 \\
&+ (4.835)^2 + (13.817)^2 + (-4.452)^2 + (16.770)^2 \\
&+ (23.939)^2 + (-16.515)^2 + (7.570)^2] \\
= \;&2861.0
\end{aligned}$$

SSE can also be obtained directly from the multiple regression computer output by selecting the value of SS (sum of squares) listed beside error. Shown here is the ANOVA portion of the output displayed in Figure 13.3, which is the result of a multiple regression analysis model developed to predict house prices. Note that the SS for error shown in the ANOVA table equals the value of $\Sigma(y - \hat{y})^2$ just computed (2861.0).

```
                                    SSE
                                   /
Analysis of Variance              /
                                 /
Source        DF      SS    /   MS        F       P
Regression    2     8189.7  /  4094.9   28.63   .000
Error        20    ( 2861.0 )  143.1
Total        22    11050.7
```

SSE has limited usage as a measure of error. However, it is a tool used to solve for other, more useful measures. One of those is the **standard error of the estimate, s_e**, which is essentially *the standard deviation of residuals (error) for the regression model.* As explained in Chapter 12, an assumption underlying regression analysis is that the error terms are approximately normally distributed with a mean of zero. With this information and by the empirical rule, approximately 68% of the residuals should be within $\pm 1s_e$ and 95% should be within $\pm 2s_e$. This property makes the standard error of the estimate a useful tool in estimating how accurately a regression model is fitting the data.

The standard error of the estimate is computed by dividing SSE by the degrees of freedom of error for the model and taking the square root.

$$s_e = \sqrt{\frac{SSE}{n - k - 1}}$$

where

n = number of observations
k = number of independent variables

The value of s_e can be computed for the real estate example as follows.

$$s_e = \sqrt{\frac{SSE}{n - k - 1}} = \sqrt{\frac{2861}{23 - 2 - 1}} = 11.96$$

The standard error of the estimate, s_e, is usually given as standard output from regression analysis by computer software packages. The Minitab output displayed in Figure 13.3 contains the standard error of the estimate for the real estate example.

$$S = 11.96$$

By the empirical rule, approximately 68% of the residuals should be within $\pm 1s_e = \pm 1(11.96) = \pm 11.96$. Because house prices are in units of \$1,000, approximately 68% of the predictions are within $\pm 11.96(\$1,000)$, or $\pm\$11,960$. Examining the output displayed in Table 13.2, 18/23, or about 78%, of the residuals are within this span. According to the empirical rule, approximately 95% of the residuals should be within $\pm 2s_e$, or $\pm 2(11.96) = \pm 23.92$. Further examination of the residual values in Table 13.2 shows that 21 of 23, or 91%, fall within this range. The business researcher can study the standard error of the estimate and these empirical rule–related ranges and decide whether the error of the regression model is sufficiently small to justify further use of the model.

Coefficient of Multiple Determination (R^2)

The **coefficient of multiple determination (R^2)** is analogous to the coefficient of determination (r^2) discussed in Chapter 12. R^2 represents *the proportion of variation of the dependent variable, y, accounted for by the independent variables in the regression model.* As with r^2, the range of possible values for R^2 is from 0 to 1. An R^2 of 0 indicates no relationship between the predictor variables in the model and y. An R^2 of 1 indicates that 100% of the variability of y has been accounted for by the predictors. Of course, it is desirable for R^2 to be high, indicating the strong predictability of a regression model. The coefficient of multiple determination can be calculated by the following formula:

$$R^2 = \frac{SSR}{SS_{yy}} = 1 - \frac{SSE}{SS_{yy}}$$

R^2 can be calculated in the real estate example by using the sum of squares regression (SSR), the sum of squares error (SSE), and sum of squares total (SS_{yy}) from the ANOVA portion of Figure 13.3.

```
                              SS_yy
                        SSE /
                  SSR /    /
Analysis of Variance    / /
                       / /
Source       DF   SS  / /    MS       F      p
Regression    2  (8189.7) /4094.9  28.63   .000
Error        20  (2861.0) 143.1
Total        22  (11050.7)
```

$$R^2 = \frac{SSR}{SS_{yy}} = \frac{8189.7}{11050.7} = .741$$

or

$$R^2 = 1 - \frac{SSE}{SS_{yy}} = 1 - \frac{2861.0}{11050.7} = .741$$

In addition, virtually all statistical software packages print out R^2 as standard output with multiple regression analysis. A reexamination of Figure 13.3 reveals that R^2 is given as

$$R\text{-sq} = 74.1\%$$

This result indicates that a relatively high proportion of the variation of the dependent variable, house price, is accounted for by the independent variables in this regression model.

Adjusted R^2

As additional independent variables are added to a regression model, the value of R^2 cannot decrease, and in most cases it will increase. In the formulas for determining R^2,

$$R^2 = \frac{SSR}{SS_{yy}} = 1 - \frac{SSE}{SS_{yy}}$$

The value of SS_{yy} for a given set of observations will remain the same as independent variables are added to the regression analysis because SS_{yy} is the sum of squares for the dependent variable. Because additional independent variables are likely to increase SSR at least by some amount, the value of R^2 will probably increase for any additional independent variables.

However, sometimes additional independent variables add no *significant* information to the regression model, yet R^2 increases. R^2 therefore may yield an inflated figure. Statisticians have developed an **adjusted** R^2 *to take into consideration both the additional information each new independent variable brings to the regression model and the changed degrees of freedom of regression.* Many standard statistical computer packages now compute and report adjusted R^2 as part of the output. The formula for computing adjusted R^2 is

$$\text{Adjusted } R^2 = 1 - \frac{SSE/(n - k - 1)}{SS_{yy}/(n - 1)}$$

The value of adjusted R^2 for the real estate example can be solved by using information from the ANOVA portion of the computer output in Figure 13.3.

THINKING CRITICALLY ABOUT STATISTICS IN BUSINESS TODAY

Assessing Property Values Using Multiple Regression

According to county assessor sources, Colorado state statute requires that all county assessors in the state value residential real property solely by a market approach. Furthermore, in the statute, it is stated that such a market approach will be based on a representative body of sales sufficient to set a pattern. No specifics on market analysis methods are given in the statutes, but there are several commonly used methods, including multiple regression. In the multiple regression approach, an attempt is made to develop a model to predict recent sales (dependent variable) by such property characteristics (independent variables) as location, lot size, building square feet, construction quality, property type (single family, condominium, townhouse), garage size, basement type, and other features. One county Web site states that "regression does not require strict similarity between property sales because it estimates the value contribution (coefficient) for each attribute. . . ." In producing a sound multiple regression model to predict property values, several models are developed, refined, and compared using the typical indicators of a good fit, such as R^2, standard error of

the estimate, F test for the overall model, and p-values associated with the t tests of significance for predictors. The final multiple regression model is then used in the estimation of property values by the appraiser, who enters into the regression model (equation) the specific measure of each independent (predictor) variable for a given property, resulting in a predicted appraised property value for tax purposes. The models are updated for currency and based on data that are never more than two years old.

Things to Ponder

1. How does the multiple regression method improve the validity of property value assessments over typical standard methods? Do you think it is more fair and equitable? If so, why?

2. Can you think of other similar possible applications of multiple regression in business?

Source: Douglas County, Colorado, Assessor's Office, at http:/www.douglas.co.us/assessor/Multiple_Regression.html, March 20, 2011, and Gunnison County Assessor's Office, at http://www.gunnisoncounty.org/assessor_assessment_process.html, March 20, 2011.

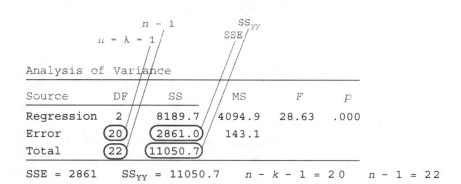

$$\text{Adj. } R^2 = 1 - \left[\frac{2861/20}{11050.7/22}\right] = 1 - .285 = .715$$

The standard Minitab regression output in Figure 13.3 contains the value of the adjusted R^2 already computed. For the real estate example, this value is shown as

$$R\text{-sq (adj.)} = 71.5\%$$

A comparison of R^2 (.741) with the adjusted R^2 (.715) for this example shows that the adjusted R^2 reduces the overall proportion of variation of the dependent variable accounted for by the independent variables by a factor of .026, or 2.6%. The gap between the R^2 and adjusted R^2 tends to increase as nonsignificant independent variables are added to the regression model. As n increases, the difference between R^2 and adjusted R^2 becomes less.

13.3 PROBLEMS

13.14 Study the Minitab output shown in Problem 13.7. Comment on the overall strength of the regression model in light of S, R^2, and adjusted R^2.

13.15 Study the Minitab output shown in Problem 13.8. Comment on the overall strength of the regression model in light of S, R^2, and adjusted R^2.

13.16 Using the regression output obtained by working Problem 13.5, comment on the overall strength of the regression model using S, R^2, and adjusted R^2.

13.17 Using the regression output obtained by working Problem 13.6, comment on the overall strength of the regression model using S, R^2, and adjusted R^2.

13.18 Using the regression output obtained by working Problem 13.11, comment on the overall strength of the regression model using S, R^2, and adjusted R^2.

13.19 Using the regression output obtained by working Problem 13.12, comment on the overall strength of the regression model using S, R^2, and adjusted R^2.

13.20 Study the Excel output shown in Problem 13.13. Comment on the overall strength of the regression model in light of S, R^2, and adjusted R^2.

13.21 Study the Minitab residual diagnostic output that follows. Discuss any potential problems with meeting the regression assumptions for this regression analysis based on the residual graphics.

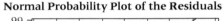
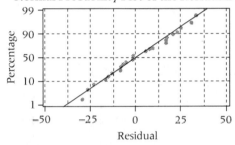
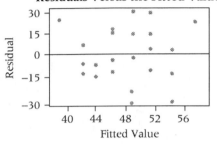
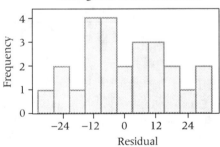

13.4 INTERPRETING MULTIPLE REGRESSION COMPUTER OUTPUT

A Reexamination of the Multiple Regression Output

Figure 13.5 shows again the Minitab multiple regression output for the real estate example. Many of the concepts discussed thus far in the chapter are highlighted. Note the following items:

1. The equation of the regression model
2. The ANOVA table with the F value for the overall test of the model
3. The t ratios, which test the significance of the regression coefficients
4. The value of SSE
5. The value of s_e
6. The value of R^2
7. The value of adjusted R^2

FIGURE 13.5

Annotated Version of the
Minitab Output of Regression
for the Real Estate Example

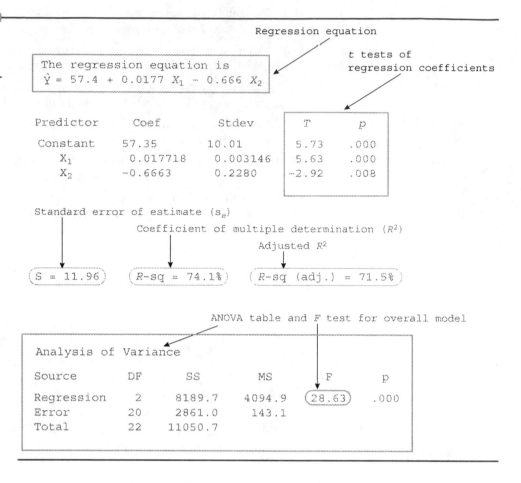

Regression equation

The regression equation is
$\hat{Y} = 57.4 + 0.0177\ X_1 - 0.666\ X_2$

t tests of
regression coefficients

Predictor	Coef	Stdev	T	p
Constant	57.35	10.01	5.73	.000
X_1	0.017718	0.003146	5.63	.000
X_2	−0.6663	0.2280	−2.92	.008

Standard error of estimate (s_e)

Coefficient of multiple determination (R^2)

Adjusted R^2

S = 11.96   R-sq = 74.1%   R-sq (adj.) = 71.5%

ANOVA table and F test for overall model

Analysis of Variance

Source	DF	SS	MS	F	p
Regression	2	8189.7	4094.9	28.63	.000
Error	20	2861.0	143.1		
Total	22	11050.7			

DEMONSTRATION PROBLEM 13.2

Discuss the Excel multiple regression output for Demonstration Problem 13.1. Comment on the F test for the overall significance of the model, the t tests of the regression coefficients, and the values of s_e, R^2, and adjusted R^2.

Solution

This multiple regression analysis was done to predict the prime interest rate using the predictors of unemployment and personal saving. The equation of the regression model was presented in the solution of Demonstration Problem 13.1. Shown here is the complete multiple regression output from the Excel analysis of the data.

The value of F for this problem is 12.21, with a p-value of .0013, which is significant at $\alpha = .01$. On the basis of this information, the null hypothesis is rejected for the overall test of significance. At least one of the predictor variables is statistically significant from zero, and there is significant predictability of the prime interest rate by this model.

An examination of the t ratios reveals that personal savings is a significant predictor at $\alpha = .001$ ($t = 4.86$ with a p-value of .0004) and that unemployment rates is a significant predictor at $\alpha = .05$ ($t = -2.85$ with a p-value of .0147). The positive signs on the regression coefficient and the t value for personal savings indicate that as personal savings increase, the prime interest rate tends to get higher. On the other hand, the negative signs on the regression coefficient and the t value for unemployment rates indicate that as the unemployment rate increases, the prime interest rate tends to decrease.

The standard error of the estimate is $s_e = 1.890$, indicating that approximately 68% of the residuals are within ±1.890. An examination of the Excel-produced residuals shows that actually 11 out of 15, or 73.3%, fall in this interval. Approximately 95%

of the residuals should be within $\pm2(1.890) = \pm3.780$, and an examination of the Excel-produced residuals shows that 14 out of 15, or 93.3%, of the residuals are within this interval.

R^2 for this regression analysis is .671, or 67.1%. The adjusted R^2 is .616, indicating that there is some inflation in the R^2 value. Overall, there is modest predictability in this model.

SUMMARY OUTPUT

Regression Statistics

Multiple R	0.819
R Square	0.671
Adjusted R Square	0.616
Standard Error	1.890
Observations	15

ANOVA

	df	SS	MS	F	Significance F
Regression	2	87.2388	43.6194	12.21	0.0013
Residual	12	42.8539	3.5712		
Total	14	130.0927			

	Coefficients	Standard Error	t Stat	P-value
Intercept	7.4196	1.943	3.82	0.0024
Unemployment Rates	−1.2092	0.425	−2.85	0.0147
Personal Savings	1.3993	0.288	4.86	0.0004

RESIDUAL OUTPUT

Observation	Predicted Prime Interest Rate	Residuals
1	10.9430	3.9070
2	12.6236	−0.5836
3	9.5901	−1.2601
4	10.4243	−1.1043
5	9.7437	0.2663
6	8.5657	−2.3157
7	7.3200	−0.1700
8	7.7466	0.5234
9	9.3946	−1.0446
10	6.6409	2.5891
11	5.3040	−0.6340
12	5.5268	−1.1868
13	5.2158	2.7442
14	6.1435	−1.0535
15	3.9276	−0.6776

13.4 PROBLEMS

13.22 Study the Minitab regression output that follows. How many predictors are there? What is the equation of the regression model? Using the key statistics discussed in this chapter, discuss the strength of the model and the predictors.

```
Regression Analysis: Y versus X₁, X₂, X₃, X₄

The regression equation is
Y = - 55.9 + 0.0105 X₁ - 0.107 X₂ + 0.579 X₃ - 0.870 X₄
Predictor        Coef    SE Coef       T        P
Constant       -55.93      24.22    -2.31    0.025
       X₁      0.01049    0.02100     0.50    0.619
       X₂     -0.10720    0.03503    -3.06    0.003
       X₃      0.57922    0.07633     7.59    0.000
       X₄      -0.8695     0.1498    -5.81    0.000
S = 9.025    R-Sq = 80.2%   R-Sq(adj) = 78.7%
```

Analysis of Variance

Source	DF	SS	MS	F	p
Regression	2	18088.5	4522.1	55.52	0.000
Residual Error	55	4479.7	81.4		
Total	59	22568.2			

13.23 Study the Excel regression output that follows. How many predictors are there? What is the equation of the regression model? Using the key statistics discussed in this chapter, discuss the strength of the model and its predictors.

SUMMARY OUTPUT

Regression Statistics	
Multiple R	0.814
R Square	0.663
Adjusted R Square	0.636
Standard Error	51.761
Observations	28

ANOVA

	df	SS	MS	F	Significance F
Regression	2	131567.02	65783.51	24.55	0.0000013
Residual	25	66979.65	2679.19		
Total	27	198546.68			

	Coefficients	Standard Error	t Stat	P-value
Intercept	203.3937	67.518	3.01	0.0059
X_1	1.1151	0.528	2.11	0.0448
X_2	-2.2115	0.567	-3.90	0.0006

Are You Going to Hate Your New Job?

In the Decision Dilemma, several variables are considered in attempting to determine whether a person will like his or her new job. Four predictor (independent) variables are given with the data set: relationship with supervisor, overall quality of work environment, total hours worked per week, and opportunities for advancement. Other possible variables might include openness of work culture, amount of pressure, how the interviewee is treated during the interview, availability of flexible scheduling, size of office, amount of time allotted for lunch, availability of management, interesting work, and many others.

Using the data that are given, a multiple regression model can be developed to predict job satisfaction from the four independent variables. Such an analysis allows the business researcher to study the entire data set in one model rather than constructing four different simple regression models, one for each independent variable. In the multiple regression model, job satisfaction is the dependent variable. There are 19 observations. The Excel regression output for this problem follows.

The test for overall significance of the model produced an F of 87.79 with a p-value of .000000001 (significant at $\alpha = .00000001$). The R^2 of .962 and adjusted R^2 of .951 indicate very strong predictability in the model. The standard error of the estimate, 5.141, can be viewed in light of the job satisfaction values that ranged from 10 to 95 and the residuals, which are not shown here. Fourteen of the 19 residuals (73.7%) are within the standard error of the estimate. Examining the t statistics and their associated p-values reveals that two independent variables, relationship with supervisor ($t = 5.33$, p-value = .0001), and overall quality of work environment ($t = 2.73$, p-value = .0162) are significant predictors at $\alpha = .05$. Judging by their large p-values, it appears that total hours worked per week and opportunities for advancement are not good predictors of job satisfaction.

SUMMARY OUTPUT

Regression Statistics

Multiple R	0.981
R Square	0.962
Adjusted R Square	0.951
Standard Error	5.141
Observations	19

ANOVA

	df	SS	MS	F	Significance F
Regression	4	9282.569	2320.642	87.79	0.000000001
Residual	14	370.062	26.433		
Total	18	9652.632			

	Coefficients	Standard Error	t Stat	P-value
Intercept	−1.469	8.116	−0.18	0.8590
Relationship with Supervisor	1.391	0.261	5.33	0.0001
Overall Quality of Work Environment	0.317	0.116	2.73	0.0162
Total Hours Worked per Week	0.043	0.121	0.36	0.7263
Opportunities for Advancement	−0.094	0.102	−0.92	0.3711

ETHICAL CONSIDERATIONS

Multiple regression analysis can be used either intentionally or unintentionally in questionable or unethical ways. When degrees of freedom are small, an inflated value of R^2 can be obtained, leading to overenthusiastic expectations about the predictability of a regression model. To prevent this type of reliance, a researcher should take into account the nature of the data, the variables, and the value of the adjusted R^2.

Another misleading aspect of multiple regression can be the tendency of researchers to assume cause-and-effect relationships between the dependent variable and predictors. Just because independent variables produce a significant R^2 does not necessarily mean those variables are causing the deviation of the *y* values. Indeed, some other force not in the model may be driving both the independent variables and the dependent variable over the range of values being studied.

Some people use the estimates of the regression coefficients to compare the worth of the predictor variables; the larger the coefficient, the greater is its worth. At least two problems can be found in this approach. The first is that most variables are measured in different units. Thus, regression coefficient weights are partly a function of the unit of measurement of the variable. Second, if multicollinearity (discussed in Chapter 14) is present, the interpretation of the regression coefficients is questionable. In addition, the presence of multicollinearity raises several issues about the interpretation of other regression output. Researchers who ignore this problem are at risk of presenting spurious results.

Another danger in using regression analysis is in the extrapolation of the model to values beyond the range of values used to derive the model. A regression model that fits data within a given range does not necessarily fit data outside that range. One of the uses of regression analysis is in the area of forecasting. Users need to be aware that what has occurred in the past is not guaranteed to continue to occur in the future. Unscrupulous and sometimes even well-intentioned business decision makers can use regression models to project conclusions about the future that have little or no basis. The receiver of such messages should be cautioned that regression models may lack validity outside the range of values in which the models were developed.

SUMMARY

Multiple regression analysis is a statistical tool in which a mathematical model is developed in an attempt to predict a dependent variable by two or more independent variables or in which at least one predictor is nonlinear. Because doing multiple regression analysis by hand is extremely tedious and time-consuming, it is almost always done on a computer.

The standard output from a multiple regression analysis is similar to that of simple regression analysis. A regression equation is produced with a constant that is analogous to the *y*-intercept in simple regression and with estimates of the regression coefficients that are analogous to the estimate of the slope in simple regression. An *F* test for the overall model is computed to determine whether at least one of the regression coefficients is significantly different from zero. This F value is usually displayed in an ANOVA table, which is part of the regression output. The ANOVA table also contains the sum of squares of error and sum of squares of regression, which are used to compute other statistics in the model.

Most multiple regression computer output contains t values, which are used to determine the significance of the regression coefficients. Using these t values, statisticians can make decisions about including or excluding variables from the model.

Residuals, standard error of the estimate, and R^2 are also standard computer regression output with multiple regression. The coefficient of determination for simple regression models is denoted r^2, whereas for multiple regression it is R^2. The interpretation of residuals, standard error of the estimate, and R^2 in multiple regression is similar to that in simple regression. Because R^2 can be inflated with nonsignificant variables in the mix, an adjusted R^2 is often computed. Unlike R^2, adjusted R^2 takes into account the degrees of freedom and the number of observations.

KEY TERMS

 **Flash Cards**

adjusted R^2
coefficient of multiple
  determination (R^2)

dependent variable
independent variable
least squares analysis
multiple regression
outliers

partial regression coefficient
R^2
residual
response plane
response surface

response variable
standard error of the
  estimate (se)
sum of squares of error (SSE)

FORMULAS

The F value

$$F = \frac{MS_{reg}}{MS_{err}} = \frac{SS_{reg}/df_{reg}}{SS_{err}/df_{err}} = \frac{SSR/k}{SSE/(N - k - 1)}$$

Sum of squares of error

$$SSE = \Sigma(y - \hat{y})^2$$

Standard error of the estimate

$$s_e = \sqrt{\frac{SSE}{n - k - 1}}$$

Coefficient of multiple determination

$$R^2 = \frac{SSR}{SS_{yy}} = 1 - \frac{SSE}{SS_{yy}}$$

Adjusted R^2

$$\text{Adjusted } R^2 = 1 - \frac{SSE/(n - k - 1)}{SS_{yy}/(n - 1)}$$

SUPPLEMENTARY PROBLEMS

CALCULATING THE STATISTICS

13.24 Use the following data to develop a multiple regression model to predict y from x_1 and x_2. Discuss the output, including comments about the overall strength of the model, the significance of the regression coefficients, and other indicators of model fit.

y	x_1	x_2
198	29	1.64
214	71	2.81
211	54	2.22
219	73	2.70
184	67	1.57
167	32	1.63
201	47	1.99
204	43	2.14
190	60	2.04
222	32	2.93
197	34	2.15

13.25 Given here are the data for a dependent variable, y, and independent variables. Use these data to develop a regression model to predict y. Discuss the output.

y	x_1	x_2	x_3
14	51	16.4	56
17	48	17.1	64
29	29	18.2	53
32	36	17.9	41
54	40	16.5	60
86	27	17.1	55
117	14	17.8	71
120	17	18.2	48
194	16	16.9	60
203	9	18.0	77
217	14	18.9	90
235	11	18.5	67

TESTING YOUR UNDERSTANDING

13.26 The U.S. Bureau of Mines produces data on the price of minerals. Shown here are the average prices per year for several minerals over a decade. Use these data and multiple regression to produce a model to predict the average price of gold from the other variables. Comment on the results of the process.

Gold ($ per oz.)	Copper (cents per lb.)	Silver ($ per oz.)	Aluminum (cents per lb.)
161.1	64.2	4.4	39.8
308.0	93.3	11.1	61.0
613.0	101.3	20.6	71.6
460.0	84.2	10.5	76.0
376.0	72.8	8.0	76.0
424.0	76.5	11.4	77.8
361.0	66.8	8.1	81.0
318.0	67.0	6.1	81.0
368.0	66.1	5.5	81.0
448.0	82.5	7.0	72.3
438.0	120.5	6.5	110.1
382.6	130.9	5.5	87.8

13.27 The Shipbuilders Council of America in Washington, D.C., publishes data about private shipyards. Among the variables reported by this organization are the employment figures (per 1000), the number of naval vessels under construction, and the number of repairs or conversions done to commercial ships (in $ millions). Shown here are the data for these three variables over a seven-year period. Use the data to develop a regression model to predict private shipyard employment from number of naval vessels under construction and repairs or conversions of commercial ships. Comment on the regression model and its strengths and its weaknesses.

	Commercial Ship	
Employment	Naval Vessels	Repairs or Conversions
133.4	108	431
177.3	99	1335
143.0	105	1419
142.0	111	1631
130.3	100	852
120.6	85	847
120.4	79	806

13.28 The U.S. Bureau of Labor Statistics produces consumer price indexes for several different categories. Shown here are the percentage changes in consumer price indexes over a period of 20 years for food, shelter, apparel, and fuel oil. Also displayed are the percentage changes in consumer price indexes for all commodities. Use these data and multiple regression to develop a

model that attempts to predict all commodities by the other four variables. Comment on the result of this analysis.

All Commodities	Food	Shelter	Apparel	Fuel Oil
.9	1.0	2.0	1.6	3.7
.6	1.3	.8	.9	2.7
.9	.7	1.6	.4	2.6
.9	1.6	1.2	1.3	2.6
1.2	1.3	1.5	.9	2.1
1.1	2.2	1.9	1.1	2.4
2.6	5.0	3.0	2.5	4.4
1.9	.9	3.6	4.1	7.2
3.5	3.5	4.5	5.3	6.0
4.7	5.1	8.3	5.8	6.7
4.5	5.7	8.9	4.2	6.6
3.6	3.1	4.2	3.2	6.2
3.0	4.2	4.6	2.0	3.3
7.4	14.5	4.7	3.7	4.0
11.9	14.3	9.6	7.4	9.3
8.8	8.5	9.9	4.5	12.0
4.3	3.0	5.5	3.7	9.5
5.8	6.3	6.6	4.5	9.6
7.2	9.9	10.2	3.6	8.4
11.3	11.0	13.9	4.3	9.2

13.29 The U.S. Department of Agriculture publishes data annually on various selected farm products. Shown here are the unit production figures (in millions of bushels) for three farm products for 10 years during a 20-year period. Use these data and multiple regression analysis to predict corn production by the production of soybeans and wheat. Comment on the results.

Corn	Soybeans	Wheat
4152	1127	1352
6639	1798	2381
4175	1636	2420
7672	1861	2595
8876	2099	2424
8226	1940	2091
7131	1938	2108
4929	1549	1812
7525	1924	2037
7933	1922	2739

13.30 The American Chamber of Commerce Researchers Association compiles cost-of-living indexes for selected metropolitan areas. Shown here are cost-of-living indexes for 25 different cities on five different items for a recent year. Use the data to develop a regression model to predict the grocery cost-of-living index by the indexes of housing, utilities, transportation, and

431

healthcare. Discuss the results, highlighting both the significant and nonsignificant predictors.

City	Grocery Items	Housing	Utilities	Transportation	Healthcare
Albany	108.3	106.8	127.4	89.1	107.5
Albuquerque	96.3	105.2	98.8	100.9	102.1
Augusta, GA	96.2	88.8	115.6	102.3	94.0
Austin	98.0	83.9	87.7	97.4	94.9
Baltimore	106.0	114.1	108.1	112.8	111.5
Buffalo	103.1	117.3	127.6	107.8	100.8
Colorado Springs	94.5	88.5	74.6	93.3	102.4
Dallas	105.4	98.9	108.9	110.0	106.8
Denver	91.5	108.3	97.2	105.9	114.3
Des Moines	94.3	95.1	111.4	105.7	96.2
El Paso	102.9	94.6	90.9	104.2	91.4
Indianapolis	96.0	99.7	92.1	102.7	97.4
Jacksonville	96.1	90.4	96.0	106.0	96.1
Kansas City	89.8	92.4	96.3	95.6	93.6
Knoxville	93.2	88.0	91.7	91.6	82.3
Los Angeles	103.3	211.3	75.6	102.1	128.5
Louisville	94.6	91.0	79.4	102.4	88.4
Memphis	99.1	86.2	91.1	101.1	85.5
Miami	100.3	123.0	125.6	104.3	137.8
Minneapolis	92.8	112.3	105.2	106.0	107.5
Mobile	99.9	81.1	104.9	102.8	92.2
Nashville	95.8	107.7	91.6	98.1	90.9
New Orleans	104.0	83.4	122.2	98.2	87.0
Oklahoma City	98.2	79.4	103.4	97.3	97.1
Phoenix	95.7	98.7	96.3	104.6	115.2

INTERPRETING THE OUTPUT

13.31 Shown here are the data for y and three predictors, x_1, x_2, and x_3. A multiple regression analysis has been done on these data; the Minitab results are given. Comment on the outcome of the analysis in light of the data.

y	x_1	x_2	x_3
94	21	1	204
97	25	0	198
93	22	1	184
95	27	0	200
90	29	1	182
91	20	1	159
91	18	1	147
94	25	0	196
98	26	0	228
99	24	0	242
90	28	1	162
92	23	1	180
96	25	0	219

Regression Analysis: Y versus X_1, X_2, X_3
The regression equation is
$Y = 87.9 - 0.256\ X_1 - 2.71\ X_2 + 0.0706\ X_3$

Predictor	Coef	SE Coef	T	P
Constant	87.890	3.445	25.51	0.000
X1	-0.25612	0.08317	-3.08	0.013
X2	-2.7137	0.7306	-3.71	0.005
X3	0.07061	0.01353	5.22	0.001

S = 0.850311   R-Sq = 94.1%   R-Sq(adj) = 92.1%

Analysis of Variance

Source	DF	SS	MS	F	p
Regression	3	103.185	34.395	47.57	0.000
Residual Error	9	6.507	0.723		
Total	12	109.692			

13.32 Minitab residual diagnostic output from the multiple regression analysis for the data given in Problem 13.30 follows. Discuss any potential problems with meeting the regression assumptions for this regression analysis based on the residual graphics.

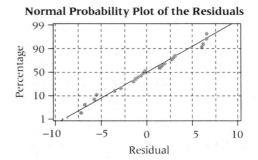

Normal Probability Plot of the Residuals

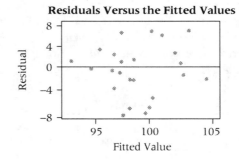

Residuals Versus the Fitted Values

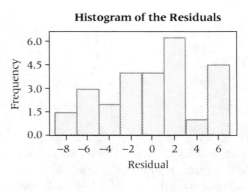

Histogram of the Residuals

1. Use the Manufacturing database to develop a multiple regression model to predict Cost of Materials by Number of Employees, New Capital Expenditures, Value Added by Manufacture, and End-of-Year Inventories. Discuss the results of the analysis.

2. Develop a regression model using the Financial database. Use Total Revenues, Total Assets, Return on Equity, Earnings Per Share, Average Yield, and Dividends Per Share to predict the average P/E ratio for a company. How strong is the model? Which variables seem to be the best predictors?

3. Using the International Stock Market database, develop a multiple regression model to predict the Nikkei by the DJIA, the Nasdaq, the S&P 500, the Hang Seng, the FTSE 100, and the IPC. Discuss the outcome, including the model, the strength of the model, and the strength of the predictors.

4. Develop a multiple regression model to predict Annual Food Spending by Annual Household Income and Non-Mortgage Household Debt using the Consumer Food database. How strong is the model? Which of the two predictors seems to be stronger? Why?

CASE

STARBUCKS INTRODUCES DEBIT CARD

Starbucks is a resounding restaurant success story. Beginning with its first coffee house in 1971, Starbucks has grown to more than 11,000 U.S. locations. Opening up its first international outlet in the mid 1990s, Starbucks now operates in more than 50 countries outside of North America. Besides selling beverages, pastries, confections, and coffee-related accessories and equipment at its retail outlets, Starbucks also purchases and roasts high-quality coffee beans in several locations. The company's objective is to become the most recognized and respected brand in the world. Starbucks maintains a strong environmental orientation and is committed to taking a leadership position environmentally. In addition, the company has won awards for corporate social responsibility through its community-building programs, its strong commitment to its origins (coffee producers, family, community), and the Starbucks Foundation, which is dedicated to creating hope, discovery, and opportunity in the communities where Starbucks resides.

In November 2001, Starbucks launched its prepaid (debit) Starbucks Card. The card, which holds between $5 and $500, can be used at virtually any Starbucks location. The card was so popular when it first was released that many stores ran out. By mid-2002, Starbucks had activated more than 5 million of these cards. The Starbucks Card has surpassed the $2.5 billion mark for total activations and reloads since its introduction. As customers "reload" the cards, it appears they are placing more money on them than the initial value of the card.

Starbucks has gone on to promote their Starbucks Card as a flexible marketing tool that can be used by individuals as a gift of thanks and appreciation for friendship or service and can be used by companies to reward loyal customers and as an incentive to employees.

Discussion

1. Starbucks enjoyed considerable success with its debit cards, which they sell for $5 to $500. Suppose Starbucks management wants to study the reasons why some people purchase debit cards with higher prepaid amounts than do other people. Suppose a study of 25 randomly selected prepaid

card purchasers is taken. Respondents are asked the amount of the prepaid card, the customer's age, the number of days per month the customer makes a purchase at Starbucks, the number of cups of coffee the customer drinks per day, and the customer's income. The data follow. Using these data, develop a multiple regression model to study how well the amount of the prepaid card can be predicted by the other variables and which variables seem to be more promising in doing the prediction. What sales implications might be evident from this analysis?

Amount of Prepaid Card ($)	Age	Days per Month at Starbucks	Cups of Coffee per Day	Income ($1,000)
5	25	4	1	20
25	30	12	5	35
10	27	10	4	30
5	42	8	5	30
15	29	11	8	25
50	25	12	5	60
10	50	8	3	30
15	45	6	5	35
5	32	16	7	25
5	23	10	1	20
20	40	18	5	40
35	35	12	3	40
40	28	10	3	50
15	33	12	2	30
200	40	15	5	80
15	37	3	1	30
40	51	10	8	35
5	20	8	4	25
30	26	15	5	35
100	38	19	10	45
30	27	12	3	35
25	29	14	6	35
25	34	10	4	45
50	30	6	3	55
15	22	8	5	30

2. Suppose marketing wants to be able to profile frequent visitors to a Starbucks store. Using the same data set already provided, develop a multiple regression model to predict Days per month at Starbucks by Age, Income, and Number of cups of coffee per day. How strong is the model? Which particular independent variables seem to have more promise in predicting how many days per month a customer visits Starbucks? What marketing implications might be evident from this analysis?

3. Over the past decade or so, Starbucks has grown quite rapidly. As they add stores and increase the number of drinks, their sales revenues increase. In reflecting about this growth, think about some other variables that might be related to the increase in Starbucks sales revenues. Some data for the past seven years on the number of Starbucks stores (worldwide), approximate sales revenue (in $ millions), number of different drinks sold, and average weekly earnings of U.S. production workers are given here. Most figures are approximate. Develop a multiple regression model to predict sales revenue by number of drinks sold, number of stores, and average weekly earnings. How strong is the model? What are the key predictors, if any? How might this analysis help Starbucks management in attempting to determine what drives sales revenues?

Sales Year	Revenue	Number of Stores	Number of Drinks	Average Weekly Earnings
1	400	676	15	386
2	700	1015	15	394
3	1000	1412	18	407
4	1350	1886	22	425
5	1650	2135	27	442
6	2200	3300	27	457
7	2600	4709	30	474

Source: Adapted from Shirley Leung, "Starbucks May Indeed Be a Robust Staple," *The Wall Street Journal,* July 26, 2002, p. B4; James Peters, "Starbucks' Growth Still Hot; Gift Card Jolts Chain's Sales," *Nation's Restaurant News,* February 11, 2002, pp. 1–2. Starbuck's Web site (February, 2008) at: http://www.starbucks.com/aboutus/Company_Factsheet.pdf.

USING THE COMPUTER

EXCEL

▪ Excel has the capability of doing multiple regression analysis. The commands are essentially the same as those for simple regression except that the *x* range of data may include several columns. Excel will determine the number of predictor variables from the number of columns entered in to **Input X Range**.

▪ Begin by selecting the **Data** tab on the Excel worksheet. From the **Analysis** panel at the right top of the **Data** tab worksheet, click on **Data Analysis**. If your Excel worksheet does not show the **Data Analysis** option, then you can load it as an add-in following directions given in Chapter 2. From the **Data Analysis** pulldown menu, select **Regression**. In the **Regression** dialog box, input the location of the *y* values in **Input Y Range**. Input the location of the *x* values in **Input X Range**. Input **Labels** and input **Confidence Level**. To pass the line through the origin, check **Constant is Zero**. To printout the raw residuals, check **Residuals**. To printout residuals converted to *z* scores, check **Standardized Residuals**. For a plot of the residuals, check **Residual Plots**. For a plot of the line through the points check **Line Fit Plots**.

▪ Standard output includes *R*, R^2, s_e, and an ANOVA table with the *F* test, the slope and intercept, *t* statistics with associated *p*-values, and any optionally requested output, such as graphs or residuals.

MINITAB

▪ Multiple regression analysis can be performed by Minitab using the following commands. Select **Stat** from the menu bar. Select **Regression** from the **Stat** pulldown menu. Select **Regression** from the **Regression** pulldown menu. Place the column name or column location of the *y* variable in **Response**. Place the column name(s) or column location(s) of the *x* variable(s) in **Predictors**. Select **Graphs** for options relating to residual plots. Use this option and check **Four in one** to produce the residual diagnostic plots shown in the chapter. Select **Options** for confidence intervals and prediction intervals. Select **Results** for controlling the regression analysis output. Select **Storage** to store fits and/or residuals.

▪ To obtain a fitted-line plot, select **Stat** from the menu bar. Select **Regression** from the **Stat** pulldown menu. Select **Fitted Line Plot** from the **Regression** pulldown menu. In the Fitted Line Plot dialog box, place the column name or column location of the *y* variable in **Response(Y)**. Place the column name(s) or column location(s) of the *x* variable(s) in **Response(X)**. Check **Type of Regression Model** as **Linear, Quadratic**, or **Cubic**. Select **Graphs** for options relating to residual plots. Use this option and check **Four in one** to produce the residual diagnostic plots shown in the chapter. Select **Options** for confidence intervals and prediction intervals. Select **Storage** to store fits and/or residuals.